Models of Society and Complex

GW01090393

Models of Society and Complex Systems introduces readers to a variety of different mathematical tools used for modelling human behaviour and interactions, and the complex social dynamics that drive institutions, conflict, and coordination. What laws govern human affairs? How can we make sense of the complexity of societies and how do individual actions, characteristics, and beliefs interact? Social systems follow regularities which allow us to answer these questions using different mathematical approaches.

This book emphasises both theory and application. It systematically introduces mathematical approaches, such as evolutionary and spatial game theory, social network analysis, agent-based modelling, and chaos theory. It provides readers with the necessary theoretical background of each toolset as well as the underlying intuition, while each chapter includes exercises and applications to real-world phenomena. By looking behind the surface of various social occurrences, the reader uncovers the reasons why social systems exhibit both cultural universals and at the same time a diversity of practices and norms to a degree that even surpasses biological variety, or why some riots turn into revolutions while others do not even make it into the news.

This book is written for any scholar in the social sciences interested in studying and understanding human behaviour, social dynamics, and the complex systems of society. It does not expect readers to have a particular background apart from some elementary knowledge and affinity for mathematics.

Sebastian Ille is an Associate Professor of Economics at Northeastern University - London, and Editor-in-Chief of the *International Social Science Journal*.

"Drawing on a rich array of historical and contemporary examples, this book provides an introduction to dynamical systems theory and how it elucidates the complex interplay of political, economic, and social factors that give rise to social norms and institutions. The exposition is exceptionally clear and tailored to different levels of mathematical preparation. It will appeal to experts as well as students across the social sciences."

— *H. Peyton Young, University of Oxford & London School of Economics, UK*

"An interdisciplinary book on complexity, a guided tour through mathematical methods ranging from evolutionary game theory, dynamical systems, Markov chains and graph theory to bifurcations and chaos, with applications to nonlinear social sciences. A rigorous introduction delivered by an intriguing storytelling approach."

— *Gian Italo Bischi, Professor of Applied Mathematics, University of Urbino, Italy*

To Anastasia
whose growing curiosity for the world
has inspired this book

– CONTENTS –

Introduction

MORE than a millennium ago, the Emperor's court was as lavish as was his harem. Yet, the poet-king Li Yu of China was confronted with a problem: his concubines and wives could substantially elevate their status by giving birth to a male heir apparent, but given their sheer numbers, the prospects of being with a child sired by the Emperor were less than slim. Meanwhile, each had potentially numerous opportunities to engage in infidelity unbeknownst to the Emperor within the palace walls. How could Li Yu ensure that the progeny was his own?

The solution is shrouded in legend according to which Li Yu asked his favourite concubine Yao Niang to wrap her feet in silk to give them the shape of a lotus. After she bound her feet, her graceful dance on the tip of her toes is said to have not only mesmerised courtiers and especially the Emperor, but has inspired envy among the other ladies of the court. The latter thus fervently adopted the practice. As delightful as this account may be, it is clearly an idealised version and probably belongs to the realm of historical fiction: given Li Yu's predicament, it seems more plausible that he recognised footbinding as a useful way to curb extramarital affairs and pregnancies.[1] Footbinding was conceived as a means of control to limit the movement of women around the palace. Types of footbinding ranged from the *three-inch golden lotus* to the less aggressive version of the *cucumber foot*, but generally, the practice severely maimed the feet - it was irreversible and painful. Yet, the Chinese elite quickly embraced footbinding since binding a daughter's feet was a hypergamous practice that opened the potential of her being accepted to the palace.[2] Adopting the practice was thus of political and economic interest to the higher social strata. It was seen as a signal of status, fertility, chastity, and virtue. Literature internalised footbinding to such a degree that it became a sign of beauty; an erotic custom that served male foot fetishism and stirred men's fantasy with a forced graceful gait. Footbinding turned into an ambiguous sign of concupiscence and purity. Probably due to a lack of historical data, it was initially assumed to be an elite practice. After all, only elite Chinese women possessed the leisure and skills to celebrate bound feet as a mark of beauty and sacrifice since they were not subject to the economic and educational constraints of female workers, farmers, or servants. Nevertheless, footbinding was soon emulated by the lower classes. While it made it impossible to work in wet rice fields, the practice was widespread in rural areas. It seemed incompatible with a society that relied heavily on labour-intensive family farming.

DOI: 10.4324/9781003035329-1

Several reasons have been discussed in the literature, such as the practice's role as a marker of social status even among the peasantry or of ethnic belonging used to distinguish oneself from the invading Mongols (Mackie, 1996). Indeed, the spread of footbinding as a more common practice overlaps with the adoption of the Han culture. Yet, footbinding was also adopted in culturally mixed areas and Manchu women embraced the practice quickly after an ineffectual prohibition of footbinding in 1847.[3] While footbinding was prevalent, it was not universal. Turner (1997) illustrates that geographic conditions seemed to have played a major role instead as footbinding was more common in hospitable areas. Bossen and Gates (2017) provide compelling arguments for another explanation. Not only was footbinding a practice to isolate women away from the eyes of strangers but contrary to common belief, it was stimulated and not deterred by the economic constraints of the peasantry. The labour cost of domestic production was low and child labour was common. In addition, income from weaving was relatively high. Women could earn more by engaging in weaving than agricultural labour. Utilising girls for weaving already at a young age and engaging them in supporting actions, such as hemp twine and reeling silk could therefore sustain a family. Furthermore, they were employed in the production of shoes, sandals, hats, and quilts. Each of these tasks happened inside the house creating little need for long-distance travel because the produce was exchanged at local markets. Footbinding inhibited the ability to play and run and compelled a girl to focus on handwork. Additionally, it was a signal. Seen both as a sign of hand-skill and as an investment towards married life, it was a testament of a wife's dedication - and to a certain degree, footbinding still allowed women to participate in heavier tasks, such as drying fruits or raising silkworms. The division of labour was simple: men plough and women weave.

The widespread custom of footbinding was quickly abandoned in the Republican era in the years following the Nationalist Revolution in 1912. Consistent with the argument of Bossen and Gates, footbinding first disappeared in urbanised areas and among the elites after literati (such as the poet Yuan Mei in the later 18th century), intellectuals, and politicians shunned the practice in their endeavour to modernise China for global trade. The reasons were again manifold. Scholars, such as Qian Yong argued that footbinding is no longer a symbol for the gentry since it has been adopted by the lower classes. Also, footbinding was seen as damaging to China's reputation and honour - a new perception of honour encouraged by the establishment of Christian missions after 1864.[4] Especially female Protestant missionaries opposed footbinding. Thus, while it was initially seen as a symbol of family honour, the changing perception turned it into a dishonourable practice.

Similarly, a young scholar by the name of Kang Youwei argued that a new status for women was necessary for China's reformation in a 10,000 word petition to the throne in 1889.[5] Already before, the Taiping Rebellion of 1850–1854 envisioned equality between men and women. Especially Christian schools established after 1860 opposed the practice, and an increasing number of Chinese from the gentry and merchant classes, who studied abroad, instituted Western ideals. Kang initiated the *Unbound Foot Association* which counted over 10,000 members at the end of the 19th century. Yet the movement was mainly centred around elite expatriate women. Eventually, the Empress Dowager Cixi issued an anti-footbinding (but non-prohibitive) edict in 1902. Despite these efforts, it took until 1911, when Sun Yat-sen banned footbinding. The practice did no longer fit the new Chinese order. The different types of footbinding indicated class in a substantially hierarchical society. It was a symbol of the old imperial world that ended with the Emperor's abdication in 1912 and made room for a new structure of social classes, one that had no need for localised control of women by men.

Yet in rural areas, Chinese held on to footbinding for several years. Fathers started to oppose footbinding while mothers still encouraged the practice since the latter were afraid of the negative signal of a *big foot* to a prospective mother-in-law. It entailed foregoing a respectable marriage and condemning her daughter to hard labour on the fields. However, the introduction of global commerce increased the availability of industrially manufactured machine-made cotton. Production shifted to iron-gear looms, which were mainly operated by men, and production moved outside the house. Meanwhile, revenues from handcrafted products declined. Consequently, the opportunity costs of footbinding became too high and peasant families started abandoning the practice. The prevalence of Christian values entailed a realisation that women can be both unbound and faithful, and schools imposed restrictions on footbinding as elementary education of girls became more important. Thus, while footbinding was almost universal in Dongting, for example, among women born before 1892, it was abandoned in less than a quarter of a century (Gamble, 1954). Similarly, the region to the south of Peking, Tinghsien, completely abolished the practice during the period from 1899 to 1919 (Mackie, 1996).

1.1 Aim and Scope

Several characteristics of the history of footbinding in China may pique our attention. While footbinding was initially a practice within the imperial court and the upper social stratum, its endorsement became increasingly and quickly widespread; not only among the gentry but eventually among commoners and peasants. We have seen that for Li Yu of China and the peasantry, footbinding was a means of control, but its main *advantage* was that bound feet were associated with different and more opaque characteristics that probably outweighed its significant costs. Over time, footbinding co-evolved with Chinese culture and arts and became increasingly ingrained in the latter, as the practice became internalised and shaped the perception of beauty. On the other hand, despite its endurance for a millennium, footbinding was abolished within a generation. Yet, revocation was not uniform across the entire population and area of China. Intellectual centres rapidly ceased to promote footbinding, whereas more rural areas, such as Shanxi, sustained the practice significantly longer. Still, also rural areas illustrated vast differences.

Footbinding is only one example of the plentiful institutions that determine the human history of habits, traditions, and in general, behaviour. **Institutions** constitute the recurrent behavioural rules that are shared by at least part of a population. They include practices, conventions, and norms to which we do not only subject our actions but which the latter reinforce.[6] Institutions are then the collectively accepted and shared code of social interactions.[7] In the context of institutions, our brief historical study of footbinding raises a number of broader questions that are part of the central themes with which we are concerned in this book:

- How are institutions adopted and when do they become prevalent?
- What makes an institution endure and when is it abolished by society?
- Under which conditions can different social practices and conventions co-exist?

- How do certain characteristics or behaviour transform into a signal that is linked to some specific qualities and how do these signals foster endorsement of a particular institution?
- How do individuals learn behavioural rules and which role do peer effects play in the evolution of institutions?
- How can we explain the co-evolutionary processes which govern institutions and which are mutually self-reinforcing?

Social systems follow certain regularities which allow us to model social behaviour and dynamics on the basis of a mathematical approach. Each chapter introduces a different mathematical technique along with various models. The mathematical technique or approach describes a particular way of interpreting actions and behaviour. The models, which apply the mathematical approach, can therefore only be abstract representations of the world, but they are adequate to replicate particular regularities of society. Nevertheless, it is still important to understand each model as a reductionist explanation of a social phenomenon. The aim cannot be a realistic representation of the real world, but only an adequate. In the end, as George Box (1976, p. 792) said: "[A]ll models are wrong".[8] Nevertheless, collectively, these models offer explanations for a wide range of social phenomena, including local and global institutional change and norm evolution, the existence of consistent institutions across different regions and periods of human society – so-called cultural universals – and localised institutions that exist alongside other accepted behavioural rules. Some of these models take account of the elements of complex systems that societies are: they are adaptive, generate scale-free networks and systems, contain different levels of aggregation, and produce emergent properties - the importance and meaning of these concepts will become clearer as we proceed with our study of complex system and social dynamics.

Nevertheless, the modelling of social behaviour in this abstract form comes at a cost. The models I discuss in this book present individuals in a stylised manner. Models involving a larger number of agents are built around the assumption that the relevant preferences and behavioural rules are largely identical across vast parts of the society under investigation. While this is certainly a strong assumption, members of the same social stratum who are faced with the same constraints and backgrounds are likely to have very similar motivations and options at hand. After all, share-croppers in a subsistence society are mainly concerned with feeding their family. In addition, the models I discuss here can be extended to a larger variety of preferences and types of agents in a straightforward manner but at the cost of a higher mathematical complexity. To understand social phenomena, we will see that it is frequently unnecessary to provide a detailed account of individual motivations, beliefs and depending on the model, even individual characteristics.

At the same time, while social behaviour emerges from individual behaviour, society cannot be understood merely on the basis of a summation of individual actions or even less so, on the basis of a *homme moyen* - the average man who is representative of the mean field approximation of a distribution - as postulated by Adolphe Quetelet almost two centuries ago (see Quetelet, 1835). Societies are formed by collectives of agents and are complex systems in which different elements, entities, and dynamics interact. The resulting social behaviour often exhibits emergent properties and can therefore be rarely adequately understood from solely analysing individual actions: the aggregate does not necessarily share the same qualitative attributes as the individuals of which it is composed. The properties of a social system are critically dependent on the social connections formed by individuals and their way of interacting. When Margarete Thatcher claimed "[..] who is society? There is no such thing!" (Thatcher, 1987), she reduced society to a mere abstract concept giving all relevance to the individual, ignoring the strategic character of their actions and the complex interplay of economic, social, political, and cultural factors that motivate social phenomena. While I give credit to the methodological individualism formulated by Max Weber and the need for a proper micro-foundation to describe a social phenomenon, we will see in future chapters that a reduction of these micro-foundations to a mere study of *the individual* is inadequate for explaining at least some aspects of society.

1.2   Some Caveats

Each of the eight mathematical approaches in this book is useful for explaining particular aspects of society. Each has not only its own potentials but also its limits, both of which I will discuss in each chapter. Again, I need to caution the reader not to over-interpret or over-generalise the results which we obtain from these models. The validity of the results in each chapter is constrained by the limiting assumptions of the underlying approach. While the approaches discussed in the early chapters of this book are more simplified and are based on stronger assumptions, the subsequent approaches are more complex and less-restrictive. Readers may fall prey to two fallacies. Some readers might be tempted to refer only to the later chapters for their work. However, abandoning restrictive assumptions does not necessarily imply a decrease in limitations. A less-restrictive approach may turn out to be unnecessarily more complex in a given context, and while being more flexible, such approaches (especially those discussed in Chapters 8 and 9 of this book) come at a cost of less control.

Another fallacy is to assume that integrating more variables improves the explanatory power of a model. While this is partially true, the inclusion of each new variable negatively affects our ability to understand the internal workings of a model and the individual impact of each variable. A scholar, therefore, faces the challenging task of balancing authenticity and tractability when designing a model. The endeavour can be approached through two different methods - from the simple to the complex or from the complex to the simple.[9] Either the scholar begins with a bare, reduced model and adds assumptions to the model until the latter adequately reflects the social phenomenon under investigation while keeping the model tractable and solvable. Alternatively, she starts with a model that almost fully describes the empirical data underlying the social phenomenon and gradually reduces the assumptions and thus, the complexity of the model up to the point that its effectiveness to satisfactorily describe the phenomenon is not compromised. The latter is ensured by testing the robustness of the model after each change. Both approaches should lead to essentially the same result - a balance that guarantees solvability or tractability on the one hand and avoids over-simplification on the other hand.

Various approaches that we study in this book follow one of two fundamental notions of social dynamics. Evolutionary game-theoretic models are studies of dynamics and equilibria. These models understand a social system as a structure that naturally *evolves* towards an equilibrium over time. Consequently, an institution is a local or global attractor of the resulting dynamical system. I will discuss the technical details later, but the intuition of a local attractor is that a particular environment can give rise to several potential solutions to social, economic, and political issues in the form of different institutional structures. A social system then settles into an institutional structure that is not too dissimilar to the initial setup. Here, history matters to a limited degree, but as long as two societies are adequately similar (and we will see what this means later on), they must eventually establish the same set of institutions. In large societies, random variations in individual actions do not affect society as a whole. This at least holds for most situations: we will further see that some rather rare initial setups at tipping points illustrate a strong sensitivity to small random variations.[10] Under these circumstances, individual actions can precipitate the evolution of one institutional solution over another or lead to a mixed state without unique institutions. In the case of a global attractor, on the other hand, history does no longer matter at all. Independent of the current characteristics of the social system, the final institutional setup is inevitable.[11]

The chaotic dynamics in Chapters 8 and 9 constitute the antithetic notion of the former social dynamics. Here, history does not only matter, some models push path dependency to its extreme. Two societies with minuscule variations in the initial institutional setup can diverge radically from each other over time. Individual actions then have a fundamental impact on the society as a whole. Popular science termed these evolutionary dynamics the *butterfly effect*. In addition, these systems are open systems. We will see that they are usually non-ergodic and cannot be studied on the basis of a Markovian system. They are path- or history-dependent and demonstrate co-evolutionary dynamics (again these concepts will become clearer subsequently).[12] How then can we align these two entirely different notions of social dynamics? An easy but unsatisfactory answer would be: it depends on the system under scrutiny. I will discuss this question in Chapter 9 in greater detail, yet as we shall see, convergence and chaos are two sides of the same coin. And I can only wholeheartedly agree with Robert May's statement: "Not only in research, but also in the everyday world of politics and economics, we would be better off if more people realised that simple non-linear systems do not necessarily possess simple dynamical properties" (May, 1976, p. 93).

Last but not least, the approaches in this book further stress the importance of an interdisciplinary perspective to competently understand and model social regularities and phenomena. It is not only the non-linearity of the social dynamics that render social systems complex, but these systems are complex because they are subject to a variety of determining factors. As our short study of footbinding in China illustrated, societies are the product of a sophisticated and compound interplay of political, social, and economic aspects that determine institutions and social dynamics.

1.3 For Whom Is This Book and How to Use It?

This book is written for any scholar, across the social sciences as well as the humanities, who is interested in developing their own mathematical models. I have done my best to increase the scope of the book and present applications beyond my discipline. At the end of this book, reader will realise that footbinding and arms races, the size of cities and the influence of celebrities on Facebook, cooperation and Persian carpets, as well as drip castles and protests have more in common than what we might believe. I further hope that this book will help readers appreciate the need for more multi- and interdisciplinary perspectives when studying social dynamics and complex systems.

The book does not expect the reader to have any prior knowledge about the different approaches, and the appendix briefly reviews the most essential concepts as well as some useful methods that have proven helpful while analysing dynamical systems. A chapter should be seen as a rather *cursory* introduction to a particular approach. I have tried to include the most essential further readings in the conclusion to each chapter for those scholars who wish to delve deeper into a subject. However, in my experience, most of the presented approaches are already sufficiently sophisticated to deliver useful insights when applied to an empirical case or context. In addition, some of the approaches can be combined (an obvious candidate being, for example, Chapters 6 and 7). At the same time, it is important to be prudent when interpreting and generalising the results an approach delivers. Consequently, I discuss the limitations of each approach as well as the connections between different approaches in the conclusion of each chapter. To improve tractability, I print a new concept in bold whenever it is first introduced and defined.

While this book has been written with a focus on self-study in mind, the content of this book can be adapted to meet the needs of a course for undergraduate and graduate students. Each chapter starts with relatively accessible examples in the earlier sections while the later sections contain more advanced material. Apart from Chapter 9, a chapter is composed of four sections in addition to an introduction and conclusion. Consequently, a judicious exposition of the first two to three sections (in addition to supplementary explanations depending on their prior background) of each chapter is suitable for undergraduate students. The full sections can be taught to graduate and postgraduate students, but it may be convenient to spread a chapter over two lectures. If a lecturer wishes to put more emphasis on evolutionary game theory, I suggest including elements from Sections A.3 and A.4 in the Appendix.

1.4 Acknowledgement

Models of Society and Complex Systems retraces the various research themes that I engaged in during the past decade, but it would have been impossible without the foundational and highly inspirational work on which this book is based. Some of these works are referenced in various chapters. I am deeply grateful to these scholars and I count myself lucky that I had the opportunity to be taught by some of them.

I take this opportunity to pay my special regards to Charles Anderton, Edgar Sanchez Carrera, Gian Italo Bischi, Habib Saadi, Laura Gardini, and Samuel Bowles for their valuable insights, thought-provoking suggestions, and very helpful comments which much improved this book. Last but not least, my sincere thanks goes to my wife Dina who had to suffer through the earliest versions of this book and yet remained married to me. Thank you for walking by my side and for being my shoulder to lean on.

Notes

1 See also Mackie (1996).
2 For the first detailed modern study of footbinding, refer to Levy (1966).
3 See Mackie (1996) and Turner (1997).

4   In fact, intellectuals, like Linag Qichao, saw footbinding as a ridiculous custom that made China the *laughingstock* to foreigners, see Appiah (2010).

5   See Volz (2007) and Appiah (2010)).

6   The difference between these concepts - practices, norms, conventions - are not clearly defined in the literature and vary across disciplines. We may define a social norm as behaviour that is based on empirical and normative expectations, whereas conventions can be seen as descriptive norms that only rely on empirically learned behaviour. Practices are habitual forms of behaviour that don't require a normative reinforcement.

7   For a broader discussion, see North (1991).

8   We may think here also of Paul Valéry's statement: "Ce qui est simple est toujours faux. Ce qui ne l'est pas est inutilisable" (Valéry, 1942).

9   This is the principle of Occam's razor, named after Franciscan friar William of Ockham who postulated: "[...] plurality must never be posited without necessity" (Scotus and García, 1912, p. 211). Ockham was probably the model for William of Baskervill in Umberto Eco's *The name of the Rose* who was played by Sean Connery in the film adaptation.

10 Such cases of *final state sensitivity* have been first described in detail in Grebogi et al. (1983).

11 But again, we will see that even in these situations, the institutional setup might be defined by a recurrent periodic pattern.

12 Theoretically, a dynamical social system can even illustrate some sort of hybrid dynamics. In these cases, two societies with similar initial setups diverge from each other over time only to converge again. This periodic repetition of divergence and convergence gives rise to a so-called **strange chaotic attractors**. However, I am not aware of historical processes that imitate these dynamics and will not cover this type of attractor here.

Game Theory: Strategic Interactions

2.1 Introduction

W E have seen in the introduction that the cultural endorsement and eventual repudiation of footbinding in China were governed by transformative social, political, and economic processes. Footbinding was a measure of control and seen as a sign of honour, identity, and distinction but also of manual skill, fertility, and modesty. It thus changed into an institution that not only fulfilled several functions but was also subject to collective and individual perceptions and actions. In this chapter, we will study some of these aspects of footbinding as well as other forms of interaction.

I further introduce an analytical toolbox that will help us model the actions of individuals depending on their expectations about others. The mutual anticipation of actions and reactions creates an interconnectedness between agents that renders their decisions strategic. With its emergence at the beginning of the 20th century, the use of game theory to study simple decentralised decision processes has become increasingly popular in the social sciences. Here, we will focus on **non-cooperative game theory** as opposed to **cooperative game theory** (also called coalitional game theory). While the latter studies the formation of coalitions and the ability of such coalitions to enforce a certain outcome, the former examines actions at the individual level based on the benefits that an action entails. The terminology, suggesting that each approach is more adapt to study a particular context, is indeed misleading. There is nothing that prevents individual actors from being cooperative or members of coalitions to have conflicting interests. In fact, cooperative game theory has the disadvantage over non-cooperative game theory that it ignores questions related to strategic bargaining within coalitions after an outcome is enforced while the latter can be used to analyse any coalitional game. Consequently, non-cooperative game theory can be applied to a wider context and provides a thorough study of decisions at the micro-level and is, thus, a more suitable tool within the context of this book.

To begin with, we have seen that women with bound feet were perceived as being of higher status, modesty, and faithfulness among the gentry and as committed to married life as well as skilled and dedicated workers among the lower classes. Footbinding gave access to hypergamy among Chinese elites and to labour specialisation among the lower classes- in short, it was seen as an institution to improve subsistence. Consequently, while the practice was not accepted

DOI: 10.4324/9781003035329-2

unanimously, it was inflicted on 50–80 percent of women (see Mackie, 1996; Bossen and Gates, 2017 who show that the prevalence of footbinding among the lower class is probably significantly underestimated). Yet, it was not adopted without resistance. Footbinding was not only opposed by influential literati and Manchu overlords, but by parents (Mackie, 1996; Appiah, 2010). It, therefore, seems puzzling why a practice is enforced even by those who initially resist it.

The following simple game-theoretic analysis will shed some light on this seemingly paradoxical behaviour. In our very simplified model, assume that parents have to choose between *binding* the feet of their daughter or to be *lenient* and refrain from footbinding. Furthermore, assume that two types of parents exist: *authoritarian* and *liberal*. Each type of parent evaluates the benefits of footbinding conditional on the behaviour of other parents. Authoritarian parents are decidedly interested in marrying off their daughters and hence, generally prefer to bind their feet. They draw a higher benefit from footbinding if other parents refrain from the custom as it increases their chances of hypergamy. They least prefer to have an unbound daughter when the custom is widely adopted. Liberal parents, on the other hand, recognise the advantage of binding their daughters' feet but prefer a situation in which footbinding is not adopted as a widespread practice which would not require their daughter to have her feet bound to be considered a marriageable match. The benefits of authoritarian parents and liberal parents are shown in Figures 2.1a and 2.1b, respectively. For the moment, we will ignore the questions of where these numbers come from and what their meaning is. It is only important to recognise that an outcome with a higher number is absolutely preferred to an outcome associated with a lower number. B denotes that a parent decides to *bind* their daughter and L indicates a *lenient* parent. The action of each type of parent defines the row, whereas the actions of the other parents determine the column of the matrices. Each parent chooses an action that is most beneficial given what they believe other parents do. Thus, the actions of other parents are considered *as given* which is indicated by the hollow letters in Figure 2.1a and 2.1b. An authoritarian parent will receive a benefit of 5 from binding if other parents also bind the feet of their daughters and a benefit of 10 from binding if others don't. Correspondingly, an authoritarian parent receives a benefit of 0 or of 2 from being lenient if other parents choose to bind or to be lenient, respectively. The bold value specifies the largest value in each row, and the direction of comparison is indicated by the small arrows. We can see that to bind is always better than to be lenient for authoritarian parents, whatever other parents do. We therefore call B (i.e. to bind) a **strictly dominant strategy**. Such a strategy does not exist for liberal parents. A closer inspection of the matrix in Figure 2.1b shows that liberal parents should do exactly what other parents are doing: it is best to bind the feet of their daughter if other parents do so and to be lenient if other parents decide not to bind the feet of their daughters. This can be seen by comparing the respective values and looking at the arrows in the matrix.

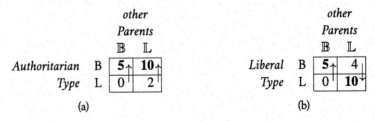

Figure 2.1: Benefit of footbinding with two types: the *authoritarian* type is shown in (a), the *liberal* type in (b).

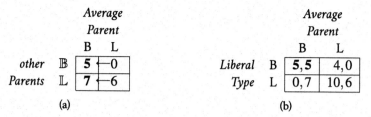

		Average Parent	
		B	L
other	B	5 ← 0	
Parents	L	7 ← 6	

(a)

		Average Parent	
		B	L
Liberal	B	5,5	4,0
Type	L	0,7	10,6

(b)

Figure 2.2: Footbinding continued: the *average* parent's actions determine the rows and benefits are shown in (a), the game between a liberal-type parent and the average parent is shown in (b).

The matrix in Figure 2.1b is, however, insufficient to understand why liberal parents would support footbinding. In fact, they are doing much better (10 compared to 5) if they assume that other parents are lenient and would therefore choose the same action. To answer this question, we need to look at the incentives and choices of the other parents. Assume that the authoritarian parents in Figure 2.1a and the liberal parents in Figure 2.1b are extreme versions of the population of parents and most parents are somewhere in between. Thus, an average parent would receive a benefit of $1/2 \times 10 + 1/2 \times 4 = 7$ (i.e. the average benefit of an authoritarian and liberal parent) if they choose to bind their daughter's feet while other parents are lenient. If the latter also choose to bind, the average parents receive a benefit of $1/2 \times 5 + 1/2 \times 5 = 5$. Similarly, the benefit of an average parent from being lenient is $1/2 \times 0 + 1/2 \times 0 = 0$ and $1/2 \times 2 + 1/2 \times 10 = 6$, respectively. Figure 2.2a illustrates the benefits, however, the matrix is transposed and the average parent and other parents exchanged their position. The average parent now determines the columns of the matrix and takes the rows (defined by the actions of other parents) as given. Average parents compare their benefits thus along the same row as indicated by the arrows in the matrix. Strategy B (i.e. to bind) is still the dominant strategy for an average parent since 7 is better than 6 and 5 better than 0.

To understand why a liberal parent will still choose to bind their daughter's feet, we need to combine the information in Figure 2.1b and Figure 2.2a. The matrix in Figure 2.2b joins the benefits of both types in a single cell. The first value in each cell of the matrix refers to the benefit of a liberal parent and the second value refers to the benefit of an average parent. When making a strategic decision, a liberal parent takes the action of an average parent into account. Knowing that an average parent has a strictly dominant strategy, which is to always choose B, it is optimal for the former to also choose B. Hence, all parties will choose to bind their daughter's feet. If you look closer at the individual benefits in Figure 2.2b you will realise that both liberal parents and average parents would be better off if they could jointly enforce a lenient solution that does not rely on footbinding (10 compared to 5 for liberal parents and 6 compared to 5 for an average parent). This kind of coordination failure can be frequently encountered in social interactions and game theory provides us with an intuitive explanation of their occurrence. Now that we have taken our first tentative step into the world of game theory, it is time to study the approach more systematically.

2.2 Definition of a Game

We call a **game** a situation in which individuals or groups (whom we call players) are confronted with a choice and the final outcome depends in part on the decisions made by other individuals.

We can separate between **simultaneous games** and **sequential games**. In the former, players either make a decision at the same time or are unaware of the other actors' choices. Both settings are essentially the same since players cannot directly observe what others are doing but can form expectations about others' actions. In a sequential game, however, players take rounds and a player who makes a move at a later round can at least partially observe what has been going on before. In addition, we can broadly differentiate between one-shot games that are played only once and repeated games in which actors meet more frequently. In the latter case, previous interactions and future expectations co-determine each player's choice. Any game specified in its **normal form** is defined by three elements: the *players* that interact strategically, their possible *actions and strategies*, and a payoff function that assigns each player a *payoff* at the end of the interaction. It is worthwhile to have a closer look at the meaning and implications of these three elements since confusion about their interpretation frequently causes misconceptions about game theory.

Players

The term **player** dates back to the first fledgling stages of game theory when it was used to study the best bets in games of chance. As much as game theory has developed beyond these confines, the definition of a player is now vastly broader. A player can be an individual or a group, a firm or a human being. We usually define the group of all players who are interacting in a game as a finite set of players $I = \{1, 2, 3, \ldots, n\}$. Depending on the context, it is sometimes more convenient to substitute the positive integers by the names or denomination of the players (i.e. teacher and student instead of players 1 and 2). In a chess game, the pieces would compose the set of players and we might define a simplified set that is reduced to only two pieces as $I = \{King, Pawn\}$. In addition, it is frequently easier to analyse a particular player, especially if players have identical properties and the player set is larger. In this case, we denote the generic player as player i and denote the other players that the former is interacting with by $-i$ (which should be interpreted as the set of players except for i). The i can then be *substituted* by any integer or name.

Strategies

Each player possesses a number of strategies. A strategy can be a simple action or a more complicated plan of conditional actions of the form "do A if C and do B if D" (while C and D might be strategies chosen by another player). Each player i has then a set of strategies defined by S_i. Using our previous example, player pawn has the choice between $S_{pawn} = \{forward, stay, beat\}$ and player king has a strategy set $S_{king} = \{forward, backward, left, right, stay\}$. From her strategy set S_i, player i chooses a strategy s_i. We call $s = (s_1, s_2, \ldots, s_n)$ a **strategy profile**. The strategy profile specifies the strategies that have been chosen and which led to a final outcome. It should be clear from the notation that the strategy profile is defined by one strategy for every player. The set S is composed of all possible strategy profiles and thus for any s it must be that $s \in S$. Imagine a two-step sequential game in which the pawn moves first and the king reacts. A strategy profile in which the pawn moves forward into one of the squares surrounding the king, followed by the king moving to his left square as a reaction, is given by $s = (forward, left)$. In this two-step example, the set S contains $3 \times 5 = 15$ different strategy profiles.

Note that for the moment, we only focused on **pure strategies** but the arguments easily extend to **mixed strategies**. A mixed strategy of player i, given by σ_i, is composed of a random mix of pure strategies. For example, in a Rock, Scissor, Paper game, an optimal mixed strategy for player i would be $\sigma_i = 1/3 Rock + 1/3 Scissor + 1/3 Paper$. In other words, player i randomly chooses one of the three pure strategies with an equal probability of one-third. Note that the probabilities are within the range of zero to one and must add up to a total of 1. Consequently, a mixed strategy that assigns a probability of one to a single pure strategy and thus, a probability equal to zero to all the other pure strategies is again a pure strategy. A mixed strategy profile is given by the collective of each player's mixed strategy choice, i.e. $\sigma = (\sigma_1, \sigma_2, \ldots, \sigma_n)$.

Payoffs

Similar to players, **payoff** should not be equated with monetary benefits but be seen as a vastly more general concept that represents a player's preferences. A payoff is a numerical representation of the benefit that the final outcome of a game bestows on an individual. As such, payoffs do include pecuniary benefits but also other aspects. Payoffs can include feelings of pain or joy, satisfaction and happiness, but also sadness and distress. Since I can feel joy by helping others, a payoff can also include the emotional or pecuniary benefit that others derive from my actions. The concept of payoff is therefore equivalent to the concept of utility as used by economists and thus, bears the same problems - something we will discuss at the end of this chapter. We define a payoff function $\pi_i(s)$ for player i that transforms a strategy profile s into a payoff (we write $\pi_i : S \rightarrow \mathbb{R}$, where $\mathbb{R}$ is the set of real numbers). Player i's payoff when choosing mixed strategy σ_i and playing against the other $(n-i)$ players' mixed strategies is given by

$$\pi_i = \sum_{s_i \in S_1} \cdots \sum_{s_n \in S_n} p_{s_1} p_{s_2} \cdots p_{s_n} \pi_i(s_1, s_2, \ldots, s_n) \tag{2.1}$$

where p_{s_l} denotes the weight that is attributed to strategy s_l. The payoff of a mixed strategy takes the expected payoff of the pure strategy profile by multiplying its likelihood by the corresponding payoff and then calculates the sum of the products over all possible strategy profiles. (Don't worry, we will have a look at an example.)

At this point, a question naturally arises. How can we measure intangible feelings and on which basis can we assign a number to a feeling of joy that for example, a child experiences if a game leads to her winning a soft toy? In fact, the *absolute* value is of little relevance, since we only need to assign a *relative value*. If we transform each payoff of player i in the payoff matrix by a so-called positive affine transformation, the game remains identical. A **positive affine transformation** alters some payoff π_i of player i into some other payoff $\hat{\pi}_i$ as follows:

$$\hat{\pi}_i = \alpha \pi_i + \beta \text{ given } \alpha > 0 \tag{2.2}$$

If we take the payoff matrix of our initial example of footbinding, we can see that a positive affine transformation changes the payoff matrix 2.2b as shown in Figure 2.3 but the game will lead us to exactly the same conclusions. The payoffs of the liberal type were transformed by choosing $\alpha = 2$ and $\beta = 5$ and for the average parent's payoffs, we have $\alpha = 1$ and $\beta = -5$.

In the absence of mixed strategies, even the assumption of relative payoffs is too restrictive, and we only require that a strictly preferred outcome is associated with a strictly higher payoff than

		average Parent	
		B	L
Liberal	B	**5,5**	4,0
Type	L	0,7	10,6

		average Parent	
		B	L
Liberal	B	**15,0**	13,−5
Type	L	5,2	25,1

Figure 2.3: Two equivalent games: The right payoff matrix has been derived from the left payoff matrix via an positive affine transformation.

an outcome which is less preferred. A typical example of such ordinal scales is the measurement of temperature. It is obvious that in winter, it is cooler outside than inside, but only by assigning a scale, i.e. a degree Celsius or Fahrenheit, to both temperatures, we can make comparable statements. Yet, as you can see, these scales are chosen arbitrarily.

Nash Equilibrium

The fundamental solution concept in game theory is the **Nash equilibrium**. In plain English, a Nash equilibrium is characterised by an outcome in which the strategy chosen by *each* player is the optimal reaction to the strategies chosen by *all the other players*. Consequently, a player takes the strategies of all other players as given and has no reason to *unilaterally* deviate from the current strategy. If this holds for all players, the outcome forms an equilibrium. The individually optimal reaction is called a **best response (strategy)**. More formally, we define some strategy profile $(s_i^*, s_{-i}^*) = (s_1^*, s_2^*, \ldots, s_n^*)$ and another strategy profile $(s_i, s_{-i}^*) = (s_1^*, \ldots, s_{i-1}^*, s_i, s_{i+1}^*, \ldots, s_n^*)$ in which player i substituted strategy s_i^* by another strategy $s_i \in S_i$ (note that player i may have any position in the strategy profile). Strategy profile $s^* = (s_i^*, s_{-i}^*)$ is a Nash equilibrium if

$$\pi_i(s_i^*, s_{-i}^*) \geq \pi_i(s_i, s_{-i}^*) \tag{2.3}$$

In other words, by choosing strategy s_i^* player i does at least as good against the strategies chosen by the other players compared to any other strategy she could have selected. If we substitute the $\geq$ sign by $>$, we call the strategy profile a **strict Nash equilibrium**, i.e. there is a unique best response for all players. The **mixed Nash equilibrium** is then defined analogously by

$$\pi_i(\sigma_i^*, \sigma_{-i}^*) \geq \pi_i(\sigma_i, \sigma_{-i}^*) \tag{2.4}$$

John Nash proved that any finite game has at least one Nash equilibrium (Nash, 1950), although the equilibrium might only exist in mixed strategies (known as the *Nash Existence Theorem*).[1] There is a straightforward way to find the mixed strategy profile σ which constitutes a Nash equilibrium. We define $\sigma = (\sigma_i, \sigma_{-i})$, where σ_i is the mixed strategy chosen by player i and σ_{-i} the mixed strategies chosen by all the other players, and let s_i and s_i' be two strategies in the strategy set S_i that are used with positive probability in player i's mixed strategy σ_i. By the *Fundamental Theorem of Mixed Strategy Nash Equilibrium*, σ is a Nash equilibrium if the following holds:

- strategies s_i and s_i' have the same payoff against σ_{-i}
- if strategy s_i'' has zero probability in σ_i, the payoff of s_i'' against σ_{-i} is less or equal to the payoff of s_i or s_i'

	A	
B	Musical	Cinema
Musical	2,1	0,0
Cinema	0,0	1,2

(a) Battle of the Sexes

	A	
B	Stag	Hare
Stag	5,5	0,3
Hare	3,0	3,3

(b) Stag Hunt (Assurance Game)

	A	
B	Cooperate	Defect
Cooperate	2,2	0,3
Defect	3,0	1,1

(c) Prisoner's Dilemma

	A	
B	Stay	Swerve
Stay	0,0	3,1
Swerve	1,3	2,2

(d) Chicken (Hawk-Dove)

	A	
B	Heads	Tails
Heads	1,−1	−1,1
Tails	−1,1	1,−1

(e) Matching Pennies

	A	
B	Gather	Hunt
Hunt	3,3	2,0
Gather	0,2	1,1

(f) Mutual Benefit

Figure 2.4: Versions of the most common 2 × 2 Normal Form Games.

Figure 2.4 provides an overview of the different types of 2×2 games in their normal form representation. Remember that the absolute payoffs in these payoff matrices are irrelevant and any other game with two players and two strategies that can be transformed into one of those in Figure 2.4 will exhibit the same properties. At this point, we should take a few moments to familiarise ourselves with the notations and to apply what we have learned so far. We take a closer look at the first game - the *Battle of the Sexes*. Exercise 2.1 asks you to do the rest of the work for the other games.

The battle of the sexes in Figure 2.4a goes as follows: assume that a couple, say *Bert* and *Anja*, are planning a night out in London. We have the player set $I = \{A, B\}$. Both players wish to spend time either at a musical or in a cinema. Hence, we can define the strategy sets $S_A = S_B = \{Musical, Cinema\}$. By some unfortunate twist of fate, their cell phone connection breaks down while they were planning their meeting leaving them with no possibility of contacting each other. Instead of returning home, they decide to sit down and employ game theory to choose their optimal venue. We further assume that they are aware that their partner is equally trained in game theory, but have no further clue what their counterpart will choose. We have four different strategy profiles $s = (s_A, s_B)$ equal to the four cells composing the payoff matrix. Anja prefers going to the cinema over the musical while Bert prefers the musical over the cinema, but both would like to spend the evening together. Thus, Anja has a payoff of $\pi_A(Cinema, Cinema) = 2$ if they watch a movie in cinema and a payoff of $\pi_A(Musical, Musical) = 1$ if both enjoy the musical but a payoff of $\pi_A(Cinema, Musical) = \pi_A(Musical, Cinema) = 0$ if they don't spend the evening together. Bert has the opposite payoff with respect to the joint evening in the cinema or the musical, and equally, has a payoff of 0 if he has to spend his time without Anja.

The battle of sexes is a typical asymmetric coordination game since players do best by choosing the same strategies. It is asymmetric since both players have different preferences over the coordinated outcomes. Other examples of a coordination game are the Stag Hunt and Mutual Benefit in Figures 2.4b and 2.4f, which demonstrate a strictly preferred outcome and are therefore called *common interest games*. We can now check which of the four strategy profiles/cells are a Nash equilibrium. Anja's actions determine the columns of the payoff matrix and Bert's actions the row of the payoff matrix. We, therefore, call Anja the **column player** and Bert the **row player**. We can see that the upper left cell, defined by strategy profile (*Musical*, *Musical*) is indeed a Nash equilibrium. If Bert deviates from this strategy profile by choosing *Cinema*, he will end up with a payoff of zero. We have $\pi_B(Musical, Musical) > \pi_B(Musical, Cinema)$. The same holds for Anja if she deviates. Remember that we only look at unilateral deviations and take the other player's strategy as fixed. Since a unilateral deviation will reduce their respective payoff to zero, none has an incentive to change their strategy and (*Musical*, *Musical*) is a Nash equilibrium. Consequently, (*Musical*, *Cinema*) and (*Cinema*, *Musical*) are unstable and not a Nash equilibrium. Repeating the test for (*Cinema*, *Cinema*) shows that also this strategy profile is an equilibrium.

Yet, there is a third equilibrium, but in mixed strategies. Based on the Fundamental Theorem, we know that each of the pure strategies that is played with positive probability should be an equally good response to the mixed strategy of the other player, i.e. they generate the same payoff. Suppose that Anja plays a mixed strategy ($\sigma_A = \alpha$ *Musical* $+ (1 - \alpha)$ *Cinema*) and Bert uses the mixed strategy ($\sigma_B = \beta$ *Musical* $+ (1 - \beta)$ *Cinema*) with $\alpha, \beta \in (0, 1)$, i.e. within the unit interval. We have

$$\pi_B(\sigma_A, Musical) = \pi_B(\sigma_A, Cinema)$$
$$\Leftrightarrow 2\alpha + 0(1 - \alpha) = 0\alpha + 1(1 - \alpha)$$

and solving for α, we obtain

$$\alpha = \frac{1}{3}$$

This implies that Anja will choose to go to the musical with a probability of 1/3 and to the cinema with a probability of 2/3.

Solving for Bert, we have

$$\pi_A(Musical, \sigma_B) = \pi_A(Cinema, \sigma_B)$$
$$\Leftrightarrow 1\beta + 0(1 - \beta) = 0\beta + 2(1 - \beta)$$

and solving for β, we obtain

$$\beta = \frac{2}{3}$$

and hence, Bert will choose to go to the musical with a probability of 2/3 and to the cinema with a probability of 1/3. This implies that both will frequent their preferred choice more often, and go to the musical with a probability of $(1/3)(2/3) = 2/9$ and to the cinema with a probability of $(2/3)(1/3) = 2/9$, but miss each other $1 - (2/9 + 2/9) = 5/9$ of the time. Using equation (2.1), their respective payoffs are given by

$$(\pi_A, \pi_B) = \frac{2}{9}(1, 2) + \frac{5}{9}(0, 0) + \frac{2}{9}(2, 1) = \left(\frac{2}{3}, \frac{2}{3}\right)$$

The first number in the rounded brackets refers to Anja's payoff and the second number refers to Bert's payoff. Both receive an expected payoff of 2/3 which is lower than if they had coordinated on a pure strategy Nash equilibrium. Would it be better, if both just flipped a coin (tails = *cinema*, heads=*musical*) and went to the cinema and musical each with a probability of 0.5? Since the likelihood of both opting for the same strategy is $(1/2)(1/2)$, the expected payoff, in this case, is given by

$$(\pi_A, \pi_B) = \frac{1}{4}(1,2) + \frac{1}{2}(0,0) + \frac{1}{4}(2,1) = \left(\frac{3}{4}, \frac{3}{4}\right)$$

Both players are better off, but can this be a Nash equilibrium? It makes sense for each player to deviate from such a strategy by only going to their preferred venue. If, for example, Anja unilaterally switches to *Cinema*, their respective payoffs are

$$(\pi_A, \pi_B) = \frac{1}{2}(0,0) + \frac{1}{2}(2,1) = \left(1, \frac{1}{2}\right)$$

and hence, it is clearly better for Bert to also switch to *Cinema*, giving him a payoff of 1 and increasing Anja's payoff to 2. Coin flipping is not an equilibrium. Indeed, both could improve over the mixed strategy Nash equilibrium by developing a coordination device that allows them to alternate between both strategies but to always predict the choice of the other. In this case, both would receive $\pi_A = \pi_B = 1.5$ on average. We will discuss the ability of players to coordinate better by using a signal in Section 2.4, after dedicating some time to the discussion of sequential games in the following section.

Exercise 2.1

(a) Show that like the *Battle of the Sexes*, both *Stag Hunt* and *Chicken* each have two Nash equilibria in pure strategies, while Prisoner's Dilemma and Mutual Benefit have only one, and Matching Pennies has none. (b) Show that the games with two Nash equilibria in pure strategies as well as matching pennies each have a Nash equilibrium in mixed strategies.

Before doing so, it is worthwhile to discuss a convenient property of Nash equilibria in relation to payoffs that extend beyond the invariance of the game's properties after a positive affine transformation, which we discussed on page 13. The best replies and the position of the interior equilibrium remain unaffected by the addition of a constant to all payoffs of some player i that she obtains given a fixed pure strategy profile s_{-i}. Let there be some pure strategy profile $\bar{s}_{-i}$ defined for the players other than i, and let the new payoffs be defined by $\hat{\pi}_i = \pi_i + \gamma_i$ if $s_{-i} = \bar{s}_{-i}$ and $\hat{\pi}_i = \pi_i$ otherwise, where γ_i is some real number. The new game defined by the payoffs $\hat{\pi}_i$ has the same pure and mixed best responses and equilibria as the original game defined by payoffs $\hat{\pi}_i$.

Figure 2.5 illustrates the transformation for a generic 2×2 game using constants r_1, r_2, s_1, and s_2. Note that the constants can also be negative. The result is intuitive since the difference between the relevant payoffs is maintained by adding or subtracting the same constant. Thus, individual preferences between the outcomes are unaffected by this transformation.

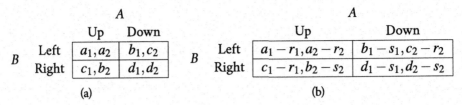

Figure 2.5: Payoff transformation by subtracting a constant that maintains the best responses and Nash equilibria.

Exercise 2.2

(a) Show that the games in Figure 2.5a and 2.5b have the same equilibrium in mixed strategies. (b) The following question is a bit tricky: show that the set of pure Nash equilibria is unaffected by any monotonic transformation of the payoffs, but mixed strategy equilibria require the more specific case of a positive affine transformation.

2.3 The Ultimatum Game

In the previous section, we have focused on interactions in which players choose an action either at the same time as the other players or are simply unaware of the strategies chosen by the latter. Yet, frequently we are exposed to situations in which one actor chooses as a first-mover and someone else reacts to the action of the former. This leads to a sequence of choices in which an earlier mover anticipates the consequences of a chosen action and a later mover takes these actions as given and chooses an optimal strategy as a response.

Pairwise interactions are habitually characterised by a situation in which somebody makes an offer and somebody else has to decide whether to accept that offer (e.g. bartering at a market, accepting a job offer or a marriage proposal, renting an apartment, etc.). The **ultimatum game**, introduced by Güth et al. (1982), is probably one of the easiest representations of such sequential games with two players. Not only this: the ultimatum game is related to our previous discussion of footbinding and its abolition. It illustrates how our sense of fairness and honour does not only influence our actions but is shaped by prevailing social customs, practices, and norms. The ultimatum game is played as follows: a *proposer* is given an amount σ which she has to split with a *responder*. The proposer is free to split the amount in any way possible and on the other hand, the responder knowing the initial amount can choose to *reject* or *accept* the offer. In the case of the former, both responder and proposer receive an amount of zero and in case of the latter, the amount is split according to the proposer's offer.

Some deliberation may be necessary before we proceed, since readers may find it easy to discard the ultimatum game as being too specific given its initial setup. Granted, how frequently are we gifted an amount of money which we are free to pass on to others? Yet, this argument misses the point of the ultimatum game. If, for example, we choose to work for a new employer, our labour will probably generate a positive return and the employer will be responsible for attributing a share of the fruits of work to us. This type of scenario holds for a large number of daily interactions. Admittedly, the ultimatum game ignores the previous history of the proposer and responder and indeed, we could easily extend the game by modelling how the proposer was able to obtain the

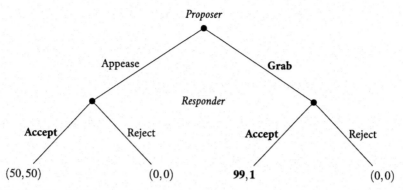

Figure 2.6: Classic version of the Ultimatum Game reduced to two strategies: dominant strategy of responder is to accept and best response of Proposer is to offer a minimum amount.

amount in the first place. This extension will evidently influence the way both players perceive each other and their respective merited amount. Before we address these questions, we will initially focus on the simple version of the game.

How much should the proposer offer? Although there are numerous ways to split this amount, it is not necessary to analyse all potential actions since we can infer the properties of the ultimatum game from a subset of strategies. We will see that two different strategies suffice for our purpose: to share the amount equally or to only offer the responder one unit of the amount. We shall denote the former strategy by *appease* and the latter by *grab*. Assume that $\sigma = 100$. Figure 2.6 presents the game in its **extensive form** as a **directed graph**. While we will discuss directed graphs in detail in Chapter 6, the interpretation of the extensive form game is relatively straightforward. We read the graph from top to bottom. The **nodes** (indicated by small circles and also called a decision node) determines which player is making a move and the **edges** (indicated by lines) emanating from the node define the possible actions of that player. The proposer is the first-mover. She occupies the **root node** and initiates the game by choosing between to appease or to grab. The following node (the so-called **child node**, and correspondingly, the root node is its **parent node**) illustrates that the responder acts after the proposer has chosen. The responder chooses whether to accept or to reject the offer. The **terminal nodes** at the bottom of the graph define the payoff of each player. The first number refers to the proposer and the second number to the responder. We can see that the directed graph looks like an inverted tree. It is, therefore, also called a **game tree** and the edges are frequently denoted as **branches**.

The best way to solve the game 2.6 is via **backward induction**. As the term indicates, we solve the game by starting at the bottom of the game tree and working our way up. The idea is that the proposer anticipates the reaction of the responder and chooses an optimal action accordingly. We first compare the responder's payoff for each action after she has been offered an equal split. Action *accept* will grant her 50 while *reject* will make her go away empty-handed. To accept is clearly the better choice. Looking at the right side of the decision tree, after the proposer offered only an amount of 1, *accepting* the offer grants the responder a payoff of 1 which is higher than a payoff of 0 if she chose to *reject*. To *accept* is the better choice for the responder in both cases – in fact, it is the better response to any non-zero offer made by the proposer – and thus, this action defines the responder's dominant strategy. Knowing that the responder always *accepts* any positive

		Responder			
		RR	RA	AR	AA
Proposer	Appease	0,0	0,0	**50,50**	50,50
	Grab	0,0	**99,1**	0,0	**99,1**

Figure 2.7: Normal Form representation of the Ultimatum Game in 2.6. Reject is denoted by *R* and accept by *A*.

amount, the proposer offers the minimum amount of 1. The result seems surprising and probably implausible. Yet, it is not a flaw in our game-theoretic approach, but the way in which we defined the game. We will postpone the discussion for a moment to study some helpful concepts in further detail. While some games are more suitable to be presented as extensive form games and others as normal form games, any game can be depicted in any of the two game presentations. Figure 2.7 shows the corresponding normal form of the extensive form game in Figure 2.6.

The responder's strategies consist of a pair of actions that are conditional on the proposer's offer. We therefore obtain four different strategies: strategy *RA* indicates that the responder rejects in case the responder chooses *appease* and *accepts* if the latter chooses *grab*. Correspondingly *AR* indicates the inverse strategy, and *AA* and *RR* specify that the responder always accepts or rejects, respectively. The Nash equilibria are shown in bold. We already identified (*Grab,AA*) as the equilibrium of the extensive form game 2.6, but why do we observe two additional equilibria in the normal form game? The second equilibrium (*Grab,RA*) leads to the same final outcome. However, if the responder believes that even a small probability exists of the proposer choosing *appease*, it is better for the former to choose strategy *AA* instead. We, therefore, call strategy *RA* **weakly dominated** by strategy *AA* and it is less likely that the responder will choose a dominated strategy. If the responder chooses to play *AR*, on the other hand, it is the proposer's best response to appease. Indeed, if the responder could make the proposer believe that he is actively committed to rejecting the low offer under *grab*, strategy profile (*Appease,AR*) is indeed an equilibrium. Going back to the extensive form game 2.6, however, shows that such a strategy is a non-credible threat and will not deter the proposer. The latter knows that once the responder is required to react to *grab*, it is better to respond by choosing *accept*. To *reject*, as dictated by strategy *AR*, is not the best response to the subordinated game initiated at the responder's choice. We, therefore, say that equilibrium (*Appease,AR*) is not **subgame perfect** and therefore, not an equilibrium of the extensive form game 2.6. We can see that both the extensive form presentation and the normal form presentation can provide us with valuable insight into the characteristics of the game.

Yet, one may still wonder why (*Appease,AR*) is not an equilibrium of the extensive form game, since it is intuitively plausible. Indeed, research has shown that individuals reject too low offers and tend to punish greedy proposers at their own cost while depending on the cultural environment, proposers offer around 30–40 percent.[2] The essential problem of the game in Figure 2.6 is that individuals are assumed to be entirely **self-regarding**. In other words, individuals are expected to evaluate their well-being independent of others, i.e. they do not contrast their benefits with those of others and ignore the latter's intentions and situation. Indeed, if given a small and inexpensive gift by a friend or $1 by a stranger to help with a bus ticket if in need, most of us would not decline the offer. Yet, in the ultimatum game, the responder knows exactly the initial amount and thus, the share that the proposer attributes to themselves. Consequently, the responder's response does not solely depend on the value of the amount given but also on the amount taken by the proposer. Individuals with a strong sense of equality and reciprocity will only accept offers close to 50 percent, while members in more individualistic societies will accept much lower offers. In addition, as alluded to in the introduction of this section, both proposer and responder may have a prior history that shapes the responder's perception of a fair offer which may be different from an equal split. Furthermore, the proposer is also not entirely self-regarding but to a certain degree, illustrates care for or familiarity with the responder and is therefore, inclined to offer more than the minimum amount.[3] This creates a situation of interdependent **social preferences** or so-called **other-regarding preferences**.[4]

Exercise 2.3

Imagine that the Chinese Emperor has to choose whether or not to impose footbinding on his wives and concubines as a fidelity-control practice. The latter have an incentive to conceive a child (preferably a son) who will elevate their standing in the Emperor's harem, but, given their numbers, are unlikely to be sufficiently frequented by the Emperor to conceive a legitimate child. The women of the Emperor's harem evidently have reasons to be unfaithful, yet footbinding would significantly limit their ability to do so. Assume that the Emperor chooses between two strategies $s_E = \{Bind, notBind\}$ and the women of his harem have equally two strategies $s_W = \{Faithful, Unfaithful\}$. Assume that the birth of a child from a faithful woman is worth 100 for the Emperor and worth 0 if the woman was unfaithful. If she is not bound, being faithful grants her 15, but being unfaithful gives her a benefit of 20. If she is bound, due to the limited mobility, being faithful gives her 10 while being unfaithful offers her 5. (a) Show and analyse the normal form game and study the equilibria. (b) It is more realistic to assume that the Emperor is a first-mover (similar to the proposer in the ultimatum game). Develop and study the sequential game both in its extensive and normal form representation.

In the following, we will extend the ultimatum game to acknowledge the social preferences of responders, but for simplicity, we ignore the social preferences of proposers. For other approaches, the reader may refer to Falk and Fischbacher (2005) and Dhami (2016). Given the amount σ to be split by the proposer and defining the responder's amount by x, we have the proposer's amount given by $\sigma - x$. The incentive to punish depends on how much the offer deviates from a normative offer ρ. Such a normative offer is in itself a function of the social environment and the factors determining the relationship between proposer and responder. It depends on the existing sharing norms within a society (Henrich et al., 2001), the intentions, alternatives and perceived degree of kindness of the proposer (Falk and Fischbacher, 2005), framing and recognised merit (Hoffman et al., 1996) as well as the total amount σ (Andersen et al., 2011). We will therefore write $\rho(\sigma)$ whenever it is necessary to indicate the dependence of the normative offer on the total amount σ. The cost of punishment is equal to the amount that the responder forgoes if they reject the offer and it may not be simply equal to x due to diminishing marginal gains of income and wealth.[5] The efficiency of punishment is determined by the amount that the proposer loses if the responder rejects the offer. Again the latter is not necessarily equal to $\sigma - x$ but depends on the responder's evaluation of the proposer's situation. A lower offer x has three effects on the responder:

- The incentive to punish increases: given a normative offer of $\rho(\sigma) < \sigma$, the incentive to punish is defined by a function of the difference between the normative and the actual offer, given by $l(\rho(\sigma) - x)$.
- The cost of punishment decreases: the perceived cost is a function of the amount not received, given by $g(x)$.
- The efficiency of a punishment/retaliation increases: the perceived impact of a rejection depends on the amount that the proposer loses, given by function $h(\sigma - x)$.

We generally assume that all functions are positive in their argument. Assuming that the proposer is aware of the responders' evaluation, their offer x must fulfil the following condition to be accepted.

$$g(x) \geq k\left(l(\rho - x), h(\sigma - x)\right) \tag{2.5}$$

where $k(.)$ is a function that describes the benefit of rejecting the offer as the relationship between the incentive to punish and the efficiency of punishment. For the purpose of illustration, assume the following simple relationships:

$$l(\rho - x) = \alpha\ (\rho - x)$$
$$g(x) = x$$
$$h(\sigma - x) = \beta\ (\sigma - x)$$
$$k\left(l(.), h(.)\right) = \alpha\ (\rho - x) + \beta\ (\sigma - x)$$

with α, β being strictly positive parameters. Setting this into equation (2.5) and solving for x gives us the optimal (payoff maximising) offer of

$$x^* = \frac{\alpha\rho(\sigma) + \beta\sigma}{1 + \alpha + \beta} \tag{2.6}$$

We assume that the parameter values are as such that the normative offer ρ exceeds the optimal offer x^*. Substituting x^* by the right side of equation (2.6) into $\rho > x^*$ and solving for β, we obtain:

$$\beta^* < \frac{\rho}{\sigma - \rho} \tag{2.7}$$

Under most circumstances (see Henrich et al., 2001, for exceptions), we can assume that $\rho \leq \sigma - \rho$ and thus, $\beta \in (0, 1)$. In order to better understand the properties of the optimal offer x^*, we study the impact of a slight increase of each of the parameters on x^* defined by the first partial derivative

$$\frac{\partial x^*}{\partial \alpha} = \frac{(1 + \beta)\rho - \beta\sigma}{(1 + \alpha + \beta)^2} \tag{2.8a}$$

$$\frac{\partial x^*}{\partial \beta} = \frac{\alpha(\sigma - \rho) + \sigma}{(1 + \alpha + \beta)^2} \tag{2.8b}$$

$$\frac{\partial x^*}{\partial \sigma} = \frac{\alpha\rho'(\sigma) + \beta}{1 + \alpha + \beta} \tag{2.8c}$$

$$\frac{\partial x^*}{\partial \rho} = \frac{\alpha}{1 + \alpha + \beta} \tag{2.8d}$$

In equation (2.8c), $\rho'(\sigma) > 0$ indicates the first derivative of ρ with respect to its argument σ (remember that ρ is a function of σ). The optimal offer increases in all arguments, i.e. all partial derivatives in 2.8 are positive.

Exercise 2.4

(a) Prove that all partial derivatives in 2.8 are positive. (b) Show that the optimal share $\xi^* = x^*/\sigma$ is independent of σ and positively depends on all other parameter values including γ, if the normative share is strictly proportional to the total amount σ, i.e. $\rho = \gamma\sigma$.

In order to determine the optimal offer based on equation (2.6), a proposer needs to have correct and precise knowledge about α, β and ρ. Yet generally, these parameter values depend on the individual responder and are unknown to the proposer. The latter therefore has only a vague idea about the optimal offer x^* when confronted with a responder. For simplicity, we will only focus on a single parameter. Assume that the normative offer ρ differs between individuals and is uniformly distributed across an interval a to b. For the random variable P, we can write

$$P \sim U(a,b) \tag{2.9}$$

Note that upper case letters denote a random variable (i.e. P) while lower case letters demonstrate the realised value (i.e. ρ) of the random variable. Figure 2.8 illustrates the uniform distribution. The probability density function $f(\rho)$ shows the probability of random variable P falling within a particular range of values, while the cumulative distribution function $F(\rho)$ returns the probability that the random variable takes a value *less or equal* to ρ.[6]

We can see from Figure 2.8a that

$$f(\rho) = \begin{cases} \frac{1}{b-a}, & \text{if } a \leq \rho \leq b \\ 0, & \text{otherwise} \end{cases} \tag{2.10}$$

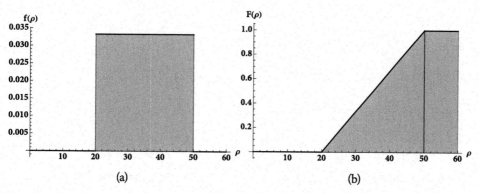

Figure 2.8: (a) shows the probability density function $f(\rho)$ and (b) illustrates the cumulative distribution function $F(\rho)$ for $a = 20$ and $b = 50$.

and correspondingly from Figure 2.8b

$$F(\rho) = \begin{cases} 0, & \text{if } \rho < a \\ \frac{\rho-a}{b-a}, & \text{if } a \leq \rho \leq b \\ 1, & \rho > b \end{cases} \qquad (2.11)$$

The proposer has to calculate the probability with which a certain offer x is accepted by the responder. Remember that the optimal offer x^*, i.e. the minimal acceptable offer for a responder, increases in ρ. Consequently, if a proposer with a critical ρ^* is just willing to accept the proposer's offer, any other responder with a lower ρ will also accept the offer. We will therefore need to know which ρ^* corresponds to an offer x. Solving equation (2.6) for ρ returns

$$\rho^* = \frac{x(1+\alpha+\beta) - \beta\sigma}{\alpha} \qquad (2.12)$$

Equation (2.12) determines the maximum normative offer at which some individual would just accept a proposer's offer of x and anyone with a higher normative offer would reject x. It hence defines a cut-off value for ρ beyond which no such offer would be acceptable. Knowing ρ^*, we can then refer to the CDF to calculate the probability p that an offer x is accepted. It is thus given by

$$p(x) = F(\rho^*(x)) = \frac{x(1+\alpha+\beta) - \beta\sigma - \alpha a}{\alpha(b-a)} \qquad (2.13)$$

Figure 2.9a illustrates an example of the probability of acceptance given an offer x (see exercise 2.5). The proposer needs to maximise the expected payoff given by

$$\pi(x) = (\sigma - x)\, p = (\sigma - x)\frac{x(1+\alpha+\beta) - \beta\sigma - \alpha a}{\alpha(b-a)} \qquad (2.14)$$

Figure 2.9b shows the expected payoff given the probability of acceptance in Figure 2.9a. Equation (2.14) illustrates how proposers weigh an increase in the probability of acceptance against a lower share if they offer a higher x. Note that the probability of acceptance of an offer x that corresponds

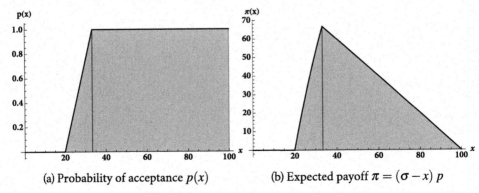

(a) Probability of acceptance $p(x)$ (b) Expected payoff $\pi = (\sigma - x)\, p$

Figure 2.9: Probability of acceptance and expected payoff $a = 20, b = 50, \alpha = 1, \beta = 0.25$, and $\sigma = 100$.

to a $\rho^* < a$ in equation (2.12) is zero and the probability reaches a maximum at $\rho^* = b$ and does not grow beyond. Consequently,

$$p(x) = 0 \text{ for any offer } x < x_l = \frac{\alpha a + \beta \sigma}{1 + \alpha + \beta} \tag{2.15a}$$

$$p(x) = 1 \text{ for any offer } x \geq x_u = \frac{\alpha b + \beta \sigma}{1 + \alpha + \beta} \tag{2.15b}$$

and in the interval $x \in (a, b)$, the expected payoff is increasing at a rate

$$\frac{\partial \pi(x)}{\partial x} = \frac{a\alpha + \beta\sigma + (1 + \alpha + \beta)(\sigma - 2x)}{\alpha(b-a)} = \frac{\alpha(\sigma - a) + \sigma}{\alpha(b-a)} - 2p \tag{2.16}$$

Equation (2.16) shows that for $p \in (0, 1)$, the slope is strictly decreasing in x and p. Consequently, the optimal offer is either given by the null of equation (2.16) if the offer is smaller than x_u, otherwise it is equal to x_u.[7] Thus,

$$x^* = \frac{a\alpha + \sigma(1 + \alpha + 2\beta)}{2(1 + \alpha + \beta)} \qquad \text{if } \sigma < \frac{\alpha(2b-a)}{1 + \alpha} \tag{2.17a}$$

$$x^* = \frac{\alpha b + \beta \sigma}{1 + \alpha + \beta} \qquad \text{if } \sigma \geq \frac{\alpha(2b-a)}{1 + \alpha} \tag{2.17b}$$

Exercise 2.5

(a) Show that if the normative offer is uniformly distributed across an interval of 20 to 50 and given $\alpha = 1, \beta = 0.25, \sigma = 100$, an offer of $x = 30$ will be accepted in three-quarters of all cases. (b) Show how the expected payoff $\pi = (\sigma - x)p$ and the optimal offer x^* are affected by changes in α.

Without any prior interaction between proposer and responder, we have $b \approx 0.5\sigma$ in most cases. Thus, inequality (2.17b) holds. Indeed, the corner solution x_u defines the optimal offer for most reasonable parameter values and is thus a good approximation for an optimal offer.[8] Using the parameters of Figure 2.9, we obtain $x^* = x_u = 33\frac{1}{3}$. At this point, it is easy to see why a proposer will make an offer that exceeds the minimum value in an ultimatum game and we can study differences between societies as shown in Henrich et al. (2001), by calibrating the normative offer (or its distribution) as well as the cost and efficiency of punishment in accordance with empirical data.

Returning to our initial discussion of footbinding, a marriage contract is in essence an ultimatum game and the implication is straightforward. The changing perception due to a more prevalent education and the adoption of Christian norms rendered the *footbinding contract* increasingly unacceptable for spouses. In the following sections, we look at two other reasons: footbinding as a signalling device, and its role as a strategic substitute and complement.

Exercise 2.6

(a) Assume that the two prisoners in Figure 2.4c have pro-social preferences. Each time a prisoner defects while the other cooperates, the former experiences an additional cost of τ. How large must τ be to turn (*Cooperate, Cooperate*) into an equilibrium and what must change to turn it into the sole equilibrium? (b) Consider the following extension of the chicken game, inspired by the hawk dove bourgeois game. Assume that some youngsters decide to not blindly swerve or stay and crash into each other, but to choose a strategy contingent on whether or not the race takes place in their *own* district. If they race against somebody in their own district, a bourgeois chooses to swerve while he will stay if the other driver comes from another district. A race with somebody of their own district occurs with probability p and against somebody of another district with probability $1 - p$. Extend the payoff matrix in Figure 2.4d by adding the bourgeois strategy. Show whether (*Bourgeois, Bourgeois*) can be an equilibrium.

2.4 Signalling, Focal Points, and Practices

Looking back at Section 2.2, we have seen that the inability to coordinate can have a major impact on the benefit that individuals draw from interactions. Bert and Anja each only have an average payoff of $2/3$ if they choose a mixed strategy and a payoff of 1 or 2 if they settle on one of the pure strategy Nash equilibria. But routinely going exclusively to the cinema can be a bit mundane after some time (definitely so for Anja and probably even for Bert). Both would indeed be better off if they could coordinate their choices. Both may use an event that is observable by both as a signal and choose their actions accordingly. For example, both could agree to always meet in the musical on a particular day of the week or month (both just have to check their calendar) or agree to go to the cinema on rainy days. Alternatively, they may choose to go to the cinema whenever Bert works late and to the musical whenever it is Anja's turn to work late, both go to the musical. As long as the event occurs roughly with a probability of $1/2$ (such as rain in the Scottish Highlands), both will have an expected payoff of about $3/2$. Since it is an optimal choice for both to stick to the agreement whenever the event occurred, this type of play forms a **correlated equilibrium** that prevents both from mis-coordinating. A correlated equilibrium needs to ensure that none of the players wants to deviate, i.e., the expected payoff therefore needs to be larger than the expected payoff under mixed strategies and consequently, the signalling device must produce a sufficiently randomised assignment of recommended actions. Further, such an assignment must be unambiguous enough to recommend a precise action for each player.

There might be situations in which no prior agreed event exists that can serve as a randomised signalling device. Imagine you are visiting a new city and have an appointment with an old acquaintance who is living there. You may have agreed to meet at the train station but upon arrival, you realise that it is so vast that at no point, you have a view over the entire station. The interaction is a simple coordination game with multiple actions that could look as in Figure 2.10. You may wait in the middle of platform 1 or the beginning of platform 10, or in front of ticket window 5. One can think of an abundance of alternatives and fill in the dotted lines and consequently, it will be difficult

	Friend			
	Platf. 10	Platf. 1	...	TW 5
Platf. 10	10, 10	0, 0	0, 0	0, 0
Platf. 1	0, 0	10, 10	0, 0	0, 0
...	⋮	⋮	⋱	⋮
TW	0, 0	0, 0	0, 0	10, 10

You appears to the left of the rows Platf. 10, Platf. 1, ..., TW.

Figure 2.10: Coordination Game: Finding your friend.

for you to find your friend. However, some strategies are more salient than others. If your friend knows from which city your train left, it is plausible to expect her to wait at the beginning of the platform of your arrival. The action to wait at the beginning of platform, say 10, thus forms a so-called **focal point**, if it is tradition to await your friend at the beginning of the platform. Still, your friend may not know your platform of arrival or follow different traditions. In this case, you will choose to wait either at the information column which has been erected at the centre of the station and has *meeting point* written on it for exactly this reason; or, in the absence of such a column, you may stand in front of the arrival board. Obviously, a focal point does not guarantee coordination, and the more diverse the perception and cultural backgrounds of players, the less likely it serves as an efficient coordination device. Yet, it is still better to opt for a salient strategy that is defined by a focal point than just randomly choosing a strategy, or in this example, to wait at some arbitrary point.

Groups of individuals may also choose to create a signal or coordination device on their own. If these signals are commonly accepted by all members of a culture, they may turn into customs and institutions. Some signals might be more strongly adhered to. For example, we tend to abide by orders of a person wearing the uniform of a law enforcement officer, we stop in front of a red traffic light or open the door if somebody knocks on it. Other accepted practices are weaker, such as waiting to let people exit an elevator before entering it or indicating your direction by setting the turn signal. Some signals might come at a substantial social cost and may reinforce socially inefficient outcomes.

In the introduction, we discussed some of the reasons for the prevalence of footbinding in China - an institution that evolved between the 10th and 12th century and lasted almost until the middle of the 20th century. Severe forms, such as the *three-inch golden lotus* were irreversible and footbinding was common among rural Han communities living in agricultural zones. As discussed in the introductory chapter, footbinding served multiple purposes. It was an ethnic and social marker and was used to ensure obedience and thus productivity of girls at an early age. In addition, Bossen and Gates (2017) illustrated several accounts in which young girls were raised to believe that bound feet would ensure a good marriage. Big feet meant marriage into a poor family. Bound feet, on the other hand, were perceived as a signal of strong willpower, a long-term commitment to married life and having acquired useful hand skills – in short, only a woman with bound feet makes a dedicated and suitable wife. A mother-in-law would therefore seek a woman with small feet as a suitable bride for her son and bound feet would ensure acceptance and respect by their future husband and mother-in-law.

Footbinding hence also served as a signal for men to find a subservient, in other words, hard-working and devoted spouse. Undoubtedly, it did not serve as a particularly efficient signal.

Not only did women suffer a tremendous cost, their inability to walk made it more difficult to employ them gainfully outside the house. In addition, footbinding obviously failed as a separating signal since the practice was indiscriminate. We can use our knowledge of game theory to get an idea why such a signal may have evolved and persisted. Assume the following simple interaction: a woman may be born as *subservient* (S) or *self-willed* (W) (whatever this may mean), any woman can choose to *bind* (B) her feet or to *desist* (D) (we ignore the role of parents for simplicity), and men can choose whether to *marry* (M) the woman or to remain *celibate* (C). Men cannot see what type of woman they are introduced to by their mothers (i.e. whether she is subservient or self-willed), but can see whether she has bound feet. This setup is evidently an oversimplification and the notion of suitability lies entirely in the eyes of the prospective husband and mother-in-law and transcends the characteristic of bound feet.

To give this game some quantifiable measures, assume that a woman is born or raised as subservient with probability p and consequently, self-willed with probability $(1 - p)$. Marriage is worth 100 to a woman, while she receives nothing if she remains celibate. A man's benefit is 100 if he marries a subservient woman or rejects a self-willed woman, but if his wife turns out to be self-willed or if he fails to marry a subservient woman, his benefit is $l < 100$. In addition, bound feet impose an additional cost of $\varepsilon \geq 0$ on him. A self-willed woman has an additional cost of $d \geq 0$ and a cost of footbinding equal to b while a subservient woman has a cost of footbinding equal to g. Parameters b and g might be equal or $b > g$, similarly cost d can be interpreted as the pressure and abuse inflicted on a presumably self-willed woman by her own or her husband's family.

The extensive form game is presented in Figure 2.11. Figure 2.11 may look daunting but the graph follows the same rules as Figure 2.6. We start with the hollow node in the middle of the graph. Initially, a woman's type is chosen by chance or fate, but historically we assign the name *Nature* to this non-strategic player. With a probability p a woman is of type *subservient* indicated by the upper node labelled with S, and with probability $1 - p$, she is *self-willed* indicated by the lower node labelled with W. Each type has the identical set of two strategies: if a woman binds her feet (indicated by B), we move along the left branch, if she desists (indicated by D), we move along the right branch. At this point, a man decides whether to marry (action M) or not to

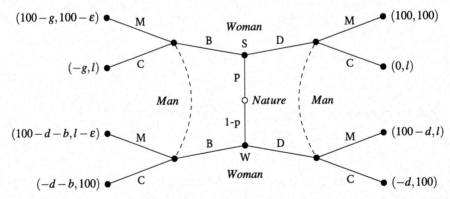

Figure 2.11: A foot binding signalling game: women are either subservient (S) or self-willed (W) and choose whether to bind (B) their feet or to desist (D) based on their type. Men choose to marry (M) or to remain celibate (C) based on the decision of the woman.

marry (action C), defining the terminal node of the decision tree and the respective payoff with the first value defining the woman's payoff and the second value the man's payoff. The dotted lines connecting a man's upper and lower decision node on the left and right sides of the graph indicate that a man is unaware of a woman's type. Since a man chooses at both connected nodes and has an identical choice of actions (C or M), he cannot infer whether he is taking an action on the upper or lower branch - in short, he does not know whether his prospective wife is subservient or self-willed. In this situation, the nodes connected by the dotted line form an **information set**.[9] Although he does not know a woman's type, he can observe whether or not her feet are bound. Thus, if a woman is subservient and binds her feet, and the man decides to marry her, we end up in the left uppermost terminal node. A woman receives a payoff of $100 - g$ and her husband, a payoff of $100 - \varepsilon$. It is difficult to study the Nash equilibria in Figure 2.11, but we can simplify our analysis by transforming the extensive form game into a normal form game, as we did with the ultimatum game. Both women and men have a set of four strategies composed of two actions. A woman has to choose whether or not to bind her feet based on her type. She therefore has strategies $S_W = \{BB, BD, DB, DD\}$. The first element in her strategy defines what she does if she is of the subservient type, the second element states her action if she is self-willed. Hence, strategy (BB) indicates that she will always bind her feet independent of her type, whereas (BD) implies that she binds her feet if she is subservient but does not do so (she desists) if she is self-willed. Correspondingly, a man's strategy depends on whether or not a woman has bound feet. His strategy set is defined by $S_M = \{MM, MC, CM, CC\}$.

Remember that only a woman knows her type but it is the stoic act of nature that determines her type. With probability p, she is subservient and with probability $1 - p$ she turns out to be self-willed. Both men and women can thus only determine their *expected payoff* prior to the realisation of the woman's type. If a woman chooses *a priori* to desist if she is subservient and to bind her feet if she is self-willed and a man only marries a woman with unbound feet, the outcome of the game is defined by strategy profile (DB, CM). With probability p, the terminal node of the game is the right uppermost node (given by path S,D,M), but with probability $1 - p$, both end up on the left lowermost node (give by path W,B,C). Consequently, a woman's payoff is $\pi_W = p100 + (1 - p)(-d - b)$ and a man's payoff is $\pi_M = p100 + (1 - p)100$. Given that both men and women have four strategies, the normal form game is defined by the 16 payoff pairs presented in Figure 2.12. A man's payoff is aligned right in the upper part of the cell above the dotted line and a woman's payoff is aligned left and written below the dotted line.

It is indeed quite cumbersome to study each cell for the existence of a unilateral improvement to find the game's Nash equilibria. A simple way to quickly determine a pure strategy equilibrium is the following: compare the woman's payoff along each column of the matrix and mark the largest payoff for each column (remember that a woman chooses the row). Now do the same for the man but compare the payoffs within the same row. With a little luck, you will find a cell in the payoff matrix for which both payoffs are marked. Since the pair of payoffs mark the largest element in their respective row and column and hence, neither a man nor a woman has any incentive to unilaterally deviate, the outcome constitutes a Nash equilibrium.

Assuming that $p > 1/2$ and $b < 100$, I have indicated the largest payoffs in bold. We can immediately see that (DD, MM) and (DD, CM) form a Nash equilibrium. Women never bind their feet and men marry them, leading to a payoff of $\pi_W = 100 + (1 - p)d$ and $\pi_M = p100 + (1 - p)l$,

	MM	MC	CM	CC
BB	$p(100-\varepsilon)+$ $(1-p)(l-\varepsilon)$ $p(100-g)+$ $(1-p)(100-d-b)$	$p(100-\varepsilon)+$ $(1-p)(l-\varepsilon)$ $\mathbf{p(100-g)+}$ $\mathbf{(1-p)(100-d-b)}$	$pl+$ $(1-p)100$ $p(-g)+$ $(1-p)(-d-b)$	$pl+$ $(1-p)100$ $p(-g)+$ $(1-p)(-d-b)$
BD	$p(100-\varepsilon)+$ $(1-p)l$ $p(100-g)+$ $(1-p)(100-d)$	$\mathbf{p(100-\varepsilon)+}$ $\mathbf{(1-p)100}$ $p(100-g)+$ $(1-p)(-d)$	$pl+$ $(1-p)l$ $p(-g)+$ $(1-p)(100-d)$	$pl+$ $(1-p)100$ $p(-g)+$ $(1-p)(-d)$
DB	$p100+$ $(1-p)(l-\varepsilon)$ $p100+$ $(1-p)(100-d-b)$	$pl+$ $(1-p)(l-\varepsilon)$ $0+$ $(1-p)(100-d-b)$	$\mathbf{p100+}$ $\mathbf{(1-p)100}$ $p100+$ $(1-p)(-d-b)$	$pl+$ $(1-p)100$ $0+$ $(1-p)(-d-b)$
DD	$\mathbf{p100+}$ $\mathbf{(1-p)l}$ $\mathbf{p100+}$ $\mathbf{(1-p)(100-d)}$	$pl+$ $(1-p)100$ $0+$ $(1-p)(-d)$	$\mathbf{p100+}$ $\mathbf{(1-p)l}$ $\mathbf{p100+}$ $\mathbf{(1-p)(100-d)}$	$pl+$ $(1-p)100$ $0+$ $(1-p)(-d)$

Figure 2.12: Normal form of a foot binding signalling game.

respectively. We call this Nash equilibrium a **pooling equilibrium** since both types of women send the same signal. In fact, any combination of strategy *MM* (always marry) and *CM* (marry women with unbound feet) is an equilibrium strategy. Note that the assumption $p > 1 - p$ is crucial to the existence of the pooling equilibrium. There is potentially a second pooling equilibrium (BB, MC) in which women always bind their feet and are married by men. This equilibrium requires that

$$p(100-\varepsilon) + (1-p)(l-\varepsilon) > pl + (1-p)100$$
$$\Leftrightarrow p > p^* = \frac{1}{2} + \frac{\varepsilon}{2(100-l)} \tag{2.18}$$

We can see that

$$\frac{\partial}{\partial \varepsilon}\left(\frac{1}{2} + \frac{\varepsilon}{2(100-l)}\right) = \frac{1}{2(100-l)} > 0$$
$$\frac{\partial}{\partial l}\left(\frac{1}{2} + \frac{\varepsilon}{2(100-l)}\right) = \frac{1}{2(100-l)^2} > 0$$

In other words, as the husband's cost of footbinding (ε) increases and/or dislike for a self-willed (expressed by $100 - l$) wife decreases, universal footbinding becomes increasingly unlikely. If, on the other hand, men are unconcerned with the bound feet of their wives ($\varepsilon = 0$), even prefer bound feet to unbound feet (see exercise 2.7) or belief that the subservient wife's devotion and dedication to hard work are essential (i.e. l is small), footbinding is likely to occur.

Relaxing the assumptions can turn the second pooling equilibrium into a **separating equilibrium** defined by (BD, MC) - subservient women bind their feet and are married, self-willed women desist and remain celibate. This equilibrium requires that

$$b > 100 > g \tag{2.19}$$

as well as

$$p(100-\varepsilon) + (1-p)100 > pl + (1-p)100$$
$$\Leftrightarrow 100 - \varepsilon > l \tag{2.20}$$

We can see that if inequality (2.20) is violated, the critical value p^* in equation (2.18) needs to exceed 1. In this case, neither the second pooling equilibrium nor separating equilibrium exists. Inequality (2.20) has a straightforward interpretation - men need to prefer a subservient woman with bound feet to a self-willed woman with unbound feet. If this is not the case, footbinding does not persist.

A woman's payoff in each of the three equilibria is given by

$$\pi_W(DD,CM) = 100 - (1-p)d$$
$$\pi_W(BB,MC) = 100 - gp - (1-p)(d+b)$$
$$\pi_W(BD,MC) = p(100-g) - (1-p)d$$

Women are always best off in the first pooling equilibrium. The men's payoffs are

$$\pi_M(DD,CM) = 100p + (1-p)l$$
$$\pi_M(BB,MC) = 100p + (1-p)l - \varepsilon$$
$$\pi_M(BD,MC) = 100 - p\varepsilon$$

The first pooling equilibrium is thus the preferable outcome for men if

$$p > \frac{100-l}{100+\varepsilon-l} = 1 - \frac{\varepsilon}{100+\varepsilon-l} \tag{2.21}$$

namely, if subservient women are sufficiently frequent and footbinding causes a significant cost for the husband (and his family).

The theory of this chapter does not enable us to study the dynamics that led to each of the equilibria and we will need to employ the approaches of later chapters, but our analysis, simple as the game may be, outlines a basic account of the process that prompted the establishment of footbinding in China akin to the empirical results of Bossen and Gates (2017). Low cost of footbinding in rural communities relying mostly on domestic immobile work and the need to marry a skilled and hard-working wife rendered footbinding socially efficient for the husbands and in-laws. Since, however for most women, the cost of remaining unmarried outweighed the cost of footbinding, the latter turned out to be an inadequate signal leading to a socially inefficient custom of universal footbinding. Once the economic transformation during China's early 20th century required increased mobility as labour shifted from de-centralised domestic work to centralised factory work, the cost of footbinding for a family escalated and the practice was eventually abandoned.

Exercise 2.7

The erotic glorification of small feet in the Chinese literature is abundant to a degree that Levy (1966) considers footbinding to have originated as a male fetish. Correspondingly, assume that footbinding does not come at a cost ε for the husband but is appreciated by men. Consequently, marrying a subservient or self-willed woman with bound feet bestows on him a benefit of $100 + \theta_M$ and $l + \theta_M$, respectively for each type of wife. (a) Would this change the results of the signalling game 2.11? (b) Assume that women also derive a positive benefit θ_W from being bound in addition to the cost of limited mobility. How large must θ_W be to destabilise the DD-pooling equilibrium?

2.5 Strategic Complements and Substitutes

Until now, we have only discussed situations in which individuals have to choose between discrete actions, yet frequently we also have to choose the intensity of an action - in other words, players can choose from a continuum of pure strategies. We do not only choose whether to consume chocolate but how much we should eat, how many years of schooling we should pursue, how much time we should dedicate to homework and to leisure activities, and so forth. Furthermore, these choices frequently depend on the level or degree that others choose to pursue a certain action. Observing others studying more encourages us to do the same. Our and others' actions form **strategic complements**. Typical examples of strategic complements are trade wars, arms races or the adoption of fashions. On the other hand, the behaviour of others can also discourage us from engaging in an activity. In this case, our actions take on the form of **strategic substitutes**. Typical examples relate to quantity competition (also known as Cournot games) and overexploitation in *tragedy of the commons* scenarios (see Bowles, 2004, Ch. 4), but again, we can think of plenty of examples that combine both effects, such as the consumption of conspicuous goods, the decision to vaccinate or to join an identity group or club.

In general, we can see that strategic complementarity occurs if a player's decision to commit more to a strategy increases the marginal benefit of the other player while engaging in the complementary action. In other words, if one player does more of an action it is beneficial for the second player to do the same. Strategic substitutability, on the other hand, ensues if doing more of an action discourages the second player to engage in that action by decreasing the marginal benefit obtained from that action. Consequently, we have the following rule for some player i observing player j, given the payoff function $\pi_i(x_i, x_j)$

$$\text{Strategic complements: } \frac{\partial^2 \pi_i}{\partial x_i \partial x_j} > 0 \tag{2.22a}$$

$$\text{Strategic substitutes: } \frac{\partial^2 \pi_i}{\partial x_i \partial x_j} < 0 \tag{2.22b}$$

Social norms, customs, and institutions are fundamentally determined by strategic complementarity and substitutability. As we have seen in the introduction to this book, footbinding, initially introduced as a form of contraceptive control to ensure the legitimacy of the heir apparent, was quickly adopted by members of the court. It spread through the ranks of the upper classes and eventually to the middle and lower classes, and over time, became increasingly extreme. "The next lower stratum, competing to provide wives and concubines to the apex, will imitate and exaggerate the fidelity-control practice so as to gain economic, social, and reproductive access to the palace." (Mackie, 1996, p. 1008). Yet later, footbinding was perceived no longer as a sign of class after the custom was increasingly appropriated by the peasantry. In addition, at the end of the 19th century, the practice was more and more regarded as dishonourable and backward by progressive scholars - detrimental to China's claim to respect by other nations. In other words, footbinding turned from a signal of honour and grace into a sign of stagnation and national shame.

We can see that in both cases, the willingness to impose footbinding on a daughter was strongly influenced by how others adopted the practice. In the former case, as more members of a higher social stratum accepted and displayed forms of footbinding, the practice became more endorsed by members of the next lower stratum. In the latter case, the members of the gentry were discouraged by the growing prevalence of footbinding among members of the lowest social classes. The essence of both dynamics can be explained using a simplified model, but I will discuss more sophisticated approaches in Chapters 5 and 9. To start with, assume a generic payoff function for stratum 1 and 2 with the respective frequency of footbinding x_1 and x_2 in each stratum.

$$\pi_i = \alpha x_i - \frac{\beta}{2}x_i^2 + \gamma x_i x_j \qquad (2.23)$$

with $i, j = 1, 2$ and $i \neq j$, and $\alpha, \beta > 0$. The initial part of the payoff function $(\alpha x_i - (\beta/2)x_i^2)$ defines a hump shape relation between the intensity of an action x_i (i.e. the frequency of footbinding in this case) and its net benefit. This relationship is plausible in the context of footbinding. Although it was considered to ensure chastity among the higher social strata and industriousness among the peasantry, we have seen that the signal is only beneficial as long as it is not too widely adopted. At the same time, footbinding came at a significant social cost. While the upper social strata had to mainly cover the additional caring cost for a bound woman, for the lower social classes footbinding limited the suitability of women for out-of-home employment. Thus across the social strata, the difference between benefits and cost is adequately reflected by a hump-shaped (but not necessarily identical) relation .

The second part of the payoff function $(\gamma x_i x_j)$ illustrates the impact of the other stratum js frequency of footbinding on the frequency of stratum i and the sign of γ will define whether the actions are strategic complements or substitutes, since

$$\frac{\partial^2 \pi_i}{\partial x_i \partial x_j} = \gamma \qquad (2.24)$$

By setting the first partial derivative of π_i with respect to x_i equal to zero and solving it for x_i, we obtain the optimal frequency x_i^* of stratum i that maximises the payoff function. The optimal frequency x_i^* is then a function of the frequency x_j in stratum j.

$$\frac{\partial \pi_i}{\partial x_i} = \alpha - \beta x_i + \gamma x_j = 0 \qquad (2.25a)$$

$$\Leftrightarrow x_i^* = r_i(x_j) = \frac{\alpha}{\beta} + \frac{\gamma}{\beta}x_j \qquad (2.25b)$$

and thus a linear function. Note that for x_i^* to be a maximum, we require that

$$\frac{\partial^2 \pi_i}{\partial x_i^2} = -\beta < 0 \qquad (2.26)$$

Hence, $\beta > 0$ is a necessary condition. Equation (2.25b) defines the **best response correspondence** (also frequently called reaction correspondence) for stratum i to the frequency of footbinding x_j of stratum j.[10] We can see that in the case of strategic complementarity, $\gamma > 0$ and the best response correspondence has a positive slope in x_j while in the case of strategic substitutes, $\gamma < 0$ and the best response correspondence is negatively sloped in x_j.

Figure 2.13a plots the best response correspondence for stratum 2 based on the frequency of footbinding in stratum 1 given by x_1 using the parameter values $\alpha = 1$, $\beta = 5.5$, and $\gamma = 4$.

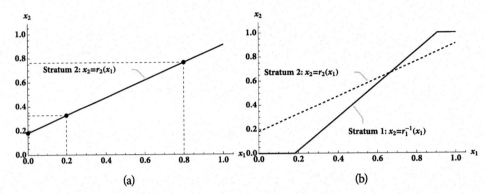

Figure 2.13: (a) illustrates the best response correspondence of stratum 2 based on the frequency of footbinding x_1 in stratum 1. (b) shows the best response correspondence of stratum 1 and stratum 2 if strategies are complementary. The intersection determines the mutual best response and the equilibrium of the interaction. Figures are drawn for $\alpha = 1$, $\beta = 5.5$, and $\gamma = 4$.

Since $\gamma > 0$ and thus, the best response correspondence has a positive slope in x_1, we can see that footbinding in stratum 2 is strategically complementary to footbinding in stratum 1. If, for example, the frequency of footbinding in stratum 1 equals 20 percent the optimal response for stratum 2 is to bind roughly one-third of the women in stratum 2. Yet, if the frequency in stratum 1 increases to 80 percent, footbinding in stratum 2 will occur at a frequency of roughly three fourth of all women. We can add the best response correspondence of stratum 1 to the graph to study the equilibrium of the interaction. However, note that the best response of stratum 1 depends on the frequency in stratum 2. We therefore have to *invert* the best response correspondence of stratum 1 by solving $x_1^*(x_2)$ for x_2. We obtain

$$x_2 = r_1^{-1}(x_1) = \frac{\beta x_1 - \alpha}{\gamma}$$

where r_1^{-1} denotes the inverse function of x_1^*. Figure 2.13b plots both best response correspondences. Since the frequencies of footbinding are restricted to the interval between zero and one, the inverse best response correspondence of stratum 1 lies on the x_1-axis until approximately 18 percent and reaches a maximum at a frequency in excess of 91 percent. This means that if the frequency of footbinding in stratum 2 is virtually zero, the practice occurs with a frequency of 18 percent among members of stratum 1. Similarly, if all women have bound feet in stratum 2, 91 percent of the women adopt the practice in stratum 1.

Given our previous discussion of the Nash equilibrium, the intuition of the equilibrium in this scenario is straightforward. An equilibrium is defined by a situation where the responses are mutually correct which happens at the intersection of the two best response correspondences. Stratum 1's best response frequency to stratum 2's frequency is equal to the frequency that induced the latter's frequency as a best response. If we solve the system of equation for $x_1 = (\alpha + \gamma x_2)/\beta$ and $x_2 = (\alpha + \gamma x_1)/\beta$ simultaneously, we obtain the equilibrium value

$$\bar{x}_1 = \bar{x}_2 = \frac{\alpha}{\beta - \gamma} \tag{2.27}$$

For the values in Figure 2.13, the equilibrium frequencies are equal to two-thirds. If stratum 1 illustrates a frequency of footbinding equal to 2/3, the best response of stratum 2 is 2/3 to which

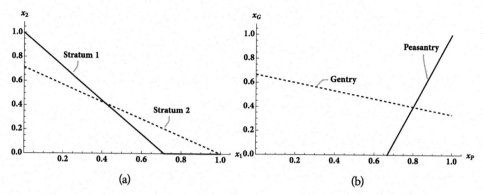

Figure 2.14: (a) shows the best response correspondence of stratum 1 and stratum 2 if strategies are substitutes using $\alpha = 5$, $\beta = 7$, and $\gamma = -5$. (b) illustrates the situation in which stratum 1's strategy is complementary and stratum 2's strategy is a substitute using $\alpha = 12$, $\beta = 18$, $\gamma_P = 6$ and $\gamma_G = -6$.

again the best response of stratum 1 is $2/3$. The numbers are identical since we defined the same parameter values for both strata. If each stratum had different values, the equilibrium would not occur at the same frequencies, but it must still hold that the frequencies are a mutual best response.[11] Figure 2.13b offers an intuition how footbinding was adopted by different social strata and eventually cascaded through society. Note that an increase in α or a value γ closer to β as well as a decrease in β will shift the equilibrium values closer to a value of one. Consequently, stronger levels of strategic complementarity and lower costs of footbinding will lead to a more frequent adoption of the practice.

Figure 2.14a illustrates a situation of strategic substitutes with parameter values $\alpha = 5$, $\beta = 7$, and $\gamma = -5$. Since $\gamma < 0$, the best response correspondences are downward sloping. Again, the equilibrium is defined by the intersection of both best response correspondences which occurs at a mutual frequency of $5/12$ according to equation (2.27). Note that in both cases, we ignore questions of how the equilibrium was accomplished and we will further investigate the dynamics in Chapter 5.[12]

Coming back to our study of footbinding, we have seen that while the adoption by the gentry encouraged endorsement of the peasantry, the inverse did not hold. Consequently, footbinding among the gentry exhibited strategic substitutability with the frequency of footbinding among peasants, but the latter was strategically complementary to the former. This situation is illustrated in Figure 2.14. The frequency of footbinding among peasants is shown on the horizontal axis and the frequency of footbinding among the upper classes on the vertical axis. An equilibrium occurs at $(x_P, x_G) = (4/5, 2/5)$. In other words, footbinding among the peasantry is at 80 percent and twice as common as it is among the gentry. In our simple model, increasing the absolute value of γ will increase footbinding among the former and decrease it among the latter.

2.6 Conclusion: The Limits of Game Theory

Scholars new to game theory frequently challenge its validity. When first exposed to the simple 2×2 games in Figure 2.4, some of the conclusions seem implausible. Intuition tells us, for example, that

$$A$$

		Cooperate	Defect
B	Cooperate	2,2	$0, 3 - \mu$
	Defect	$3 - \mu, 0$	$1 - \varepsilon, 1 - \varepsilon$

Figure 2.15: Prisoner's dilemma with pro-social preferences.

the two prisoners would not turn each other in. After all, these two jailbirds must have collaborated on several heists and intuitively, we expect them to adhere to a sort of honour among thieves.

While game theory is not devoid of some concerns, the previous example is not one of them. The prisoner's dilemma is not specified to reflect the situation we have in mind.[13] That does not mean we cannot easily include mutual regard, respect, and honour in the game. Assume that turning your fellow thief in comes with a negative payoff of μ if a player is the only snitch, and if both snitch on each other, the negative impact is equal to ε. Intuitively, it should hold that $\mu > \varepsilon$ and we could even imagine a negative value for ε if turning the other player in is considered poetic justice. The transformed payoff matrix of our more *prosocial* version of the game is illustrated in Figure 2.15. If both ε and μ are sufficiently small, mutual defection remains the sole Nash equilibrium of the game. If, however, both parameters exceed a value of 1, the dominant strategy is to cooperate, and if $\mu > 1$ and $\varepsilon < 1$, the game turns into a coordination game with two pure strategy Nash equilibria and another equilibrium in mixed strategies. It is therefore important to pay close attention to the accompanying narrative that provides context to the game and not to over-interpret the information given. The classic prisoner's dilemma with purely self-regarding preferences is all about contrasting individual good and public good. By pursuing a strategy that is individually optimal, both prisoners fail to reach a socially optimal outcome that would have minimised their sentence. It is an antithesis to the Smithian Invisible Hand.

Yet, this does not mean that game theory has no inherent problems. To understand the latter, we need to discuss the implicit assumptions we make by presenting preferences in a payoff matrix or as payoff functions. Preferences are expressed in the form of binary relations. The preference ordering $x \succ y$ is read as some alternative x is strictly preferred to some other alternative y, the relation $x \simeq y$ means that the individual is indifferent between alternatives x and y, and the combination $x \succeq y$ implies that x is weakly preferred to y (i.e. the individual is either indifferent or prefers x strictly over y). Let there be three alternatives, x, y, and z. Preferences then need to meet two criteria:

Completeness: $x \succeq y$ or $y \succeq x$

Transitivity: $x \succeq y$ and $y \succeq z$ imply that $x \succeq z$

The completeness assumption (or axiom) guarantees that any player can compare any two alternatives. Notice that it also includes the reflexive relation $x \succeq x$, i.e. an alternative x is weakly preferred to itself. Transitivity, on the other hand, ensures that there are no loops in the preference relation. These two axioms seem sufficient to ensure that the preferences can be reflected as payoffs. Given a fixed number of alternatives, any player can tabulate these alternatives to reflect her preferences. She writes the most preferred alternatives into the top row of the table and then those less preferred in the lower rows. Alternatives about which the player is indifferent are listed in the same row and no alternative that is strictly preferred is in the same or a lower row than another less preferred alternative. Since her preferences are complete, each alternative must find a position in the table, and because her preferences are transitive, no alternative can be found in more than one cell of the table. We can then assign a payoff value to each row of the table, with the highest value given to the top row and the lowest value to the bottom row.

So far so good, but we need to avoid another issue that is exemplified by the following short narrative: Sidney Morgenbesser, a philosopher at Columbia University, once was given the choice between apple pie and blueberry pie. He initially orders apple pie, but shortly thereafter, the waitress returns to tell him that cherry pie is also on the menu. At this point, he opts for blueberry pie. Morgenbesser's preferences are complete and transitive, but they are reversed after he is confronted with a second choice set. According to his ordering, $apple \succ blueberry$ given the set $\{apple, blueberry\}$ and $blueberry \succ apple$ if given the set $\{apple, blueberry, cherry\}$. Preferences therefore need to meet a third criterion:[14]

> **Independence of irrelevant alternatives:** The preference of x over y is independent of context.

Before we are all set, we need to relate preferences with choices and implicitly assume another axiom:

Given the strategies and associated outcomes that are available to a player, the latter will choose a strategy that leads to an expected outcome that ranks highest in her preference ordering.[15]

If preferences meet all the above axioms, we call them **consistent**. Acts of altruism or spite can be presented on the basis of consistent preferences. The selfish homo economicus has little to do with game theory. As long as preferences are consistent, they are considered rational. Consequently, donating to charity is a rational choice as long as it ranks highest in a person's preference ordering. While this raises philosophical questions as to whether altruistic acts are truly altruistic, it demonstrates that game theory adequately represents any type of (consistent) social preferences as long as the game is correctly specified.

Supporters of the axioms refer to an evolutionary argument. Simply speaking, inconsistent preferences are subject to exploitation (the so-called *money pump*) and selection pressure will therefore promote individuals with more consistent preferences in the long run. In other words, consistent preferences have been instilled by environmental forces over time, and we are genetically and socially programmed to act rationally. Yet, critics raise several issues with the first three axioms, some of which I will briefly discuss in the following.[16]

Completeness requires that a player has not only knowledge about the alternative outcomes, but she must also have experienced them at least once to allow for a comparison. In one-shot games, we must assume that a player is able to infer preferences from an earlier engagement with a different player and that her preferences are independent of the player with whom she engages. Yet, this still requires that at least one time, she chooses an action that leads to an unfamiliar outcome for which no preference relation yet exists.[17]

Behavioural research (including behavioural economics) has shown that individuals demonstrate intransitive preferences under certain circumstances (e.g., inter-temporal decision-making violates the transitivity axiom if an individual discounts future payoffs hyperbolically). A more critical issue is that transitivity does not hold for aggregates. Lecturers of microeconomics, for instance, frequently but probably unintentionally treat such aggregates as individuals (firms and households) and tend to substitute the prisoners by two companies in the prisoner's dilemma. While this provides a more intuitive context for students as it is easier to convince them of the selfish character of businesses, the decisions of companies are a process that involves more than one individual. The **Condorcet paradox** shows that a majority decision by three individuals about three different alternatives can lead to intransitive choices. Depending on which two alternatives are compared first, any of the three alternatives can come out on top.[18]

Discussion surrounding the independence axiom spawned another amusing anecdote: An elderly English lady is invited for tea. Given the choice between staying at home and joining the tea party, she opts for the latter. Shortly before she leaves her house, she hears that cocaine is served during the tea. The mannerly lady is scandalised at such an offer and rejects the invitation. At first glance, this is a violation of the axiom. After all, she has no obligation to snort cocaine. Yet for the English, having tea is an utterly social event. The provision of cocaine entails information about the attendees and thus changes the quality of the event. Independently of how we interpret the anecdote, it should be clear that the definition of the alternatives needs to include any information that is relevant to the player. While the axiom simplifies the analysis by requiring only a definition of the relative preference across pairs of options making them independent of the larger choice set, we need to specify very carefully the nature of these options.

Unfortunately, the three axioms are not enough to apply the Nash solution concept. In an influential paper, Aumann and Brandenburger (1995) demonstrate the conditions for a Nash equilibrium. In a two-player game, a Nash equilibrium entails that the rules of the game (i.e. the strategy sets and payoff functions of both players), the rationality of players and their conjectures are *mutual* knowledge. Games among a larger group of players require a common prior and *common* knowledge of the conjectures in addition. Common priors demand a prevailing process by which players form beliefs about the states of the world. Mutual knowledge requires a reciprocal understanding (I know that you know, and you know that I know), whereas common knowledge is not satisfied by a universal understanding (we all know that everybody else knows), but by an infinite iteration of this knowledge (we all know, that all know, that all know, etc.).

Looking at the mutual knowledge requirements for two-player games (and ignoring a discussion of common knowledge for simplicity), we can see that game theory imposes an exceedingly demanding theory of mind on each player. Each player needs to possess empathy to such a degree that she can form a correct preference ordering for all players involved as well as anticipate their logical reasoning. However, the multi-dimensionality of preferences and their interrelation with social identities turns the ordering of preferences across different alternatives into a difficult task (see also Sen 2002; Young 2008; Ille 2017). Since a player needs to adjudicate between alternatives in a rational manner, she needs to devise an optimal way to reduce the cognitive load that this action requires. Yet, this creates a problem of infinite regress: the optimal answer to a problem involves determining an optimal heuristic to identify the optimal answer. To accomplish this, a player needs to find the optimal heuristic to determine the optimal heuristic, ad infinitum.

Connected to this problem is the non-uniqueness of the solution algorithm. Different algorithms may lead to different optimal strategies. Yet at the same time, the solution algorithm frequently requires a symmetry in the players' approaches. We have seen that the Battle of the Sexes in Figure 2.4a has a mixed equilibrium in which Anja and Bert go to the musical with a probability of 1/3 and 2/3, respectively. Both mixed strategies are mutually best responses. Obviously, the mixed strategy does not preclude the risk of a mis-coordination (indeed in 5/9th of the cases) in which case both Anja and Bert will show up at different places and receive a payoff of zero. They may therefore be inclined to minimise their potential loss by playing a maximin strategy. Appendix A.2.1 shows that Anja's maximin strategy is to attend the musical two-thirds of the time giving her a minimum payoff of two-thirds - the same as if she played her mixed strategy. Yet, it is not Bert's best response to choose his maximin strategy of one-third. If Anja chooses $\alpha = 2/3$, he will do better by only going to the musical and he thus chooses $\beta = 1$. Anja's best response is then to mimic him, leading to the pure strategy Nash equilibrium (*Musical, Musical*).

As we have seen above, however, a player must be sure to a reasonable degree about the other player's conjecture and thus solution algorithm. We further require that probabilities can be attributed to actions and states, and that these, in the form of priors, are commonly known. Yet, frequently we are faced with situations of ambiguity, in which we have a vague idea of the likelihood of events. Binmore (2009, Chapter 10.8) suggests a solution in the form of *muddled* strategy equilibria. Although the approach is mathematically compelling, it is questionable whether we can expect players to apply such a complex solution algorithm to determine their strategy. Alternative, approaches to the standard definition of rationality have been developed over the years and some have been remarkably correct and intuitive in their predictions, but again they suffer from such a high degree of mathematical sophistication that we may doubt that any evolutionary process could have internalised such complex thought processes.[19]

The evolutionary games, which I will discuss in the following chapters, therefore take a different approach to modelling players' choices. Subsequent approaches assume that players determine an action or behavioural rule based on their observations in past periods or by imitating peers, thereby alleviating many of the problems I discussed in the conclusion of this chapter.

Further Reading

Fudenberg and Tirole (2005) is one of the main textbooks and a thorough overview of game theory. An easy introduction is offered by Binmore (2007), and Gintis (2000a) strikes a good balance between accessibility and a more technical approach that explains the theoretical underpinnings.

Notes

1 A finite game is defined by a finite number of players, each having a finite number of pure strategies.
2 See Güth and Tietz (1990); Henrich et al. (2001); Falk et al. (2003); Henrich et al. (2006); Fischbacher et al. (2009) for examples.
3 The interested reader may refer to a truncated version of the ultimatum game, called the *dictator game*. In this game, the responder is left without a choice and has to accept whatever they are given by the proposer - in this case, adequately termed the *dictator*. Although the dictator does not fear any consequences of a low offer, most individuals attribute a significant amount to the responder.
4 A significant literature in behavioural economics is concerned with non-standard preferences. Important concepts are endowment effects, reference dependence, and loss aversion, as well as the interplay between reasoning and belief, see, for example, Bénabou and Tirole (2011, 2016) and Gino et al. (2016).

5   Diminishing marginal gains (economists speak of diminishing marginal utility) of wealth imply that richer individuals benefit less from a specific additional amount than poorer individuals. Similarly, we do not benefit equally from each additional Dollar, Pound or Euro we receive as income. A salary increase of $100 is perceived as more beneficial by someone with a low income than someone else with a high income. Similarly, the negative feeling after a financial loss does not grow proportionally to the amount lost.

6   Note that the probability density function is the derivative of the cumulative distribution function.

7   To determine whether the optimal offer is the corner solution x_u, we need to check whether condition (2.16) is negative at $p = 1$ - remember that the slope of the payoff function is strictly decreasing in p and the optimum is given by $\partial \pi(x)/\partial x = 0$. If the slope is not negative at this point, it is also not negative for any smaller value of p and so $x^* = x_u$. Substituting $p = 1$ in the second part of the equation in (2.16) and solving for σ returns the conditions in (2.17). In case, we have no corner solution since (2.16) is negative at $p = 1$, we set the first part of the equation equal to zero and solve for x to obtain the optimal offer.

8   You may try $\sigma = 100$, $\alpha = 10$, $\beta = 1$, $a = 20$, and $b = 80$ as a counter-example. In this highly egalitarian society with a strong incentive to punish norm deviations, the optimal offer is $x^* = 62.5$.

9   For nodes to be part of the same information set, we further assume that any actions a player has chosen and that led to these nodes are identical. If a different action had led to a different node with an identical set of actions, a player could still infer their position on the game tree simply by remembering what led them there - a property called *perfect recall*.

10 *Correspondence* instead of best response *function* or reaction *function* is the mathematically more generic term. The difference between correspondence and function is that the former assigns a set of reactions that are a best response to a particular action while the latter is the special case in which there is only one unique reaction.

11 If the parameters were chosen such that $x_1 = 2/3$ is a best response to $x_2 = 1/3$, then an equilibrium must entail that $x_2 = 1/3$ is also a best response to $x_1 = 2/3$.

12 Moving from a static study to a dynamic study of the strategic substitutes and complements in Figures 2.13b and 2.14a shows that the interior equilibrium is only stable if the absolute slope of the best response correspondence of the strategy defined by the horizontal axis (also called abscissa) is larger in absolute values than the best response correspondence of the other strategy. In our examples, stratum 1s best response correspondence is always steeper than stratum 2s best response correspondence.

13 In fact, misspecification can explain a number of seeming paradoxes in game theory, such as the Traveler's Dilemma (Basu, 1994). By introducing a regret element, further lowering the stated amount is eventually more costly than the malus applied.

14 A slightly more technical version of the independence axiom is: If $x \succeq y$ given choice set T, and if $x, y \in S \subset T$, then $x \succeq y$ given choice set S.

15 This last axiom is somewhat tautological, if we infer preferences from revealed behaviour (i.e., if a player chooses some strategy s over some other strategy s', the outcome associated with s must be preferred over the outcome associated with s'.)

16 For further discussion, refer to Binmore (1994) and Gintis (2009).

17 If we infer preferences from revealed actions, a player demonstrates preferences via her choice and illustrates complete preferences as long as she always makes a choice, but this still does not ensure consistency. We require that her preferences are **coherently extendible**, i.e. while learning her preferences, she remains consistent.

18 For details, see Marquis de Condorcet (1785). Arrow (1951) provides a generalisation known as *Arrow's impossibility theorem* in social choice theory.

19 For an example of such an alternative approach, see Ille (2012).

Evolutionary Game Theory and Dynamical Systems: Decentralised Decision-Making and Spontaneous Order

3.1 Introduction

FOOD sharing is common among foraging bands, but the degree and mode of sharing differ across hunter–gatherer communities leading to varying degrees of reciprocity and willingness to share. For example, Chipewyan and Kootenai women distribute meat on behalf of their husbands. Alaskan Eskimos only share within but not between families. The Ache are most likely to share with kin as a reciprocal action while among the Ju/'hoansi, the spoils go to the owner of the arrow that killed the prey and food exchange is ensured by trading arrows. The Mikea and the !Kung regularly encourage reciprocity via verbal abuse, jesting or pleas of hunger. To evade this so-called demand sharing, Mikea conceal their cooking from others and Gunwinggu lie to other band members about their success in hunting (for further details, refer to Kelly, 2013, Ch. 6).

Furthermore, communities encourage repeated trading and gift-giving at a young age to enculturate sharing, thereby internalising the need to reciprocate and creating an intrinsic motivation to share. The ritual of sharing is frequently perceived as more important than the value of the good which is shared. Giving to others often incurs a future liability or indebtedness. Failure to share or to reciprocate, on the other hand, commonly results in social punishment while free-riders may resort to tolerated scrounging (i.e. tolerated theft) to ensure that they can appropriate food in the absence of reciprocal sharing.

In this chapter, we will study the impact of various factors on the sharing norms found in hunter–gatherer societies to explain the plethora of institutional setups. These factors include the cost of punishment, the benefit of sharing or free-riding or the intrinsic benefit of the process of sharing with others in addition to kin selection and reciprocal altruism - and in return, these factors are determined by the social and natural environment in which foraging bands interact. For example, the risk of social punishment depends on group size which affects the frequency of repeated interactions and the risk of encountering free-riders. The benefits from sharing are contingent on the variability in individual returns (a forager gathers more than needed on one day

DOI: 10.4324/9781003035329-3

and less on another day), low correlation between foragers leading to low variability in collective returns (if one forager does better another does worse) and roughly equal foraging abilities (on average, all foragers gather the same amount and no need to specialise exists). In addition, early socialisation and enculturation of sharing internalises the need to give and affect the intrinsic motivation to share with others.

For our study, we will make use of **evolutionary game theory**, which is an appropriate tool to analyse the **dynamical systems** that govern conventions, practices, and norms. In this framework, I generally assume that interactions take place between members of a larger community. Members base their choices on social learning: new behavioural rules are acquired after encountering and by observing others. After having observed the benefits that a certain behavioural rule accrues to another member, the new behaviour is replicated by imitation if it seems more beneficial than the old behaviour.

The evolutionary approach is thus distinct from the classic non-cooperative game-theoretic approach we used in Chapter 2. The classic approach models interactions between a very small number of individuals whose actions are based on best response actions. I assumed that an individual chooses a behaviour that maximises her benefits given her expectation about the behaviour of the other player. Yet, as we have seen in the previous discussion, a best response does not only require mutual knowledge of the available actions, the interacting individuals' preferences and consistency of choices but also the cognitive ability to compare the expected benefit of each action - not only for oneself but also for those with whom the player is interacting. The evolutionary approach does not necessitate these stringent assumptions on the rationality of individuals to trace the evolution of the behaviour within a group over time. No prior knowledge of the various alternative behavioural rules nor any sophisticated optimisation process is required. Change in behaviour is motivated by a prevalence of distinct behavioural rules which illustrate a difference in affective valence or functional value for an individual. Individuals are therefore only assumed to be able to compare the benefits of a particular behavioural rule by observation and to imitate such behaviour. In addition, infrequent replication errors or idiosyncratic behaviour continuously introduces randomness into the social learning process which enables us to study the impact of behavioural innovation and the evolutionary relevance of behavioural patterns in a society in the long run.

Nevertheless, both approaches are not as dissimilar as we may expect. Evolutionary game theory determines evolutionary long-run equilibria which are Nash equilibria in the classic non-cooperative approach.[1] Yet, the inverse does not necessarily hold true - not all Nash equilibria are evolutionarily stable, i.e. do not persist in the long run if they are subjected to infrequent idiosyncratic behaviour. Consequently, by explicitly modelling the dynamics leading to an evolutionary equilibrium, we are able to eliminate Nash equilibria which are implausible in larger societies.

In the following, I develop a simplified model that presents the reasons for the varying degrees of sharing. However, I ignore crucial motivators, such as kin and reciprocal altruism. (Thus, we may interpret a social outcome without universal sharing as a convention in which sharing only occurs between kin or those who have exchanged food before). Evidently, a comprehensive model should include these factors and the approach is flexible enough to do so. Since the principal aim is here to render the concepts and the approach accessible, the models serve mainly an illustrative purpose. While we content ourselves with the most basic models, the latter still provide valuable insights into the principal factors that drive and consolidate particular sharing norms.

3.2 The Continuous Replicator Model

To start our simple model, I focus on the replication process of different behavioural rules and the existence of potential evolutionary equilibria that define a social norm before I analyse their evolutionary pertinence (i.e., whether they persist in the long run) in the next section. Assume that members of a population or community can choose between two behavioural rules or strategies, i.e. they can be *sharers* or *loners*. Members of a community can freely choose their strategy before each interaction. However, to make our lives easier, I trace the proportion of society members who adhere to each behavioural rule. Let x be the proportion of members who choose to share. Since the proportions need to sum to 100 percent, the relative frequency of members who prefer to be a loner and not to share is therefore given by $(1-x)$. Consequently, we only need to trace x, i.e., the proportion of *sharers*, and can directly infer the proportion of *loners* and thus the population distribution. Furthermore, we define the first-order ordinary differential equation

$$\dot{x} = \frac{dx}{dt} = f(x) \tag{3.1}$$

In other words, $\dot{x}$ denotes the change in proportion x after an infinitesimally small period $\Delta t \to 0$ has passed. Based on the form of $f(x)$, equation (3.1) allows us to track the forces determining the rate of change in the composition of our population.

We assume that individuals randomly meet and observe each other. If one of these individuals believes that they could have done better by imitating the behaviour of another member, they will switch their behavioural rule. Given the proportion x of sharers and the corresponding proportion of $(1-x)$ loners, the probability of choosing a sharer who then encounters a loner is simply given by $x(1-x)$ which is half of the probability that two members of different behavioural rules are matched. Sharers will only reconsider their behavioural rule, if they encounter a loner who has gained a larger benefit, and correspondingly, loners will only switch if they encounter a more successful sharer. Maintaining the terminology of Chapter 2, I define π_s as the payoff of sharers and correspondingly, π_l as the payoff of loners. I can then write our simplified process of social learning as[2]

$$\dot{x} = x(1-x)(\pi_s - \pi_l) \tag{3.2}$$

Equation (3.2) is a special case of the **continuous replicator equation** with two behavioural rules.[3] While the change in x depends on the sign of $\dot{x}$, the $x(1-x)$ term defines the speed of change and is largest if $x = 0.5$, i.e., the community is well-mixed. The former implies that if on average sharers do better (worse) than loners, the proportion x will increase (decrease). As such, the replicator equation models vicarious reinforcement. Note that both π_s and π_l are functions that may have x as an argument, meaning that individual benefits may depend on the current population distribution. The $x(1-x)$ term constrains x to the unit interval, i.e. $x \in (0,1)$. As x gets closer to its extrema 0 and 1, the $x(1-x)$ term becomes smaller and change seizes to happen.

Instead of modelling the individual social approaches to sharing across different foraging bands, I will focus our attention on the different *degrees* of sharing norms in this section. Assume that a sharer's payoff is defined as

$$\pi_s = \alpha_s + \beta_s x \tag{3.3}$$

Parameter α_s defines an intrinsic gain that a sharer obtains from sharing, while parameter β_s determines the benefit that she obtains from mutual exchange with others which minimises variability in food availability.

A loner profits from free-riding and tolerated scrounging, but bears the cost of social punishment. I can define the payoff of a loner as

$$\pi_l = \alpha_l + \beta_l x - \gamma x^2 \tag{3.4}$$

Equivalent to the definition of the payoff of sharers, parameter α_l defines the intrinsic value of being a loner, and parameters β_l and γ specify the expected food obtained from tolerated scrounging or free-riding, and the cost of social punishment, respectively. To keep the model as simple as possible, I do not explicitly model the evolution of social punishment in the form of public beating, ostracism, or gossip but simply assume that the social costs quadratically increase in the proportion of sharers. Consequently, a small number of sharers are proportionally less able to punish loners compared to a community consisting mostly of sharers. Using (3.2) and defining $\alpha = \alpha_s - \alpha_l$ and $\beta = \beta_s - \beta_l$, I can write the replicator dynamic for this social process as

$$\dot{x} = x(1-x)\,(\alpha + x(\beta + \gamma x)) \tag{3.5}$$

Note that while I assume that all parameters in equations (3.3) and (3.4) are strictly positive, α and β can have negative values if the intrinsic value of a loner exceeds the value of a sharer or if scrounging conveys a larger return than sharing, respectively.

We define a **fixed point** (or stationary point) as a point x^* for which $\dot{x} = f(x^*) = 0$, i.e. once the dynamical system (3.1) reaches this point, the proportion of sharers (and thus the proportion of loners) does no longer change over time. We may, therefore, call a fixed point also an equilibrium point. Given the process in equation (3.2), a fixed point always occurs whenever all members of the population are either sharers or loners (these are **pure fixed points**), and if $\pi_s = \pi_l$ (potentially defining **interior fixed points**). Further remember that since x denotes a relative frequency, the variable cannot take a negative value nor exceed 1 and any interior fixed point must remain within the unit interval $x \in (0,1)$. Equation $\pi_s = \pi_l$ may therefore have no solution, one solution, or several solutions. For the specific case defined by equation (3.5), we obtain two potential interior fixed points in addition to the general pure (strategy) fixed points.

$$x_1^* = 0 \tag{3.6a}$$

$$x_2^* = 1 \tag{3.6b}$$

$$x_3^* = \frac{-\beta - \sqrt{\beta^2 - 4\alpha\gamma}}{2\gamma} \tag{3.6c}$$

$$x_4^* = \frac{-\beta + \sqrt{\beta^2 - 4\alpha\gamma}}{2\gamma} \tag{3.6d}$$

For the existence of the interior fixed points $x_3, x_4 \in (0,1)$, it must hold

For x_3^*: $2\gamma > -\beta - \sqrt{\beta^2 - 4\alpha\gamma}$ and $\beta < -\sqrt{\beta^2 - 4\alpha\gamma}$

For x_4^*: $2\gamma > -\beta + \sqrt{\beta^2 - 4\alpha\gamma}$ and $\beta < \sqrt{\beta^2 - 4\alpha\gamma}$

The first condition stems from the fact that the numerator needs to be smaller than the denominator for a fraction to be smaller than 1; the second condition is a consequence of the strictly positive denominator, which requires that the numerator is also strictly positive for the fraction to be greater than 0. Thus, x_3^* can only exist within the unit interval if $\beta < 0$.

For the moment, assume that $\gamma = 0$, i.e. no form of social punishment exists. The dynamical system displays three fixed points instead of four. The single interior fixed point is given by

$$\hat{x}_3^* = -\frac{\alpha}{\beta} \tag{3.8}$$

It must hold that $|\beta| > |\alpha|$, where $|.|$ denotes the absolute value, and α and β must be of opposite sign for $\hat{x}_3^*$ to be interior. In other words, the return from tolerated scrounging must be higher than the benefits from sharing if the intrinsic value of being a sharer is higher than the intrinsic value of being a loner.

Exercise 3.1

(a) Define the replicator equation (3.2) for each of the 2×2 games in Figure 2.4 on page 15. (b) Find the fixed points. Are the fixed points identical to the Nash equilibria?

We can analyse in which way a change in one of the parameter values affects the position of the interior fixed point. While this is easy to see from equation (3.8), the most elegant way to study the impact of a parameter is by examining the first partial derivative. Remember that a partial derivative tells us the impact of a minuscule increase of a variable or parameter on our dependent variable (in our case $\hat{x}_3^*$) while all other variables and parameters remain constant. We have the following

$$\frac{d\hat{x}_3^*}{d\alpha} = \frac{-1}{\beta} \tag{3.9a}$$

$$\frac{d\hat{x}_3^*}{d\beta} = \frac{\alpha}{\beta^2} \tag{3.9b}$$

In other words, the effect of an increase in the difference between the intrinsic values of sharers and loners depends on whether or not scrounging conveys a larger benefit than sharing. Note that equations (3.9a) and (3.9b) must be of equal sign. For example, if scrounging is more beneficial than sharing, $\beta < 0$ and equation (3.9a) is positive implying that a relative increase in the intrinsic value of sharing shifts the interior equilibrium to the right (i.e. to a distribution with a higher proportion of sharers). In addition, since the intrinsic value of sharers must be higher than the intrinsic value of loners, equation (3.9b) is positive and an increase in the benefits from sharing relative to scrounging and free-riding will also shift the interior equilibrium to the right.

Since $\gamma = 0$, both π_s and π_l are linear in x, i.e., if the payoffs are drawn in a diagram with x as the independent variable, both payoff functions define a line, as shown in Figure 3.1. Notice that the intercept on the (π_s, π_l)-axis at $x = 0$ is simply α_s for π_s and α_l for π_l and their respective slopes are defined by the value of β_s and β_l. Since π_3^* is determined by the population distribution at which $\pi_s - \pi_l = 0$, the interior equilibrium lies at the corresponding intersection of the payoff functions, i.e., at the intersection of the solid line with each of the dashed lines in Figure 3.1.

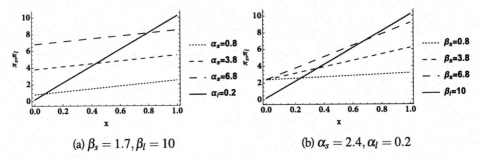

Figure 3.1: Expected payoffs of sharers and loners: the solid line shows $\pi_l(x)$ and the dashed lines show $\pi_s(x)$ for various parameter values.

This raises a question: why does the impact of α and β depend on the respective sign of the other? It seems plausible to assume that an increase in the intrinsic value of being a sharer or the return from sharing should generally benefit sharers and therefore increase their frequency in the population. Indeed this assumption is correct, and it is not contradicted by the results in equation (3.9a) and (3.9b). The answer lies in the different roles that the interior fixed point can play in reference to the pure fixed points. To better understand this phenomenon, we study the stability of the fixed points in closer detail in the following.

Exercise 3.2

Since the best replies and the position of the interior equilibrium remain unaffected by the addition of a constant according to our discussion on pages 17–18, any symmetric 2×2 game can be transformed into

	U	D
u	α, α	$0,0$
d	$0,0$	β, β

(a) Show that this is the case. (b) Define the replicator equation in a game with one population. How are the fixed points affected by the signs of α and β (both are negative, positive, or of different sign)?

3.3 Regime Change, Stability and Bifurcation

The replicator equation reproduces a system of social learning in which individuals learn by imitating more successful members of their society. However, it is reasonable to assume that sporadically, individuals commit errors and do not adopt a better behavioural rule. As a consequence, a population will fluctuate around a fixed point. It is therefore important to understand the impact of such fluctuations. We might think of a ball being placed on the top of a hill which will roll downhill after an ever so slightly push. Contrarily, a ball being placed in a valley between two hills will return back to its original position after being pushed. The same situations can occur after a small perturbation in the distribution of sharers and loners.

We define the set of states that the system defined by equation (3.2) can take as its **state space**. Consequently, the number of variables needed to define the state of our population of sharers and loners determines the dimensionality of the state space. Since we trace only x over time, the state space is one-dimensional and can illustrate three different types of fixed points.

- **Node**: This is an **asymptotically stable** fixed point since any population distribution in its vicinity converges to this point over time. It is also called a *sink*. (More precisely, asymptotically stable means that the fixed point is Liapunov stable, i.e., any distribution close to the point remains within its vicinity, and further the fixed point is attracting.)
- **Repellor**: This is an **unstable** fixed point since any population distribution in its vicinity moves away from this point over time. It is also called a *source*.
- **Saddle Point**: This is a **halfstable** fixed point since any population distribution will converge to this point from one side and move away from the other side.

Nodes and repellors are considered to be **structurally stable** while saddle points in a one-dimensional system are **structurally unstable** for reasons which become clear later in this section. It will also become obvious why saddle points are named as such in the Section 3.4.

Remember that the stability of a fixed point depends on how a population reacts to small fluctuations around a fixed point, i.e. does a change to the population distribution further destabilise the composition of the population or does the latter return back to the original distribution? We therefore evaluate the system's behaviour at some new distribution $(x^* + \varepsilon)$ where ε denotes a small perturbation away from a fixed point. Consequently for $\dot{x} = f(x)$, we have the following[4]

For $\varepsilon > 0$:

If $f(x^* + \varepsilon) > 0 \Rightarrow$ fluctuations lead away from the fixed point x^*

If $f(x^* + \varepsilon) < 0 \Rightarrow$ fluctuations return to the fixed point x^*

The inverse holds for $\varepsilon < 0$.

The first (partial) derivative of a function measures exactly this: the impact of an infinitely small increase of the function's argument (x in this case) on the dependent variable ($\dot{x}$ in this case). Since $\dot{x} = 0$ at a fixed point x^*, an infinitesimally small increase in x can render $\dot{x}$ either positive or negative, implying that x either further increases or decreases. Thus, if the first derivative at a fixed point is negative, the small increase in x entails a subsequent small decrease of the population distribution. The population returns back to the fixed point and the equilibrium is thus asymptotically stable. Contrarily, if the first derivative at the fixed point is positive, the share x further increases after an initial small increase, thereby pushing the population further away from the fixed point. The equilibrium is unstable. The value of the derivative at the fixed point is called the **eigenvalue** or **characteristic value** which is defined as

$$\lambda = \left. \frac{df(x)}{dx} \right|_{x=x^*} \tag{3.10}$$

where the $|$ symbol denotes that we evaluate the derivative at a fixed point x^*. Table 3.1 summarises the relationship between the eigenvalue and the stability of the fixed point. The zero eigenvalue is a special case and I postpone the discussion of the three possibilities to the end of this section. Coming back to our example, the first derivative of $f(x)$, as defined in equation (3.5), with respect

Table 3.1

Stabilities given the characteristic value λ

Eigenvalue	Second derivative	Type of fixed point
$\lambda < 0$		Node: asymptotically stable fixed point
$\lambda > 0$		Repellor: unstable fixed point
	Same sign	Saddle point: halfstable fixed point
$\lambda = 0$	Left positive/Right negative	Node: stable fixed point
	Left negative/Right positive	Repellor: unstable fixed point

to x is

$$\frac{df(x)}{dx} = \alpha(1 - 2x) + x(\beta(2 - 3x) + \gamma x(3 - 4x)) \tag{3.11}$$

For the moment, I will maintain our assumption that $\gamma = 0$. Consequently, we need to study (3.11) at each of our three fixed points. Substituting the fixed point values for x leads to

$$\left.\frac{df(x)}{dx}\right|_{x=0} = \alpha \tag{3.12a}$$

$$\left.\frac{df(x)}{dx}\right|_{x=-\frac{\alpha}{\beta}} = -\frac{\alpha(\alpha + \beta)}{\beta} \tag{3.12b}$$

$$\left.\frac{df(x)}{dx}\right|_{x=1} = -\alpha - \beta \tag{3.12c}$$

Remember that existence of the interior equilibrium requires that $|\alpha| < |\beta|$ and α and β are of different signs. Consequently, the signs of the first derivatives in equation (3.12) alternate. If $\alpha > 0$, the interior fixed point x_3^* at $-\alpha/\beta$ requires that $\beta < 0$ and $|\beta| > \alpha$. Consequently, equation (3.12b) is negative. The pure fixed points are repellors and the interior fixed point is a node. If $\alpha < 0$ the latter is a repeller, while $x = 0$ and $x = 1$ are nodes. In the absence of an interior fixed point (i.e., α and β have the same sign, or $|\beta| < \alpha$), the derivatives at $x = 0$ and $x = 1$ have opposite signs.

This alternating stability is a common feature of one-dimensional dynamical systems. Figure 3.2 illustrates the reason. Note that the one-dimensional state space is just a line - the x-axis ranging from zero to one. Figure 3.2 plots the function $\dot{x}$ as a dotted line and for illustrative purposes, the tangent at the interior fixed point.[5] Whenever the dotted line is above the axis, $\dot{x}$ is positive and the dynamics push the system to the right. If the dotted line is below the axis, the opposite occurs. I ignore momentarily the special case at which $\dot{x}$ is just tangent to the x-axis: if $\dot{x}$ cuts the x-axis from below at the interior fixed point as we move to the right, the function can only cut the axis from above at the pure fixed points as shown in Figure 3.2a. If, on the contrary, function $\dot{x}$ intersects with the x-axis from above at the interior fixed point, it can only cut through the axis from below at the pure fixed points as shown in Figure 3.2b.

The arrows in Figure 3.2 illustrate the dynamics of our system.[6] In Figure 3.2a, any population distribution to the left of the interior fixed point at $-\alpha/\beta$ will converge to $x = 0$ and the region between 0 and $-\alpha/\beta$ is called **the basin of attraction** of $x_1^* = 0$. Any point to the right will converge to $x = 1$ and the region of the rightward arrow between $-\alpha/\beta$ and 1 defines the

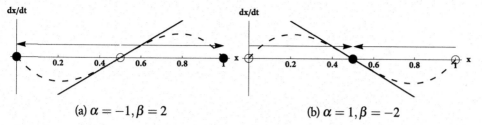

(a) $\alpha = -1, \beta = 2$ (b) $\alpha = 1, \beta = -2$

Figure 3.2: Plot of the state space of the one-dimensional system: the solid circles mark the (stable) nodes and the empty circles the repellors, the arrows indicate the direction of the dynamics. In addition, the dotted line illustrates $\dot{x}$ and the solid line shows the tangent at the interior fixed point.

basin of attraction of $x_2^* = 1$. The interior fixed point determines the border between the two basins of attraction which is called a **separatrix**. In Figure 3.2b, the entire state space to the right of $x = 0$ and to the left of $x = 1$ defines the basin of attraction of the interior fixed point. We can now see that both figures are the only two alternatives given a one-dimensional system with three equilibria. Consequently, stabilities need to alternate, which explains the alternating signs in equation (3.12).

We can now make sense of our results in equation (3.9). If β is negative, the interior fixed point is stable and we are in the situation presented in Figure 3.2b. By equation (3.9a), an increase in α shifts the interior equilibrium to the right. Since the interior fixed point is the only asymptotically stable equilibrium, any increase in α increases the frequency of sharers x. Yet, if β is positive, the interior equilibrium is unstable as shown in Figure 3.2a, and by equation (3.9a), an increase in α shifts the interior fixed point to the left. In this case, the interior equilibrium is a separatrix. A left move of the latter increases the basin of attraction of the $x^* = 1$ equilibrium in which the population is composed only of sharers. This implies that an increase in α increases the likelihood of converging to $x = 1$ and is therefore also beneficial for sharers. To see this, we might imagine that when individuals initially form a community, they choose to be a sharer or loner at random. Thus, any point in the state space can define the initial distribution and a larger basin of attraction implies that more points converge to a fixed point.[7] In addition, since random errors push a population away from a fixed point, the basin of attraction defines the number of errors that need to occur to shift a population from one node to another. The basin of attraction, therefore, defines the robustness of a convention - I will discuss this property in further detail in Chapter 4.

The alternating stability is not always given in a one-dimensional dynamical system. To see this, I now drop the assumption that $\gamma = 0$. In this case, the system in equation (3.5) illustrates the four fixed points previously defined in equation (3.6) and the first derivative as given in equation (3.11). The derivatives at the four fixed points are then

$$\left. \frac{df(x)}{dx} \right|_{x=x_1^*} = \alpha \tag{3.13a}$$

$$\left. \frac{df(x)}{dx} \right|_{x=x_2^*} = -\alpha - \beta - \gamma \tag{3.13b}$$

$$\left. \frac{df(x)}{dx} \right|_{x=x_3^*} = \frac{(\beta + \gamma)\left(\beta^2 - 4\alpha\gamma\right) - 2\alpha\gamma\delta + \beta\delta(\beta + \gamma)}{2\gamma^2} \tag{3.13c}$$

$$\left.\frac{df(x)}{dx}\right|_{x=x_4^*} = \frac{(\beta+\gamma)\left(\beta^2-4\alpha\gamma\right)+2\alpha\gamma\delta-\beta\delta(\beta+\gamma)}{2\gamma^2} \tag{3.13d}$$

with $\delta = \sqrt{\beta^2-4\alpha\gamma}$. The complicated derivatives for the interior fixed points make it difficult to see under which conditions a point is stable or unstable. As a first step, consider Figure 3.3. Here we see the change in the dynamics if we increase α for a given value of β and γ. Starting with $\alpha = 0.8$ in Figure 3.3a, the left interior fixed point is stable and the right interior fixed point is unstable. As α increases, function $f(x)$ shifts up and the interior fixed points approach each other. At $\alpha = 1$ in Figure 3.3b, both interior fixed points collide and are just tangent to the x-axis. Further increasing α in Figure 3.3c eliminates the interior fixed points. The system undergoes a **tangential bifurcation**.[8]

In Table 3.1, we defined a saddle point as halfstable. We can see the rationale in Figure 3.3b. Population distributions to the right of the saddle point are attracted, any distribution to its left diverges and asymptotically approaches $x = 1$. Remember that the value of $\dot{x}$ determines the rate of change of x. Therefore, as the distribution approaches the saddle node from the left, the function approaches the x-axis and convergence progressively slows down up to the saddle point at which change comes to a halt. At this point, only a random error can lead the system to cross the saddle point. Once this occurs, the rate of change picks up and convergence accelerates towards $x = 1$. Figure 3.3d shows how the system behaves at a minuscule distance from the x-axis. (I substituted $\beta = -6$ at which the function is tangent for the slightly larger value of $\beta = -5.999$). Within a few periods, the distribution approaches $x = 1/3$ but then remains around this value for 800 periods only to suddenly converge to $x = 1$ afterward.

We can calculate the parameter value for the saddle point by simply setting $x_3^* = x_4^*$ since the interior fixed points need to collide. From equation (3.6c) and (3.6d), we can see that this requires the root of the numerator δ to equal zero. Given that $x^* \in (0,1)$ for any interior fixed

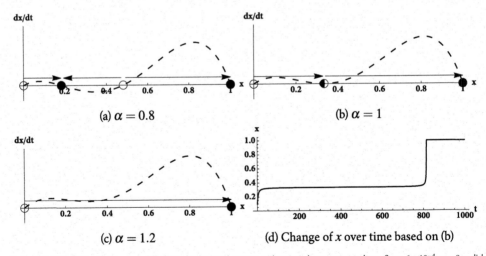

(a) $\alpha = 0.8$

(b) $\alpha = 1$

(c) $\alpha = 1.2$

(d) Change of x over time based on (b)

Figure 3.3: Plot of the state space of the one-dimensional system with general parameter values: $\beta = -6+10^{-4}$, $\gamma = 9$: solid circles indicate nodes, empty circles indicate repellors and half-shaded circle indicate the saddle point (which is stable from the right and unstable from the left). Arrows indicate the direction of the dynamics. In addition, the dotted line illustrates $\dot{x} = f(x)$. Figure 3.3d illustrates the change of x over time for the situation depicted in Figure 3.3b.

point, we have

$$\beta_{saddle} = -2\sqrt{\alpha\gamma} \qquad (3.14)$$

which must also be the zero of the functions (3.13c) and (3.13d). Equation (3.14) tells us that some critical combination of intrinsic values of sharing and scrounging as well as a cost of social punishment exists at which a slight reduction in the benefits from scrounging or more efficient ways of identifying free-riders can induce a sudden shift from a mostly non-sharing norm to one in which every member is a sharer (i.e., a switch from the dynamics in Figure 3.3a to those in Figure 3.3c). We say that a *bifurcation* occurs at β_{saddle}. Setting this value into (3.6c) or (3.6d) returns the position of the saddle point at

$$x^*_{saddle} = \sqrt{\frac{\alpha}{\gamma}} \qquad (3.15)$$

at which we obtain, as expected, the eigenvalue $\lambda = 0$. Consequently, we have to check the value of the second derivative and we see that it is positive around the saddle point.[9] Given conditions (3.14) and (3.15), it must further be that $\gamma > \alpha > 0$ and $\beta < 0$.

The eigenvalue of x_1^* given by equation (3.13a) is therefore positive. Consequently, $x = 0$ is a repellor which implies that the saddle node will be tangent to the x-axis from above. We call this a **saddle I**, while a saddle tangent from below is called a **saddle II**. This answers the question of the sign of the eigenvalues in equation (3.13) and hence, the stability of the fixed points if both interior fixed points are within the unit interval. The eigenvalue of x_1^* and x_4^* are positive while the eigenvalues of x_2^* and x_3^* are negative.

We can now also see why the saddle point is considered to be structurally unstable. Small changes to a parameter fundamentally change the stability of the interior fixed point(s). As we change one of the three parameters only slightly, the interior fixed points collide and mutually extinguish each other. This characteristic is not mandatory for any fixed point with a zero eigenvalue. The bottom part of Table 3.1 also listed the requirements for a node and a repellor which are structurally unstable. Figure 3.4 illustrates an example of a node and a repellor with a zero eigenvalue. We observe that both fixed points are also an inflection point of $\dot{x}$, i.e. the curvature of the graph changes. Since the curvature of a function is defined by its second derivative, the second derivative is equal to zero at the fixed point and the sign of the second derivative to its left is different from the sign to its right - the second derivative is positive to the left of the node in Figure 3.4a and negative to its right, and negative to the left of the repellor in Figure 3.4b and positive to its right.

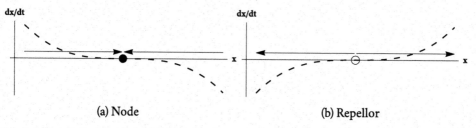

(a) Node   (b) Repellor

Figure 3.4: Examples of structurally unstable fixed points with eigenvalue $\lambda = 0$.

3.4   Multi-Population and N-Strategy Games

So far, we have studied systems that have only two behavioural rules and could be sufficiently described as a one-dimensional dynamical system. In an n-dimensional system, the population distribution at time t is defined by

$$x(t) = (x_1(t), x_2(t), \ldots, x_n(t))$$

where $x_i(t)$ defines the proportion (or frequency) of members choosing behaviour i. The rate of change of $x(t)$ can be described by the set of time evolution equations

$$\dot{x}_1 = \frac{dx_1}{dt} = f_1(x_1(t), x_2(t), \ldots, x_n(t))$$

$$\dot{x}_2 = \frac{dx_2}{dt} = f_2(x_1(t), x_2(t), \ldots, x_n(t))$$

$$\vdots$$

$$\dot{x}_n = \frac{dx_n}{dt} = f_n(x_1(t), x_2(t), \ldots, x_n(t))$$

(3.16)

The **Jacobian matrix** of the dynamical system is defined by all first-order *partial* derivatives. For system (3.16), the Jacobian at a fixed point $x^* = (x_1^*, x_2^*, \ldots, x_n^*)$ is given by

$$J = \begin{bmatrix} f_{11} & f_{12} & \cdots & f_{1n} \\ f_{21} & f_{22} & \cdots & f_{2n} \\ \vdots & \vdots & \ddots & \vdots \\ f_{n1} & f_{n2} & \cdots & f_{nn} \end{bmatrix}_{x=x^*}$$

(3.17)

where f_{ij} is short for[10]

$$f_{ij} = \frac{\partial f_i(x_1, x_2, \ldots, x_n)}{\partial x_j}$$

(3.18)

The stability of the fixed point x^* then depends on the sign of the real parts of the eigenvalues of the Jacobian matrix J. Simply speaking, if all eigenvalues of J at x^* have negative real parts, the fixed point is (asymptotically) stable. Some of the readers might be unfamiliar with the meaning of eigenvalue and real part. To better understand the meaning of this statement and the underlying intuition, I will limit our discussion to two-dimensional dynamical systems, before I apply what we have learnt to a slightly more complex example.

A two-dimensional system may represent a situation in which two populations interact and each population is defined by two behavioural rules, or alternatively, we have a single population that has three behavioural rules. Both situations are defined by the time evolution equations

$$\dot{x}_1 = f_1(x_1, x_2)$$
$$\dot{x}_2 = f_2(x_1, x_2)$$

Any fixed point (x_1^*, x_2^*) satisfies

$$0 = f_1(x_1^*, x_2^*)$$
$$0 = f_2(x_1^*, x_2^*)$$

and we obtain the Jacobian at the fixed point

$$J^* = \begin{bmatrix} f_{11} & f_{12} \\ f_{21} & f_{22} \end{bmatrix} \tag{3.21}$$

Assume for a moment that $f_{12} = \partial f_1/\partial x_2 = 0$ and $f_{21} = \partial f_2/\partial x_1 = 0$. The **eigenvalues** of the Jacobian are simply its diagonal elements, i.e.,

$$\lambda_1 = f_{11} = \frac{\partial f_1}{\partial x_1}$$

$$\lambda_2 = f_{22} = \frac{\partial f_2}{\partial x_2}$$

Under this assumption, the motions or dynamics of x_1 and x_2 are independent around the fixed point, i.e. the change in x_1 does not depend on x_2 and the converse also holds. Since we have a two-dimensional system and any population distribution is defined by a tuple (x_1, x_2), the state space is defined by a two-dimensional plane. The change in the population distribution, subsequent to a small disturbance which pushed it away from the fixed point in the x_1-direction or x_2-direction or a combination of both, is then only defined by the marginal impact of x_1 along the x_1-direction and the marginal impact of x_2 along the x_2-direction of the plane. In other words, if the population slightly increased in x_1 after some idiosyncratic behaviour, we only need to check the sign of the first partial derivative $\partial f_1/\partial x_1$ to see whether the small increase in x_1 is followed by a subsequent decrease in x_1 which returns the system back to the initial fixed point. In this case, the partial derivative and thus, λ_1 must be negative. The logic for a small fluctuation in the x_2-direction is analogous and therefore defined by the sign of λ_2. We obtain the results shown in Table 3.2.

It is clear that both eigenvalues do not necessarily have the same sign. If, for example, $\lambda_1 < 0$ and $\lambda_2 > 0$, any fluctuation around the fixed point along the x_1-axis will be self-stabilising, yet any fluctuation along the x_2-axis will initiate a movement away from the fixed point. The surface of the state space will take the form of a saddle, as shown in Figure 3.5. The figure plots the **potential function** V for this dynamical system $f_1 = -(x_1 - 0.5)$ and $f_2 = (x_2 - 0.5)$ and visualises the saddle. For the potential function $V(x_1, x_2)$ it must hold that $f_1 = -(\partial V/\partial x_1)$ and $f_2 = -(\partial V/\partial x_2)$.[11] A cross-section along the x_1-axis of the saddle shows a valley while a cross-section along the x_2-axis illustrates a hill. We can now imagine a ball being placed at the centre of the saddle at $(x_1^*, x_2^*) = (0.5, 0.5)$. If the ball is pushed back and forth only along the x_1-axis, it will slide back to its original point. If it is, however, only nudged slightly along the x_2-axis, it will roll

Table 3.2

Stabilities given the characteristic values λ_1 and λ_2 for $f_{12} = 0$ and $f_{21} = 0$

λ_1	λ_2	Type of fixed point
< 0	< 0	Node: stable fixed point
> 0	> 0	Repellor: unstable fixed point
> 0	< 0	Saddle point: unstable fixed point
< 0	> 0	Saddle point: unstable fixed point

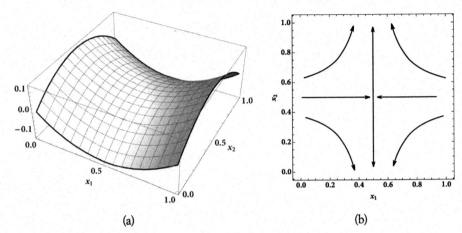

(a)   (b)

Figure 3.5: (a) Saddle type surface (showing potential function $V = \frac{x_1^2 - x_1}{2} - \frac{x_2^2 - x_2}{2}$) in a two-dimensional state space with a saddle point at $(x_1^*, x_2^*) = (0.5, 0.5)$, (b) The corresponding stable and unstable manifold in the state space.

down the hill away from the original fixed point. Figure 3.5b shows the **vector field** on the state space, i.e. a collection of arrows indicating the magnitude and direction of the dynamics.

In this case, the straight line parallel to the x_1-axis and going through (x_1^*, x_2^*) constitutes the **stable manifold** (also called **in-sets**) as is shown by the two straight vectors pointing towards the fixed point. Any initial condition on the stable manifold converges asymptotically to the fixed point (i.e., $(x_1(t), x_2(t)) \to (x_1^*(t), x_2^*(t))$ as $t \to \infty$). The straight line parallel to the x_2-axis and going though the fixed point is called the **unstable manifold** (or **out-sets**). The straight vectors point away from the fixed point, indicating that any initial condition converges to the fixed point if we go backward in time (i.e., $(x_1(t), x_2(t)) \to (x_1^*(t), x_2^*(t))$ as $t \to -\infty$). In more general terms, the stable and unstable manifolds are smooth curves that are tangent to the **eigenvectors** at the equilibrium point, which for this particular system are $(1, 0)$ and $(0, 1)$.[12] We can see that the unstable and stable manifold divide the state space into four regions (or quadrants) and any population distribution starting in one of the quadrants will follow a hyperbolic dynamic and remain within that quadrant. (Notice that this only holds in the close vicinity of the fixed point for non-linear systems.) Consequently, the saddle point is hyperbolic. The one-dimensional saddle point in the previous section was structurally unstable and had a zero eigenvalue. This latter fixed point is nonhyperbolic. If fact, we define any fixed point, whose eigenvalues have only non-zero real parts, a **hyperbolic point**. If the Jacobian has a zero eigenvalue at the fixed point, the latter is a **nonhyperbolic point**.

If all values of the Jacobian given in equation (3.21) are non-zero, the stability analysis is more complicated, since x_1 and x_2 are interdependent. If, for example, some idiosyncratic choice slightly increases x_1 it does not only change the sign of f_1, but since x_1 is also an argument of f_2 the change will either increase or decrease x_2. The latter, in return, has an impact on both f_1 and f_2. Luckily, it is still sufficient to calculate the eigenvalues of the Jacobian. You may think of the eigenvalues as an indicator for the factor by which our dynamical system is squeezed (the absolute value is smaller than one) or stretched (the absolute value is larger than one) along the axes of transformation after a small fluctuation. Only if a small fluctuation around a fixed point leads to a push back (whether as a squeeze or stretch) in the opposite direction, the fixed point is stable. Consequently, this backward push requires that the eigenvalues all have a negative real part.

For the moment, I have stressed the term *real part*, indicating that an eigenvalue can also include an *imaginary part*. To see this, we first have a look at the **characteristic equation** for λ of the Jacobian (3.21) given by

$$\lambda^2 - (f_{11} + f_{22})\lambda + (f_{11}f_{22} - f_{12}f_{21}) = 0 \tag{3.23}$$

Solving (3.23) returns two eigenvalues

$$\lambda_{+,-} = \frac{f_{11} + f_{22} \pm \sqrt{(f_{11} + f_{22})^2 - 4(f_{11}f_{22} - f_{12}f_{21})}}{2} \tag{3.24}$$

We then define λ_+ as the **eigenvalue** with the positive square root, and λ_- as the eigenvalue with the negative square root. Notice that the **trace** of the Jacobian is defined as $Tr(J) = f_{11} + f_{22}$ and its **determinant** is $\Delta(J) = f_{11}f_{22} - f_{12}f_{21}$. We can, therefore, rewrite (3.24) as

$$\lambda_{+,-} = \frac{1}{2}\left(Tr(J) \pm \sqrt{Tr(J)^2 - 4\Delta(J)}\right) \tag{3.25}$$

Further notice that $\Delta(J) = \lambda_+ \times \lambda_-$ and $Tr(J) = \lambda_+ + \lambda_-$. We can also see that an eigenvalue has an imaginary part if the value in the square root is negative, which implies that $Tr(J)^2 - 4\Delta(J) < 0$ and in which case we call the fixed point a **focus**. If the eigenvalues have an imaginary part, the dynamics caused by an idiosyncratic action will *spin* the direction of the trajectories. A **trajectory** (or **orbit**) defines a sequence of x values at successive time intervals. It tells us how the population distribution is moving through the state space after starting out from a specific distribution. With these results in mind, Table 3.3 presents the generalised version of Table 3.2.

You may also find the terminology spiral node instead of stable focus and spiral repellor instead of unstable focus in the literature. Table 3.3 assumes that none of the eigenvalues is zero, i.e. all of the fixed points are hyperbolic. Furthermore, I ignore $\Delta(J) = \frac{1}{4}Tr(J)^2$ which is considered to be a *degenerate case*.[13] If $0 > \Delta(J)$, the square root is larger than $Tr(J)$ and hence the eigenvalues have opposite signs, which explains the saddle point in the right column of Table 3.3. The other columns are a consequence of the sign of the term under the square root in equation (3.25). In this case the sign of the real part is defined by the sign of the trace of the Jacobian. Notice that if the square root in equation (3.25) is negative, the eigenvalues can be written as

$$\lambda_{+,-} = \frac{1}{2}\left(Tr(J) \pm i\Omega\right) \tag{3.26}$$

Table 3.3

Stabilities of fixed points for the two-dimension state space

	$\frac{1}{4}Tr(J)^2 < \Delta(J)$	$0 < \Delta(J) < \frac{1}{4}Tr(J)^2$	$0 > \Delta(J)$
$Tr(J) < 0$	Stable focus	Node	Saddle point
$Tr(J) > 0$	Unstable focus	Repellor	Saddle point

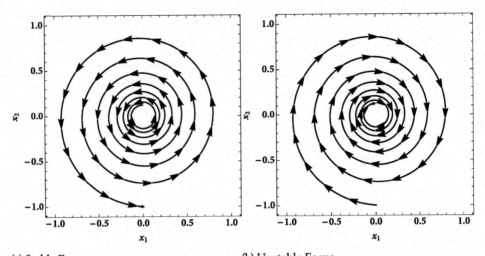

(a) Stable Focus:
$\dot{x}_1 = -x_1 + 20x_2, \dot{x}_2 = -20x_1 - x_2$

(b) Unstable Focus
$\dot{x}_1 = x_1 - 20x_2, \dot{x}_2 = 20x_1 + x_2$

Figure 3.6: Examples of fixed points with eigenvalue $\lambda_{+,-} = \frac{1}{2}Tr(J) \pm i\Omega$.

where Ω defines the imaginary part and is given by

$$\Omega = \sqrt{|Tr(J)^2 - 4\Delta(J)|}$$
$$= \sqrt{|(f_{11} + f_{22})^2 - 4(f_{11}f_{22} - f_{12}f_{21})|}$$

Figure 3.6 provides an example of a stable and unstable focus. If, however, the eigenvalues have only an imaginary part but no real part since $Tr(J) = 0$, the trajectories illustrate a closed loop which we call a **cycle**. If the trajectories spiral toward this cycle and eventually move along the cycle, it is called a **limit cycle**.[14]

What remains to be done is to define the replicator dynamics for equation (3.16). The replicator dynamics for the general case are

$$\dot{x}_1 = f_1 = x_1(\pi_1 - \phi)$$
$$\dot{x}_2 = f_2 = x_2(\pi_2 - \phi)$$
$$\vdots$$
$$\dot{x}_n = f_n = x_n(\pi_n - \phi)$$

(3.27)

with ϕ being the average individual benefit defined as $\phi = x_1\pi_1 + x_2\pi_2 + \ldots + x_n\pi_n$. Thus, whenever a behavioural rule grants an individual a higher benefit than what is obtained by the average individual in the population, its proportion will increase. Remember that a fixed point is defined by a population distribution in which no change occurs. This is the case for any population distribution in which $x_k = 1$ and $x_j = 0$ for any k and all $j \neq k$, i.e. whenever a behavioural rule is adopted by all members of society. We find that $\pi_k = \phi$ for such a behavioural rule k while the first frequency term x_j in all the other replicator equations is zero. Thus, the system in equation (3.27) is stable. It is easy to check that for the case of two behavioural rules for some population *i* with respective frequencies $x_{i1} = x_i$ and $x_{i2} = 1 - x_i$ as in the previous sections, equation (3.27) simplifies to

$$\dot{x}_i = x_i(1 - x_i)(\pi_{i1} - \pi_{i2})$$

which renders it equivalent to (3.2).

Exercise 3.3

Repeat exercise 3.2 but assume that players of two different populations interact. (You will therefore need to define two frequencies.) (a) Show that the interior fixed point is a saddle point in games with α and β greater zero. (b) Compare the dynamics for α and β smaller than zero to the one-population case. Show that the stabilities of the fixed points differ.

3.5 Three Strategies with One and Two Populations

Foraging societies differ vastly with respect to their degree of egalitarianism, i.e. equal access to food and technology. To counteract attempts by individuals to dominate other members, egalitarian communities use ritualisation and social conventions to establish self-reinforcing egalitarian norms. In inegalitarian communities, on the other hand, power over others stems from prestige acquired in previous interactions or access to decisive resources. For example, the Pintupi and Ju/'hoansi form egalitarian groups with socially enforced consensual rules of access to land. The Chumash transformed from an egalitarian foraging society into a people with social divisions. Others, like the Kwakwak'awakw and Nuuchahnulth, define their claim for property and resources based on their family lines (Kelly, 2013, Ch. 9).

In the following, I will use the results of the previous section to study a simple model of sharing practices. Although this model is too stylised to take account of the social and environmental factors which contribute to various degrees of sharing among group members (see again Kelly, 2013 for a very detailed exposition), the model provides us with a general intuition about the dynamics that reinforce a sharing convention once it is established. I start with the assumption that members of a community meet randomly and haggle about splitting a resource or good. Each member can choose between demanding *low* (L), *medium* (M) or *high* (H). Furthermore, assume that a medium demand is the will to equally share a resource. If joint demands exceed the resource, both members fail to agree and are left with no return, since the resource or good does not materialise as both members are necessary for its creation. In other words, sharing only occurs if a high demand is matched by a low demand or a medium demand by a low or medium demand. The normal form game is defined by payoff matrix

$$
\begin{array}{c}
 \\
L \\
M \\
H
\end{array}
\begin{array}{c}
\begin{array}{ccc}
L \quad\quad & M \quad\quad & H
\end{array} \\
\left(
\begin{array}{ccc}
\alpha, \alpha & \alpha, 0.50 & \alpha, \beta \\
0.50, \alpha & 0.50, 0.50 & 0, 0 \\
\beta, \alpha & 0, 0 & 0, 0
\end{array}
\right)
\end{array}
\qquad (3.28)
$$

with $\alpha < 0.5 < \beta$. The three Nash equilibria are shown in bold. Notice that if $\alpha = 1 - \beta$, matrix (3.28) represents a standard **Nash demand game**. If, however, $\alpha < 1 - \beta$, an egalitarian split is more efficient (in the sense that it allows a higher total benefit) than an inegalitarian split. The latter, on the other hand, is more efficient than the former if $\alpha > 1 - \beta$.

I define x as the proportion of L-players, y as the proportion of H players and $z = 1 - x - y$ as the proportion of M-players and as before, I assume that paring is sufficiently random to ensure that the likelihoods of encountering a member who chooses low, medium or high are equal to the respective proportions in the population. The respective payoffs are then given by

$$\pi_x = \alpha \tag{3.29a}$$

$$\pi_z = 0.5(x+z) \tag{3.29b}$$

$$\pi_y = \beta x \tag{3.29c}$$

where the index indicates the behavioural rule. Correspondingly, we define the replicator dynamics

$$\dot{x} = x(\pi_x - \phi) \tag{3.30a}$$

$$\dot{y} = y(\pi_y - \phi) \tag{3.30b}$$

with $\phi = x\pi_x + y\pi_y + (1 - x - y)\pi_z$. Notice that only two replicator equations are sufficient, since the proportions need to sum to 1 and we can directly infer the proportion of members who demand medium by subtracting the proportions of the other behavioural rules from 1. I therefore substitute the proportion z in the average benefit ϕ by $(1 - x - y)$. In the one-population case with an n different strategies, the system is therefore sufficiently defined by $(n - 1)$ replicator dynamics where n can be any natural number greater than one.

The *dimensionality* of the state space is equal to the number of replicator equations. Therefore, the state space forms a **unit 2-simplex** in our example, i.e. the state space is a two-dimensional equilateral triangle of side length 1. Figure 3.7 demonstrates the way this type of state space is usually presented. On the left, point $(0.4, 0.2)$ is plotted in a regular Cartesian coordinate system. Since the proportions are restricted to the unit interval and need to sum to one, the Cartesian plane is limited by the straight line $(1 - x)$ to its right. The state space therefore constitutes a right triangle within which any population distribution must remain. Its vertices define distributions in which every member adopts the same behavioural rule. For visual elegance, I slant the unit simplex and set the interior angles to $60°$, which renders the simplex symmetric as shown in the right part of Figure 3.7.[15] Any point on its right edge defines a population distribution in which no member chooses to demand medium. Correspondingly any point on the left edge or lower edge defines a distribution that lacks a demand for low or high, respectively.

I use the simplex to illustrate the **best response areas** of the Nash demand game. Figure 3.8a plots these for $\alpha = 0.25$ and $\beta = 0.75$ in the unit simplex. Any member who finds herself confronted with a population distribution in the blue area maximises benefits by choosing to demand medium. For a distribution in the red area, it is best to demand low and in the yellow area, benefits are maximised by demanding high. The unit simplex in Figure 3.8b shows the vector field indicated by the arrows, which retraces the trajectories and thereby indicates the direction of the dynamics. The figure further illustrates the zero **isoclines**. An isocline (or isoparametric curve) is a curve of constant value (zero in this case). These zero isoclines are also called **nullclines**. The red, brown,

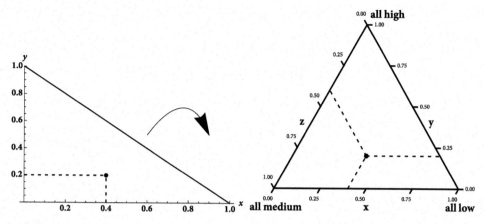

Figure 3.7: Transformation of the unit simplex.

and blue lines show the nullclines, indicating the loci at which a respective proportion does not change, i.e., the points at which the corresponding time derivative $\dot{x}$ (red), $\dot{y}$ (brown) or $\dot{z}$ (blue) equals zero. In fact, the nullclines and the vector field are connected. The sign of a time derivative must change sign as we cross the respective nullcline, since at this point it is equal to zero. For example, if we start at an initial distribution to the left of the brown nullcline for $\dot{y}$, the subsequent distribution must decrease in the share of members who choose high, since $\dot{y} < 0$ to the left of the brown nullcline and $\dot{y} > 0$ to its right. Similarly, we can see that to the right of the blue curve, z decreases and increases to its left, while x increases above the red curve and decreases below.

A fixed point always exists at the vertices of the unit simplex, as we have seen in the previous section. In addition, a fixed point occurs at the intersection of all nullclines (here at $x = \alpha/\beta$ and $y = 1 - 2\alpha$) or at a point on one of the edges of the simplex at which the nullclines of the non-zero proportions intersect. We can see in Figure 3.8b that the system has two stable nodes: a pure node (or asymptotically stable equilibrium) in which all members choose medium and an interior node

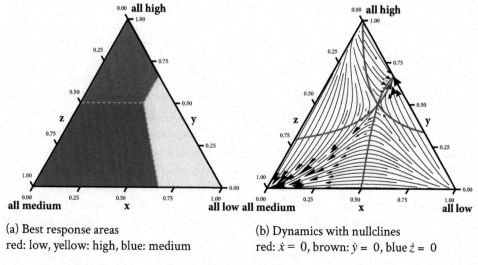

(a) Best response areas
red: low, yellow: high, blue: medium

(b) Dynamics with nullclines
red: $\dot{x} = 0$, brown: $\dot{y} = 0$, blue $\dot{z} = 0$

Figure 3.8: Unit simplices for the three Strategy Nash Demand Game with $\alpha = 0.25$, $\beta = 0.75$.

at the right edge of the simplex in which the population is composed of members who choose low and high. From the previous discussion, it should be clear that $\pi_x = \pi_y$ at this equilibrium. Setting equations (3.29a) and (3.29b) equal, and solving for x and y gives us

$$x = \frac{\alpha}{\beta}$$

$$y = 1 - \frac{\alpha}{\beta}$$

We can easily verify that it does not pay off to demand medium in this context. We have $\pi_x = \pi_y = \alpha$ and $\pi_z = \alpha/(2\beta)$. Since $\beta > 0.5$ by definition, it holds that the benefit of choosing medium is lower than α. Checking the eigenvalues at the fixed points shows that only two equilibria have negative eigenvalues for $0 < \alpha < 0.5$ and $0.5 < \beta < 1$. We obtain

$$\text{For: } (x,y) = (0,0)$$

$$\lambda_- = -0.5$$

$$\lambda_+ = \alpha - 0.5$$

and

$$\text{For: } (x,y) = (\frac{\alpha}{\beta}, 1 - \frac{\alpha}{\beta})$$

$$\lambda_- = \frac{\alpha \left(0.25 - 0.5\sqrt{(0.5-\alpha)^2} + 0.5\alpha - \beta \right)}{\beta} = \frac{\alpha^2}{\beta} - \alpha$$

$$\lambda_+ = \frac{\alpha \left(0.25 + 0.5\sqrt{(0.5-\alpha)^2} + 0.5\alpha - \beta \right)}{\beta} = -\frac{\alpha(\beta-0.5)}{\beta}$$

The basin of attractions of the two nodes depends on α and β. Figure 3.9 shows the basins for different parameter values. Red defines the interior fixed point's basin of attraction while blue illustrates the basin of attraction of the egalitarian fixed point. The point at the centre of the unit simplex is at $(x,y) = (1/3, 1/3)$ - a completely randomised mix of the population at which all behavioural rules occur with equal frequency. In Figure 3.9a, we can see that such a random initial distribution will converge to the egalitarian fixed point at $(x^*, y^*) = (0,0)$ if $\alpha = 0.25$ and $\beta = 0.75$. In fact for any pair given by $\beta = 1 - \alpha$ and $0 < \alpha < \beta < 1$, its basin of attraction covers the fully randomised distribution. In Figure 3.9b, we see that this does not hold if the sum of α and β exceeds 1. In this case, a fully randomised distribution converges to the mixed fixed point at $(x^*, y^*) = (\alpha/\beta, 1 - \alpha/\beta)$. The latter thus occurs if an inegalitarian sharing convention allows for additional benefits. For example, a hunter's ability to successfully hunt large game bestows on him higher prestige that enables him to appropriate a larger share of the spoils and attain a higher reproductive success (Alvard and Gillespie, 2004). Furthermore, if resources vary but are defensible and dense while competition for these resources is high, we observe that systems of land tenure evolve. In contrast, Kelly (2013, p. 242) lists a number of social and environmental factors that render an inegalitarian convention more attractive to foragers.

You may have realised that the best response areas in Figure 3.8a do not perfectly overlap with the basins of attraction in Figure 3.9a. This is caused by the frequency term in each replicator.

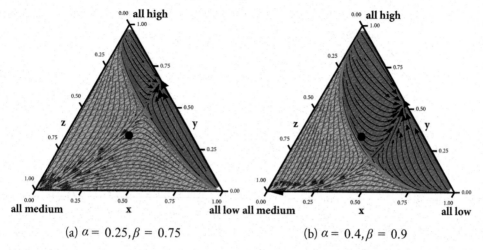

(a) $\alpha = 0.25, \beta = 0.75$ (b) $\alpha = 0.4, \beta = 0.9$

Figure 3.9: Unit simplices for the three Strategy Nash Demand Game: coloured regions illustrate the basins of attraction of the mixed and pure node.

For example, we can see that the best response area for choosing *high* covers the entire lower right part in Figure 3.8a, but the basin of attraction of the node *all medium* includes the area with a high x value and a very low y value. At $x = 0.75$, $y = 0.09$ and thus, $z = 0.16$, we obtain $\pi_z \approx 0.45$ and $\pi_y \approx 0.56$. Consequently, it is best to choose high. Yet, remember that according to the replicator dynamics, a proportion increases if it offers a benefit larger than the population's average benefit and it increases at a rate proportional to its current proportion. Since $\phi \approx 0.31$, both z and y increase, but since members choosing medium are more abundant than those who choose high, the proportion of the former grows more rapidly and hence, the population converges to the all medium fixed point.[16]

So far, we have ignored any stratification which attributes meat and property according to characteristics like sex or heritage within a group. For example, Aka men consume higher amounts of meat than Aka women. Women in Aboriginal societies are subject to male authority. Yet, Pintuoi women consider themselves as equal while Yaraldi women are equal to men in religious affairs, have a say in the selection of their marriage partner, but are punished for promiscuity while men are not. In contrast, members of different Kwakwak'awakw villages are ranked according to their village (Kelly, 2013, Ch. 9). To better understand the dynamics leading to these different conventions, assume that members of a foraging band can be divided into two subgroups (group 1 and group 2) based on a common attribute (e.g., kin, gender). Furthermore, for simplicity, suppose that interaction only takes place between members of different subgroups (e.g., we are only interested in interactions between women and men). We can then extend the replicator dynamics as follows

$$\pi_{1x} = \alpha \tag{3.31a}$$

$$\pi_{1z} = 0.5(x_2 + z_2) \tag{3.31b}$$

$$\pi_{1y} = \beta x_2 \tag{3.31c}$$

$$\pi_{2x} = \alpha \tag{3.31d}$$

$$\pi_{2z} = 0.5(x_1 + z_1) \tag{3.31e}$$

$$\pi_{2y} = \beta x_1 \tag{3.31f}$$

where the indices now specify not only the behavioural rule but also the subgroup. The replicators in equation (3.30a) need to be extended accordingly.

$$\dot{x}_1 = x\left(\pi_{1x} - \phi_1\right) \tag{3.32a}$$
$$\dot{y}_1 = y\left(\pi_{1y} - \phi_1\right) \tag{3.32b}$$
$$\dot{x}_2 = x\left(\pi_{2x} - \phi_2\right) \tag{3.32c}$$
$$\dot{y}_2 = y\left(\pi_{2y} - \phi_2\right) \tag{3.32d}$$

with $\phi_1 = x_1\pi_{1x} + y_1\pi_{1y} + (1 - x_1 - y_1)\pi_{1z}$ and $\phi_2 = x_2\pi_{2x} + y_2\pi_{2y} + (1 - x_2 - y_2)\pi_{2z}$.

We can see that the dimensionality of the state space is equal to the number of strategies minus one for each population summed over all populations while the shape of each space is defined by the combined unit simplices of each population. A two-population game in which each population has two strategies can be represented by a square, three populations each with two strategies by a cube, a two-population game in which one population has two and the other three strategies by a triangular prism. But starting with two populations and three strategies for each, it becomes difficult to graphically represent the state space. Our two-population Nash demand game would require a four-dimensional representation. Nevertheless, the following approach makes it possible to get an idea about the dynamics: Figure 3.10a plots the best response area for sub-population 2. However, note that I switched the x and y axes and consequently, the red area denotes the populations for which high is best response. If the population distribution is in the yellow area, it is best to choose low, but in the blue area it is still best to choose medium. Figure 3.10b superimposes Figure 3.10a on Figure 3.8a, since the latter figure illustrates the best response areas for population 1. We can see that in the red area, it is a best response for members of sub-population 1 to choose low and for members of sub-population 2 to choose high. This forms a mutual best response. The inverse occurs in the yellow area. In the blue area, it is a mutual best response to choose medium for each member independent of their affiliation. Since a mutual

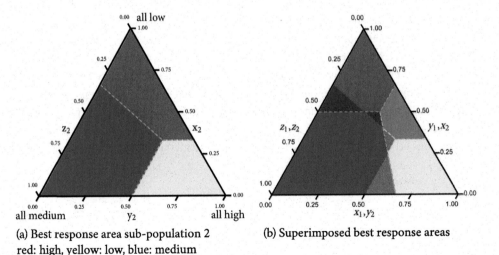

(a) Best response area sub-population 2
red: high, yellow: low, blue: medium

(b) Superimposed best response areas

Figure 3.10: Best response areas for two sub-population interactions.

best response indicates an equilibrium (refer to Chapter 2) and this holds in the area around the vertices, it is thus intuitive that each vertex constitutes a node of system (3.32).

In fact, while we end up with 16 fixed points, only the three vertices have eigenvalues with a non-positive real part and are therefore asymptotically stable. We obtain the following

$$\text{For: } (x_1, y_1, x_2, y_2) = (0,0,0,0)$$
$$\lambda_1 = -0.5$$
$$\lambda_2 = \alpha - 0.5$$
$$\lambda_3 = -0.5$$
$$\lambda_4 = \alpha - 0.5$$

and

$$\text{For: } (x_i, y_i, x_j, y_j) = (0,1,1,0)$$
$$\lambda_1 = -\alpha$$
$$\lambda_2 = -\alpha$$
$$\lambda_3 = 0.5 - \beta$$
$$\lambda_4 = \alpha - \beta$$

for $i, j = \{1,2\}$ and $i \neq j$ (meaning that we can substitute the i-index in the previous equations by 1 or 2 and the j-index by the other value, since the inegalitarian nodes are symmetric and have the same set of eigenvalues). We observe that the mixed node in the one-population game splits into two pure nodes in the two-population version of the Nash demand game in which one sub-population is faced with the lower share while the other sub-population is able to extract a higher cut of the shared resource.

Exercise 3.4

Assume the following payoff functions for frequencies x, y, and z in a single population: $\pi_x = \alpha x$, $\pi_y = \beta y$, and $\pi_y = \gamma y$, with $\alpha, \beta, \gamma > 0$. (a) Define the replicator equations (using $z = 1 - x - y$). (b) Determine the potential function. (c) Plot the nullclines in the unit simplex and deduce the position and stability of the equilibria. (d) Confirm your results.

3.6 Conclusion

This chapter covered two elementary aspects that are central to the study of social systems - the analysis of dynamical systems and differential equations, and the replicator equations (or dynamics). The former applies to any dynamic process, and since I defined institutions as evolutionary equilibria, the notion of asymptotic stability is a recurrent element in future chapters. The results of this chapter, such as the criteria for stability, the graphical presentation of the state space and vector field, will thus prove indispensable later on. We will see that some of the criteria depend on whether the dynamical system is defined as a continuous or a discrete process, but the underlying logic remains identical. First-order derivatives and eigenvalues play a significant role for the stability of an equilibrium and I have therefore summarised the most basic rules of differentiation in Section A.1.1 of the Appendix. While we have only studied one, two, and four-dimensional systems in this chapter, it should further be clear that the solution algorithms and criteria apply to any system of higher dimensionality. Yet, even systems of lower dimensionality can prove to be challenging to analyse. Sections A.5 and A.6 in the Appendix provide some additional helpful techniques that can considerably simplify the analysis of a system's dynamics and equilibria.

The second element – replicator dynamics – represents a simple way of modelling social learning. Its particular elegance stems from the sole need to model the individual benefits of a specific behavioural rule as a payoff function. Once each behavioural rule or strategy is assigned a payoff function, the social system can be analysed with the tools I discussed here. Replicator dynamics are based on some stringent assumptions, but most essentially, they constitute a shift away from the overly sophisticated cognitive assumptions of the more classic game theoretical approaches. Individuals simply adopt a strategy by learning from peers. No additional knowledge and cognitive abilities but those that are necessary to replicate the behavioural rule are necessary. In this regard, replicator dynamics add the evolutionary component to game theory, but eliminate the actual *game* element, since they dispense with any kind of strategic interaction. Agents only imitate, they do not anticipate and project the consequences of their actions. At the same time, interactions occur completely randomly and are not subject to any structure. Where classic game theory is too ambitious in its idea of men, replicator dynamics are probably too undiscerning, which is why future chapters take a middle-of-the-road approach. Nevertheless, the capacity and sophistication of replicator equations make them an essential tool for studying social dynamics. Sections A.3 and A.4 therefore provide greater details and extensions of the approach.

Even in the simple context of this chapter, we have seen that replicator equations can demonstrate complex dynamics and allow us to study the impact of environmental changes on the stability of fixed points. We have seen that under certain conditions, even minor change in one or two parameters can lead to bifurcations and thus drastic changes of the prevailing institutions.

Applications and Relation to Other Chapters

The theory of dynamical systems can be applied to any non-static social context. The concept of nodes or asymptotically stable fixed points (also frequently called evolutionarily stable equilibria in this context) is particularly interesting in cases in which we observe that a social system illustrates certain regularities and the notion of a basin of attraction gives us an idea of why particular norms, conventions or practices occur more frequently than other solutions to social problems. I will discuss this further in Chapter 4. While the former define social institutions and therefore, the context in which social actors interact, they also constitute the outcome of such interactions. The replicator dynamics are an elegant and flexible approach to model these *co-evolutions* of various social institutions. They allow us to convert the benefit that individual obtain from a particular behavioural rule (to remain consistent with Chapter 2, I used the term *payoff function*) into a dynamical system to which we can apply the theory we studied in this chapter. The standard replicator dynamic assumes that encounters between members of one society/population are completely random. We can relax this assumption and will study models in which peer effects and social networks play a role in Chapter 7. In addition, the replicator dynamic presented here is in continuous time. This formulation makes the analysis of the dynamical system easier but we may want to analyse interactions that occur periodically. We discuss recurrence relations and briefly, the replicator in discrete time in Chapter 5. Although many social systems illustrate regularities, it is not a given that dynamics lead to stable institutions that are invariant to any small idiosyncratic action nor can we directly infer the nature of these institutions based on some defined set of external conditions. The so-called butterfly effect comes to mind, and the discussion of bifurcations gave us a very tentative exposure to this behaviour. These interesting dynamics will be further developed in Chapter 9.

Further Reading

Readers interested in a thorough and detailed exposition of evolutionary game theory and replicator dynamics should refer to Weibull (1997). A slightly less technical and more applied discussion of the topic is offered in Gintis (2000a, Chs. 8 and 9). This book is especially interesting for those readers who are also interested in the topics of Chapters 2 and 4. Bowles (2004) and Boyd and Richerson (1985, 2005) offer a number of applications. Though the former is concerned with an economic treatment while the latter focus on anthropological topics, the models discussed in this literature offer inspiration for applications in other contexts of the social sciences. Another application can be found in Ille (2021) in which agents choose a combination of two different types of behavioural rules. The resulting replicator equations capture a simple form of multi-level selection and the feedback effect between both sets of rules. Furthermore, the concept of evolutionary stability is important when considering the long-term impact of policies. A combined approach, using empirical data and replicator dynamics, can identify suitable policies that lead to a persistent institutional transformation after a one-time implementation (see, for example, Ille and Peacey, 2019).

Those readers who are interested in a wider discussion of dynamical systems and also in the material discussed in Chapter 9, should refer to Hilborn (1994), Strogatz (2015), and in particular Sandholm (2010). The latter is an exceptional exposition that offers a wide range of examples and applications to readers, and is an excellent source for inspiration. A more concise and technical overview is offered by Guckenheimer and Holmes (1983).

Notes

1 To be slightly more precise, an evolutionary equilibrium of the replicator dynamic is a Nash equilibrium of the stage game, where each stage is a repetition of the *same* base game.

2 It may seem more plausible to write the dynamic process as $\dot{x} = 2x(1-x)(\pi_s - \pi_l)$, given that we study the case in which a sharer meets a loner as well as the inverse case. Remember that the results of a game are unaffected by a positive affine transformation of the payoffs, and we can simply divide all payoffs by 2. We will later see that the form of equation (3.2) is consistent with the general form of the continuous replicator equation as well as with its derivation in Section A.3.

3 The discrete-time versions are defined in equations (5.22) and (5.23) in Chapter 5.

4   In the context of evolutionary game theory, we encounter the concept of *evolutionarily stable strategy*. For any two behavioural rules, i.e., (mixed or pure) strategies σ_1 and σ_2, we assume that σ_1 is an incumbent rule, but the population is *infiltrated* by a small share ε of individuals, who chooses σ_2 (frequently called a mutant). A strategy σ_1 is evolutionarily stable if $\pi(\sigma_1, \varepsilon\sigma_2 + (1-\varepsilon)\sigma_1) > \pi(\sigma_2, \varepsilon\sigma_2 + (1-\varepsilon)\sigma_1)$. The first argument in the payoff function π denotes the strategy chosen by an individual and the second argument is the expected strategy of their opponent. This is equivalent to the condition: $\pi(\sigma_1, \sigma_1) \geq \pi(\sigma_2, \sigma_1)$ and if $\pi(\sigma_1, \sigma_1) = \pi(\sigma_2, \sigma_1)$, then $\pi(\sigma_1, \sigma_2) > \pi(\sigma_2, \sigma_2)$ for all $\sigma_2 \neq \sigma_1$. In other words, the evolutionarily stable strategy is a best response against itself, and if the mutant strategy is equally good, then the evolutionarily stable strategy is a best response against the mutant strategy. I shall here suffice with the simpler exposition based on replicator dynamics, since any evolutionarily stable strategy is asymptotically stable in the replicator dynamics. In other words, a stable equilibrium of the replicator dynamics is also an evolutionarily stable strategy and the inverse (for further details, refer to Weibull, 1997, pp. 36–37 and pp. 100–113). Since a Nash equilibrium is not necessarily asymptotically stable, any evolutionarily stable state is a Nash equilibrium, but the inverse does not hold.

5   Further note that Figure 3.2a illustrates the dynamic version of an assurance (or coordination) game, and Figure 3.2b is equivalent to the Hawk-Dove game, both of which I discussed in Chapter 2.

6   The arrows indicate the vector field.

7   We could argue that individuals initially flip a coin and hence, a large population is originally situated at a distribution of $x = 0.5$. Any such population will converge to the fixed point whose basin of attraction covers more than half of the state space.

8   We frequently also find the term **saddle-node bifurcation** in the literature, which is more frequently used in two-dimensional systems. More generally, a bifurcation occurs if a fixed point changes stability. Consequently, as the dynamics change from those in Figure 3.2a to those in Figure 3.2b, the system undergoes a bifurcation.

9   At β_{saddle}, we have $d^2 f / dx^2 = -2\left(2\sqrt{\alpha\gamma}(1-3x) + \alpha + 3\gamma x(2x-1)\right)$, which simplifies to $-2\alpha + 2\sqrt{\alpha\gamma} > 0$ at x_{saddle}.

10 Notice that there is a minor change in notation for the first derivatives. While $\frac{df}{dx}$ denotes a first (order) derivative, $\frac{\partial f_i}{\partial x_j}$ is the first (order) *partial* derivative of function f_i at x_j. Function f_i has more than one argument and thus, the ∂ indicates that I treat the other arguments as constant.

11 Consequently, the fixed point are the extrema of V, i.e. those points at which the (partial) derivatives are zero, and the fixed point is stable if it is a local minimum of V.

12 The manifolds in Figure 3.5b can be easily inferred for the example. In simple terms, we can think of a vector (a, b) as an indicator of how a point/vector is *adjusted* along the two axes. For $(1, 0)$ and $(0, 1)$, all of the vectors parallel to the axes belong to one of the eigenvectors and no shortening or extension occurs along the axes, but the direction along the x_1-axis is flipped, i.e. it decays to the fixed point, since the corresponding eigenvalue of $(1, 0)$ is -1, whereas the eigenvalue of $(0, 1)$ is 1.

13 In this unlikely case, only note that the fixed point is either a star if we obtain two independent eigenvectors. Alternatively, if there is just one independent eigenvector, we have a **degenerate critical point**, and for $t \to \infty$ and $t \to -\infty$, all trajectories are parallel to the eigenvector and the trajectories look like a vortex squashed in the direction orthogonal to the span of the eigenvector.

14 Note that a limit cycle (both attracting or repelling) exist also in some cases in which $Tr(j) \neq 0$, see supercritical and subcritical Hopf bifurcations.

15 More correctly, Figure 3.7 as well as the following figure show a *projection* of the unit simplex.

16 In Chapter 2, we discussed that strictly and weakly dominated strategies can be ignored under certain circumstances. This assumption does not strictly hold in the evolutionary context. Here, we have an example in which the dominated strategy to play medium is not eliminated.

Markov Chains and Stochastic Stability: Understanding Cultural Universals

4.1 Introduction

In 3200 BCE, the bustling city of *Uruk* must have been an impressive sight. Founded on the union of two earlier settlements some eight centuries earlier, it has since grown into a metropolis of unprecedented size. Over 40,000 inhabitants are living in the Sumerian city that spreads across an area of over five square kilometres. While a remarkable spectacle for its time, a modern observer would recognise some familiar patterns. Protected by a monumental city wall that reaches a height of seven metres, a system of canals and streets connects Uruk to the Euphrates and the agricultural area surrounding the city. Its inhabitants no longer produce for self-sufficiency, but benefit from division of labour. Individuals specialise in a craft and Uruk's districts are clustered by profession. Some inhabitants are specialised in trade or fishing, others in the production or the construction of houses, monuments, and public architecture. Few are administrators, responsible for the distribution of goods, employment of labour, mediation, and legal enforcement. These administrators constitute a rich and privileged class. At its top, Uruk is ruled by a king of divine descent. Priests worship the goddess *Inanna* and the sky god *An* in the *White Temple* - a structure raised on a platform with sloping sides and towering at 20 metres above all other monumental buildings.[1] The temple's outer walls are covered in white gypsum plaster to reflect sunlight and signal Uruk's political power and divine position from afar. More importantly, Uruk's reliance on trade and its immense size (it is more than twice as large as any other city at that time) encumbers keeping record of the number of goods demanded, supplied, and exchanged or of the labour and type of workers needed for new projects. Administrators are therefore adopting an abstract way of keeping track - the first *cuneiform script*. Pictograms are gradually substituted by abstract glyphs and form symbols that not only depict the number and type of goods but also represent monosyllabic words and phonemes. Scribes use the new script to record quantities, the political history of Uruk as well as epic poems (most notably, the *Epic of Gilgamesh*).

Across the history of mankind, we find that most of these characteristics are recurrent, even universal: the design of larger cities, the division of labour, beliefs and worshipping, a hierarchical political structure, the need to record history and epic tales. While we might argue that

DOI: 10.4324/9781003035329-4

institutions and other forms of interactions have been propagated and adopted across time and in various regions of the world, this does not explain the consistency across institutions that evolved organically and are not centrally designed, such as labour specialisation or the topology of cities.

Similarly, we may wonder why in the presence of several solutions to problems of coordination, a majority of societies gravitate towards mostly identical answers in the long run. Our discussion of coordination problems in the past two chapters has shown that even simple interactions with more than one strategy tend to have more than one (Nash) equilibrium. Equilibrium refinements, such as those discussed in Appendix A.2, allow us to discriminate between equilibria and reduce the number of possible solutions, but they require a high degree of cognitive sophistication. Other criteria, such as focal points that we studied in Chapter 2.4 are not free of ambiguity and can still lead to miscoordination. Moreover, different criteria may still identify different equilibria requiring yet another heuristic to operate as a discrimination criterion for these refinements. The evolutionary approach in Chapter 3 eliminates implausible unstable equilibria but again, it does not necessarily identify a unique equilibrium. We have seen that institutions, as solutions to coordination problems, are history-dependent. A dynamical system will converge to a stable outcome in the vicinity of the initial state (which we called the equilibrium's basin of attraction). A different history and thus, an initial state that is defined by another distribution of the behavioural strategies may lead to different institutions. Yet, it is implausible that all societies with the same set of institutions coincidentally started with similar initial distributions of behavioural rules, individual characteristics, and environments. In this chapter, we will discuss a different evolutionary approach that by and large converges to a single equilibrium, independent of the initial state of a population. It can explain the recurrent patterns of institutions that we observe across various cultures and eras.

Simultaneously, we will address another issue of the evolutionary approach of Chapter 3. The replicator equations model interactions in a fixed environment on the basis of completely random matching. The dynamics assume that individuals, after reflecting on past interactions, imitate behaviour from others who tended to fare better. Obviously, this implies certain stringent assumptions. First, the system is independent of time, i.e. payoffs are either constant or only affected by the strategy distribution in the population. Time is not a variable of the system. This issue is of minor relevance if individuals ignore the impact of time or if institutional fundamentals are relatively robust, i.e. it is legitimate to ignore technology and environmental change. If fundamentals are not perpetual, the problem of time homogeneity can be addressed by extending the replicator dynamics and adding a corresponding variable. Similarly, the approach discussed in this chapter can be easily adapted to account for the impact of time. For ease of exposition, I ignore the problem here and will therefore only discuss *time-homogeneous* processes in this chapter.

I will, however, address a second problem of the replicator equations. The latter assume that the social dynamics can be adequately represented on the basis of population averages. This requires two conditions. First, individuals are expected to follow a relatively naive approach to social learning based on the simple premise: what is good, on average, for someone else is also good for me. Using average payoffs seems less plausible if gains are subject to considerable fluctuations or if individual preferences are not homogeneous. Second, the standard replicators require that a population is large and mixing of individuals occurs sufficiently randomly. However, we will see that the approach discussed here is independent of population size and can account for a degree of stochasticity in a more sophisticated manner. Instead of expected values, we model dynamics on the basis of transition probabilities. While this does not directly account for the possibility of purely local interactions (which we address in Chapters 7 to 8), it allows us to define stochastic dynamics that are specific to each state in the state space.

4.2 Markov Chains

To simplify matters, I assume that a society is composed of only two members. We might think here of a simple coordination game similar to the Battle of the Sexes in Chapter 2. Yet instead of having opposing preferences, the couple shares a common interest and the interaction is defined by the payoff matrix in Figure 4.1. Anja and Bert either prefer to meet at the musical or prefer to meet at the cinema, depending on the relative values of a and b in this symmetric game. Obviously, for $a, b > 0$, the game has two Nash equilibria: $\{Musical, Musical\}$ and $\{Cinema, Cinema\}$. We have seen that any symmetric 2×2 coordination game can be transformed into payoff matrix 4.1 (see pages 17–18 as well as exercise 3.2). The game is therefore exemplary for any social interaction in which the participating agents have identical preferences. In Chapter 2, we have further discussed why it is a best response to follow the equilibrium strategy, yet we ignored the question of how Anja and Bert ended up at such an equilibrium in the first place. Without any expectations or other form of knowledge, neither would know whether they should go to the cinema or the musical in the Battle of the Sexes in Figure 2.4a on page 15. Admittedly, the common interest character of the game in Figure 4.1 might lead us to conclude that the equilibrium with the higher payoff is a focal point, but this requires that both players have a common understanding about each other's payoffs. While the approach in Chapter 3 offers a solution based on social learning, the long-run equilibrium depends on the initial population distribution.

However, we might think of another plausible heuristic. Instead of recollecting whether others have fared better with a certain behaviour in the past, individuals remember what others have done during past interactions. A player then chooses a best response to the frequency at which others have chosen an action or strategy - a process called **adaptive learning**. If Bert observes that Anja went to the cinema more frequently in the most recent weeks, he will choose to do the same. This heuristic does not avoid miscoordination, but we will see that over time, Anja and Bert will converge to one of the two equilibria. Assume the simplest case: both Anja and Bert recollect the past two interactions and choose an action correspondingly. Given memory length $m = 2$ and the number of players $n = 2$, a state is defined by $\{s_A^{t-2} s_A^{t-1}; s_B^{t-2} s_B^{t-1}\}$, where s_A^k and s_B^k define Anja's and Bert's actions in period k, respectively. Since each player has two actions at their disposal (i.e. $S_i = \{M, C\}$), the state space is composed of $4^2 = 16$ states. To render the exposition clearer, I will ignore the order of the players in each state. Since players are symmetric, it is unnecessary to separate between, for example, states $(CC; MM)$ and $(MM; CC)$. The state space is then given by

		Anja	
		Musical	Cinema
Bert	**Musical**	a, a	$0, 0$
	Cinema	$0, 0$	b, b

Figure 4.1: *Accord* of the sexes with common interests.

the following ten states: $(MM;MM)$, $(MM;MC)$, $(MM;CM)$, $(MM;CC)$, $(MC;MC)$, $(MC;CM)$, $(MC;CC)$, $(CM;CM)$, $(CM;CC)$, and $(CC;CC)$.

For the moment, let us assume that $a = b$ and therefore, none of the equilibria is strictly preferred. Whenever Bert observes that Anja chose once C and once M in previous periods, he flips a coin and chooses one of the two strategies with equal probability. If however, Anja chose an identical strategy during the last two interactions, he chooses her strategy. The same holds for Anja. If both are, for example, in state $(CM;CM)$, both players flip a coin. The oldest memory is forgotten, and the latest memory is replaced by the new action. The new state is then $(M*;M*)$, since both players chose M in period $t - 1$, leading to one of four possible states that occur with equal probability: $(MM;MC)$, $\{MC;MM\}$, $(MC;MC)$, and $(MM;MM)$. The first two states are identical (remember, we ignore the order of our players). Thus, state $(CM;CM)$ leads to states $(MC;MC)$ or $(MM;MM)$, each with probability 0.25, and state $(MM;MC)$ with probability 0.5. We can represent the transition probabilities from one states to another in a **probability transition matrix**. In our case, the probability transition matrix is of dimension 10×10, since a population can transition from each of the ten states to one of the nine other states in the next period or remain in the current state. Yet, some of the transitions may occur with zero probability. Let P be such a matrix and $p_{l,k}$ be the probability of moving from some state l to some state k. Keeping the order of states as in the previous paragraph, i.e. $(MM;MM) \to \#1$, $(MM;MC) \to \#2$, $(MM;CM) \to \#3, \ldots$, the probability transition matrix P is given by Figure 4.2. The starting state defines the position of the row vector and the column represents the state in the next period. State $(CM;CM)$ is in position 8 and its corresponding row vector is $(0.25, 0.5, 0, 0, 0.25, 0, 0, 0, 0, 0)$ based on the previously calculated probabilities. Since a row vector defines all transition probabilities to which a state can move, the sum of the elements of each row vector in the matrix sum to 1. The transition probabilities from equilibria $(MM;MM)$ and $(CC;CC)$ are given by row vectors 1 and 10, respectively. None of the players wishes to move out of the equilibria and consequently, the probability of remaining in these states equals 1 for each. States 1 and 10 each form a special case of a **recurrent class**. The latter defines a set of states that can be reached from any state within the set with a positive probability in a finite number of steps - they *communicate*- but any state in the set does not communicate with any other state outside the set. Notice that state $(MM;CC)$ (state #4) is not an equilibrium, since it switches to state $(MC;CM)$ (state #6), and thus, $p_{4,6} = 1$.

$$P = \begin{pmatrix} 1 & 0 & 0 & 0 & 0 & 0 & 0 & 0 & 0 & 0 \\ 0 & 0 & 0.5 & 0 & 0 & 0.5 & 0 & 0 & 0 & 0 \\ 0.5 & 0.5 & 0 & 0 & 0 & 0 & 0 & 0 & 0 & 0 \\ 0 & 0 & 0 & 0 & 0 & 1 & 0 & 0 & 0 & 0 \\ 0 & 0 & 0 & 0 & 0 & 0 & 0 & 0.25 & 0.5 & 0.25 \\ 0 & 0 & 0.25 & 0.25 & 0 & 0.25 & 0 & 0 & 0 & 0 \\ 0 & 0 & 0 & 0 & 0 & 0 & 0.25 & 0 & 0.5 & 0.5 \\ 0.25 & 0.5 & 0 & 0 & 0.25 & 0 & 0 & 0 & 0 & 0 \\ 0 & 0 & 0 & 0 & 0 & 0.5 & 0.5 & 0 & 0 & 0 \\ 0 & 0 & 0 & 0 & 0 & 0 & 0 & 0 & 0 & 1 \end{pmatrix}$$

Figure 4.2: Probability transition matrix.

By defining an initial state as a ten-dimensional row vector v_s and multiplying it with the probability transition matrix, we obtain the next state. If, for example, Anja and Bert are currently in state $(CM;CC)$, the initial state is defined as $\vec{v}_9 = (0,0,\ldots,1,0)$. The state in the following period is $\vec{v}_9 \times P = (0,0,0,0,0,0.5,0.5,0,0,0)$. In other words, Anja and Bert find themselves either in state $(MC;CM)$ or $(MC;CC)$ with equal probability. We can now see how the approach works for larger populations. If, for example, the population is composed of 100 couples and half of the couples are in state $(CM;CC)$ and the other half in state $(MM;MC)$, the initial state is $\vec{v}_{(0.5*2,0.5*9)} = (0,0.5,\ldots,0.5,0)$. In the next period, the population is in state $(0,0,0.25,0,0,0.5,0.25,0,0,0)$. We can generalise this to

$$v^{t+1} = v^t P \tag{4.1}$$

and we have

$$v^{t+2} = v^{t+1} P = v^t P^2 \tag{4.2}$$

In other words, to calculate the state in period two, it suffices to multiply the current state with the square of the probability transition matrix. By extension, we obtain

$$v^{t+n} = v^t P^n \tag{4.3}$$

Based on a state at time t, we can predict any future state of the system without the need for any information about the states prior to t. Such a process is called a **Markov chain**. The matrix in Figure 4.2 defines a **time-homogeneous** Markov chain since the transition probabilities are independent of time. Since it is always best for both players to choose M in state $(MM;MM)$ and C in state $(CC;CC)$, both states are **absorbing states**. Once, Anja and Bert have reached one of these states, they remain there forever.

It is therefore interesting to study the behaviour of the system in the long run. Intuitively, since we have two absorbing states, both players should eventually settle on one of them. Based on equation (4.3), it suffices to calculate

$$P^* = \lim_{n \to \infty} P^n \tag{4.4}$$

and the probability transition matrix converges to the matrix shown in Figure 4.3. This is a fairly interesting result. Apart from the leftmost and rightmost column vectors, all column vectors in P^* are composed of only zeros. As expected, Anja and Bert eventually wind up in one of the absorbing states. The elements in the leftmost vector tell us the probabilities with which both will only meet at the musical, the rightmost column vector shows the probabilities for winding up at the cinema for good given some initial state. Adaptive learning therefore gives us a more detailed explanation than best response. Not only does it identify the Nash equilibria as absorbing states, but it shows how Anja and Bert can form correct beliefs and thus eventually completely avoid miscoordination. By continuously increasing n in equation (4.4), we can see that convergence is relatively slow. It takes around 35 periods before miscoordination happens with a chance of less than 1 percent. Furthermore, we can use the information in Figure 4.3 to predict the final distribution of a population with a larger number of couples. If, for example, couples are initially uniformly distributed across all initial states, or start in any combination of states $(MM;CC)$ and $\{MC,CM\}$, half of all couples will eventually go to the cinema and the other half to the musical.

$$P^* = \begin{pmatrix} 1 & 0 & 0 & 0 & 0 & 0 & 0 & 0 & 0 \\ 2/3 & 0 & 0 & 0 & 0 & 0 & 0 & 0 & 0 & 1/3 \\ 5/6 & 0 & 0 & 0 & 0 & 0 & 0 & 0 & 0 & 1/6 \\ 1/2 & 0 & 0 & 0 & 0 & 1 & 0 & 0 & 0 & 1/2 \\ 1/3 & 0 & 0 & 0 & 0 & 0 & 0 & 0 & 0 & 2/3 \\ 1/2 & 0 & 0 & 0 & 0 & 0 & 0 & 0 & 0 & 1/2 \\ 1/6 & 0 & 0 & 0 & 0 & 0 & 0 & 0 & 0 & 5/6 \\ 2/3 & 0 & 0 & 0 & 0 & 0 & 0 & 0 & 0 & 1/3 \\ 1/3 & 0 & 0 & 0 & 0 & 0 & 0 & 0 & 0 & 2/3 \\ 0 & 0 & 0 & 0 & 0 & 0 & 0 & 0 & 0 & 1 \end{pmatrix}$$

Figure 4.3: Probability transition matrix.

Exercise 4.1

So far, we assumed that Anja and Bert have no preference for any of the two options. Now assume that $a < b$ in the game of Figure 4.1. (a) For the same memory length $m = 2$, define the probability transition matrix. (b) What are the absorbing states? (c) After how many periods will Anja and Bert end up in an absorbing state independent of the initial state?

So far, we have assumed that Anja and Bert are able to properly calculate the frequency of past actions and define the best response to this frequency distribution. Yet, it is reasonable to assume that both sporadically commit errors. After all, adaptive learning results from cognitive and informational limitations of players. It is thus consistent to assume that erroneous actions ensue from time to time. We therefore add the assumption that both Anja and Bert commit an error now and then, and do not choose the best response to the two past interactions they remember. To make this case more interesting, let us further assume that such errors are state-dependent. If one of the two players remembers the other to have chosen musical in the past two interactions, they will go to the cinema with probability λ. If the player, however, remembers that the other player went to the cinema in the past two periods, musical is chosen with a probability ε. Such state dependency can have several reasons. In general terms, players might have a preference for one outcome and deviation is thus less likely. In this case, the error rate would inversely correlate with the payoffs at this state. In our example with identical payoffs, causes may be behavioural idiosyncrasies, differences in external circumstance or the coordination device used. By perturbing the Markov process, $(MM;MM)$ and $(CC;CC)$ are no longer absorbing states. The two-player population will move from $(MM;MM)$ to $(MM;MC)$ if one of the players makes a mistake and does not choose a best response. This situation happens with a probability of $2(1-\lambda)\lambda$. Also, both could make a mistake and move to $(MC;MC)$ with probability λ^2. Hence, Anja and Bert remain in state $(MM;MM)$ with a probability of $1 - 2(1-\lambda)\lambda - \lambda^2 = (1-\lambda)^2$.

The probability transition matrix of the perturbed Markov process is then defined as in Figure 4.4. Since any state can be reached from any other state after some time with positive probability, the process is **irreducible**. Furthermore, the process is **aperiodic** and does not return to the same state at regular intervals. Since these two conditions hold, the Markov chain is **ergodic**.[2]

$$\begin{pmatrix}
(1-\lambda)^2 & 2(1-\lambda)\lambda & 0 & 0 & \lambda^2 & 0 & 0 & 0 & 0 & 0 \\
0 & 0 & (1-\lambda)/2 & \lambda/2 & 0 & (1-\lambda)/2 & \lambda/2 & 0 & 0 & 0 \\
(1-\lambda)/2 & \frac{1}{2} & 0 & 0 & \lambda/2 & 0 & 0 & 0 & 0 & 0 \\
0 & 0 & \varepsilon(1-\lambda) & \varepsilon\lambda & 0 & (1-\varepsilon)(1-\lambda) & (1-\varepsilon)\lambda & 0 & 0 & 0 \\
0 & 0 & 0 & 0 & 0 & 0 & 0 & \frac{1}{4} & \frac{1}{2} & \frac{1}{4} \\
0 & 0 & \frac{1}{4} & \frac{1}{4} & 0 & \frac{1}{4} & \frac{1}{4} & 0 & 0 & 0 \\
0 & 0 & 0 & 0 & 0 & 0 & 0 & \varepsilon/2 & \frac{1}{2} & (1-\varepsilon)/2 \\
\frac{1}{4} & \frac{1}{2} & 0 & 0 & \frac{1}{4} & 0 & 0 & 0 & 0 & 0 \\
0 & 0 & \varepsilon/2 & \varepsilon/2 & 0 & (1-\varepsilon)/2 & (1-\varepsilon)/2 & 0 & 0 & 0 \\
0 & 0 & 0 & 0 & 0 & 0 & 0 & \varepsilon^2 & 2(1-\varepsilon)\varepsilon & (1-\varepsilon)^2
\end{pmatrix}$$

Figure 4.4: Probability transition matrix with state-dependent errors.

In this case, assigning specific values to λ and ε transforms P^* into a matrix that is composed of identical row vectors. This implies that after some time, it does not matter at which state the process started. The initial beliefs of Anja and Bert are irrelevant in the long run and any previous history does ultimately not play a role. For example, if we assume that $\lambda = \varepsilon = 0.1$, P^* converges to

$$\begin{pmatrix}
0.216 & 0.087 & 0.087 & 0.048 & 0.009 & 0.156 & 0.087 & 0.009 & 0.087 & 0.216 \\
\vdots & \vdots & \vdots & \vdots & \vdots & \vdots & \vdots & \vdots & \vdots & \vdots \\
0.216 & 0.087 & 0.087 & 0.048 & 0.009 & 0.156 & 0.087 & 0.009 & 0.087 & 0.216
\end{pmatrix}$$

We see that each row vector in P^* is identical. The vector equals the **invariant distribution** $\vec{\pi}$ of the Markov process which is defined by

$$\vec{\pi} = \vec{\pi}P \tag{4.5}$$

Thus, if we multiply the invariant distribution vector with the matrix in Figure 4.4, we re-obtain the vector (I invite you to check). Looking at the invariant distribution, we can see that each of the previously absorbing states is visited in only 21.6 percent of the time, and in more than half of time, Anja and Bert find themselves in another state. If both are less likely to commit errors, we would expect that states $(MM;MM)$ and $(CC;CC)$ occur more frequently. Reducing the error rates to 0.001 changes the invariant distribution to $(0.4936, 0.002, 0.002, 0.001, 0., 0.0039, 0.002, 0., 0.002, 0.4935)$. As we decrease the perturbation, Anja and Bert find themselves going to the cinema or the musical in 98.72 percent of the time. Further reducing the error eventually causes both to coordinate virtually every time. Since cinema and musical generate the same payoff, the time spent in each is equally split.

> **Exercise 4.2**
>
> At $\lambda = \varepsilon = 0.001$, how much time are Anja and Bert expected to spend at or close to state $(MM;MM)$ before switching to state $(CC;CC)$?

What happens, if for some reason both probabilities are not equal? Assume that $\lambda = 0.01$ and $\varepsilon = 0.001$. Thus, a transition away from $(MM;MM)$ occurs more frequently than from $(CC;CC)$. The invariant distribution assigns a probability of 8.53 percent to the former state and of 89.20 percent to the latter state. Bert and Anja spend most of their time in the cinema.

$$\begin{pmatrix}
(1-\lambda)^2 & 2(1-\lambda)\lambda & 0 & 0 & \lambda^2 & 0 & 0 & 0 & 0 & 0 \\
0 & 0 & (1-\lambda)^2 & (1-\lambda)\lambda & 0 & (1-\lambda)\lambda & \lambda^2 & 0 & 0 & 0 \\
(1-\lambda)^2 & 2(1-\lambda)\lambda & 0 & 0 & \lambda^2 & 0 & 0 & 0 & 0 & 0 \\
0 & 0 & \varepsilon(1-\lambda) & \varepsilon\lambda & 0 & (1-\varepsilon)(1-\lambda) & (1-\varepsilon)\lambda & 0 & 0 & 0 \\
0 & 0 & 0 & 0 & 0 & 0 & 0 & (1-\lambda)^2 & 2(1-\lambda)\lambda & \lambda^2 \\
0 & 0 & (1-\lambda)^2 & (1-\lambda)\lambda & 0 & (1-\lambda)\lambda & \lambda^2 & 0 & 0 & 0 \\
0 & 0 & 0 & 0 & 0 & 0 & 0 & \varepsilon(1-\lambda) & (1-\varepsilon)(1-\lambda)+\varepsilon\lambda & (1-\varepsilon)\lambda \\
(1-\lambda)^2 & 2(1-\lambda)\lambda & 0 & 0 & \lambda^2 & 0 & 0 & 0 & 0 & 0 \\
0 & 0 & \varepsilon(1-\lambda) & \varepsilon\lambda & 0 & (1-\varepsilon)(1-\lambda) & (1-\varepsilon)\lambda & 0 & 0 & 0 \\
0 & 0 & 0 & 0 & 0 & 0 & 0 & \varepsilon^2 & 2(1-\varepsilon)\varepsilon & (1-\varepsilon)^2
\end{pmatrix}$$

Figure 4.5: Probability transition matrix with state-dependent errors.

If you have done exercise 4.1, you have seen that Anja and Bert will eventually always go to the cinema in the unperturbed Markov chain if both prefer cinema to musical and have not started in state $(MM; MM)$. In view of the previous results, this scenario raises an interesting question: is there a trade-off between the error rates and the payoffs? Intuitively, as long as the error rate is inversely correlated with the payoffs of the coordination game, the stochastic process should identify the preferred outcome as the most frequent meeting place. Yet, what happens if the error rates are not inversely correlated with the payoff in a state? Assume the equilibrium payoffs $a > b$, and hence, all states, except for (CC, CC), will converge to state (MM, MM) in the unperturbed Markov process. The transition matrix of the perturbed process is given by Figure 4.5

If $\lambda = \varepsilon$ and both are sufficiently small, the invariant distribution will assign a value close to one to state (MM, MM), and P^* will converge to the unperturbed case as ε and λ approach zero. Anja and Bert shift to strategy M if the other person has chosen musical at least once during the past two interactions. Thus convergence to (MM, MM) happens more frequently. If $\lambda < \varepsilon$, this effect is only reinforced and at the same time, it renders an *escape* from this state less likely. Based on Foster and Young (1990), we call (MM, MM) a **stochastically stable state**. As the errors converge to zero, the invariant distribution assigns a positive probability to the state.

The interesting case occurs if $\lambda > \varepsilon$. For $\lambda = 0.1$ and $\varepsilon = 0.00001$, we obtain $\vec{\pi} = (0.03\ 0.01\ 0.01\ 0.00\ 0.00\ 0.00\ 0.00\ 0.00\ 0.00\ 0.96)$. In other words, state (CC, CC) occurs in 96.4 percent of all interactions, whereas Anja and Bert find themselves in state (MM, MM) only 2.6 percent of the time. Figure 4.6 illustrates the results of a simulation of one million interactions. State (CC, CC) occurs with a relative frequency of 96.2 percent and (MM, MM) with a relative

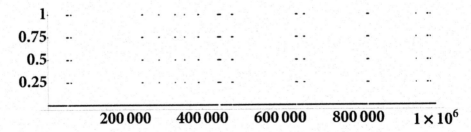

Figure 4.6: Agent-based simulation of stochastic play with memory and sample size 4 among two players, and state-dependent error $\varepsilon = 0.00001$, and $\lambda = 0.1$. Values illustrate the share of M play in the collective memory of both players, thus 0 illustrates state (CC, CC) and a value of 1 represents (MM, MM).

frequency of 2.5 percent despite Anja's and Bert's preferences for spending time at the musical – a coordination failure. The simulation generates results that are very close to our calculations. Apart from very short periods, both end up always going to the cinema. Thus, although going to the musical is the stochastically stable state if both error rates converge to zero at roughly the same rate, cinema is the habitual venue for both if the error rate in this state converges to zero at a significantly faster rate than the error rate close to state (MM, MM).

4.3 Stochastic Stability

In the next step in our analysis, we could move on to study the actual battle of the sexes scenario as in Figure 2.4a on page 15, in which Bert prefers musical but Anja would rather pick cinema. The game is no longer symmetric. We have four different error probabilities, two for each player and the state space consists of 16 states. If we, however, wish to have a slightly more realistic memory size, say for example a size of 4, we end up with $8^2 = 64$ states. While the analysis of the 16 states is daunting, 64 states is impractical. If we then increase the number of players, the solution in the previous section becomes entirely infeasible. Luckily, previous work by Peyton Young (1993) and others have simplified the approach.

Similar to before, we assume that two populations, composed of Berts and Anjas, interact in some sort of coordination game. This game can have a common interest, as in Figure 4.1 in which both players strictly prefer the same outcome (such as meeting at the musical for $a > b$), but it can also be a non-symmetric game with opposing interests. In each interaction, only two players (one from each population) are randomly matched and interact. Similar to before, we assume that individuals base their choice on past interactions. If we have a player population larger than two, a player does not only resort to their own memory but asks around to gather information about the past actions of other players. Hence, an Anja samples from the memory of past actions of Berts to form an expectation about the action her matched Bert will choose. Respectively, a Bert does the same. I further assume that the size of a player's sample does not exceed half of the collective memory size.[3] In addition and as before, some players randomly but sporadically commit errors, they either experiment or remember and report wrongly. Consequently, with a small probability, a player might sample erroneous past actions at a frequency that makes her changes her best response.

The general coordination game is given in Figure 4.7a. We assume that $\hat{a}_i > d_i$ and $\hat{b}_i > g_i$ for $i = \{A, B\}$. If payoffs for Anjas and Berts are different, i.e. the payoff matrix is not symmetric, interactions take place between two distinct populations. An Anja from the group of Anjas is always matched with some Bert from the Bert group, and vice versa. In other words, neither a Bert interacts with another Bert nor an Anja with another Anja. If, however, anybody can interact

		Anja	
		Musical	Cinema
Bert	Musical	$\hat{a}_B, \hat{a}_A$	g_B, d_A
	Cinema	d_B, g_A	$\hat{b}_B, \hat{b}_A$

(a)

		Anja	
		Musical	Cinema
Bert	Musical	a_B, a_A	$0, 0$
	Cinema	$0, 0$	b_B, b_A

(b)

Figure 4.7: Two equivalent generic coordination games with $a_i = \hat{a}_i - d_i$ and $b_i = \hat{b}_i - g_i$.

with anybody else, independent of their gender, the game is characterised by a single population of homogeneous players. In this case, payoffs are symmetric and we can drop the indices from the payoffs. Following Chapter 2.2 and defining α_i as the relative frequency at which player i chooses to go to the musical, the mixed strategy equilibrium is given by

$$\alpha_i^* = \frac{\hat{b}_i - g_i}{\hat{a}_i - g_i - d_i + \hat{b}_i} \tag{4.6}$$

We can further simplify our analysis. In Chapter 2.2, we have seen that a normal form game is unaffected by a transformation of the payoff matrix after adding the *same* (positive or negative) constant to all payoffs associated to the same strategy of the other player (see pages 17–18). In other words, we can add a constant to all values of the row player that are in the same column without changing the game dynamics. Similarly, we can add some value to all of the column player's payoffs that are in the same row. Choosing appropriate values, we can simplify the payoff matrix in Figure 4.7a. Subtract d_B from Bert's payoffs linked to Anja choosing musical, and g_B from Bert's payoff if Anja plays cinema. Similarly, subtract d_A from Anja's payoff in the row for musical and g_A in the row for cinema. Redefining $a_i = \hat{a}_i - d_i$ and $b_i = \hat{b}_i - g_i$ returns the simplified payoff matrix in Figure 4.7b. The mixed strategy frequency is then

$$\alpha_i^* = \frac{b_i}{a_i + b_i} \tag{4.7}$$

which is identical to equation (4.6) but simplifies notation. From Chapter 3, we know that this interior equilibrium is unstable, given $a, b > 0$ and is a separatrix, i.e. the interior fixed point defines the basins of attraction of the pure strategy equilibria. It is best to go to the cinema if $\alpha < \alpha^*$ and to the musical if $\alpha > \alpha^*$. Consequently, infrequent errors will only temporarily push a population away from a pure strategy equilibrium. If errors occur cumulatively, however, repeated displacement of the population away from the pure equilibrium state can push the system over to the basin of attraction of the other pure strategy equilibrium.

Consider a simple scenario in which we have two larger player populations and both Anjas and Berts sample five interactions in previous periods and choose a best response to their sample. Let α_i be the frequency at which a player population went to the musical during these five interactions. From the perspective of an Anja, the number of occurrences are used as a proxy of a Bert's current play which can range from 0 to 5. From the perspective of an Anja, states then correspond to a frequency of α_B ranging from 0 to 1 in steps of 0.2. We can represent the states by the balls in Figure 4.8. Now assume that the game is defined by $a_A = a_B = 3$ and $b_A = b_B = 5$ in the payoff matrix of Figure 4.7b. The separatrix is $\alpha^* = 5/8$. Thus, if Musical occurs at a rate higher than 0.625 in the sample, it is a best response to choose the same.

We can determine the minimum number of instances of musical that an Anja needs to sample so that musical is a best response by calculating the product of α^* and the sample size. Since

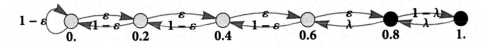

Figure 4.8: Illustration of the transition probabilities.

the players' sample and thus the number of states is finite, we need to calculate the corresponding (next highest) integer value which is given by

$$r^s_{\mathscr{M}} = \lceil s\alpha^* \rceil = \lceil 5 \times \frac{5}{8} \rceil = \lceil 3.125 \rceil = 4 \tag{4.8}$$

with s being the size of the sample. The function $\lceil \cdot \rceil$ denotes the ceiling function that returns the least integer greater than or equal to the argument. Similarly, we need to find the minimum frequency for cinema, so that the latter strategy is a best response.

$$r^s_{\mathscr{C}} = \lceil s(1 - \alpha^*) \rceil = \lceil 5 \times \frac{3}{8} \rceil = \lceil 1.865 \rceil = 2 \tag{4.9}$$

It is therefore a best response for Anja to choose musical if this action occurs at least four times in her sample, but cinema is the optimal choice if Berts have gone to the cinema at least twice in the sample. Thus, in the light grey states in Figure 4.8, Anja should choose cinema and in the black states, she should opt for musical.

In line with our previous discussion, assume that Berts and Anjas are prone to errors that depend on the frequency of musical in past interactions. Errors occur at a rate of ε as long as musical has been played at a frequency less than α^* and at a rate of λ if musical occurs more frequently in the collective memory. Imagine that both Anjas and Berts have met at the cinema for a long time, and past memory therefore consists only of cinema plays. How many errors on the Berts' side need to consecutively occur at a minimum for an Anja to choose musical as her best response? Looking at the transition probabilities in Figure 4.8 and from our previous calculations in equation (4.8), we can see that Berts must have collectively made the error at least four times in the past, so that Anja has a positive chance to sample all four times of musical and only once cinema. At this point, our Anja chooses musical as her best response. With positive probability, the same or another Anja can now sample musical four times yet another time. If this event is repeated yet another two times, a Bert has now a positive chance to sample musical four times. At this point, it is also optimal for Bert to choose musical. Thus, it needs a minimum of four erroneous musical choices by Berts to set in motion a sequence of events that eventually end up in a situation in which both populations only choose to go to the musical. The population shifts from remembering only going to the cinema to only going to the musical. Since payoffs are symmetric, the same shift can be brought about by four erroneous choices among Anjas. We can apply the same logic and calculate the minimum number of consecutive errors required to induce a shift towards cinema after a long time of only going to musicals and obtain that only two errors are needed.

Since both player populations have the same payoffs, the separatrix given by α^* is identical for Anjas and Berts. However, if each player population has a different payoff structure and the game is not symmetric, the likelihood of transition depends on which population initiated the shift. To simplify notation, I define a state in which all players' memory only contains cinema by $\mathscr{C}$ and a state which it is only composed of musical by $\mathscr{M}$. A transition from $\mathscr{C}$ to $\mathscr{M}$ requires $\lceil s\alpha^*_A \rceil$ errors if initiated by Berts, but $\lceil s\alpha^*_B \rceil$ errors if it is initiated by Anjas. For example, assume, we keep the previous payoffs for Berts (i.e. $a_B = 3, b_B = 5$), then such a transition still requires four errors within the Anja population. If we assume that Anjas have a payoff $a_A = b_A = 10$, we obtain $\alpha_A = 1/2$ and thus $\lceil s\alpha^*_A \rceil = 3$. Hence, only three erroneous musical choices among the Berts is sufficient to shift from $\mathscr{C}$ to $\mathscr{M}$. The minimum number of errors needed for the transition is the minimum of 4 and 3. Assuming, for the moment, that errors occur at the same rate, i.e. $\varepsilon = \lambda$, we follow Young (1993) and define the minimum resistance of moving from $\mathscr{C}$ to $\mathscr{M}$ by

$$r_{\mathscr{M}} = \min\{\lceil s\alpha_A^*\rceil, \lceil s\alpha_B^*\rceil\} \qquad (4.10a)$$

Equally, the **minimum resistance** of moving from $\mathscr{M}$ to $\mathscr{C}$ (also called, the **stochastic potential** of $\mathscr{C}$) is defined as

$$r_{\mathscr{C}} = \min\{\lceil s(1-\alpha_A^*)\rceil, \lceil s(1-\alpha_B^*)\rceil\} \qquad (4.10b)$$

while equations (4.8) and (4.9) define the minimum resistances for a symmetric game. Young has shown that if the error converges to zero and transitions become increasingly unlikely, the invariant distribution gives all weight to the state with the smallest minimum resistance, i.e. the state into which transition is most likely. Since we have only two attracting states, the former is also the state out of which a transition is least likely. Plugging in our previous results, we obtain $r_{\mathscr{M}} = 3$ and $r_{\mathscr{C}} = 2$, and hence, always going to the cinema will be the stochastically stable equilibrium.

Exercise 4.3

(a) Develop a transition graph similar to Figure 4.8 for a memory size of ten. (b) Show that for $a_A = a_B$ and $b_A = b_B$, the resistances in equation (4.10) determine the risk dominant equilibrium (see Appendix A.2.2) as the long-term convention.

As we have seen before, we might be in a scenario in which error rates vary depending on the state of the system and the population. We can extend Young's approach to take account of the four different error rates (two for each population). Remember that we assumed $a_A = 10$, $a_B = 3$, $b_A = 10$, $b_B = 5$, and $s = 5$. If errors occur independently, the maximum probability of a transition, induced by Anjas, from $\mathscr{C}$ to $\mathscr{M}$ is then ε_A^4 and from $\mathscr{M}$ to $\mathscr{C}$, is λ_A^2. Similarly, if it is initiated by the erroneous choices of Berts, the maximum probabilities are ε_B^3 for $\mathscr{C}$ to $\mathscr{M}$ and λ_B^3 for $\mathscr{M}$ to $\mathscr{C}$.

Note that we can express the error rates in terms of a *baseline* error ε. For example, we can choose ε_A as a baseline error and define $\varepsilon^{\gamma_A} = \lambda_A$. Focusing only on transitions initiated by the Anja population, for the moment, we compare a transition from $\mathscr{C}$ to $\mathscr{M}$ at a probability of ε^4 to a transition from $\mathscr{M}$ to $\mathscr{C}$ at a probability $\varepsilon^{2\gamma_A}$. Since the error rates are within the unit interval, $\varepsilon^4 > \varepsilon^{2\gamma_A}$ if $4 < 2\gamma_A$ and $\varepsilon^4 < \varepsilon^{2\gamma_A}$ if $4 > 2\gamma_A$. Consequently, if $\gamma_A < 2$, the likelihood of a transition from $\mathscr{C}$ to $\mathscr{M}$ initiated by Anjas is lower than the likelihood of the inverse transition. For example, assume that $\varepsilon_A = 0.01$ and $\lambda_A = 0.001$ (hence $\gamma_A = 1.5$), the maximum transition probability from $\mathscr{C}$ to $\mathscr{M}$ is 10^{-8} and from $\mathscr{M}$ to $\mathscr{C}$a, it is 10^{-6} and thus a hundred times more likely.

We can see that a comparison of the transition likelihoods only requires to compare the exponents, if we express all errors in terms of the baseline error. We define $\gamma_i(\sigma)$ as the corresponding γ exponent of the baseline error of population i in the basin of attraction of state σ. For example, if as before, we take $\varepsilon_A = 0.01$ as the baseline and assume $\lambda_A = 0.001$, $\varepsilon_B = 0.0001$, and $\lambda_B = 0.001$, we have $\gamma_A(C) = 1$, $\gamma_A(M) = 1.5$, $\gamma_B(C) = 2$, $\gamma_B(M) = 1.5$. Assuming that errors maintain their relative size (i.e. $\gamma_i(\sigma)$ is invariant) as all errors converge to zero at the same rate, the extended minimum resistances are

$$r_{\mathscr{M}}^{\gamma} = \min\{\lceil s\alpha_A^* \rceil \gamma_B(C), \lceil s\alpha_B^* \rceil \gamma_A(C)\} \tag{4.11a}$$

$$r_{\mathscr{C}}^{\gamma} = \min\{\lceil s(1-\alpha_A^*) \rceil \gamma_B(M), \lceil s(1-\alpha_B^*) \rceil \gamma_A(M)\} \tag{4.11b}$$

Applying the results in equation (4.11) to our previous parameters returns

$$r_{\mathscr{M}}^{\gamma} = \min\left\{\lceil 5 \times \frac{1}{2} \rceil \times 2, \lceil 5 \times \frac{5}{8} \rceil \times 1\right\} = 4 \tag{4.12a}$$

$$r_{\mathscr{C}}^{\gamma} = \min\left\{\lceil 5 \times \frac{1}{2} \rceil \times 1.5, \lceil 5 \times \frac{3}{8} \rceil \times 1.5\right\} = 3 \tag{4.12b}$$

Consequently, Anja and Bert will find themselves going to the cinema virtually all times as the error rates converge to zero. Both have established a **convention** which in this case is to go to the cinema. However, the convention is critically dependent on the sample size. If instead of sampling five interactions, both sample only three, the minimum resistances are

$$r_{\mathscr{M}}^{\gamma} = \min\left\{\lceil 3 \times \frac{1}{2} \rceil \times 2, \lceil 3 \times \frac{5}{8} \rceil \times 1\right\} = 2 \tag{4.13a}$$

$$r_{\mathscr{C}}^{\gamma} = \min\left\{\lceil 3 \times \frac{1}{2} \rceil \times 1.5, \lceil 3 \times \frac{3}{8} \rceil \times 1.5\right\} = 3 \tag{4.13b}$$

In this case, both will eventually settle on musical as the convention. Including a state-dependent sample size is a straightforward extension of the previous argument and the resistances in (4.11) (see exercise 4.4).

Exercise 4.4

Show that including a state-dependent sample size of the form $s_i(\sigma)$ leads to the following resistances:

$$r_{\mathscr{M}}^* = \min\{\lceil s_A(C)\alpha_A^* \rceil \gamma_B(C), \lceil s_B(C)\alpha_B^* \rceil \gamma_A(C)\} \tag{4.14a}$$

$$r_{\mathscr{C}}^* = \min\{\lceil s_A(M)(1-\alpha_A^*) \rceil \gamma_B(M), \lceil s_B(M)(1-\alpha_B^*) \rceil \gamma_A(M)\} \tag{4.14b}$$

4.4   Benefit and Caveats

Young (1993) showed that the minimum resistances in equation (4.10) can be used to determine the stochastically stable equilibrium in more complex games with a larger number of strategies. The same holds for the extension in equations (4.14) and (4.11). This approach is therefore an elegant way of defining conventions in more sophisticated interactions. It has several advantages over the replicator dynamics presented in Chapter 3.3. While both social imitation and adaptive play encapsulate the limitation of human cognition and decision-making, the form of adaptive play that we study in this chapter builds on a different perception of the role of idiosyncrasies and stochastic effects. In the previous chapter, we studied the asymptotic stability of an equilibrium assuming that disturbances (or mutations) occur sufficiently infrequently. An equilibrium is perturbed only a very limited number of times before individuals again adopt behavioural rules or strategies that are more beneficial. A population therefore never leaves the basin of attraction of an equilibrium. In this chapter, however, we assume that these stochastic effects continuously perturb the dynamic process in a way that perturbations accumulate at instances to such a degree that a population escapes the basin of attraction of an equilibrium and moves from one node to the next. Consequently, a population drifts across the state space over time and moves from one equilibrium to another. However, we have seen that not all equilibria occur at the same frequency - some are more accessible than others. The time spent at an equilibrium is thereby defined by the number of errors or stochastic shocks that need to occur to move a population out of its basin of attraction into the basin of attraction of another equilibrium, which we called resistance. As such errors die out, the time a population spends in the state of the smallest minimum resistance is infinitely longer than the time spent in the other states. Applying the stochastic stability approach therefore seems to have two advantages. First, it shows that long-run dynamics are not path-dependent. It is irrelevant where the population started since it can reach any state with positive probability. Second, if resistances differ, stochastic stability will identify a single equilibrium allowing us to explain behavioural rules of a population in the long run. Combining these two advantages demonstrates that minor differences in the incentive structure and choice set between cultures eventually lead to the same institutions.

Yet, some theoretical and practical weaknesses impose some limitations. The resistances in equation (4.10) illustrate some rather unintuitive behaviour (see also Bowles, 2004, Chapter 12): to see this, assume for simplicity that the sample size is identical for all players and sufficiently large, so that we can ignore the ceiling function in equation (4.10) and divide all values by s. The simplified resistances are

$$\tilde{r}_{\mathcal{M}} = \min\{\alpha_A^*, \alpha_B^*\}$$
$$\tilde{r}_{\mathcal{C}} = \min\{(1 - \alpha_A^*), (1 - \alpha_B^*)\}$$

I further assume that Anjas and Berts play the Battle of the Sexes. As in Chapter 2, Berts prefer to go to the musical while Anjas have a preference for going to the cinema. Consequently, $\alpha_B^* < 0.5 < \alpha_A^*$ and $r_{\mathcal{M}} = \alpha_B^*$ and $r_{\mathcal{C}} = (1 - \alpha_A^*)$. Remember that the former denotes the resistance of a transition from $\mathcal{C}$ to $\mathcal{M}$, and the latter from $\mathcal{M}$ to $\mathcal{C}$. The transition from $\mathcal{C}$ to $\mathcal{M}$ is induced by the erroneous play of Anjas, while the opposite transition is induced by Berts' errors. In other words, the population that benefits most from an equilibrium is responsible for moving *out* of this equilibrium (see exercise 4.5). The individuals' behaviour is therefore inconsistent with their incentives. However, the implausible result can be solved by rendering the error rates dependent on the potential loss of player i where potential loss $l_i(s_i^*)$ is defined as the difference between the payoff obtained if the chosen optimal response s_i^* is correct against the other player and if it is not (see also van Damme and Weibull, 1998, and for a similar approach Bergin and Lipman, 1996). For the general payoffs in matrix 4.7b, we have $l_i(M) = a_i - 0$ and $l_i(C) = b_i - 0$. Assuming that a higher potential loss makes a player less prone to errors, we obtain

$$\begin{aligned} l_A(M) < l_A(C) &\Rightarrow \varepsilon_A(M) > \varepsilon_A(C) \Rightarrow \gamma_A(M) < \gamma_A(C) \\ l_B(M) > l_B(C) &\Rightarrow \varepsilon_B(M) < \varepsilon_B(C) \Rightarrow \gamma_B(M) > \gamma_B(C) \end{aligned} \tag{4.15}$$

and assuming that both populations react roughly equally to the same potential loss, it further holds that $\gamma_B(C) < \gamma_A(C)$ and $\gamma_B(M) > \gamma_A(M)$. If players are sufficiently sensitive to losses, the resistances are given by $r_{\mathcal{M}} = \alpha_A^* \gamma_B(C)$ and $r_{\mathcal{C}} = (1 - \alpha_B^*)\gamma_A(M)$.[4] Keep in mind that while a loss-dependent error rate addresses the inconsistency of who initiates the change in convention, stochastic stability ignores deliberate choice and remains limited to explaining organic change.

> ### Exercise 4.5
>
> Show that payoff-dependent sample sizes, as defined by equation (4.14), with identical error rates for all players and states imply that a population is responsible for the transition from its preferred equilibrium.

A second problem is that the resistances do not identify a convention if the error rates are identical and the sample is limited in size. Since we calculate the next greatest integer, a small sample size can lead to a situation, in which $\lceil s\alpha_A^* \rceil = \lceil s\alpha_B^* \rceil = \lceil s(1 - \alpha_A^*) \rceil = \lceil s(1 - \alpha_B^*) \rceil$ (take the example in equation (4.13) for instance and assume an identical error rate for all states). Consequently, if the sample size is too small, the convention is exclusively determined by the error rates. The argument may seem mainly academic. After all, individuals are likely to examine their environment closely before making meaningful choices, and therefore larger sample rates are not only plausible but realistic. However, this raises a third problem with the approach.

Not only is the approach ambiguous about the forces that reduce the error over time and the assumption that errors converge to zero seems implausible in most realistic contexts, but in addition, resistances do not only increase with the sample rate but also as the error rates converge to zero. Consequently, transitions between equilibrium states are extremely rare if error rates are small and sample rates are high. Figure 4.9 shows the simulations for one million interactions for the respective parameter values used to calculate the resistances in equations (4.12) and (4.13). At a first glance, the simulations seem to confirm the analytical results. The calculation of the resistances in equation (4.12) determined cinema as the convention, and the resistances with the smaller sample size in equation (4.13) identified musical as the convention.

However at closer inspection, we can see that no complete transition occurred during the entire simulations. The same holds true if we increase the number of interactions even further to 100 million interaction periods. While the population size does not affect results (for simplicity, the simulations have only one player in each population), the initial memory of interactions from which players first draw their sample determines the convention. In each simulation, a player's

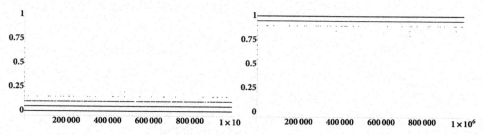

(a) Simulation with parameters used for (4.12). (b) Simulation with parameters used for (4.13).

Figure 4.9: Errors defined by $\lambda_A = 0.001$, $\lambda_B = 0.001$, $\varepsilon_A = 0.01$, and $\varepsilon_B = 0.00001$. Values illustrate the share of M play in the collective memory of both players, thus 0 illustrates state $\mathcal{C}$ and a value of 1 represents $\mathcal{M}$.

initial memory in period 0 is composed of a random order of five instances of musical and the same number of instances of cinema. Each player has an equal chance of sampling more cinema or more musical and it is more likely that a first sample includes roughly an equal number of instances for each strategy. If sample size equals 5, Anja therefore adopts both strategies with equal likelihood. Bert, on the other hand, opts for cinema if his sample includes more than one instance of past cinema play and he is significantly more likely to choose the latter strategy. After a few interactions, Bert will mostly have played cinema which is eventually a best response for Anja. If the sample size is only 3, Anjas and Berts select whichever strategy occurs more frequently in their sample. Consequently, both equilibria are equally likely to be a convention in this case. In fact, if we repeat the simulation in Figure 4.9b several times, each equilibrium is chosen with roughly equal probability. Thus, if the error rates are heterogeneous but too low so that no further shift occurs after each player's memory almost only contains instances of a single strategy, the convention is given by $\mathcal{M}$ if the state independent resistance $r_{\mathcal{M}}$ is less than half the sample size. Equivalently, $\mathcal{C}$ is the convention of $r_{\mathcal{C}} < s/2$. Otherwise, $r_{\mathcal{C}} = r_{\mathcal{M}}$ and each equilibrium has a 50 percent chance of defining the convention.

If we repeat the simulation with higher error rates but otherwise the same parameters, the most common state coincides with the predictions based on equation (4.14) (see Figure 4.10). However, in this case, the state-dependent resistances no longer determine a pure long-term convention, but a state around which a society gravitates most frequently. Due to the high error rates, pure states $\mathcal{C}$ and $\mathcal{M}$ occur with relatively low probability. I thus define $\tilde{\mathcal{C}}$ and $\tilde{\mathcal{M}}$ as a state in which the respective strategy ensues in at least 90 percent of the past memory (i.e. for a memory of size 20, state $\tilde{\mathcal{C}}$ transpires if each player goes to the cinema at least 18 times during the past interactions). In the simulation with sample size 5 in Figure 4.10a, $\tilde{\mathcal{C}}$ occurs at a frequency of 49 percent while $\tilde{\mathcal{M}}$ occurs at a rate of one-tenth of a percent. At the lower sample rate of 3 illustrated in Figure 4.10b, state $\tilde{\mathcal{C}}$ and $\tilde{\mathcal{M}}$ materialise at a frequency of 3.5 percent and 87.5 percent, respectively.

Consequently, stochastic stability can only serve as an explanation for the existence of well-defined institutions, if error rates remain low. Yet, as we have seen, low error rates render transitions very sporadic implying that a society spends a significant amount of time at an institution before eventually moving to a state of lowest resistance. Not only is the approach then no longer

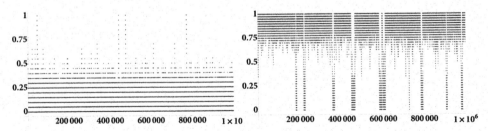

(a) Simulation with parameters used for 4.12 and memory size 10.

(b) Simulation with parameters used for 4.13 and memory size 20.

Figure 4.10: Simulation parameters identical to Figure 4.9, but errors are defined by $\lambda_A = 0.06$, $\lambda_B = 0.05$, $\varepsilon_A = 0.1$, and $\varepsilon_B = 0.03$. Values illustrate the share of M play in the collective memory of both players, thus 0 illustrates state $\mathcal{C}$ and a value of 1 represents $\mathcal{M}$.

a discrimination criterion to select a long-term institution since societies can remain locked in an equilibrium by chance, but it is also debatable whether such a process is still time-homogeneous, since environmental factors are prone to change in the *very* long run. I will address these issues in the next section.

4.5 Loss Sensitivity and Idiosyncratic Errors

Ultimately, while stochastic stability can explain organic institutional change, the need for sporadic conventional shifts requires strong restrictions on the sample and error sizes. It is rather questionable whether these restrictions are met across societies. In addition, I relied on fairly simplifying and improbable assumptions to develop the resistances with a loss-dependent error. The potential loss is considered constant across the basin of attraction of a convention. Thus, for example, at a sample rate of 20 and the previously assumed payoffs of $a_A = b_A = 10$, Anja will consider musical as the convention whenever this strategy occurs more frequently in her sample. Consequently, her potential loss from erroneously choosing musical equals 10 independent of whether Bert went to the cinema 11 or 20 times. To solve these issues, I extend the way in which a sample affects the likelihood of an erroneous choice and thus, the error size. If, for example, Anja's sample contains 10 instances of each cinema and musical, she has no knowledge whether Bert follows a convention. It is intuitive to assume that Anja chooses a strategy at random in this case. The probability that Anja adopts musical or cinema is then 50 percent for each strategy. If, however, her entire sample consists of only one strategy, say she samples cinema 20 times, she is least likely to opt for musical. Assuming that Anja and Bert sample musical at a frequency of α_i for $i = A, B$, we extend (4.15) by defining their potential loss as

$$\tilde{l}_i(M) = \alpha_i \, a_i - (1 - \alpha_i) \, b_i \text{ if } \alpha_i \geq b_i/(a_i + b_i) \qquad (4.16a)$$
$$\tilde{l}_i(C) = (1 - \alpha_i) \, b_i - \alpha_i \, a_i \text{ if } \alpha_i < b_i/(a_i + b_i) \qquad (4.16b)$$

Using the previous numbers, if Anja samples both strategies at an equal rate, her (perceived) potential loss is zero, but equals $a_A = 10$ if she samples only one strategy. We can interpret α_i as the rate at which a player expects the other type to experiment. At $\alpha_A = 0.5$, an adventurous Bert just flips a coin and any strategy is a good choice for Anja. If $\alpha_A = 1$, Bert is a rather conservative, non-experimenting guy who just goes to musicals whereas at $\alpha_A = 0$, he seems to be fixated on going to the cinema. We obtain the resistances in equation (4.14) as a special case, if players assume that their counterpart is never experimenting.

Under the redefined potential loss $\tilde{l}_i(M)$, we therefore no longer assume that error rates are small across the entire unit interval. We will see that this imposes an additional barrier to the transition between equilibria. To streamline the argument, assume that payoffs are symmetric, i.e. $a_A = a_B = a$ and $b_A = b_B = b$. For clarity, I define α_s as the share of musical occurrences in a player's sample, and α as the share of musical occurrences in the collective memory, i.e. the recollection of past interactions. It is unlikely that samples are consistently biased and on average $\alpha \approx \alpha_s$. When a society composed of Anjas and Berts transitions from one possible convention to another, it eventually has to cross the region in which past memory has a distribution approximately equal to $\alpha^* = b/(a+b)$. In this area of the state space, most of the samples then include a share of musical

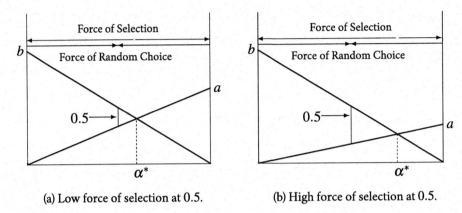

(a) Low force of selection at 0.5.   (b) High force of selection at 0.5.

Figure 4.11: Illustration of the interplay of the force of selection and the force of random choice for two coordination games based on expected payoffs.

play that is also roughly equal to $b/(a+b)$. Both Bert and Anja choose musical or cinema with equal probability, since both strategies have the same expected payoff and potential loss is zero. This drives the population towards $\alpha = 0.5$ at which point past memory contains an equal number of musical and cinema. We shall call this push towards $\alpha = 0.5$ the *force of random choice*. At the same time, individuals are inclined to choose whichever strategy grants a higher payoff. This force, which we may call the *force of selection*, compels the population to move along the basin of attraction towards either equilibrium $\mathscr{C}$ at $\alpha = 0$ or $\mathscr{M}$ at $\alpha = 1$. The force of random choice is strongest at α^* and weakest at $\alpha = 0$ and $\alpha_m = 1$ and pushes towards the centre of the unit simplex. In turn, the force of selection points in the inverse direction; it is strongest at $\alpha = 0$ and $\alpha = 1$ and weakest at α^* and pushes a population to the pure states. Figure 4.11 offers a graphical interpretation of the forces based on two symmetric coordination games. The bold lines in both figures show the expected payoff for going to the cinema and the musical given frequency α. Keep in mind that the force of selection increases with the potential loss. The latter equals the absolute distance of the two expected payoff lines as per equation (4.16). Expected payoffs for each strategy are identical where the straight lines intersect at $\alpha^* = b/(a+b)$, and potential loss as well as the force of selection are zero. Individuals choose each strategy with equal likelihood, pushing the memory towards $\alpha = 0.5$. Since, however, $\alpha^* > 0.5$, expected payoffs at $\alpha = 0.5$ differ and cinema is a better choice than musical. The vertical line (indicated by the arrow) highlights the potential loss at this state. Furthermore, at the pure states, the potential loss at $\mathscr{C}$ is given by b and the potential loss at $\mathscr{M}$ equals a.

In Figure 4.11a, we can see that at $\alpha = 0.5$, the difference between the expected payoffs is rather small. In this case, the force of random choice exceeds the force of selection and succeeds in continuously pushing the population towards a memory state close to $\alpha = 0.5$. The loss-dependent error rate imposes a barrier that impedes the transition between states. On the other hand, at $\alpha = 0.5$ in Figure 4.11b, the expected payoff of going to the cinema significantly surpasses the expected payoff from choosing musical. Since the potential loss is considerable at this state, errors happen with a lower frequency and Anja and Bert mostly choose to go to the cinema. The force of selection is now stronger than the force of random choice which eventually leads to $\mathscr{C}$ at $\alpha = 0$. In addition, a is significantly smaller in Figure 4.11b compared to 4.11a, rendering a movement away from $\mathscr{M}$ more likely. In this case, the loss-dependent error rate, hence, encourages transitions from $\mathcal{M}$ to $\mathcal{C}$. However, the opposite transition is again subject to the barrier imposed by random choice. Altogether, since the force of random choice drives a population towards $\alpha = 0.5$ and the relative strength of each of the two forces at this state dictates the long-term dynamics, the payoff distance between both strategies at $\alpha = 0.5$ critically determines the accessibility of a convention, i.e., the pure strategy state. We can therefore speculate that an equilibrium's basin of attraction plays a crucial role for determining the long-term convention.

To test the hypothesis, assume that the error rate is given by

$$\varepsilon_\gamma = \frac{1}{2}\left(1 - \left(\frac{|\alpha_s a - (1-\alpha_s)b|}{\alpha_s a + (1-\alpha_s)b}\right)^\phi\right)$$

$$\varepsilon_\alpha = \max\left\{\varepsilon_\gamma, \varepsilon_{min}\right\}$$

(4.17)

While the loss-dependent error ε_α mainly depends on the nature of ε_γ, the minimum error ε_{min} ensures a strictly positive lower bound. As the population converges to $\alpha = 0$ and $\alpha = 1$, the ratio in equation (4.17) approaches 1 and ε_γ converges to zero. In the absence of a lower bound, once a population reaches $\mathcal{C}$ or $\mathcal{M}$ by chance, the state will persist indefinitely. A small error of ε_{min} ensures that a population does not get stuck in these two states and transitions across the state space remain possible. Figure 4.12 plots ε_γ for $\alpha \in [0,1]$ and different ϕ. We can see that the latter controls an individual's sensitivity to potential losses. The exponent ϕ is inversely correlated with the sensitivity to small losses. At $\phi = 1$, the individual error rate decreases linearly with the loss, while for larger ϕ an individual's reaction is less pronounced and an individual demonstrates a degree of indifference towards small losses.

Figure 4.13 represents the results of two sets of simulations for $\phi = 2$, i.e. a case in which small losses tend to be ignored. In each simulation set, a is fixed at a particular value while b starts at the lowest value b_{min} in the first simulation and increases by an increment of δ after each simulation run. Since each of the two sets is composed of 21 individual simulations, payoff b reaches a maximum at $b_{max} = b_{min} + 21\delta$. Each histogram in Figure 4.13 illustrates the frequency distribution of the α states across the simulation. The first set of simulation uses $a = 10$, $b \in (2, 23)$ (i.e. $\delta = 1$) as well as a memory of length $m = 200$ and a sample of size $s = 100$. We assume that only two players interact. Each simulation runs for one million interaction periods and for each period, the computer records $\alpha \in [0, 1]$ in the collective memory, i.e. the relative frequency of

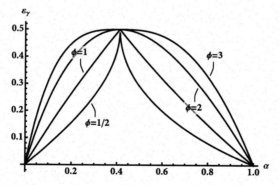

Figure 4.12: Error ε_γ for different exponents ϕ.

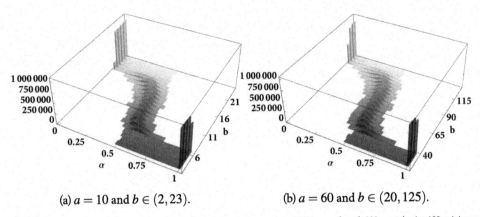

(a) $a = 10$ and $b \in (2, 23)$.   (b) $a = 60$ and $b \in (20, 125)$.

Figure 4.13: The histograms of strategy M players for two simulation sets, $n = 21$. Memory length 200, sample size 100, minimum error $\varepsilon_{min} = 0.0001$.

musical during the past 200 interactions for both players. State $\mathscr{C}$ corresponds to $\alpha = 0$ and $\mathscr{M}$ to $\alpha = 1$. Figure 4.13a depicts the histograms for each of the 21 simulations. We can see that at $b \in (2, 5)$, the population centres around $\mathscr{M}$ while at $b \in (20, 23)$, Anja and Bert end up at the cinema almost every time. However, for values of b in between 5 and 20, both are unable to establish a clear convention. Compared to the original approach with fixed error rates, there are a few things to notice. The minimum error is only 0.0001 while the memory and sample sizes are rather large making the assumptions more realistic. We have seen that a simulation with a state independent error would simply have chosen the equilibrium with a higher payoff and the population would never leave the vicinity of this state. In the case of a loss-dependent error, small minimum error rates do not limit interactions to the neighbourhood of $\mathscr{C}$ or $\mathscr{M}$ since the frequency at which errors occur is no longer independent from other errors. Each error increases the likelihood of the following error and thus memory distributions are more likely to shift towards the centre of the state space.

Furthermore, random choices impose an additional barrier to the transition process. A convention requires more than being a state of smallest resistance. It also necessitates a minimum payoff differential - either b does not exceed 5 or the payoff of going to the cinema must be at least 20. We observe a similar behaviour for the higher payoffs in Figure 4.13b. State $\mathscr{M}$ is a convention for $b \leq 30$, while state $\mathscr{C}$ is a convention for $b \geq 120$. Notice that for $a = 10$ and $b = 5$, the separatrix is $\alpha^*_{\mathscr{M}} = 1/3$. The same holds for $a = 60$ and $b = 30$. Plugging in the other values shows that state $\mathscr{C}$ is a convention if the separatrix is at least at $\alpha^*_{\mathscr{C}} = 2/3$. In other words, either $\mathscr{C}$ or $\mathscr{M}$ require a basin of attraction of at least $2/3$ in order to define a convention in the long run. This result is reminiscent of the $1/3$ law found for other evolutionary processes in the case of weak selection (for the Moran process, see Nowak et al., 2004 and for the Wright-Fisher process, see Imhof and Nowak, 2006). Yet, we will see that this rule is not universal but contingent on how sensitive individuals are towards losses and thus ϕ.

Since the sensitivity to losses is inversely correlated with the force of random choice, the latter increases in ϕ. At higher sensitivities, a population more frequently hits the lower bound ε_{min} thus bringing the dynamics closer to the original model with small state independent errors. The minimum basin of attraction and hence, the resistance needed for a convention decrease. At higher

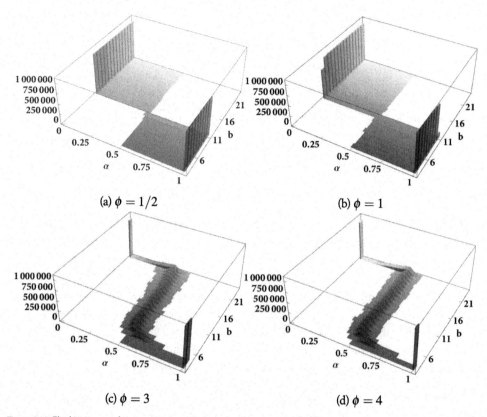

(a) $\phi = 1/2$

(b) $\phi = 1$

(c) $\phi = 3$

(d) $\phi = 4$

Figure 4.14: The histograms of strategy M players for two simulation sets and parameters identical to Figure 4.13a at $a = 10$ and $b \in (2,23)$. Minimum error is $\varepsilon_{min} = 10^{-4}$ for 4.14a and 4.14b and $\varepsilon_{min} = 10^{-6}$ for 4.14c and 4.14d.

ϕ and a lower sensitivity, the basin of attraction of the convention must be larger, otherwise Anjas and Berts will be drawn towards a mixed state in which they frequently choose a location at random. By this logic, the minimum basin of attraction required for a convention must depend on ϕ. The simulations in Figure 4.14 illustrate the dynamics for different ϕ while keeping the same parameter values as in Figure 4.13a. Remember that each simulation is initiated with a memory that is defined by a random distribution at $\alpha = 0.5$ with an equal number of cinema and musical play. For $a > b$, the basin of attraction of $\mathcal{M}$ exceeds the basin of attraction of $\mathcal{C}$, and the inverse holds for $a < b$. At $\phi = 1/2$, we observe that a population cannot escape the pure equilibrium state whose basin of attraction exceeds 0.5 as is shown in Figure 4.14a.[5] In Figure 4.14b, we can see that the same holds true at $\phi = 1$, but transitions occur at $a = b = 10$ and $\mathcal{C}$ and $\mathcal{M}$ materialise with roughly equal frequency. Simulations with $\phi > 1$ illustrate more interesting results. We have seen that at $\phi = 2$ the minimum basin of attraction required for a convention is 2/3. In Figure 4.14c, $\mathcal{M}$ is the conventional state for $b < 4$ while and $\mathcal{C}$ requires $b > 28$, implying that the minimum size of the basin of attraction increases to approximately 3/4 at $\phi = 3$. The critical values for $\phi = 4$ are given by $b < 3$ and $b > 37$ indicating a minimum basin of attraction of roughly 4/5.

We observe that ϕ and the minimum basin of attraction required for a convention are positively correlated. Figure 4.15 studies the relation in further detail based on simulations at $a = 100$ which offer a greater resolution than the previous simulations using $a = 10$. As expected,

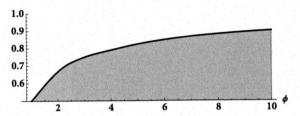

Figure 4.15: The minimum basin of attraction based on the sensitivity to losses ϕ, given $a = 100$ and $\varepsilon_{min} \in [10^{-10}, 10^{-6}]$.

a lower sensitivity to losses increases the minimum basin of attraction. Intuitively, societies that are more inclined to experiment and willing to ignore small losses will have a harder time to define a commonly accepted convention. We can see here that the relation is concave - an increase from $\phi = 1$ to $\phi = 2$ has the largest impact, but further increases in ϕ lead to a diminishing increase of the minimum basin of attraction. The loss-dependent error rate defined in equation (4.17) is a more realistic reflection of the way in which individuals make choices on the basis of plausible error and sample sizes and offers a more nuanced model of organic institutional change. While it still allows us to identify a unique equilibrium state that will define a convention in the long run, it does so only under the additional condition illustrated in Figure 4.15. At $\phi \leq 1$, a loss-dependent error leads to the same states as those predicted by the resistances in equation (4.10), even if the payoffs are non-symmetric and have opposing preferences, like in the Battle of the Sexes.[6]

The existence of loss-dependent errors thus does not preclude the convergence to a unique equilibrium. Coming back to our initial discussion, stochastic stability can then explain the existence of *cultural universals* (for example, the use of language, symbols, and names; the definition of property right, status, and leadership; the belief in higher beings, see also Lévi-Strauss, 1968; Brown, 1991). In addition, the results tell us more about the character of these universal conventions. A society will only converge to a unique convention if is a *sufficiently* more *efficient* solution. The two terms require further elaboration. Sufficiency relates to the positive correlation between the insensitivity to losses and the minimum size of the basin of attraction. We have seen that at $\phi = 2$, convergence requires either $a > 2b$ or $2a > b$ - one solution must be twice as good as the alternative. While the quantitative results depend on the specific error function in equation (4.17), the qualitative results, i.e. that a lower sensitivity translates into the need for a greater premium, are more comprehensive. The second point relates to the nature of this premium and the meaning of greater efficiency. We may think here of efficiency in terms of a higher payoff at the convention. After all, if both Bert and Anja benefit much more from going to the musical instead of the cinema, they will eventually always go to the former. Yet, it is important to note that the simple relation that $a > \sigma b$ or $b > \sigma a$ (with σ depending on the minimum basin of attraction) only holds for payoff matrices with zero off-diagonal values as in Figure 4.7b. The relation does not apply to general payoff matrices as in Figure 4.7a, i.e. if miscoordination bears an individual benefit. The relationship is more complex in this case but will not be further explored here for reason of conciseness.

Before finalising this chapter, one last point needs further discussion. While we established the relationship between the minimum basin of attraction for a convention and ϕ for symmetric payoffs ($a_A = a_B$ and $b_A = b_B$), it is natural to ask how results are affected if Berts and Anjas have different preferences. I will limit the discussion to $\phi = 2$ and an asymmetric version of an *Accord*

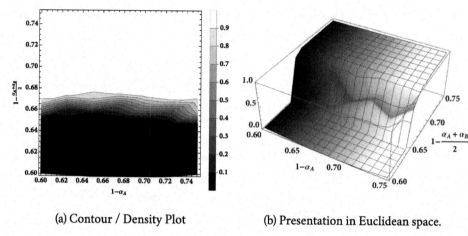

(a) Contour / Density Plot   (b) Presentation in Euclidean space.

Figure 4.16: Frequency of Musical plays based on basin of attraction of $\mathcal{M}$, given by $(1 - \alpha_A^*)$ and the average basin of attraction across both populations, given by $1 - \frac{\alpha_A^* + \alpha_B^*}{2}$. Black indicates a frequency of zero, while white indicates a relative frequency of 1. Simulations use $s = 200$, $m = 400$, $\phi = 2$.

of the Sexes game, with which we started this chapter and in which both Anjas and Berts prefer the same state but not to the same degree. Assume that $a_A > b_A$ and $a_B > b_B$ and thus, both groups prefer musical over the cinema. In the symmetric case, we have seen that $a_i > 2b_i$ has to hold for both to converge to the convention musical. Figure 4.16 presents the frequency of states at which the memory of past play (with $m = 400$) contains more than 99 percent of musical play. The figure shows the relation between $1 - \alpha_A^* = a_A/(a_A + a_B)$, i.e. the basin of attraction of $\mathcal{M}$ only for Anjas, and the average basin of attraction $(1 - \alpha_A^* + 1 - \alpha_B^*)/2$. Figure 4.16a presents the results in a density plot. The colour gradient illustrates the frequency of states at which each group's memory contains more than 396 instances of musical. Black indicates zero occurrences and white a frequency of 100 percent after one million interaction periods. We can see that a transition occurs at approximately $(1 - \alpha_A^* + 1 - \alpha_B^*)/2 = 2/3$ independent of the value of $1 - \alpha_A^*$. The same is illustrated in Figure 4.16b with the frequency plotted on the z-axis. We can see a clear falloff below 0.66. At an average basin of attraction of 0.65, Anjas and Berts are unable to coordinate and are drawn towards $\alpha = 0.5$, yet above an average basin of attraction of 0.67, Anjas and Berts quickly settle on cinema. In other words, the two-thirds rule for $\phi = 2$ also applies to non-symmetric games, but it applies to the *average* basin of attraction. If one group has only a mild preference for musicals, the other group needs to fancy the latter proportionally more for it to be an institution.

4.6   Conclusion

I have started our analysis in this chapter by using Markov chains to study the dynamic transition between states across the state space. Combining Markov chains with adaptive learning presents both a realistic and sophisticated explanation of the ability of individuals to form consistent expectations and to coordinate. We have further seen that the process by which individuals use the frequency of past actions to determine their future choices converges to a unique state if individual judgement is subject to sporadic mistakes. A population of players will find itself mostly in a state into which transition is most likely. Once individual errors vanish, the population occupies this state indefinitely and the latter turns into a convention. Since convergence to the conventional state occurs independently of the initial state, i.e. the process is not path-dependent, stochastic stability offers a possible description of the process leading to cultural universals. Yet while the resistances offer an elegant alternative to studying the underlying Markov chain in detail, the improbable way in which errors are expected to occur limits the approach. I therefore introduced state-dependent and loss-dependent error rates. Both extensions provided a more realistic representation of individual decision-making but the latter imposed the need for a payoff premium on a convention, i.e. as the individual sensitivity to small losses decreases, a population only converges to a state of coordination if the latter grants a sufficiently superior benefit to individuals. In other words, universals occur if they establish a significantly better solution to a coordination problem than any alternative.

While the loss-dependent error imposes additional conditions on a convention and thus on cultural universals, it explains their evolution in a more realistic context with larger sample and error sizes. In addition, it provides a realistic narrative of when and how errors converge to zero. This has several implications. A state independent error rate suggests an independence between errors, while loss-dependent errors render the likelihood of a non-best response conditional on the occurrences of previous erroneous choices. At the outset, we assumed that individuals sample a population to form an understanding of whether a convention exists. A sample is then taken as a signal of the convention and as the sample becomes more mixed, the signal is noisier and individuals are prone to commit errors. Yet, this interpretation requires that individuals are entirely oblivious to prior information (i.e. they have just been exposed to a new social environment) or of their past experience (why else would they go around to sample). We can, however, interpret the process in a slightly different manner. Instead of as a signal of the convention itself, we can also read sampling as a process to understand how willing members of society are to uphold or question a convention. The dependence between errors is then not only a logical consequence but a necessity. It changes the social dynamics into a more deliberate process and shares the fundamental other-regarding motivation of strategic choice with the threshold approach discussed in Chapter 5.

Although I limited the discussion in this chapter to coordination games, stochastic stability offers interesting insights when applied to other games. For example, the stochastically stable state of a two-population Hawk-Dove game depends on the harshness of the conflict when playing opposing strategies (which depends on the ratio of benefits to costs) and the rate at which players sample past interactions. If conflict entails significantly losses, a better knowledge of past actions is advantageous to a population. However, contrary to intuition, less knowledge (i.e. a smaller sample size) is more profitable if the cost of conflict is low (see Bilancini et al., 2022).

Applications and Relation to Other Chapters

While Chapter 3 and this chapter offer an evolutionary approach to game theory, they differ radically not only in their underlying mathematics but also in their perspective. The former models social imitation between agents with very limited cognitive abilities. Random mutations only determine the evolutionary stability of an equilibrium. The approach of this chapter relies on a more sophisticated representation of individual actions. Players remember the past history of play, form expectations, and choose an optimal response to these expectations. Infrequent, random error play an essential role for determining a smaller set of *plausible* institutions than the previous approach. The perspective is therefore more long-term compared to evolutionary game theory. The population fluctuates between equilibra, which can take an enormous amount of interactions, especially when the error rate converges to zero. Consequently, the suitability of each approach depends on the sophistication of the individuals and the duration of their interactions we wish to model. Furthermore, while the approaches in this chapter, similar to 3 and 5, assume an unconstrained and completely random matching process, Chapter 7 will show that strictly local interactions can lead to different institutions.

Further Reading

The initial publications on stochastic stability by Foster and Young (1990), Young (1993), and Kandori et al. (1993) led to a relatively large but also very technical literature. The assumption of the stochastic stability approach that errors are state and payoff independent has been criticised in Bergin and Lipman (1996) and van Damme and Weibull (1998), but some easier introductions are offered by Young (1998), Gintis (2000a, Chapter 10), Durlauf and Young (2001, Chapter 5) as well as Bowles (2004, Chapter 12). Examples of other notable contributions are Turnovsky and Weintraub (1971), Blume (1993), Ellison (1993, 2000) and Samuelson (1994, 1997).

Notes

1 Inanna will later be worshipped as *Ishtar* by the Babylonians and Assyrians. A blue gate dedicated to the goddess led to the inner city of Babylon. The Ishtar Gate can now be seen in the Pergamon Museum in Berlin.

2 An ergodic Markov chain describes a process through which any state can be reached from any other state in any limited number of steps. If all elements of the transition matrix have a strictly positive value, the number of steps required is one and the matrix is ergodic. If the process is periodic, it will cycle between a number of states and will never reach any other state in a limited number of steps once the process has reached a periodic state. Additionally, if the transition matrix has a value of 1 in one of the elements on the main diagonal, the process will remain in this state once reached. The Markov chain in Figure 4.2 is therefore reducible and not ergodic.

3 The implication will become clear as we proceed with the argument. The idea is that a player needs to have a memory that is sufficiently long for erroneous play to appear sufficiently frequently in the sample and the shift in best response then also needs to occur sufficiently frequently. A slightly more correct constraint is that the size of the joint sample should not exceed the memory size m, i.e. $s_A + s_B \leq m$.

4 In addition, under certain regularities (see Ille, 2015 for details), the resistances with state-dependent error and sample sizes still identify the same convention as the simpler resistances in equation (4.10).

Furthermore, we can use the approach to better understand the impact of risk aversion on the convention. Assume, for simplicity, a symmetric Battle of the Sexes defined by the payoff matrix

A

		Musical	Cinema
B	Musical	a,b	$0,0$
	Cinema	$0,0$	b,a

with $a > b$. Denoting α as the frequency of musical, we have $\alpha_A^* = a/(a+b)$ and $\alpha_B^* = b/(a+b)$. If errors and sample sizes are state independent, both $\mathcal{M}$ and $\mathcal{C}$ are conventions with equal frequency as the error converges to zero.

Now let us assume that Berts are more risk-averse and therefore sample more at the same payoff compared to Anjas. If the probability of an error is the same across both populations and all states, we can ignore the error while calculating the resistances. In addition, we may assume that the sample size is sufficiently large to ignore the ceiling function. We can then multiply all values by $a+b$ and obtain $\tilde{r}_{\mathscr{C}} = \min\{s_A(C)a, s_B(C)b\}$ and $\tilde{r}_{\mathscr{M}} = \min\{s_A(M)b, s_B(M)a\}$. Since by assumption, Anjas have a lower sample rate than Berts at the same payoff, we have $s_A(M) < s_A(C) < s_B(M)$ and $s_(M) < s_B(C) < s_B(M)$, leading to

$$\tilde{r}_{\mathscr{M}} = s_A(M)b < \min\{s_A(C)a, s_B(C)b\} = \tilde{r}_{\mathscr{C}}$$

In other words, the convention is defined by going to the cinema where the less risk-averse population obtains a higher payoff.

For the case of state-dependent error size, define two positive, strictly increasing and concave functions u and v as such that $u(0), v(0) = 0$ with $u'(.), v'(.) > 0$ and $u''(.), v''(.) < 0$. Let $\gamma_A(M) = v(b)$, $\gamma_A(C) = v(a)$, and $\gamma_B(M) = u(a)$, $\gamma_B(C) = u(b)$. If the sample size is state independent, we can ignore it and define the resistances as $\tilde{r}_{\mathscr{C}} = \min\{au(b), bv(a)\}$ and $\tilde{r}_{\mathscr{M}} = \min\{bu(a), av(b)\}$. Furthermore, we assume that $u(\omega) > v(\omega)$ for $\omega = M, C$. Note that we have $v(a)/a < v(b)/b$ and $u(a)/a < u(b)/b$ (i.e. both functions are concave), and $u(a) > v(a) > v(b)$ and $u(a) > u(b) > v(b)$ (both functions are strictly increasing and the former assumption). If $au(b) < bv(a)$, then it must be that $a/b < v(a)/u(b) < v(a)/v(b)$ and thus we have a contradiction. Therefore, $\tilde{r}_{\mathscr{C}} = bv(a)$.

If $\tilde{r}_{\mathscr{M}} = av(b)$, then $\tilde{r}_{\mathscr{M}} > \tilde{r}_{\mathscr{C}}$. Also if $\tilde{r}_{\mathscr{M}} = bu(a)$, we obtain $\tilde{r}_{\mathscr{M}} > \tilde{r}_{\mathscr{C}}$. In both cases, the convention is defined by musical where the more risk-averse population obtains a higher payoff. Thus, risk aversion can have opposing effects based on whether it influences the sample or the error size based on the realistic assumption that individuals demonstrate a diminishing sensitivity to losses (see Kahneman and Tversky 1979).

5 Notice that the results are not entirely symmetric. In the simulation, the stochastic sampling process pushed the population into the basin of attraction of $\mathscr{M}$ for $a = b = 10$ and thereafter no further transition occurred. Repeating the simulations several times, the convention will be defined by $\mathscr{C}$ in half of the simulations and $\mathscr{M}$ in the other half.

6 For example, the convention is defined by $\mathscr{C}$ if $a_A = 75$, $b_A = 25$, $a_B = 25$, $b_B = 80$, and $\phi = 1/2$ at $s = 100$. Using these values in the resistances defined by equation (4.10) determines the same convention.

Individual Threshold Models and Public Signals: Fads, Riots, and Revolutions

5.1 Introduction

A FTER John Ballard was told: "there will be hell to pay tomorrow" (see Congressional Record, 1959, p. 13607) by a British stableman, he rushed off to relay the information to William Dawes and Paul Revere. The latter two speculated that the British were to attack the towns of Lexington and Concorde after they heard rumours earlier that day. Ballard's information only confirmed their suspicion. Revere and Dawes decided to warn the surrounding communities. Both took a different path to Lexington to raise as much support as possible. Revere took off to the North while Dawes took a route to the South of Boston. During his *Midnight Ride*, Revere mobilised a large number of people on his way to Lexington by telling colonial leaders of the oncoming *Regulars*. Leaders then sent out riders to spread the word. By the end of the day, around 40 riders travelled through the region. Dawes, on the other hand, was less successful. While he carried the same news, the numbers his message reached and incited were much fewer. Nevertheless, both had been able to marshal enough resistance at Lexington, when the British began their march the next morning. Because of Dawes' and Revere's swift action, the colonial militia defeated the British troops in Concorde, starting the American Revolutionary War.

Over 230 years later, in 2008, Egyptian workers organised a strike. Israa Abdel Fattah, together with a few friends, established a Facebook page to call for a nationwide strike in support of the workers. The April 6 Youth Movement gained over 100,000 Facebook users who joined to express their solidarity with the workers. On the day of the strike, some 60,000–80,000 people marched the streets of Mahalla city, where the strikes originated. Other political parties joined the strike but the movement did not develop the same momentum elsewhere as citizens followed the call for strike and stayed at home. Again in early 2011, Abdel Fattah organised a group of 20 protesters to go down to the centre of Cairo. She filmed their protest and disseminated the videos via Facebook. Soon, hundreds joined the small group on Tahir Square, only to be followed by thousands and eventually tens of thousands to ultimately topple the president in office, Hosni Mubarak.

A young woman by the name of Kitty Genovese was less successful in rallying people when she returned to her home in Queens, New York, after a late shift. Unbeknownst to her, she was

DOI: 10.4324/9781003035329-5

followed by Winston Moseley. After she parked her car one Friday morning in 1964, Moseley approached her with a knife. Genovese ran to her apartment and was stabbed twice in front of the building. After she screamed for help, a neighbour shouted at Moseley from his window. Her assailant fled the premises only to return after several minutes to attack her again. She was stabbed several times and succumbed to her injuries. While the incident lasted several minutes and occurred in front of the building, none of the 38 neighbours, who watched from their windows, came to Kitty Genovese's help. Two neighbours claimed to have called the police but only minutes after the attack (for a critical analysis of the case, refer to Kassin, 2017).

The events in the United States and Egypt share a common characteristic. Initially, an individual or a very small group exerts social influence on individuals outside the group. The latter choose to adopt the former's action or belief which leads to an ever growing number of joining members. The belief or action then cascades through the population and the initially small group grows through imitation into a large part of society. Not only information, like news (whether fake or real) and beliefs spread through word of mouth in cascades. This type of dynamics is pervasive. Fads, social movements, pandemics and even crime can be understood as processes of social cascades. The *Broken Window Theory* (Wilson and Kelling, 1982), for example, suggests that the existence of minor anti-social behaviour and crimes can promote more serious types of crime. In the late 1960s, Philip Zimbardo parked a car in the Bronx, New York. He popped the hood of the car and removed its number plates. Within minutes, the car was looted, most of its valuable components stolen the same day and it was reduced to a complete wreck within three days. Zimbardo repeated the experiment in Palo Alto, California. The car remained untouched for over a week. When it started to rain, a passerby shut the hood. Eventually, Zimbardo and his group decided to take measures and sledgehammers in their own hands. Initially, no one in the group wanted to initiate the destruction, but after the first blow, more and more students joined the process, temporarily getting carried away by their destructive urges (Zimbardo, 1969).

Yet, as the example of Kitty Genovese shows, these cascades are sometimes cut short or do not even emerge. None of the neighbours called the police in time. After one tenant shouted to leave her alone, it temporarily startled her assailant, but no other neighbour joined and made their way down to the street to help Genovese. In this chapter, we study the dynamics of these cascades and the necessary conditions for their occurrence. The approach studied here mainly relies on the initial work of (Granovetter, 1978) and (Schelling, 1978, Ch. 3). We will see that the actions of only a few, maybe even one individual, can lead to significantly different population dynamics and equilibria, which will help us understand the so-called *bystander effect* that led to Genovese's death.

While these cascades apply to a large array of social contexts, they are fundamentally driven by three different types of social imitation (see also Sunstein, 2002; Lesourne et al., 2002; Skyrms, 2010):

- **Positive imitation**: This type of imitation occurs if an individual A believes that another individual B has a knowledge advantage. In this case, an action (such as running in a particular direction during an earthquake) creates an informational externality in the form of a public signal. As the public signal grows stronger, more individuals believe in the information contained in the signal. In so doing, the signal becomes even stronger and can dominate private knowledge. A coordination failure then occurs if the private knowledge is correct and the public knowledge incorrect (e.g., following the crowd although knowing that hiding under a table is more secure).

- **Normative imitation**: While A might not believe in the informational value of an action or that a statement is the truth, she decides to follow others assuming such behaviour to be expected from her. In this case, an individual action creates a reputational externality. Individually, the action might be considered detrimental, but it is still adopted out of fear of social sanctions (e.g., under peer pressure, an individual engages in an action that she considers morally wrong). Again, we can readily think of social scenarios in which normative imitation leads to coordination failures (e.g., drug consumption).

- **Preferential imitation**: In contrast to normative imitation, the action of individual B modifies the benefit that A obtains by engaging in the same action. Consequently, the existence of a network externality entails preferential imitation. For example, if most of A's peers adopt a particular software that uses a proprietary file system which cannot be used by any other software (like Microsoft Word in the old days), it is best for A to use the same software, even in the absence of peer pressure.

An **externality** defines the impact of an action on a third party. The consequences of such an action are not properly accounted for by the originator, i.e., they are not *internalised*, and can be a cost or a benefit. We then speak of negative or positive externalities, respectively.

Depending on the specific context, these three types of imitation can overlap making a clear distinction difficult or an individual can be motivated by two or all types of imitation. Such a distinction is irrelevant for the underlying analytical models presented in Sections 5.2 to 5.4, since we ignore individual motivations and only focus on the reaction (i.e. the conditional belief or action) of each individual when confronted with the actions and beliefs of others. Yet, it is important to keep in mind that a distinction of the type of imitation can be pertinent for the interpretation of a model's results. In the following, we will start with the simplest case and generalise the approach thereafter. It will become clear that the analyses in the previous chapters are helpful to understand the approach, especially with regard to the equilibrium analysis.

5.2   Thresholds in a Single Population

Following Granovetter (1978), we begin with the easiest setup in which an individual forms a belief based on the actions of all the other members and does not discriminate between them. Further assume that such a belief is binary and may entail a particular action or choice. This definition is sufficiently broad to encompass an ample variety of scenarios. We can imagine, for example, the situation in which an individual has to choose whether some information is wrong or correct, whether restaurant A is a better option than restaurant B, whether she should go outside and protest or stay at home, or follow a fashion or not. In contrast to previous chapters, we assume that agents are heterogeneous. Each agent acts on an individual threshold that determines either a critical number of other individuals or a share of the population. If the number of other agents (or the share of the population), who opted for a particular action or some belief, is equal or exceeds that threshold, she will join them in their action or belief. In other words, if my threshold to enter the newly opened Thai restaurant around the corner is ten, I will only give it a try under the condition that I observe at least ten other customers sitting in the restaurant.

To get a feeling for the dynamics, we can think of a very simple discrete uniform distribution in a population with 100 individuals. One individual has a threshold of 0 and is frequenting the restaurant even if no other client entered. The former might be the nephew of the owner, a Thai foodie, someone who simply likes the ambience or has a crush on the waitress. An individual threshold should therefore be seen as the result of a set of preferences and potentially a sophisticated decision process. Note that identical thresholds do not indicate identical preferences but may be purely coincidental. Continuing with the hypothetical distribution, assume that a second individual has a threshold of 1, a third individual of 2 and so on until the last individual has a threshold of 99. Upon seeing the owner's nephew in the restaurant, the individual with threshold 1 enters, which encourages the individual with threshold 2 and so forth setting in motion a domino effect until eventually all 100 places all filled.

While this process seems simple, the dynamics illustrates a number of interesting character-istics. The assumption of agents with heterogeneous characteristics is not merely an extension of a simpler model, contrary to other models discussed in this book. (Indeed, the premise that interac-tions take place between rather similar individuals only made most of the results in Chapters 2 and 3 possible.) The dynamics are critically dependent on the notion that individuals demonstrate a variation in their attributes. For example, assume that all agents are identical and have a threshold of 10 percent. In this case, everyone is willing to join but only as long as each of the individuals observes that the action is already carried out by 10 percent. Thus, even in a group of ten people, the indispensable first-mover is missing, since no one is willing to take the first step. This type of coordination failure explains the reaction after the stabbing of Kitty Genovese. The work by John Darley and Bibb Latané (1968; 1968) showed exactly the same result. Individuals are less likely to act and help if they find themselves in larger groups.

Furthermore, small changes to the distribution can lead to significant alterations of the dynamics. For example, a slight change in the uniform distribution by modifying the threshold of a single individual blocks the domino effect at exactly this person. Assume the latter's original threshold changes from 3 to 4. In this case, the sequence ends with the owner's nephew and two other customers, since no other customer has the necessary threshold to increase the number further. The (now two) individuals with threshold 4 decide to eat somewhere else. In larger societies, we can imagine a redundancy of thresholds, but if the right person is removed from the distribution, the social dynamics of two social systems can appear entirely different despite their threshold distributions being essentially indistinguishable.

In the following, we assume that the population is large enough to ensure a sufficiently smooth distribution of the individual thresholds in such a way that the domino effect is not interrupted. Let x be the proportion of a population engaging in a particular action. At the same time, x must then also denote the period's critical threshold value and any person with an individual threshold equal or lower to the critical threshold value will join the action in the next period. The frequency distribution of the thresholds across the population is given by $f(x)$ and the cumulative distribution function (CDF) by $F(x)$. Remember that $F(x)$ indicates the share of a population or number of individuals (depending on the way we define a threshold) with a threshold equal or less than x. In other words, $F(x)$ are those who engage in the action or share the belief upon seeing x. To make this more intuitive, imagine a simple example: assume that at some period $t = 1$, precisely 30 out of 100 individuals share a belief. The number of agents who share the belief in the next period is then given by all those with a threshold of less or equal to 30 percent, i.e. $F(0.3)$. Let these be half of the population and thus $0.5 = F(0.3)$. In the following period ($t = 2$), the share of the population who adopt the belief is given by $F(0.5)$. The process thus defines an **iterated map** that can be represented by the difference equation

$$x_{t+1} = F(x_t) \tag{5.1}$$

In contrast to the dynamical systems, which we studied in Chapter 3, the dynamics in equation (5.1) are not continuous in time but model a system with discrete periods of time. Thus, while we define an equilibrium as a state in which the share of individuals x^* remains constant over time, the criteria for stability are not identical. Given equation (5.1), an equilibrium is defined by $x_{t+1} = x_t$, and thus

$$x^* = F(x^*) \tag{5.2}$$

In other words, the share of individuals with a threshold equal to or less than x^* corresponds exactly to the share that is already actively engaging in the action or follows the belief. Extending the previous example, the equilibrium would be reached if $0.5 = F(0.5)$. Upon seeing half of the population, precisely the same share accepts the belief and the population has reached an equilibrium in $t = 3$.[1] Note that this does not necessarily imply that the same individuals are involved in each period, but that the number that abandons a belief or action is exactly offset by those who initiate it.

In Chapter 3, we have seen that the evolutionary stability of an equilibrium depended on the first (partial) derivatives of the replicator dynamics. The interpretation was that an increase in the share of those who play a certain strategy by one additional individual either encourages another individual to opt for that strategy if the first derivative is positive or discourages another individual if the first derivative is negative. The population returns to its original equilibrium state in the latter case. In the discrete case, however, change does not occur gradually, i.e. continuously but in discrete time periods. Intuitively, we may ask what happens if a population is currently in equilibrium at x^* and the number of actors increases by a small amount ε? Assume that $x_1 = x^* + \varepsilon$ and consider $x_2 = F(x_1)$. If $x_2 > x_1$, the new share of individuals is larger than the initial perturbed value, and the population increases and moves away from the equilibrium point. If, however, the new share x_2 lies somewhere between x^* and x_1, the distance towards x^* decrease in future periods and the population returns to the equilibrium after a few iterations. However, we have ignored to possibility that the dynamics are cyclic. In this case, the population might move to some share $x_2 < x^*$. If $|x^* - x_2| > |\varepsilon|$ (or more generally, if $|x^* - x_{t+1}| > |x^* - x_t|$), the population spirals away from the equilibrium. If, to the contrary $|x^* - x_{t+1}| < |x^* - x_t|$, the population jumps between values to the left and right of x^* but eventually closes the gap and returns to the equilibrium. Figure 5.1 illustrates all four cases. Note that since $F(x) \in [0, 1]$, the function is tangent to the abscissa once it hits the lower bound (at $x < 2/30$ in Figure 5.1b and $x > 0.72$ in Figure 5.1d) and parallel to the abscissa at the upper bound (at $x > 22/30$ in Figure 5.1b).

The points where the value on the ordinate (i.e., x_{t+1}) equals the value on the abscissa (i.e., x_t) are situated on the 45° line. Consequently, an equilibrium, given by $x^* = F(x^*)$, occurs at the intersection of the $F(x)$ function and that line. As before, I will use the terms *fixed point* and

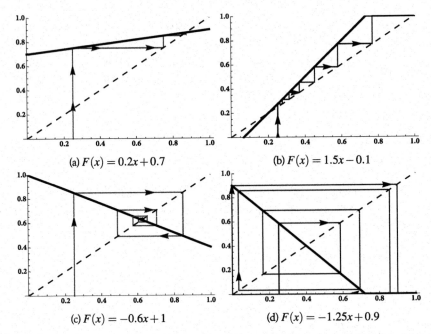

(a) $F(x) = 0.2x + 0.7$

(b) $F(x) = 1.5x - 0.1$

(c) $F(x) = -0.6x + 1$

(d) $F(x) = -1.25x + 0.9$

Figure 5.1: Function $F(x)$ is shown in bold, the 45° line as the dotted line, and the trajectory in grey. All iterations start at $x_0 = 0.25$ and arrows indicate the direction of movement.

equilibrium interchangeably. We can see that the distribution of the thresholds increases in x in the top row figures, but in Figure 5.1a it cuts the 45° line from above, while in Figure 5.1b, it cuts the line from below. Whenever the CDF $F(x)$ is above the 45° line, $F(x_t) > x_t$ and the share of the population willing to join an action upon witnessing a share x is higher than the initial share x of those who already engaged in the action. If $F(x)$ is below the 45° line, $F(x_t) < x_t$ and the share decreases in the next period. Since $F(x_t) > x_t$ to the left of x^* and $F(x_t) < x_t$ to its right, the equilibrium is an attractor in Figure 5.1a. Since the inverse holds for the intersection in Figure 5.1b, x^* is unstable. The population decreases to the left of x^* and converges to $x = 0$. To its right, the population increases and converges to $x = 1$.

In the bottom row figures, the distributions decrease in x. Note that the first derivative of the CDF is the probability density function, which is non-negative. Figure 5.1c and 5.1d therefore do not depict a CDF. While I include the discussion of the two cases here for completeness, I postpone the discussion of these cases to later chapters and focus on the cases shown in the top row of Figure 5.1. Before I do so, notice that the negative slope of $F(x)$ causes the interesting effect that the population shifts between points to the left and right of the intersection. In Figure 5.1c, the function has an absolute slope smaller than 1 and with each shift, the population spirals closer to the equilibrium. In Figure 5.1d, the absolute slope of $F(x)$ is greater than 1 and with each shift, the population overreacts and diverts from the equilibrium to eventually shift periodically between $x_1 = 0$ and $x_2 = 0.9$. From the previous discussion and the graphs, we can infer the following stability criterion[2]

$$x^* \text{ is a (asymptotically) stable fixed point, if } \left| \frac{dF(x)}{dx} \right| < 1 \text{ evaluated at the fixed point } x^*$$

(5.3)

$$x^* \text{ is an unstable fixed point, if } \left| \frac{dF(x)}{dx} \right| > 1 \text{ evaluated at the fixed point } x^*$$

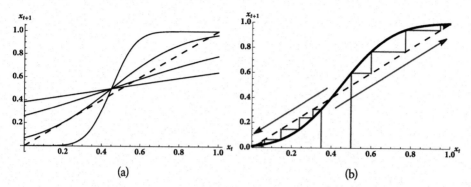

Figure 5.2: (a) shows four different CDFs with mean $\mu = 0.45$ and standard deviation $\sigma = \{0.1, 0.3, 0.7, 1.5\}$. The curve becomes flatter as σ increases. (b) has asymptotically stable fixed points at $x_1^* = 0.015$ and $x_2^* = 0.997$. The vectors illustrate the general dynamics and basins of attraction, and the grey zig-zag lines show the population paths for $\mu = 0.45$, $\sigma = 0.2$ and initial conditions $x_{01} = 0.35$, $x_{02} = 0.50$.

Remember that the first derivative shows how the function scales in the neighbourhood of a point. The result in equation (5.3) is intuitive in the context of CDFs. A derivative of greater or smaller than 1 implies that the function expands or shrinks around the fixed point. However, a CDF can intercept the 45° line more than once. Since the stability in this case is defined by whether $F(x)$ crosses the 45° line from above or below (ignoring tangent points), if $F(x)$ is continuous, stable and unstable fixed points alternate as we increase x_t, similar to the one-dimensional continuous system discussed in Chapter 3.

Consider, for example, a normal distribution with mean μ and standard deviation σ. Figure 5.2a illustrates in which way different CDFs intersect the 45° line. The distributions only vary with respect to their standard deviation. Increases to the standard deviation render the curve flatter upon which it only intersects the 45° line once. At lower values of σ, however, the CDF of the normal distribution crosses the line three times and thus, has three fixed points. Figure 5.2b demonstrates this case in closer detail. The first intersection occurs from above at $x_1^* = 0.015$. The CDF then intersects from below at $x_2^* = 0.399$ and meets the 45° line again at $x_3^* = 0.997$. Given the condition in equation (5.3), only x_1^* and x_3^* are stable. The figure depicts the population path towards each of the equilibria. Equilibrium x_2^* constitutes a separatrix that segregates the basin of attractions of the stable fixed points.

Exercise 5.1

(a) Define a possible distribution for each of the examples in the introduction and show the equilibrium path. (b) Study the system $x_{t+1} = \sin(\alpha x_t)$ for $x_t \in [0, 1]$ and $\alpha \in (0, 2]$. (c) The graphical stability analysis in Figure 5.1 extends to the best-response correspondences in Chapter 2. Show graphically that the interior equilibria of Figures 2.13b, 2.14a, and 2.14b are stable. (Hint: Keep in mind that instead of reacting to itself, a group reacts to the adopters in the other group.)

This makes for some interesting implications if we give some non-mathematical meaning to these results. Define individuals with a threshold of zero who hence act or share a belief without observing anybody else as *nonpartisan*.[3] In a small group of five members, two nonpartisans are sufficient to ensure that the entire group acts. Larger groups then need a proportionally larger number of nonpartisans to reach x_3^*. In larger groups, a higgly piggly bunch of people is less likely to contain the adequate number of nonpartisan members to push the entire group over the separatrix, while a smaller group might just have the necessary number to reach the upper equilibrium.

This observation indicates that the dynamics of groups composed of random individuals are influenced by the size of the group. Two groups of diverse size can converge to different equilibria although the thresholds of their members are derived from the same probability distribution. Before we look at this in more detail, I discuss some other implications of Figure 5.2a. An increase of the standard deviation stretches the CDF around the mean. At around $\sigma^* = 0.298$, the CDF is tangent to the $45°$ line. At values below σ^*, the system has three fixed points. At σ^*, the system undergoes a saddle-node bifurcation similar to the continuous case which we discussed on pages 50–51. At a standard deviation that is slightly larger than σ^*, the population initially appears to settle close to the tangent point only to eventually but abruptly converge to the higher stable fixed point, leading to dynamics similar to Figure 3.3a on page 50.

pages 50–51

Exercise 5.2

Show that for an exponential threshold distribution given by CDF $F(x, \lambda) = 1 - e^{-\lambda x}$, as well as $\lambda > 1$ and $x > 0$, the system has only a single fixed point, which is (a) stable and (b) increasing in λ.

Figure 5.3a illustrates not only the bifurcation but also the non-monotonic relation between σ and the stable fixed points x^* (see also Granovetter, 1978 for a similar result). At $\sigma < \sigma^*$, the system has two stable fixed points and an interior unstable fixed point. The two lower fixed points approach each other as the standard deviation increases, and at $\sigma > \sigma^*$, the lower fixed points collide and disappear while the only remaining upper stable fixed asymptotically converges to $x^* = 0.5$ as σ grows. The joint effect of the mean and the standard deviation on the stable fixed points is shown in Figure 5.3b. For large σ, the mean has no impact on neither the stability nor position of the fixed point which is at around $x^* = 0.5$. At small values of σ and μ, the system has a single stable fixed point at $x^* = 1$. As μ increases, the system bifurcates leading to two stable fixed points close to $x_1^* = 0$ and $x_2^* = 1$. Once μ exceeds a critical size, the higher equilibrium disappears and the system remains at the only stable fixed point at $x^* = 0$.

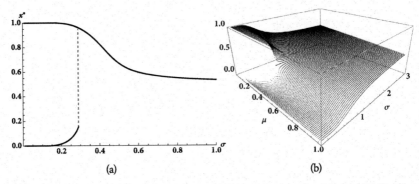

Figure 5.3: (a) presents x^* as a function of σ and given $\mu = 0.45$ and (b) presents x^* as a function of $\mu \in [0.1, 1]$ and $\sigma \in [0.1, 3]$.

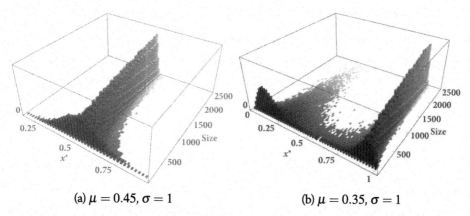

Figure 5.4: Based on 100,000 simulations, the histograms show the frequency of the realised equilibrium values x^* based on individual thresholds drawn randomly from a normal distribution and given various group sizes. (a) has a stable fixed point at $x^* = 0.533$, (b) has a stable fixed point at $x^* = 0.901$.

I return to the question of how group size affects social dynamics. Intuitively, if the individual thresholds are sampled randomly from a given distribution, a larger group is more likely to be representative of the distribution. Consequently, the equilibria defined by equation (5.1) are more probable to emerge in larger groups. Smaller groups, however, are more likely to contain gaps in the distribution and the domino effect is cut short. In this case, the population persists at a lower stable fixed point. On the other hand, the repercussion of the individual act of joining an action or sharing a belief is stronger, since each individual pushes a share x_t by a marginal value of $1/n$. Thus, the two effects operate diametrically in smaller groups. Figure 5.4 shows the simulation results as a histogram of the relative frequencies of the equilibria across groups of different size. In each of the 100,000 simulations per group, members are assigned an individual threshold defined by a random number that is drawn from the normal distribution. For $\mu = 0.45$ and $\sigma = 1$, the CDF intersects the $45°$ line once from above at $x^* = 0.533$. In Figure 5.4a, we can see that the standard deviation around the stable fixed point decreases with the group size as expected. Smaller groups have a higher probability to activate a larger share of members, but these groups are also more likely to remain trapped at a lower equilibrium. Independent of the group size, the population most frequently converges to $x^* = 0.533$, giving us some confidence that the model remains a good predictor also for smaller groups. Figure 5.4b shows the results for $\mu = 0.35$ and $\sigma = 1$. While the CDF intersects the $45°$ line only once from above at $x^* = 0.901$, the CDF is almost tangent to the $45°$ line at approximately $\hat{x} = 0.30$ because of its stronger s-shaped form. Smaller groups tend to remain stuck around $\hat{x}$, turning it into a pseudo-equilibrium.

To summarise results, while the dynamics in large groups follow the model closely, it only provides an approximation for the behaviour of smaller randomly sampled groups for three reasons. On the one hand, smaller groups have insufficient redundancies of the thresholds so that the domino dynamics may terminate prematurely if a necessary threshold is not part of the group. On the other hand, such small groups can also overshoot, since the marginal impact of an individual's action on others is stronger and a higher proportion of other agents is activated. In addition, the differences between the thresholds of members in modest-sized groups are not sufficiently small and the CDF cannot be approximated by a smooth continuous CDF. In the case of Kitty Genovese, probably two factors were at play and led to her death. Thirty-eight onlookers constituted a group that was too large for the first neighbour, who shouted at Moseley to trigger a sufficiently strong impact on the group to set in motion a cascade. Other onlookers needed at least a second nudge to react. At the same time, the group was too small to have sufficiently close and redundant thresholds. In a much larger group, more neighbours might have needed less encouragement to engage with the killer (working as law enforcement officers or security guards) and thus trigger the support of others.

5.3 Thresholds in More Than One Population

The model in the previous section can be generalised to any number of populations each with a binary action. I assume that the members of each population only choose whether to participate in one particular action. The frequency of members in population $i = 1, \ldots, k$ engaging in such an action is given by x_i. At time $t + 1$, the system is then defined by

$$
\begin{aligned}
x_1(t+1) &= F_1\left(x_1(t), x_2(t), \ldots, x_k(t)\right) \\
x_2(t+1) &= F_2\left(x_1(t), x_2(t), \ldots, x_k(t)\right) \\
&\vdots \\
x_k(t+1) &= F_k\left(x_1(t), x_2(t), \ldots, x_k(t)\right)
\end{aligned}
\tag{5.4}
$$

We can see that the system is the discrete version of the dynamical system we studied earlier in Chapter 3 on page 52. The equilibrium $x^* = (x_1^*, x_2^*, \ldots, x_k^*)$ is analogously defined by

$$
x_i^* = F_i(x_1^*, x_2^*, \ldots, x_k^*)
\tag{5.5}
$$

for all i. Alternatively, we can slightly modify the system of equations (5.4) to take account of the absolute numbers instead of shares. Let N_i be the population size of population i. The numbers of members of i who engage in the action in period t is then given by $n_i(t) = x_i(t)N_i$. System 5.4 turns into

$$
\begin{aligned}
n_1(t+1) &= N_1\, F_1\left(\frac{n_1(t)}{N_1}, \frac{n_2(t)}{N_2}, \ldots, \frac{n_k(t)}{N_k}\right) \\
n_2(t+1) &= N_2\, F_2\left(\frac{n_1(t)}{N_1}, \frac{n_2(t)}{N_2}, \ldots, \frac{n_k(t)}{N_k}\right) \\
&\vdots \\
n_k(t+1) &= N_k\, F_k\left(\frac{n_1(t)}{N_1}, \frac{n_2(t)}{N_2}, \ldots, \frac{n_k(t)}{N_k}\right)
\end{aligned}
\tag{5.6}
$$

and equivalently, an equilibrium $n^* = (n_1^*, n_2^*, \ldots, n_k^*)$ is obtained if it holds for all i that

$$
n_i = N_i\, F_i\left(\frac{n_1^*(t)}{N_1}, \frac{n_2^*(t)}{N_2}, \ldots, \frac{n_k^*(t)}{N_k}\right))
\tag{5.7}
$$

The stability of an equilibrium is determined by the eigenvalues of the system's Jacobian matrix evaluated at the fixed point. This again looks rather similar to the analysis in Chapter 3, but in the discrete case and equivalently to the analysis in the previous section, the eigenvalues must have an absolute value less than one and the system oscillates if eigenvalues are negative.[4]

Assume that the system is composed of two populations A and B. The equilibrium is given by[5]

$$n_A^* = N_A \, F_A(n_A^*/N_A, n_B^*/N_B)$$

$$n_B^* = N_B \, F_B(n_A^*/N_A, n_B^*/N_B)$$

We calculate the first partial derivatives to obtain the Jacobian

$$J^* = \begin{bmatrix} \dfrac{\partial n_A(t+1)}{\partial n_A(t)} & \dfrac{\partial n_A(t+1)}{\partial n_B(t)} \\[2ex] \dfrac{\partial n_B(t+1)}{\partial n_A(t)} & \dfrac{\partial n_B(t+1)}{\partial n_B(t)} \end{bmatrix} \Bigg|_{n_A^*, n_B^*} \tag{5.8}$$

and determine the eigenvalues at the equilibrium values n_A^* and n_B^*. The system is stable if the two eigenvalues λ_1 and λ_2 of this Jacobian are larger than -1 and smaller than 1, or if they are complex numbers, the complex conjugates have modulus less than 1.[6]

In some cases, we are unable to obtain a well-defined solution for the eigenvalues. In this case, it is frequently helpful to refer to the **Jury conditions** to implicitly determine whether the system is stable at the fixed point. I have provided the conditions for two- and three-dimensional system in the appendix (see Section A.6.3). For a two-dimensional system, we have

$$|Tr(J^*)| < 1 + \Delta(J^*) < 2 \tag{5.9}$$

It then suffices to ascertain the upper bound of the absolute value of the trace as well as the lower and upper bound of the determinant to verify the stability of a fixed point.

5.4   Two Populations with Uniform Distributions

In the following, we will study a simple two-dimensional system to better understand some of the properties that can lead to a growing divide in opinion and cause political polarisation. While I ignore the contributing properties of social networks (which we cover in Chapter 6.5) as well as other behavioural effects, such as menu effects and confirmation bias, we will see that under certain conditions, the distribution of opinions of those who engage in a political discourse might not be representative of the collective's opinion.

Assume that the population size of a group sharing a belief or political conviction A is given by N_a and similarly the number of those who are of the opposite conviction B is given by N_a. Members of each group have the choice to publicly express their opinion on social media. They will do so based on the share of individuals who share their belief on these platforms. Each individual has a threshold that determines whether she joins the discourse by comparing the number of those with a different belief to those who share her conviction. If the share of others compared to her own peers is small, she joins the platform and engages in the discourse. If the share of others is high, she will abstain. In the following, I will develop a more general version of the linear tolerance threshold distribution in Granovetter and Soong (1988) and Schelling (1971) to keep matters as simple as possible and similarly assume that the share of individuals willing to engage decreases linearly with the number of individuals who do not share the conviction.

Let the number of As who engage in discourse at time t be a_t and the corresponding number of Bs be b_t. Members of group A are hence interested in the ratio $r_a = b_t/a_t$ and equivalently, Bs make their choice contingent on the ration $r_b = a_t/b_t$. The tolerance thresholds are linearly distributed according to

$$
\begin{aligned}
F_a(r_a) &= 1 - \frac{r_a}{R_a} = 1 - \frac{b_t}{R_a a_t} \text{ for } A \\
F_b(r_b) &= 1 - \frac{r_b}{R_b} = 1 - \frac{a_t}{R_b b_t} \text{ for } B
\end{aligned}
\tag{5.10}
$$

The parameters R_a and R_b determine the maximum tolerated ratio and hence, the tolerance level of each group. At $r_i > R_i$ for $i = a, b$, none of the members of the group is willing to join the platform to engage in a discussion. A higher R_i therefore indicates that a group is either more tolerant or more willing to face a discourse. Due to the absence of engagement by As and Bs at $r_A > R_A$ and $r_B > R_B$, respectively, the dynamics in equation (5.6) need to be defined for the four different scenarios.

If $b_t/a_t < R_a$ and $a_t/b_t < R_b$

$$
a_{t+1} = N_a\left(1 - \frac{b_t}{R_a a_t}\right)
\tag{5.11a}
$$

$$
b_{t+1} = N_b\left(1 - \frac{a_t}{R_b b_t}\right)
$$

If $b_t/a_t \geq R_a$ and $a_t/b_t < R_b$

$$
a_{t+1} = 0
\tag{5.11b}
$$

$$
b_{t+1} = N_b\left(1 - \frac{a_t}{R_b b_t}\right)
$$

If $b_t/a_t < R_a$ and $a_t/b_t \geq R_b$

$$
a_{t+1} = N_a\left(1 - \frac{b_t}{R_a a_t}\right)
\tag{5.11c}
$$

$$
b_{t+1} = 0
$$

If $b_t/a_t \geq R_a$ and $a_t/b_t \geq R_b$

$$
a_{t+1} = 0
\tag{5.11d}
$$

$$
b_{t+1} = 0
$$

Note that the dynamics for $a_t = b_t = 0$ are indeterminate, but $a_t = 0, b_t = N_b$ and $a_t = N_a, b_t = 0$ are fixed points. The interior fixed points for $a_t/b_t < R_b$ and $b_t/a_t < R_a$ are the simultaneous solution to

$$
a^* = N_a\left(1 - \frac{b^*}{R_a a^*}\right)
\tag{5.12}
$$

$$
b^* = N_b\left(1 - \frac{a^*}{R_b b^*}\right)
$$

and the Jacobian is

$$J = \begin{bmatrix} \dfrac{\partial a_{t+1}}{\partial a_t} = \dfrac{N_a b_t}{R_a a_t^2} & \dfrac{\partial a_{t+1}}{\partial b_t} = \dfrac{-N_a}{R_a a_t^2} \\[3mm] \dfrac{\partial b_{t+1}}{\partial a_t} = \dfrac{-N_b}{R_b b_t^2} & \dfrac{\partial b_{t+1}}{\partial b_t} = \dfrac{N_b a_t}{R_b b_t^2} \end{bmatrix} \tag{5.13}$$

with eigenvalues

$$\lambda_1 = 0$$
$$\lambda_2 = \frac{N_a b_t}{R_a a_t^2} + \frac{N_b a_t}{R_b b_t^2} \tag{5.14}$$

Since the eigenvalues in equation (5.14) are non-negative, a fixed point is stable if λ_2 (evaluated at the fixed point) is smaller than 1. We can see that the size of the second eigenvalue depends on the two groups sizes and tolerance levels. Figure 5.5a plots the $\{a^*, b^*\}$ tuples of the interior fixed points in relation to the size of group B. The system undergoes a bifurcation at $N_b^l = (25/16)(71 - 3\sqrt{105}) \approx 62.91$ and at $N_b^h = (25/16)(71 + 3\sqrt{105}) \approx 158.97$. For values of $N_b < N_b^l$, only one interior fixed point exists with values of a^* and b^* increasing in N_b. The interior fixed point is unstable. For $N_b^l < N_b < N_b^h$, the system has three interior equilibria of which one fixed point is asymptotically stable. At the stable fixed point, b^* increases in N_b, but contrary to the other fixed points, a^* decreases in N_b. For $N_b^h \leq N_b$, the system bifurcates again and collapses to one interior unstable fixed point. Figure 5.5b also shows the fixed points, but this time in relation to the tolerance level of group B. Again, we observe a regime shift. For $R_b \leq 9/4$, the single interior equilibrium is unstable. For higher tolerances, the system has again one stable and two unstable interior fixed points.

A graphical analysis of the dynamics will help us to better understand these characteristics. In Chapter 3, I plotted the nullclines for each frequency (i.e. $\dot{x}_i = 0$) to study the dynamics around the fixed points. In the discrete context, we can do something very similar by mapping out the nullclines at which no quantitative change occurs (i.e. $N_i F_i(r_i) - i = 0$ with $i = a, b$). Solving

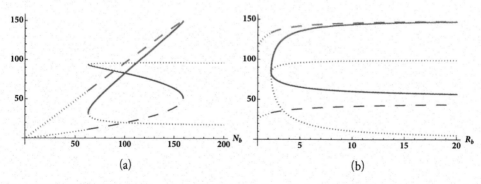

(a) (b)

Figure 5.5: Values of a^* are shown in blue, values of b^* are shown in brown. Dotted and dashed lines show the corresponding value for the two unstable interior equilibria, solid lines show the values for the stable interior equilibrium: (a) shows the equilibrium quantities in relation to the population size of group B for $R_a = R_b = 6$ and $N_a = 100$, (b) shows the equilibrium quantities in relation to the tolerance level of group B for $R_a = 6$, $N_a = 100$, and $N_b = 150$.

$a^* = N_a F_a(b_t/a^*)$, we obtain a parabola defined by

$$\hat{b} = \frac{R_a a(N_a - a)}{N_a} \tag{5.15}$$

as shown in Figure 5.6. The parabola defines the area in which the direction of the dynamics change. It intersects the abscissa at $a = 0$ and $a = N_a$ and has a maximum at[7]

$$a^{max} = \frac{N_a}{2} \text{ and } \hat{b}^{max} = \frac{N_a R_a}{4} \tag{5.16}$$

From the first equation in (5.10), we can see that the number of individuals in group A who engage in the next period decreases in b_t, since $\partial F_a(r_a)/\partial b_t = -N_a/(R_a a_t)$. Thus, below the parabola, i.e. at low values of b, the number of engaging members in A expands, while at higher values of b above the parabola, the number contracts. The arrows then show the corresponding direction of the social dynamics.

Adding the parabola for group B at $b^* = N_b F_b(a_t/b^*)$ to Figure 5.6 generates Figure 5.7. The latter figure does not only determine the system's fixed points but also their stability. The same logic applies to dynamics determined by the parabola for group B, only that the graph is flipped and turned at a $90°$ angle. To the left of the parabola of group B (i.e., at lower values of a), the number of engaging members increases, to its right the number decreases. Based on this, Figure 5.7 defines the direction of the movement for each of the six regions. For example, in the region below both parabolas, both a and b increase which is indicated by an arrow pointing right, a second arrow pointing upwards and an interior arrow that combines the direction of both. The arrows for the other areas are obtained in the same way.

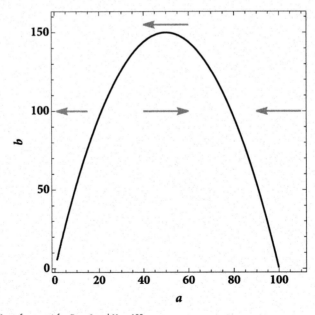

Figure 5.6: The nullcline of group A for $R_a = 6$ and $N_a = 100$.

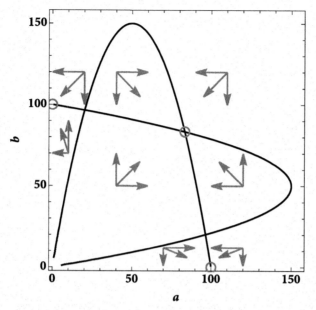

Figure 5.7: The nullclines for $R_a = R_b = 6$ and $N_a = N_b = 100$. The stable interior equilibrium lies at $(a^*, b^*) = (250/3, 250/3)$. The other two stable fixed points are at $(0, N_b)$ and $(N_a, 0)$.

As we have seen in Chapter 3, an intersection of the nullclines marks a fixed point. In Figure 5.7, we obtain three interior fixed points. By equations (5.11b) and (5.11c), two additional pure fixed points exist at $(N_a, 0)$, and $(0, N_b)$. While the second eigenvalue is indeterminate for these two equilibria, Figure 5.7 helps us to determine their stability. The stable interior fixed point is defined by the intersection of the decreasing arms of both parabolas (indicated by the circle). The arrows show that the two other interior equilibria are saddle points. The origin is unstable and thus, the number will increase if at least one individual engages, while the two pure fixed points at $(N_a, 0)$, and $(0, N_b)$ are stable. Since the stable fixed points are asymptotically attracting, the initial conditions define whether engagement occurs between representative shares of each group or whether only a single belief is shared on the platform.

The relative shape of the parabolas defines the number of equilibria and their stability. Given the results in equations (5.15) and (5.16), the parabola extends to the right and its maximum increases linearly as the size of the respective group grows. While the width of the parabola is unaffected by changes in the tolerance level of the group, its maximum increases linearly as the group becomes more tolerant.[8] Figure 5.8 plots the parabola for group A in relation to various

> **Exercise 5.3**
>
> There are minor differences between a game defined in terms of equation (5.4) or (5.6) if we consider that *numbers of joiners* can only be integers. (a) Show that for the game discussed in this section and $R_a = R_b = 5$, we obtain three interior stable fixed points at $(79, 80)$, $(80, 80)$, and $(80, 79)$. (b) Generalise the result of this game for any parameter value.

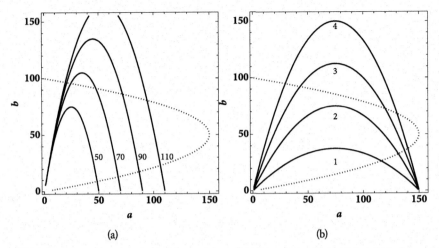

Figure 5.8: The nullclines for (a) different population sizes $N_a = \{50, 70, 90, 110\}$ and (b) different tolerances $R_a = \{1, 2, 3, 4\}$.

groups sizes and tolerance levels. Consistent with Figure 5.5a, the parabolae only intersect once at group sizes below $N_a = 63$. At higher group sizes, we observe three intersections until $N_a \geq 159$ beyond which the parabola for A only intersects the parabola for B on its increasing branch. Similarly, the parabolae only intersect once at tolerance values below or equal to $9/4$ which is consistent with Figure 5.5b. Once tolerances exceed this value, the system maintains three interior fixed points and their position only changes marginally at higher levels of tolerance.

In Figure 5.7, we have seen that a stable interior equilibrium necessitates an intersection of the downwards sloping branches of both parabolae. Consequently, as Figure 5.5a shows, marginal changes to the group sizes can radically alter the stability of the interior fixed point. The group sizes at which such an interior fixed point is asymptotically stable can be within a rather small interval. Figure 5.9 depicts two scenarios that illustrate small differences in the population size of group B but fundamentally different dynamics. In Figure 5.9a, the two nullclines intersect on the upward sloping branch of the parabola of group A and the downward sloping branch of the parabola of

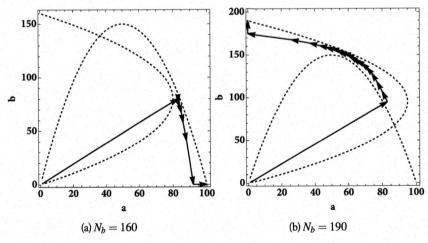

(a) $N_b = 160$ (b) $N_b = 190$

Figure 5.9: Dynamics for two different population sizes, given $N_a = 100$, $R_a = 6$, and $R_b = 2$.

group B. The figure illustrates the path that the population takes towards the equilibrium starting at $(a_0, b_0) = (1, 1)$. While the numbers for both groups increase in the first period to $(83, 80)$, the numbers of group B decline rapidly thereafter and the population converges to $(100, 0)$. In Figure 5.9b, the nullclines intersect on the downward sloping branch of the parabola of group A and the upward sloping branch of the parabola of group B causing the population to converge to $(0, 100)$. Neither of the two equilibria is representative of the belief distribution in the underlying population. An increase of the population by merely 18 percent leads to diametrically opposed public opinions.[9]

5.5 Extensions with Individual Preferences and Choices

While so far we assumed that an individual's threshold is determined by some underlying preferences and expectations, we have not explicitly modelled the underlying decision process. In most cases, it may be adequate to ignore the individual micro-level decision variables and only characterise the aggregate threshold distribution. Yet in other cases, the population thresholds may not follow a standard CDF and we can gain additional insights by explicitly modelling the individual decision function.

Assume that engaging in the action entails a benefit π_i^e for an individual i and abstaining grants a benefit of π_i^a. Individuals only chooses to act if $\pi_i^e > \pi_i^a$. We can define a decision function $\pi_i = \pi_i^e - \pi_i^a$ and suppose that π_i is a function of the share of individuals who opt for the action, given by x, and a variable θ_i that is determined by the individual's preferences. Let us further assume that the individuals can be order according to their θ_is and that the set of all θ_is, given by $\theta = \{\theta_1, \theta_2, \ldots \theta_n\}$ is defined by some arbitrary distribution, similar to the CDF of the thresholds in the previous section. We can then find an agent j who is indifferent between engaging and abstaining in some period t and let her individual preference value be θ_t^*. The individual is indifferent between joining and abstaining, and thus separates the population into those who engage and those who abstain. For some share x_t, we have the following

$$
\begin{aligned}
x_{t+1} &= F(\theta_t^*) \text{ if all } i \text{ with } \theta_i \leq \theta_t^* \text{ join the action, and the rest abstains} \\
x_{t+1} &= 1 - F(\theta_t^*) \text{ if all } i \text{ with } \theta_i > \theta_t^* \text{ join the action, and the rest abstains}
\end{aligned}
\tag{5.17}
$$

To give this some meaning, imagine that individual i has to choose whether to follow her private information or a public signal. Again, we can think of a multitude of examples, such as the choice between going to a favourite pub and trying a new place or between believing some information or following the crowd. For simplicity, assume that all individuals have the same private information. The decision function of i is given by

$$
\pi_i^{priv} = \theta_i \alpha - (1 - \theta_i) x
\tag{5.18}
$$

and represents the net benefit that i obtains from following her private information. Parameter α is the value of the private information and x the share of the population that follows the public signal and hence the latter's strength, while θ_i determines the relative weight that each individual places on the public and private component. Note that the decision function can also be defined in terms of the benefit of following the public signal, i.e. $\pi_i^{pub} = (1 - \theta_i) x - \theta_i \alpha$, leading to the same results (see exercise 5.4).

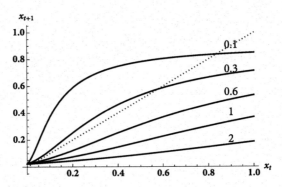

Figure 5.10: $F(\sigma^*)$ for different values of α given a normal distribution with $\mu = 0.6$ and $\sigma = 0.3$.

Solving $\pi_i = 0$ for θ_i, we obtain the critical value at

$$\theta^* = \frac{x}{\alpha + x} \tag{5.19}$$

Since $\partial \pi_i / \partial \theta_i > 0$, those individuals with $\theta_i \leq \theta^*$ follow the crowd while those with $\theta_i > \theta^*$ continue to act based on their private information, leading to the following recurrence relation

$$x_{t+1} = F\left(\theta_t^* = \frac{x_t}{\alpha + x_t}\right) \tag{5.20}$$

Note that if $F(\theta^*)$ is strictly increasing and $d\theta^*/dx > 0$, it must hold that $F(\theta^*)/d\theta \times d\theta^*/dx > 0$. (We will discuss the case if $d\theta^*/dx \not> 0$ in greater detail in Chapter 9.) If $F(\theta^*)$ is the CDF of a normal distribution, the intersection with the 45° line then depends not only on the mean and standard deviation as shown in Figures 5.2b and 5.3 but also on the value of α. Given that $\theta^*(0) = 0$ and $\partial \theta^*/\partial \alpha = -x/(\alpha + x)^2$, an increase in α flattens $F(\theta^*)$ (as shown in Figure 5.10). Consequently, this leads to the expected result – a higher importance of private information decreases the stable fixed point or renders it unstable and hence, reduces the share of individuals who follow the public information.[10]

Exercise 5.4

(a) Show that the dynamics are equivalent if the decision function is defined in terms of those who follow the public signal instead, i.e. $\pi_i^{pub} = (1 - \theta_i)x - \theta_i\alpha$. (b) How does the analysis change if $\pi_i^{pub} = \theta_i x - (1 - \theta_i)\alpha$? (c) Instead of a normal distribution, assume that the system given by equation (5.20) is defined by a linear distribution of the weights given by $F(\theta) = \beta + (1 - \beta)\theta$ and study its properties.

The analysis easily carries over to the multi-population case of which I will discuss an extension of the previous example. Imagine that individuals are either members of population 1 or 2. Similarly to the single-population case, assume that an individual i has the following payoff function if she is a member of 1 or 2, respectively.

$$\pi_{i1} = \alpha_1 \theta_{i1} - (1 - \theta_{i1})x_1x_2$$
$$\pi_{i2} = \alpha_2 \theta_{i2} - (1 - \theta_{i2})x_2x_1$$

(5.21)

where x_1 and x_2 denote the share of the population that believe in the public information. In this case, we assume that a complementarity between the beliefs of both populations exist. By following the public information, members of one population send a reinforcing signal to the members of both populations.

The critical weights are then defined by

$$\theta_k^* = \frac{x_1x_2}{\alpha_k + x_1x_2} \text{ with } k = 1, 2$$

Again, assume that θ_{i1} and θ_{i2} are normally distributed with some mean μ_1 and μ_2 and some standard deviation σ_1 and σ_2, respectively. Figure 5.11a shows the nullclines for $0 = F(x_1) - x_1$ as a solid curve and $0 = F(x_2) - x_2$ as a dashed curve. Beneath the nullcline for population 1, the share x_1 decreases and above the curve the share increases. Similarly, to the right of the dashed nullcline for population 2, the share x_2 increases and to its left the share decreases. The s-curved nullclines define three interior fixed points, two are stable while the central equilibrium is a saddle point. However, this only holds for intermediate values of α_1 and α_2 as is shown in Figure 5.11b. As expected, at low values both populations fully adopt the public information while at high α values, all members (except those who are nonpartisan and have a threshold of 0) adhere to their personal information. At medium levels, the system bifurcates and is defined by two interior stable fixed points as in Figure 5.11a. While, in essence, these results are no different from those discussed in the initial sections of this chapter, explicitly defining the choice function allows for greater

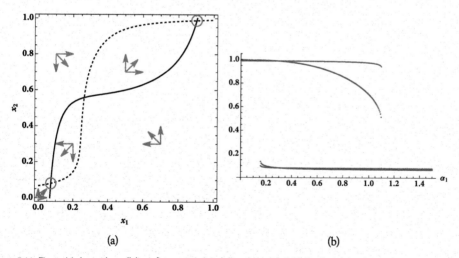

(a)   (b)

Figure 5.11: Figure (a) shows the nullclines for $x_1 = F(x_1)$ (solid) and $x_2 = F(x_2)$ (dashed) and the dynamics given parameters $\alpha_1 = 0.7$, $\alpha_2 = 0.3$, $\mu_1 = \mu_2 = 0.3$, and $\sigma_1 = \sigma_2 = 0.2$. (b) illustrates the stable equilibrium values of x_1 (blue) and x_2 (brown) for different α_1 values and parameters as in (a).

flexibility. The possible relationships between the individual choice function and the shares in each group affect the slope of the nullclines and can lead to asymmetric and cyclic outcomes (see exercise 5.5).

Exercise 5.5

(a) Assume that the payoff functions are given by

$$\pi_{i1} = \alpha_1 \theta_{i1} - (1 - \theta_{i1})x_1(1 - x_2)$$
$$\pi_{i2} = \alpha_2 \theta_{i2} - (1 - \theta_{i2})x_2(1 - x_1)$$

Show that the nullclines are downward sloping and define the interior fixed points.

(b) Assume that the payoff functions are given by

$$\pi_{i1} = \alpha_1 \theta_{i1} - (1 - \theta_{i1})x_1(1 - x_2)$$
$$\pi_{i2} = \alpha_2 \theta_{i2} - (1 - \theta_{i2})x_2 x_1$$

Under which conditions do we observe cyclic behaviour?

By explicitly modelling the choice function in a threshold model, the latter seems similar to the discrete replicator dynamics, of which we have studied the continuous version in Chapter 3. Different versions of the discrete replicator dynamics exist and the most broadly used types are

$$x_i(t+1) = x_i(t) + \gamma(\pi_i - \phi)x_i(t) \tag{5.22}$$

where $\phi = x_1\pi_1 + x_2\pi_2 + \ldots + x_n\pi_n$ is the average payoff in the population and $\gamma \in (0,1]$ is a scaling factor that ensures that x_i remains within the unit interval. If $\gamma = 1$, we can see that $\Delta = x_i(t+1) - x_i(t)$ is equivalent to the continuous version in equation (3.27) on page 56. Alternatively, we can define the discrete replicator equation as

$$x_i(t+1) = \frac{\lambda + \pi_i}{\lambda + \phi}x_i(t) \tag{5.23}$$

where $\lambda \geq 0$ is some baseline fitness, i.e. the natural growth rate of x_i, and defines the smoothness of the transition from one period to the next, since a higher baseline fitness reduces the periodical impact of the payoff-based change.

While both these replicator dynamics and the threshold model characterise a process of social imitation in discrete time, the described processes are not identical, but differ essentially in two aspects. Social imitation and learning in the replicator dynamics are driven by differences in payoffs obtained by distinct strategies. Individuals meet, compare their past success and adopt a new strategies with positive probability if the latter seems to be more efficient.[11] In the threshold model, on the other hand, individuals indirectly infer that a strategy is better, but not through an observation of the individual performance but only of the sheer numbers. This links to the second fundamental difference. The replicator dynamics assume that individuals are rather homogeneous for two reasons. If other players are characterised by entirely different attributes and preferences, a player cannot ensure that a strategy that is successful for any of the other players is also beneficial for her. Additionally, the replicators rely on a simplified mean-field approximation, i.e., population dynamics can be approximated by averages. On average, a member of population i is more likely to adopt a strategy $\hat{s}_i$ over any other strategy s_i if $\pi_i(\hat{s}_i, \sigma_{-i}) > \pi_i(s_i, \sigma_{-i})$. In contrast, the cascading dynamics of the threshold model require that individuals are heterogeneous. In a homogeneous population, the dynamics would only be a binary, one-period decision. Second, we have seen that in this case, averages are inadequate approximations. Small changes to the distribution of large populations do not affect the average, but they can interrupt the domino dynamics and lead to radically different fixed points.

A word of caution is therefore necessary: it is tempting to combine both approaches to cover a broader variation of social imitation (e.g., via a convex combination of the approaches or a two-stage approach) and in this case, the decision to act does not only depend on the simple observation of a number of other actors but also on the payoff benefits. However, while mathematically feasible, the underlying assumptions about the population properties for each approach render a combination logically inconsistent. The population would then need to be heterogeneous with regard to a critical element (such as the weights σ in the public signal example) but sufficiently homogeneous in all other aspects that describe the individual preferences.

5.6 Conclusion

The approach of this chapter explains various social phenomena, such as information cascades, market bubbles, political polarisation and radicalisation, mass gatherings, social movements and at a larger scale, revolutionary waves. At its core and in contrast to most of the other approaches we see in this book, is the need for heterogeneity among agents, since the dynamics are critically dependent on these inherent differences between individuals. Yet, another characteristic is even more striking. Small differences, imperceptible at an aggregate scale, change the characteristics of the system's fixed points fundamentally. The absence or presence of a single individual could mean the difference between a localised *argy-bargy* and an all-out revolution.

Applications and Relation to Other Chapters

While I have stressed the similarity and differences between the results in Chapter 3 and this chapter, extensions of the threshold model link the approach to other chapters. The model ignores the role of social structure since individuals observe the actions of *all* other members in the group. In Chapter 6, we will see that social networks exhibit properties that render the connections between members of the same social network inegalitarian. Most members are sparsely connected but a few members form highly connected hubs. Given the indirect connections between members of the same social network, the feedback effects in a *spatial* version of the threshold model can generate interesting results. We can further assume that hubs, in the form of social influencers, have an impact on a large number of individuals, but at the same time, a less critical marginal impact on each of their neighbours compared to less connected close-knit friends and family members (see Chapter 6 for details). By taking account of the varying impact of neighbours and attaching different weights to their actions, the threshold model shares similarities with the sandpile model discussed in Chapter 8, in which we observe similar cascading dynamics. Additionally, we might further assume that not all neighbours encourage, but some discourage an action. Such an extended model illustrates dynamics that are chaotic and is discussed in Chapter 9.

Further Reading

The approach was originally defined in Granovetter (1978) and Schelling (1978) and interesting extensions are offered by Granovetter and Soong (1988) and Granovetter and Soong (1986). Timur Kuran used very similar models to explain voting behaviour, preference falsification, path dependency of collective decisions, and ethnification as a self-reinforcing process (see Kuran, 1987a,b, 1998). While literature on the threshold model is limited, numerous other models of herd behaviour and information cascades exist, see for example Bikhchandani et al. (1992), Banerjee (1992), Choi (1997) and Kirman (2011), as well as Young (1998) who formalised the results in the context of evolutionary game theory.

Notes

1   Note that there is a different way to interpret the equilibrium condition in equation (5.2). The difference in x between two period is given by $\Delta x = x_{t+1} - x_t$. At the fixed point no change occurs between subsequent periods, thus $\Delta x = 0$. Substituting and rearranging leads to the equilibrium condition $F(x_t) = x_t$.

2   The criterion can also be derived using a Taylor series expansion. Let x_0 be a point close to the equilibrium value x^*. The trajectory starting at x_0 can then be approximated by

$$x_1 = F(x_0) = F(x^*) + \frac{dF(x)}{dx}|_{x^*}(x_0 - x^*)$$

$$= x^* + \frac{dF(x)}{dx}|_{x^*}(x_0 - x^*)$$

and thus

$$\frac{x_{t+1} - x^*}{x_t - x^*} = \frac{d(F(x))}{dx}|_{x^*} \tag{5.24}$$

If the derivative is smaller than 1 in absolute terms, the next iteration brings the population closer to the equilibrium value.

3   These are what Granovetter calls *instigator*. Since the application here goes beyond riots or protests, I opt for a more neutral denomination.

4   Similar to the continuous case, oscillation also occurs with complex eigenvalues. However, the ensuing oscillations are trigonometric in nature (sine and cosine functions) with periodicity $2\pi/Im(\lambda)$.

5   The solution extends to the case of relative shares defined in equation (5.4).

6   Remember that the eigenvalues are the roots of the characteristic equation and if complex, come in pairs of the form $\lambda_1 = a + ib$ and $\lambda_1 = a - ib$, i.e. as complex conjugates. The modulus of the two complex numbers is then $|\lambda_1| = |\lambda_2| = \sqrt{a^2 + b^2} = \sqrt{\lambda_1 \lambda_2}$.

7   Remember that we obtain the maximum a_t^{max} through the first-order condition, i.e. by setting $\partial b_t^* / \partial R_a = 0$ and solving for a_t. The corresponding value for n_b is derived by plugging the value back into equation (5.15).

8 More generally, we have

$$\frac{\partial b^*}{\partial N_a} = \frac{R_a a_t^2}{N_a^2} > 0$$

$$\frac{\partial b^*}{\partial R_a} = \frac{a_t(N_a - a_t)}{N_a} > 0$$

(5.25)

9 Similar results are obtained by small changes in the tolerances of the groups.

10 While it is not obvious from Figure 5.10, a higher α also shifts the unstable interior fixed point upwards and thus increases the invasion barrier for more s-shaped distributions at lower standard deviations.

11 To see why equation (5.22) describes an imitation process (see also Bowles 2004, Chapter 2 for the case with two strategies), assume that individuals can imitate 1 to n different strategies and their share in the population is given by $x_1, \ldots, x_n$, respectively. For imitation to occur, members of two different strategies must meet. The probability of a member choosing s_i meeting a member playing s_k is the product of their frequencies $x_i x_k$. Two possibilities can occur in this situation: either $\pi_i \geq \pi_k$ or $\pi_i < \pi_k$. In the former case, the s_k-player imitates the s_i-player with probability $\lambda(\pi_i - \pi_k)$ leading to an increase of x_i. In the latter case the inverse occurs with probability $\lambda(\pi_k - \pi_i)$, thus reducing x_i. We can differentiate between both cases via two indicator functions, $\rho_{\pi_i \geq \pi_j}$ and $\rho_{\pi_i < \pi_j}$, that take on the value of 1 if the condition in the subscript is fulfilled and 0 otherwise. The new value of x_i after an interaction with a s_k-player is

$$x_i(t) + \rho_{\pi_i \geq \pi_j} \lambda \, x_i(t) x_k(t)(\pi_i - \pi_k) - \rho_{\pi_i < \pi_j} \lambda \, x_i(t) x_k(t)(\pi_k - \pi_j)$$
$$= x_i(t) + \lambda \, x_i(t) x_k(t)(\pi_i - \pi_k)$$

since $\rho_{\pi_i < \pi_j} = 1 - \rho_{\pi_i \geq \pi_j}$. We can generalise this result to all possible interactions

$$x_i(t+1) = x_i(t) + \lambda x_i(t)\left(x_1(t)(\pi_i - \pi_1) + \ldots + x_n(t)(\pi_i - \pi_n)\right)$$
$$= x_i(t) + \lambda x_i(t)\left(\pi_i - (x_1(t)\pi_1 + \ldots + x_n(t)\pi_n)\right)$$
$$= x_i(t) + \lambda x_i(t)\left(\pi_i - \phi\right)$$

The derivation of the definition in equation 5.23 is straightforward, since the numerator is the sum of the payoff and baseline fitness, and the denominator renormalises the population to 1.

Social Networks and Graph Theory: Small World Effects and Social Change

6.1 Introduction

During the second half of the 1960s, an Aboriginal Australian tribe, the *Martu*, was resettled when an Australian-British programme built a ballistic missile testing range on their territory. The Martu lived in the Western Dessert and relied on hunting and gathering as well as burning. Seasonal burning, or more accurately, *patch mosaic burning* was used to flush out prey and expose their tracks and dens. The displacement of the Martu caused significant ecological changes. Not only did the lack of pyrodiversity curtail biodiversity, since the burnt patches offered a habitat for dingos, lizards, kangaroos, and various plants, but uprooting the Martu caused the extinction and near extinction of several small-bodied mammals, birds and reptiles. Invasive species, such as cats, foxes and camels, on the other hand, became more pervasive. While the Martu were resettled in their homelands in the 1980s, the biotope never returned to its old pattern (see Crabtree et al., 2019).

During the same period that the Martu left the Western Dessert, Stanley Milgram conducted a set of experiments to trace how different people are connected. In a study with Jeffrey Travers (1969), Milgram contacted a group of 296 volunteers, 196 in Nebraska and 100 participants in the Boston area and asked them to send a document to a Boston stockbroker. But the procedure had a catch. The document could not be sent directly to the stockbroker but only to somebody with whom the sender was acquainted on a first-name basis. The latter then had to send the document again to a first-name acquaintance and so on, until it eventually reached the stockbroker. Participants of the study were only given some general information about the stockbroker: name, address, occupation, and place of employment as well as additional information about his college, military service, and wife.

Travers and Milgram tracked the path of each document and recorded who passed on a document. This allowed them to record the number of intermediaries. In the study, 453 inter-mediaries were involved but not all sent on a document. In the end, 64 documents reached their target. Travers and Milgram found that, on average, it took 5.2 intermediaries to reach the Boston stockbroker. Documents, which were initially sent directly from the Boston area took

DOI: 10.4324/9781003035329-6

only marginally fewer intermediaries (4.6 on average) - a surprising result. While we can argue that those documents which required the involvement of more people were less likely to reach their target, individuals had also insufficient information to choose the most efficient sequence of intermediaries. Frigyes Karinthy's concept of *six degrees of separation* was empirically validated.

Shortly thereafter, during the early 1970s, Mark Granovetter studied how people are getting a job and published his research in a book of the same title (Granovetter, 1995). He discovered that more than half of his interviewees found a job through a personal contact. These contacts were either family friends and social acquaintances or a person known from work. Younger, early-career workers and those who were actively searching for a new position relied mainly on social contacts and older, more established as well as highly educated workers resorted predominantly to professional contacts. In addition, these contacts were not necessarily directly employed in the new firm or were employers but were business contacts or otherwise indirectly connected to the employer.

All three events have more in common than the period during which they occurred. They illustrate the major importance of social ties. All of us interact in complex social networks, and the type and number of connections we form with others crucially define our opportunities. In the following, we will study what determines whether a member of a social network is an influential and central actor. With the right connections, we can have substantial influence on other members of the social network. For example, according to Crabtree et al. (2019), the Western desert food web includes 173 unique species and 1,149 feeding links, and the exclusion of the Martu had a fundamental impact on the feeding links of the food web. The Martu were super-generalists and consumed roughly half of the other species. Their absence did not only have an impact on the species they ate but also those that were eaten by prey hunted by the Martu. We will have a closer look at various different network topologies and the role of highly connected network members in this chapter. At the same time, the research of Travers and Milgram demonstrates that despite their size, social networks tend to connect any two members through only a few intermediaries. We will therefore further study why certain social networks exhibit so-called **small-world** properties.

Since most of our analysis of social networks makes use of a branch of mathematics that studies graphs (therefore called *graph theory*), I will use the terms *graph* and *network* interchangeably.

6.2 Definitions and Elementary Measures

The following definitions will help us understand the general characteristics of social networks. Networks are composed of two elementary building blocks: nodes (or vertices and sometimes called points) and links (or ties and edges). **Nodes** constitute the interacting elements of a network. Within the context of social networks, nodes frequently define the interacting agents of a social network. These agents can be individuals or aggregates, such as firms, cities or states. If a node represents an agent, it can be understood as a strategic decision-maker who reacts to other members of the network. We discuss such scenarios in closer detail in Chapter 7. However, the concept of a node is much broader. Based on the context, a node can also be a device (e.g., computer or relay), an opinion (e.g., a social media thread), an action, etc. **Links** define the connection or relationship

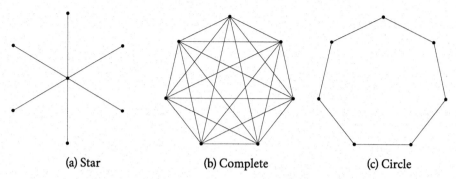

(a) Star   (b) Complete   (c) Circle

Figure 6.1: Characteristic networks.

between nodes. Consequently, two nodes form the endpoints of a link. Figure 6.1 depicts three characteristic network topologies. Nodes are normally shown as small circles and links as straight lines connecting two circles.

The set of n different nodes is given by $N = \{1, 2, 3, \ldots, n\}$. The connection between two nodes i and j is defined by $l_{i,j} \in \{0, 1\}$. In other words, variable $l_{i,j}$ is binary and either takes on a value of 0 or of 1, and a link is established between i and j in the latter case. We follow convention and assume that $l_{i,i} = 0$, i.e. that any node i is not linked to itself. If the direction of the link (a directed link is also called an *arc*) does not play a role, i.e. the network is **undirected**, we have $l_{i,j} = l_{j,i}$. Such a case occurs, if we, for example, analyse neighbourhoods. If i is a neighbour of j, then also the converse is true. If, however, the direction of the link is important (such as in a network showing friendships or the exchange of goods), we may have the situation that $l_{i,j} \neq l_{j,i}$ and hence the network is **directed**. For example, we may have the case in which node 3 is desperately in love with node 1, but the latter has no feelings for the former. However, a directed network does not exclude the possibility of a bi-directional connection (both 1 and 4 are madly in love with each other - sadly for node 3). Figures 6.2a and 6.2b show a directed and undirected network, respectively. The total number of nodes, given by n, of a graph g is called its **order** and given the set of links L, the total number of links defined by $|L|$ determines its **size**. Both networks are of the same order ($n = 4$), but their sizes differ since the directed network has six links while the undirected network consists of four links. In a **complete network**, as in Figure 6.1b, all nodes are connected to all other nodes. A complete graph obtains the maximum size equal to $n(n-1)/2$ if the graph is undirected and equal to $n(n-1)$ if the graph is directed.

We can see that the set of nodes N and the set of links L are thus sufficient to describe a network g, given by $g = (N, L)$, as long as we assume that nodes and links are homogeneous, i.e.,

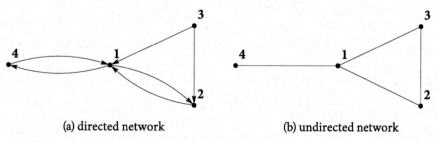

(a) directed network   (b) undirected network

Figure 6.2: Network examples.

no idiosyncratic attribute other than the number of links extending from or into a link are relevant. I will discuss the heterogeneous case later in this chapter.

We can further represent the network in the form of a matrix that presents the existence of a link $l_{i,j}$ for each pair of nodes. The row determines the node from which a link emanates and the column defines the receiving node. This matrix must therefore be a square matrix with the number of columns and rows equal to n (i.e., its dimension is $n \times n$) and each element in the matrix either has value 0 or 1. The **adjacency matrix** G has thus the form

$$G = \begin{pmatrix} l_{1,1} & l_{1,2} & \cdots & l_{1,n} \\ l_{2,1} & l_{2,2} & \cdots & l_{2,n} \\ \vdots & \vdots & \ddots & \vdots \\ l_{n,1} & l_{n,2} & \cdots & l_{n,n} \end{pmatrix} \tag{6.1}$$

and the adjacency matrices for networks Figure 6.2a and 6.2b are shown in Figure 6.3.

Note that the node labels are only added for reasons of clarity. Since nodes are not expected to be self-connected (i.e., $l_{i,i} = 0$), the main diagonal of an adjacency matrix is filled with zeros. In the directed network, node 3 connects to node 2 (i.e., $l_{3,2} = 1$) while node 2 is not connected to node 3 (i.e., $l_{2,3} = 0$) both of which are shown in bold in Figure 6.3a. The undirected network, however, ignores the direction of a link and it must hold that $l_{3,2} = l_{2,3} = 1$. Since $l_{i,j} = l_{j,i}$ for all links in such a network, the adjacency matrix of an undirected network must be symmetric, in other words, the values are mirrored along its main diagonal.

The adjacency matrices in Figure 6.3 tell us which node is directly linked to another node. Yet, we can use the matrix to determine which node is connected to another node after a certain number of steps. The nodes that can be reached after two steps are given by $GG = G^2$. Hence, G^k shows the nodes that can be reached after k steps. Figure 6.4 presents the square and cube of the two adjacency matrices of the directed and undirected network. The first element of the adjacency matrix in Figure 6.4a shows that there are two options to reach node 1 from itself in two steps in the directed network, and indeed, we can go from 1 to 4 and back and from 1 to 2 and back. There is only one way for 3 to reach 2 (i.e., via 1) and no way to reach itself within two steps, nor any number of steps for that matter, since no link is leading to 3. Consequently, the value is also empty in G^3 of the directed network. However, in the undirected network, two options exist to reach 3 in two steps ($3 \to 1 \to 3$ and $3 \to 2 \to 3$) and as well as in three steps ($3 \to 1 \to 2 \to 3$ and $3 \to 2 \to 1 \to 3$).[1]

$$\begin{array}{c} \quad 1\ 2\ 3\ 4 \\ \begin{array}{c}1\\2\\3\\4\end{array} \begin{pmatrix} 0 & 1 & 0 & 1 \\ 1 & 0 & 0 & 0 \\ 1 & 1 & 0 & 0 \\ 1 & 0 & 0 & 0 \end{pmatrix} \end{array} \qquad \begin{array}{c} \quad 1\ 2\ 3\ 4 \\ \begin{array}{c}1\\2\\3\\4\end{array} \begin{pmatrix} 0 & 1 & 1 & 1 \\ 1 & 0 & 1 & 0 \\ 1 & 1 & 0 & 0 \\ 1 & 0 & 0 & 0 \end{pmatrix} \end{array}$$

(a) directed network (b) undirected network

Figure 6.3: Adjacency Matrix of the directed and undirected network.

$$\begin{pmatrix} 2 & 0 & 0 & 0 \\ 0 & 1 & 0 & 1 \\ 1 & 1 & 0 & 1 \\ 0 & 1 & 0 & 1 \end{pmatrix} \qquad \begin{pmatrix} 0 & 2 & 0 & 2 \\ 2 & 0 & 0 & 0 \\ 2 & 1 & 0 & 1 \\ 2 & 0 & 0 & 0 \end{pmatrix} \qquad \begin{pmatrix} 3 & 1 & 1 & 0 \\ 1 & 2 & 1 & 1 \\ 1 & 1 & 2 & 1 \\ 0 & 1 & 1 & 1 \end{pmatrix} \qquad \begin{pmatrix} 2 & 4 & 4 & 3 \\ 4 & 2 & 3 & 1 \\ 4 & 3 & 2 & 1 \\ 3 & 1 & 1 & 0 \end{pmatrix}$$

(a) directed G^2 (b) directed G^3 (c) undirected G^2 (d) undirected G^3

Figure 6.4: The square and cube of the adjacency matrices in Figure 6.3.

Exercise 6.1

(a) Determine the adjacency matrix G for each of the graphs in Figure 6.1. Keep in mind that all three graphs are undirected. (b) What are the general characteristics of G if the graph is complete?

We say that element $g_{i,j}^k$ in G^k computes the number of walks of length k between node i and node j. A **walk** is a sequence of steps along linked nodes between any two nodes i and j in network g. Based on the previous discussion, we can see that its length is simply the number of links that lie on this walk. A walk composed of distinctive links is called a **trail** and a trail composed of distinctive nodes is called a **path**.[2] The **shortest path** between two nodes i and j is simply the path with the fewest number of links. If any two nodes of a graph are linked via a path, the graph is **connected**, otherwise it is **disconnected**. We can refine this definition further for directed graphs. If a path between any two nodes of a directed graph exists in any two directions (i.e., any node can be reached from any other node), the directed graph is considered to be **strongly connected**. If the latter is not the case, the graph is either **weakly connected**, if any nodes can be reached under the assumption that the direction of a link is irrelevant (i.e., we transform the directed graph into an undirected graph) or disconnected (i.e., such a transformation still does not render all nodes accessible). Any sub-graph of an undirected graph that contains all the nodes that are directly or indirectly connected via a path is a **(connected) component** of g. If, for example, g has n nodes with $n - 1$ nodes being connected and the remaining node has a degree of zero, graph g has two components. If the sub-graph comprises only connected nodes in a directed graph, we call it a **strongly connected component**. If any two nodes in the sub-graph are only connected if we ignore the direction of a link, we term it a **weakly connected component** of g.

By definition, a path can never lead back to a node whereas a trail can do so under the condition that a link is not used twice. In this case, a trail is called a **cycle** since the starting and end node are identical. If a connected undirected graph has no cycles, i.e., the path between any two nodes is unique, we call it a **tree**. We have seen an example of a tree (in this case, a game tree) in (2.7) in Chapter 2.

Exercise 6.2

(a) Show that the path between any two nodes in a tree is unique. (b) How can the adjacency matrix G be used to determine whether a graph is connected?

In order to better understand the attributes of a social network, we analyse both its local characteristics, which study the individual qualities of a node or link, as well as its global characteristics, which look at the network as a whole but are partially derived from individual measures. The basic local characteristics help us identify the most influential or central actors in a social network.

In a directed graph, we separate between **out-neighbours** of some node i, who are those nodes that have a link coming from i and her **in-neighbours**, whose links point towards i. Formally, we define out-neighbours as $N_i^d(g) = \{k \in N | l_{ik} = 1\}$ which means that the set of outgoing neighbours of a node i is composed of all those nodes in the set of nodes N that have a link from i to themselves. In-neighbours are given by $N_{-i}^d(g) = \{k \in N | l_{ki} = 1\}$. Note that the definitions only differ with respect to the direction of the link (i.e., $l_{ik} = 1$ for out-neighbours instead of $l_{ki} = 1$ for in-neighbours).

Since an undirected graph ignores the direction of a link and therefore, $l_{ik} = l_{ki}$, the set of in-neighbours is identical to the set of out-neighbours, and we just speak of **neighbours** in this context. It suffices to define the set of neighbours in an undirected graph identically to the set of out-neighbours as $N_i(g) = \{k \in N | l_{ik} = 1\}$. The number of neighbours of i in an undirected graph is

$$\eta_i(g) = |N_i(g)| = \sum_{k=1}^{n} l_{ik} \tag{6.2}$$

and we call $\eta_i(g)$ the **degree** of node i. Equivalently, we can define the **out-degree** and **in-degree** of node i, respectively, as

$$\eta_i^d(g) = |N_i^d(g)| = \sum_{k=1}^{n} l_{ik}$$

$$\eta_{-i}^d(g) = |N_{-i}^d(g)| = \sum_{k=1}^{n} l_{ki} \tag{6.3}$$

The degree (as well as in-degree and out-degree) of node i can range between 0 (i.e., i is unconnected) to $n - 1$ (i.e., i is connected to all other nodes in g). If all nodes of a network have the same degree, we call this graph a **regular graph** while a regular *directed* graph is composed of nodes that have the same in-degree as well as out-degree. The complete network in Figure 6.1b and the circle in Figure 6.1c are examples of a regular network.

> **Exercise 6.3**
>
> Show that in any graph g, there is an even number of odd degree nodes.

Using a graph's adjacency matrix, we can directly determine the in-degree and out-degree of node i. The sum of elements of the *column* vector at position i defines the former and the sum of the elements in the *row* vector at i the latter. Looking at Figure 6.3a, the in-degree of node 1 is 3 and of node 3 is 0, while their out-degrees are both 2 (use Figure 6.2a to double-check). Since the adjacency matrix of an undirected graph is symmetric, it is of no importance if we take the sum of the values of a column vector or the corresponding row vector. We have $\eta_1(g) = 3$ and $\eta_3(g) = 2$ (use Figures 6.3b and 6.2b to check the result).

The following applies to all three degree types alike, but to keep the exposition concise, I will focus on the undirected network. The **degree distribution** of graph g is a vector whose elements are given by the fraction of nodes with a degree j, i.e., by $P(j) = n_j/n$ where n_j defines the number of nodes with degree j. Note that the fractions need to sum to 1. Summing the elements of each row vector of the adjacency matrix in Figure 6.3b returns $\{3, 2, 2, 1\}$ and the total number of nodes is $n = 4$. The degree distribution for the simple example in Figure 6.2b is therefore $P = (0, 1/4, 1/2, 1/4, 0, \dots, 0)$, i.e. one node each with a degree of 1 and 3, and two nodes with a degree of 2.

We can define the **average degree** in a network g either on the basis of the individual degree of each node or the degree distribution,

$$\bar{\eta}(g) = \frac{1}{n}\sum_{k=0}^{n-1} \eta_k(g) = \sum_{j=0}^{n-1} P(j)j \tag{6.4}$$

Using our example, we have $(3+2+2+1)/4 = 2$ using the first approach, and $1/4 \times 1 + 1/2 \times 2 + 1/4 \times 3 = 2$ using the second approach.

The **(geodesic) distance** $d(k, j)$ between nodes k and j is given by the length (i.e., the number of steps) of their shortest path. If no path between k and j exists, we assume that their distance is infinite. The **eccentricity** of node k measures how far k is from the most distant node in g, i.e.,

$$\varepsilon(k) = \max_{i \in N} d(k, i) \tag{6.5}$$

In Figure 6.2b, the shortest path between nodes 4 and 2 is $(4 \rightarrow 1 \rightarrow 2)$ and thus, their distance is 2, which is also each nodes' eccentricity.

The **radius** of g is the minimum eccentricity of any node in g

$$r = \min_{k \in N} \varepsilon(k) \tag{6.6}$$

A **central node** j has the minimum eccentricity of any node in g, i.e., $\varepsilon(j) = r$, while the **diameter** of the network is the maximum eccentricity across all nodes

$$d = \max_{k \in N} \varepsilon(k) \tag{6.7}$$

Thus, if on the contrary, node j has an eccentricity equal to the network diameter, i.e., $\varepsilon(j) = d$, it is a **peripheral node**. The average distance from any node k to all other nodes in g can be simply calculated as

$$\bar{d}_k = \frac{1}{n-1}\sum_{j=1}^{n} d(k, j) \tag{6.8}$$

The **characteristic path length** of graph g is then

$$\bar{d} = \frac{1}{n}\sum_{k=1}^{n} \bar{d}_k = \frac{1}{n(n-1)}\sum_{k=1}^{n}\sum_{j=1}^{n} d(k, j) \tag{6.9}$$

In other words, the characteristic path length is the average of the individual average distance of a node to any other node on the graph.

The **density** of g is defined as the ratio of its size over the maximum size of a network of the same order. We have seen that a complete network has the maximum number of links, given by $n(n-1)/2$ for an undirected graph and $n(n-1)$ for a directed graph. The density of g is thus defined as

$$D = \frac{2|L|}{n(n-1)} \text{ for an undirected graph}$$

$$D = \frac{|L|}{n(n-1)} \text{ for a directed graph}$$

(6.10)

i.e., the size of graph g with n nodes divided by the number of links of a complete graph with the same number of nodes.[3]

6.3   Centralities

Based on the nodes' individual characteristics, we can evaluate their importance in a network. These indicators of importance are not unique but depend on what we consider relevant for our analysis. Each of the **centrality measures** focuses on a particular element of importance.

Degree Centrality

The most straightforward and probably easiest centrality measure is **degree centrality**. As the name indicates, degree centrality assesses a node's status in terms of its degree (i.e., its number of links). We define the degree centrality of node k as

$$C_D(k) = \eta_k(g)$$

(6.11)

Commonly, degree centrality is expressed in terms of the maximum possible degree in the network. Remember that a network is composed of n nodes and thus, the maximum possible degree is given by $n-1$ illustrating the case that the node connects to all other nodes in the graph. The normalised degree centrality of node k is simply

$$C_{\tilde{D}}(k) = \frac{\eta_k(g)}{n-1}$$

(6.12)

In a directed network, degree centrality extends in a straightforward manner. We define the in-degree centrality on the basis of a node's in-degree and correspondingly, the node's out-degree centrality is derived by using the out-degree in equations (6.11) or (6.12). Node 1 in Figure 6.2b has a degree centrality of $C_D(1) = 3$ while it has an in-degree centrality of $C_D^d(-1) = 3$ and an out-degree centrality of $C_D^d(1) = 2$ in the directed graph in Figure 6.2a. The normalised degree centrality is simply equal to the previous values divided by 3.

We can further extend this concept to the level of the entire graph. The **degree centralisation** of a graph g is defined as the cumulative difference between the node with the highest degree centrality and the degree centrality of all other nodes in g relative to the maximum possible centralisation. That may sound confusing but we will take this measure step-by-step.

Remember that the maximum possible degree in a connected network is $n-1$ while the minimum possible degree is 1. Thus, the maximum possible centralisation is obtained in a network in which all nodes are connected to a central node, i.e., a star. The difference in degree centrality of the central node and any other node in this type of network is $(n-1)-1 = (n-2)$. There are $n-1$ other nodes in the network. The difference between the degree centrality of the central node and itself is obviously 0. Consequently, the normalised cumulative difference of the star network relative to the maximum attainable normalised degree is $(n-1)(n-2)/(n-1) = n-2$. Take the star network in Figure 6.1a. The graph has $n=7$ nodes, the maximum degree is equal to the central node's degree centrality of 6, and the 6 other nodes have a degree centrality of 1. For the star, we have therefore a difference of six times $(6-1)$, giving us $6(6-1)/6$ as a normalised difference.

Let i^* be the node with the highest degree centrality in g. Taking the former result into account to determine the denominator, the degree centralisation of any g is

$$C_D(g) = \frac{\sum\limits_{k=1}^{n} (C_D(i^*) - C_D(k))}{(n-1)(n-2)} = \frac{\sum\limits_{k=1}^{n} (C_{\tilde{D}}(i^*) - C_{\tilde{D}}(k))}{n-2} \qquad (6.13)$$

We have seen that node 1 in Figure 6.2b has the highest degree centrality in the graph, which is equal $C_D(1) = 3$. Applying equation (6.13) to the graph in Figure 6.2b leads to

$$C_D(6.2b) = \frac{(3-2)+(3-2)+(3-1)}{(4-2)(4-1)} = \frac{2}{3}$$

Exercise 6.4

Show that the degree centralisation of a star is always equal to 1, and the degree centralisation of any regular network is 0.

Betweenness Centrality

Degree centrality ignores the specificities of a network's topology and assumes that the importance of a node is entirely defined by its level of connectedness. We can think of several instances in which such an approach does not identify the most important node of a network. For example, we can think of a situation in which a small number of groups exchange information via a middleman. The latter is crucially important for the flow of information but may only be connected to one or two members of each group. Consequently, degree centrality will not identify the most important member in such a network. In this case, we can measure the importance of a node by looking at the frequency at which the shortest paths between any two nodes in the network make use of a node.

Let the total number of shortest paths from any node i to some other node j be $\sigma_{i,j}$ and let the number of shortest paths passing through node k be $\sigma_{i,j}(k)$. The **betweenness centrality** is defined as[4]

$$C_B(k) = \sum_{i \neq k \in N} \sum_{j \neq k \in N} \frac{\sigma_{i,j}(k)}{\sigma_{i,j}} \qquad (6.14)$$

We can normalise the betweenness centrality measure by dividing (6.14) by the number of pairings, excluding node k, that exist in a network. The number of pairings is $(n-1)(n-2)$ in a directed network and half of that number in an undirected network since the direction of the path is irrelevant in the latter case. This can be seen by looking at the star in Figure 6.1a: a peripheral node can connect to $n-2=5$ other peripheral nodes. Since there are $n-1=6$ peripheral nodes, the number of paths is 30. However, since a shortest path from any node i to a node j is equivalent to a shortest from j to i, the shortest paths are counted twice. We therefore obtain 15 paths in the undirected star. The normalised betweenness centrality of node k is

$$C_B^d(k) = \sum_{i\neq k\in N}\sum_{j\neq k\in N}\frac{\sigma_{i,j}(k)}{\sigma_{i,j}}\frac{1}{(n-1)(n-2)} \text{ for directed graphs}$$

$$C_{\tilde{B}}(k) = \sum_{i\neq k\in N}\sum_{j\neq k\in N}\frac{\sigma_{i,j}(k)}{\sigma_{i,j}}\frac{2}{(n-1)(n-2)} \text{ for undirected graphs}$$

(6.15)

Looking at the graph in Figure 6.2b again, and excluding any shortest path initiating or terminating at node 1, we can see that the undirected graph has three different shortest paths ($2\leftrightarrow 3, 2\leftrightarrow 4$, $3\leftrightarrow 4$). The latter two shortest path travel via node 1 and we thus, obtain a betweenness centrality for node 1 equal to

$$C_B(1) = \frac{\sigma_{2,3}(k)}{\sigma_{2,3}} + \frac{\sigma_{2,4}(k)}{\sigma_{2,4}} + \frac{\sigma_{3,4}(k)}{\sigma_{3,4}} = \frac{0}{1}+\frac{1}{1}+\frac{1}{1} = 2$$

(6.16)

In the directed network of Figure 6.2a, four shortest paths exist that do not have node 1 as a starting or final node (i.e., $2\rightarrow 4, 3\rightarrow 2, 3\rightarrow 4, 4\rightarrow 2$), leading to

$$C_B^d(1) = \frac{\sigma_{2,4}(k)}{\sigma_{2,4}} + \frac{\sigma_{3,2}(k)}{\sigma_{3,2}} + \frac{\sigma_{3,4}(k)}{\sigma_{3,4}} + \frac{\sigma_{4,2}(k)}{\sigma_{4,2}} = \frac{1}{1}+\frac{0}{1}+\frac{1}{1}+\frac{1}{1} = 3$$

(6.17)

Exercise 6.5

Show that all other nodes, both in the directed network and the undirected network in Figure 6.2, have a betweenness centrality of 0. Why is this the case?

Closeness Centrality

In addition to her level of connectedness and the role she plays for establishing connections, an individual's importance is also defined by how closely she is placed to any other individual within the social network. While betweenness centrality measures how well an individual serves as a bridge between other members of a social network, **closeness centrality** evaluates how central her position is. As before, we defined the geodesic distance (i.e. the length of the shortest path) between two nodes i and j by $d(i,j)$. The closeness centrality of a node k is

$$C_C(k) = \frac{1}{\sum_{i\neq k}d(i,k)}$$

(6.18)

In other words, closeness centrality is defined as the reciprocal of the total distance from all other nodes in g to node k. Thus, the node with the closest proximity to all other nodes has the highest closeness centrality. The normalised closeness centrality is obtained by multiplying equation (6.18) by the smallest possible aggregate distance $n - 1$ and is given by

$$C_{\tilde{C}}(k) = \frac{n-1}{\sum\limits_{i \neq k} d(i,k)} \tag{6.19}$$

For the graph in Figure 6.2b, we obtain

$$C_{\tilde{C}}(1) = \frac{3}{1+1+1} = 1 \text{ and}$$

$$C_{\tilde{C}}(2) = 3/4, C_{\tilde{C}}(3) = 3/4, C_{\tilde{C}}(4) = 3/5$$

You may realise that this definition of closeness centrality can impose some problems if it is applied to a weakly connected directed graph or an unconnected graph. Node 3 in the graph of Figure 6.2a is not reachable, leading to a distance of infinity. To solve this issue, we assume that $1/\infty = 0$. Consequently, isolated notes have a closeness centrality of zero. We then redefine the closeness centrality for a directed graph as

$$C_{\hat{C}}(k) = \frac{\rho}{\sum\limits_{i \neq k} d(i,k)} \tag{6.20}$$

with ρ being equal to the number of nodes connected to k via a path from i. For the graph in Figure 6.2a, the redefined closeness centralities are

$$C_{\hat{C}}(1) = 1, C_{\hat{C}}(2) = 3/4, C_{\hat{C}}(3) = 0, C_{\hat{C}}(4) = 3/5$$

Alternatively, we can make use of the **harmonic centrality** as suggested by Dekker (2005) and Rochat (2009)

$$C_H(k) = \sum\limits_{i \neq k} \frac{1}{d(k,i)} \tag{6.21}$$

This looks rather similar to the definition of the closeness centrality in equation (6.18), but there are two differences. Instead of summing over all distances and then taking the reciprocal, the harmonic centrality is calculated by summing the reciprocals of the distances.[5] In addition, the direction of the distances is inverted. Instead of considering the paths from any other node to some node k, we consider the inverse paths starting at k. The difference is irrelevant if the graph is undirected but will obviously change results in a directed graph.[6] The normalised version of the harmonic centrality is then equivalently given by

$$C_{\hat{H}}(k) = \frac{1}{n-1} \sum\limits_{i \neq k} \frac{1}{d(k,i)} \tag{6.22}$$

For the directed graph in Figure 6.2a, we have

$$C_{\hat{H}}(1) = \frac{1}{3} \left(\frac{1}{1} + \frac{1}{\infty} + \frac{1}{1} \right) = 2/3 \text{ and,}$$

$$C_{\hat{H}}(2) = 1/2, C_{\hat{H}}(3) = 5/6, C_{\hat{H}}(4) = 1/2$$

The harmonic centralities for the undirected graph in Figure 6.2b are

$$C_{\hat{H}}(1) = 1, C_{\hat{H}}(2) = 5/6, C_{\hat{H}}(3) = 5/6, C_{\hat{H}}(4) = 2/3$$

Other Centralities

Instead of considering only the immediate neighbours of a node, we might be interested in the quality of these neighbours in the sense of their respective importance within the network. A person might be highly connected, but these connections themselves are of rather little importance in the network. In contrast, another person might have only a few connections, but these connections take a central role in the network and are highly influential. Consequently, it does not only matter to know a lot of people but who you know. Other types of centrality therefore generalise the degree centrality measure, but instead of considering only the direct neighbours of a node, **Katz centrality**, **eigenvector centrality**, **Bonacich's power centrality** and **PageRank centrality** address this issue by considering the nodes connected to these neighbours, and so on.

We will only cover the general ideas behind these centralities: Katz centrality acknowledges all nodes that are accessible from a node but weighs the importance of a distant node according to a weighing factor $\alpha^{d(k,i)}$ with $\alpha \in (0,1)$ and exponent $d(k,i)$ being the distance between node k and i. Eigenvector centrality (or eigencentrality) considers the connectedness of the neighbours of a node k, as well as the connectedness of their neighbours, and so forth. Bonacich (1987) proposed an extension of the degree centrality that combines two opposing elements: centrality and power. If a node's neighbours are themselves highly connected, the node is central, but her neighbours can easily revert to other neighbours to influence the network, while if her neighbours have only a small degree, she is powerful since her neighbours depend on her. PageRank centrality extends eigenvector centrality by taking into account the direction of a link and its weight. Note that these are only the most common forms of centrality measures, and numerous other centralities have been developed in recent years.[7]

The extension of degree centrality to the network level, as we have seen in equation (6.13), can be generalised and applied to any type of centrality. Let $C_x(k)$ be the centrality measure of node k and let $Cx(i^*)$ be the node with the highest such measure in g. We further define $\mathscr{G}$ as the collection of all possible graphs with n nodes and let

$$\hat{D}_x = \max_{g' \in \mathscr{G}} \left[\sum_{k=1}^{n} (C_x(i;g') - C_x(k;g')) \right]$$

be the largest sum of differences for centrality C_x for any network with the same order. The **(Freeman) centralisation** for network g is given by

$$C_x(g) = \frac{\sum_{k=1}^{n} (C_x(i^*;g) - C_x(k;g))}{\hat{D}_x} \tag{6.23}$$

We have seen before that the maximum difference in degree centrality is obtained in a star for which we obtain $\hat{D}_D = (n-1)(n-2)$. Substituting the latter in equation (6.23) returns equation (6.13).

A star also maximises the sum of the differences for closeness centrality. The aggregate difference of the closeness centralities, in this case, is equal to $\hat{D}_C = (n-2)/(2n-3)$, and the **closeness centralisation** can be written as

$$C_C(g) = \frac{2n-3}{n-2} \sum_{k=1}^{n} (C_C(i^*) - C_C(k)) = \frac{2n-3}{(n-2)(n-1)} \sum_{k=1}^{n} (C_{\tilde{C}}(i^*) - C_{\tilde{C}}(k)) \tag{6.24}$$

Show that the aggregate difference between the central node in a star and the other nodes is indeed equal to $\hat{D}_C = (n-2)/(2n-3)$ for the closeness centrality and $\hat{D}_{C\tilde{x}} = (n-2)(n-1)/(2n-3)$ for the normalised closeness centrality. To show this, proceed in a manner that is analogous to our previous discussion of degree centralisation.

So far, I mainly focused on the individual characteristics of nodes to identify the most central and influential members of a social network. We are also interested in determining whether a network exhibits particular groups that interact more strongly within a network. While a social network may be composed of only a single component, and thus all members are either directly or indirectly connected, some sub-graphs can form more tightly connected communities.

The probably easiest community detection measure is a **clique**. A clique is formed by a subset of nodes and their respective links if any two nodes in this subset are directly connected. Consequently, a clique forms a sub-graph of g that is complete, i.e., everybody in the clique is connected to everybody else. For example, nodes 1, 2, and 3 in the undirected graph of Figure 6.2b form a clique.

A triplet is formed by three nodes that are either connected by two undirected links (an **open triplet**) or three undirected links (a **closed triplet**). The **global clustering coefficient** is then the fraction of closed paths of length two over all paths of length two or

$$C = \frac{\text{number of closed triplets}}{\text{number of open and closed triplets}} \tag{6.25}$$

It is therefore a measure of *triadic closure*. In simple terms, two members of a social network who are connected to the same individual tend also to form a connection between each other to achieve cognitive balance (Heider, 1946; Granovetter, 1973). The undirected graph of Figure 6.2b has three closed triplets ($2 \to 1 \leftarrow 3$, $1 \to 2 \leftarrow 3$, $1 \to 3 \leftarrow 2$) and two open triplets ($4 \to 1 \leftarrow 3$ and $4 \to 1 \leftarrow 2$). Hence, the global clustering coefficient for this graph is $3/5$.

Another immensely insightful measure is **modularity**. In simple terms, we measure how much the number of links in a particular sub-graph (i.e., a group) differs from a fictitious sub-graph of the same order and degree distribution in which all nodes are connected randomly. In other words, modularity provides us with a measure of how likely a community of members in a social network is not connected by mere chance. The modularity of a community (or partition) of network g is given by (for details, refer to Newman (2006) and the Appendix A.7).

$$Q(c) = \frac{1}{2m} \sum_{ik} \left(G_{ik} - \frac{\eta_i(g)\eta_k(g)}{2m} \right) \delta(c_i, c_k) \tag{6.26}$$

with $\delta(c_i, c_k)$ being an indicator function that has a value of one if the community of node i, given by c_i, is equal to the community of k, given by c_k and zero otherwise, thus summing only over the nodes that we consider to be in the same community. Consequently, modularity provides us with a measure of how likely a selected set of members in a network is connected through reasons other than chance and hence, form a distinctive community within the social network. By splitting a network into communities that maximise equation (6.26), we can identify the community structure of a graph.

Blondel et al. (2008) suggested an efficient algorithm to identify communities. The algorithm follows an iterated two-step approach. In the first step, each individual node of a network is initially assigned its own individual community. The algorithm then calculates the increase in modularity of a node, if some other node i is added to the community of the former. Node i is moved to the community that experienced the largest positive increase in modularity. This step is repeated for all nodes until a shift of a node to another community no longer leads to a positive increase in modularity for any community. In the second step, the nodes of each community are recombined into a singular node, thus forming a new and condensed network. Links between two nodes in this new network bear a weight that is equal to the number of links that connect the members in the original network who are now condensed into a singular node.[8] Step 1 then follows step 2 and the sequence is reiterated as long as the algorithm produces a positive increase in modularity. The algorithm is known as the **Louvain method**.

6.4   Application

In the following, I will apply our knowledge to study power relations and activism in graphs of different sizes. The network centrality measures identify influential and central actors while modularity detects communities of tightly connected members within a network. These are efficient techniques to analyse the political and economic power relations in formal and informal networks and help us better understand the historic rise of single individuals. For example, Padgett and Ansell (1993) studied the political and economic influence of early Renaissance Florentine families to determine the factors leading to the rise of the Medici. Applying the previously discussed centrality measures explains the sudden emergence of this particular family on the political stage of the Republic of Florence. Strategic alliances, and partnerships as well as intermarriages played a vital role in their ascension to power. But it was not only the number of connections but also the quality of these connections that paved the way for their coming to power in the 15th century. Social network analysis can reveal remarkable insights into historic socio-economic phenomena.

At the same time, organically grown social networks illustrate properties that render the exchange of information in network of substantial order particularly efficient and at the same time, robust against external interventions. Social network analysis identifies the elements that determine a network's robustness and its weak points. For example, individuals can occupy a critical position as they lie on various shortest paths between different members and their removal from the network would severely disrupt the flow of information. Yet, at the same time, networks can exhibit numerous redundancies and the shortest paths between individuals are not unique. The presence of a particular individual thus becomes inessential for the exchange of information in the network.

Political Power Play in Feudal Japan

I will commence our analysis by turning to the study of historical networks. We will study a small network based on James Clavell's novel *Shōgun*. While the novel does not offer a entirely historically correct and neutral account of feudal Japan, the characters and events are based on existing historical figures and the novel offers a broadly correct version of the events surrounding

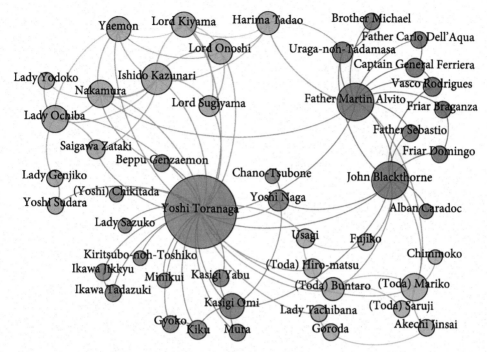

Figure 6.5: Shōgun network showing degree centrality and modularity.

Tokugawa Ieyasu and William Adams.[9] The simple network is therefore not just an illustrative proof of concept but demonstrates the strengths of social network analysis for historical and political analyses in addition to being an efficient means to studying prose narratives.

Figure 6.5 shows the small network composed of 49 main characters connected by 96 links.[10] Obviously, ambiguity about what constitutes a connection between two characters exists, such as whether an antagonistic relationship should be represented by a link. Additional complications arise due to shifting alliances. I have therefore decided to illustrate any type of relation by a link, but the following results are robust to marginal changes in the network structure. The size of a node shows its relative degree centrality and the colour shows its community based on the Louvain method. We can see that the two main characters, Yoshi Toranaga (Tokugawa) and John Blackthorn (Adams), as well as Blackthorn's part-time teacher and main antagonist Father Alvito are most strongly connected. Since the story mainly centres around these characters, their high centrality degree is no surprise. Yet more remarkably, the Louvain method correctly identified the novel's different factions without any additional information but purely based on the network topology. The green group is composed of the Toranaga's Japanese rivals and enemies. Toranaga's own faction is shown in violet and characters linked to Mariko, whose loyalty is torn between Blackthorn and Toranaga constitute the blue faction. The remaining faction shown in orange consists of the foreigners who follow their own political and economic agenda.

Toranaga illustrates the highest centrality value across all measures confirming his unique standing in the network and his ability to form persuasive political alliances. This does not hold for other characters. Figure 6.5 focuses on the direct connections between characters but ignores

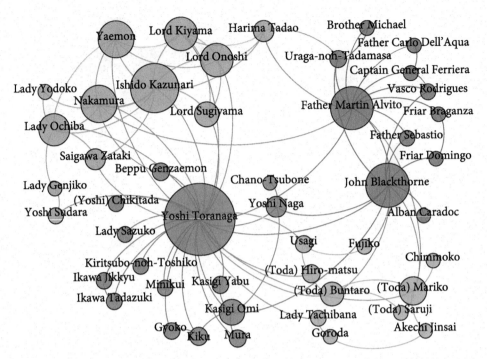

Figure 6.6: Shōgun network showing eigenvector centrality and modularity.

the quality of these connections. Toranaga's main antagonist Ishido does not seem to play any vital role. While his relatively low degree centrality does not identify him as a crucial political force, his relatively few ties with other network members are mainly caused by the story's limited focus on his character. Yet, if we look at the quality of the political ties between characters, the image changes. Ishido takes a central role in the network based on the character's eigenvector centrality scores. This is visualised in Figure 6.6, which expresses a node's eigenvector centrality by its size. While Toranaga has an eigenvector centrality of 1, Ishido has the second highest score of 0.49. Remember that the eigenvector centrality is a generalisation of the degree centrality that takes into account the degree of a node's neighbours as well as their neighbours' degree and so on. Being linked to highly connected neighbours leads to a higher score even if the node itself has only a few connections. The higher centrality score reflects Ishido's ability to form alliances with powerful political actors in the novel and thus act as the principal political foe of the novel.

This simple network analysis shows that no single optimal centrality measure exists to determine a member's political influence and power. Consequently, there is no hierarchy between the various centrality measures for the topological study of a network, but these measures operate in conjunction.

The Small-World Networks in the Middle East

With the creation of social network sites during the first decade of this century, our practices of forming social rapports, communicating with peers, and spreading information have changed significantly. The consumption of news and information has increasingly shifted from more classical news outlets, such as newspapers and news on public television, to news and entertainment websites and especially social media. While this development has made it difficult for the average person to discern unsubstantiated claims from validated facts, it has also allowed for a decentralised and mostly unsupervised communication.

It is therefore no surprise that social media like Facebook, Twitter, and Instagram have become powerful tools for political activism and social movements. Since the Arab Spring in 2010, individuals have become politically active on Twitter and Facebook where social movements have gathered momentum before the latter turned into widespread non-virtual protests. On the one hand, political activism on social media can make it easier not only for scholars but also for state organisations to study the topology and size of the network without the need to physically infiltrate the system, allowing them to identify members more easily. In addition, control of large hubs can be used to diffuse misinformation. On the other hand, numerous advantages offset these risks and social online movements demonstrate structures that differ from more orthodox ways of political activism. We will see that these networks are characterised by a small diameter and eccentricity as well as a low degree centrality of most members. Consequently, while most members are only directly connected to a small share of other members, the geodesic distance between any two members remains small (a property that came to be known as **small-world networks**). This topology creates a polyarchal hierarchy in which, in addition to no longer being restricted to physical contact, information can reach any member quickly and efficiently. Furthermore, the small distance between members implies a significant redundancy in shortest paths between them. The exchange of information thus does no longer critically depend on a few intercalated individuals, and communication between any two members is not disrupted if a few individuals leave the network. Furthermore, a single member can only identify the small group of nearest neighbours but has no direct contact with most members in the network. Besides the option to discard one's identity and physical characteristics, the decentralised structure of networks on social media can offer activists considerable protection against persecution.

My co-author and I analysed the social networks that are formed by Middle Eastern secularists in the aftermath of the Arab Spring. Secularists use social media to escape peer pressure and social exclusion that voicing their religious views would entail. Although secularist groups and pages on Facebook form networks that drastically vary in terms of order, from a few hundred members to several hundred thousand, the diameter and the density of these networks are mostly small. For example, the largest network we studied is composed of 300 thousand nodes and has a diameter of 4 and a density of 0.

In the following, we will have a closer look at a medium-sized network composed of $4,622$ nodes and $18,713$ links. The graph has been constructed from the past 999 threads on the Facebook page. A node represents either a user or a post. Whenever a user initiates a post or responds to a post, a link is formed between the user and the post, but not between users. Users who answer to a post and are thus part of the same thread are indirectly connected through the node that defines the initial post. We may therefore think of an individual thread as a star network. However, since a user can answer multiple posts, the former interconnects to the latter. The network hence takes the form of 999 interconnected stars.

Let $\mathfrak{N}$ be the set of types of nodes and $\mathfrak{J}$ the set of types of links. If the network is composed of multiple types of nodes or links (i.e., $|\mathfrak{N}| > 1$, or $|\mathfrak{J}| > 1$), these links and nodes form a

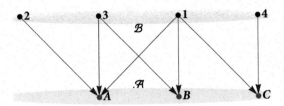

Figure 6.7: Sample of a bipartite graph whose projection corresponds to Figure 6.2b. Set $\mathcal{A}$ corresponds to posts and set $\mathcal{B}$ to users.

heterogeneous graph. Otherwise (i.e., $|\mathfrak{N}| = 1$, or $|\mathfrak{I}| = 1$), the social network is a **homogeneous graph**. Since nodes can be either users or posts, the graph is heterogeneous. Furthermore, users are only connected to posts but not to other users. Let $\mathcal{A}$ and $\mathcal{B}$ be the set of posts and users, respectively. The two sets are independent and disjoint. Any node in $\mathcal{B}$ connects to a node in $\mathcal{A}$, but no link connects nodes of the same set. We call such a graph **bipartite**. Figure 6.7 illustrates a simplified example of a directed bipartite graph. Node 1 in set $\mathcal{B}$ is linked to all nodes in set $\mathcal{A}$. Consequently, the graph has only one component since all nodes are either directly or indirectly connected.

Similarly, for the secularist graph, the 3, 623 users are connected via posts but no user is directly connected to another user. Indeed, we can interpret the network both as a directed and an undirected graph. The nature in which we choose to represent a bipartite graph depends on the context we are interested in and the information we intend to extract from the graph analysis. A directed graph implies that a user connects to a post by writing a comment. Thus, a directed link leads from a user node to a post node. This representation suggests a hierarchy among the two types of nodes - posts act as the central focus of communication. While some measures, such as in-degree and out-degree, are symmetric and it therefore does not matter whether a link extends from a user to a post or the opposite, other measures are severely affected by the form in which we represent the graph. The shortest paths can only be calculated along the direction of links and hence the geodesic distance between two nodes is either one or infinite. The former is only the case on a path from a user to a post while the latter holds for the inverse path and for any two nodes that are of the same type. Centrality measures, such as betweenness and closeness can therefore not offer any helpful insight.

It is therefore often-times easier to consider the connections between the type of nodes as symmetric, i.e., a post connects to a user as much as a user connects to a post. If at least some users respond to a sufficiently large variety of posts, the undirected bipartite graph has only a single component and geodesic distances are finite. This case also holds for the graph we study here.

We first concentrate on the directed bipartite graph. Figure 6.8a depicts its out-degree distribution. We can see that the vast majority of the degrees are concentrated within the single-digit range. Yet, this representation is not particularly meaningful since the graph drops off rapidly after three degrees. In these cases, the degree distribution is better presented in a *double logarithmic plot* or *log-log scale*. In other words, both the ordinate, showing the relative frequency, and the abscissa, showing the degree, do not scale linearly but exponentially at a base of 10, as shown in Figure 6.8b.[11] In the log-log scale, we can see that the degree distribution is approximately linear up to a degree of 30. This linear pattern in log-log scale does not occur by chance and we will have a closer look at the reasons in the following section, but for the moment, I focus on the implications. Approximately 40 percent of the nodes are connected to only a single neighbour. Nodes with a

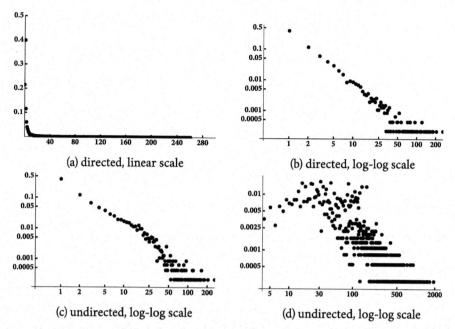

Figure 6.8: (a) and (b) show the out-degree distribution of the bipartite graph. (c) show the degree distribution of the undirected version of the bipartite graph, and (d) shows degree distribution of the unipartite projection.

higher number of neighbours occur significantly more sporadically as their degree increases and only a few nodes are connected to a vast number of other nodes. The highest degree centrality score is 261, but the share of nodes with a degree exceeding 20 is only 3 percent in the directed graph. The network is therefore composed of a majority of nodes that are only weakly connected and a small number of highly connected activists.

A very similar pattern can be observed for the undirected bipartite graph, shown in Figure 6.8c. The degree distribution as well as the previously discussed statistics remain roughly identical. While this type of distribution implies that deleting a randomly chosen node does not affect the network topology on average and thus the flow of information, it also indicates that informational exchange may be severely hindered if a highly connected node were to be deleted (which includes also posts in the undirected network). The first column in Table 6.1 provides additional data on the properties of the undirected bipartite graph. The graph's low degree centralisation, density, and average degree confirm that the network is mostly composed of only lowly connected nodes. Nevertheless, the network diameter and the characteristic path length demonstrate that no node is far away from any other node in the network. The path connecting the two nodes that are furthest apart has only seven intermediate nodes and on average, it takes only four steps (and thus three intermediate nodes) to connect to any other node. Furthermore, the bipartite structure renders any closed triplets impossible while open triplets are formed between any two users who responded to the same post. Consequently, the global clustering coefficient is zero.

A **unipartite projection** of the bipartite graph reduces the number of types to a single type and creates a homogeneous graph. If we change the relation $\mathcal{B} \rightarrow \mathcal{A} \leftarrow \mathcal{B}$ in the graph in Figure 6.7 into a $\mathcal{B} \leftrightarrow \mathcal{B}$ relationship, we obtain the undirected graph of Figure 6.2b. Applying the same

Table 6.1

Network characteristics of undirected secularist networks

	Bipartite	Unipartite
Global clustering coefficient	0.0	0.788
Network diameter	8	4
Degree centralisation	0.055	0.493
Characteristic path length	3.972	2.103
Average degree	8.100	129.640
Network density	0.002	0.036

approach to the secularist network leaves us with a unipartite graph that is either only composed of posts or users. Thus, a unipartite projection generates two new graphs with an order equal to the number of nodes of each type in the original bipartite graph. In our context, the unipartite graph composed only of users is more illuminating and relevant. The new graph is composed of 3,623 users and has a size of 235,104 links. The unipartite projection connects a user to any other user that responded to the same post. They form a complete sub-graph. Consequently, the graph becomes much denser, which is shown in Figure 6.8d and the second column of Table 6.1. Although the degree distribution still shows a negative and somewhat linear relationship for degrees larger than 20, it is more dispersed, positive, and approximately linear for smaller degrees.[12] A low degree indicates that a user must have initiated or responded to a post to which few other users responded. On a social platform, such as Facebook, these conditions do not hold for most users. Yet, only a small number of users will respond to almost every post and most users will not come in direct contact with a significant number of other users. This explains the shape of the distribution in Figure 6.8d, which peaks at around a degree centrality of 20.

We have seen that the bipartite graph does not allow for closed triplets. If projected into a unipartite representation, any post to which at least three users responded will form a complete sub-graph with a clustering coefficient equal to one. The relatively low network density indicates that the network is composed of numerous interconnected complete sub-graphs that result in a high degree centralisation. Half of the nodes have a degree larger than 112 and the complete sub-graphs imply a high redundancy of shortest paths.

Similarly, looking at equation (6.14) shows that a low betweenness centrality either indicates that a particular node lies only very rarely on the shortest paths connecting any two other nodes and/or that the shortest paths between the latter are numerous. Given the complete sub-graphs created by the unipartite projection, we would assume that the betweenness centrality of most nodes is small. Indeed, Figure 6.9a shows that more than half of the nodes have a betweenness centrality of 1. The highest centrality at 342,469 corresponds to a normalised betweenness centrality of roughly 5 percent.[13] The redundancy of shortest paths between nodes entails that erasing a random node from the graph has no significant effect on communication across the network. Information exchange is further aided by the low geodesic distance between nodes. Figure 6.9b shows that most nodes are only two steps away in the unipartite graph and four steps away in the bipartite graph.[14] The redundancies and short distance between members render communication efficient and strengthen the robustness of the network, making it difficult for state actors to disrupt

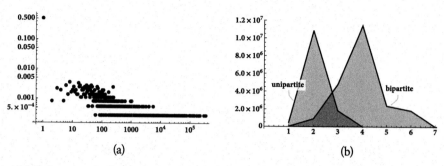

Figure 6.9: (a) betweenness distribution of unipartite graph, (b) distribution of geodesic distance of undirected bipartite and unipatite graphs.

social networks by randomly excluding members from the network. The relatively high average degree of this particular network, however, imposes a risk of identification on members, since a single individual is able to reveal numerous other members entailing the need to obscure their identity and create *fake* accounts.

For the sake of brevity, this section only delineates a very cursory analysis of the secularist network, but even this short analysis exposes the basic properties of the graph and testifies to the explanatory power of the statistical measures we have studied in the earlier sections. The study further indicates the way in which social media transform not only communication but forms of activism.

6.5 Preferential Attachment and the Power Law

In the previous section, I have mentioned that the linear degree distribution as shown in Figures 6.8b and 6.8c is not uncommon. This linear relationship if plotted in a log-log scale is defined as a **power law distribution**.

A power law tells us that a quantity y can be expressed by the power of another quantity x according to following equation

$$y = f(x) = \alpha x^{-\tau} \tag{6.27}$$

In our case, x defines the degree of a node while y determines the fraction of nodes of the former degree. It is important to note that power laws are a rather universal characteristic that is studied not only in biology and physics but they are a property of numerous social systems beyond social networks (see Zipf, 1949 for various examples). We will come across other examples in Chapter 8.

If two quantities are correlated according to a power law distribution, a double logarithmic plot describes a straight line. This is simply a mathematical consequence of the power law. We can transform equation (6.27) by applying the logarithm to both sides of the equation which is the same transformation we obtain by plotting our data in log-log scale. We get

$$\log y = \beta - \tau \, \log x \tag{6.28}$$

with $\beta = \log \alpha$ being the intercept and $-\tau$ the slope of the line.

In addition, the power law has a number of interesting properties. First, it is **scale invariant**. With this we mean that changing the scale at which we measure x (e.g. in degrees Celsius or

Fahrenheit, in centimetres or miles, US dollars or British Pounds, etc.) proportionally scales quantity y. To see this, imagine we scale x by some amount γ, then

$$g(x) = \alpha \left(\gamma x \right)^{-\tau} = \gamma^{-\tau} f(x) \qquad (6.29)$$

in other words, function $g(x)$ in equation (6.29) is directly proportional to function $f(x)$ in equation (6.27).

Why is a power law distribution so common in social systems in general and in social networks in particular? Barabási and Albert (1999) suggested a simple model of **preferential attachment**. Preferential attachment is a process that distributes quantities according to how much individuals already possess. It is frequently called the **Matthew Effect** - in simple terms, the rich become richer and the poor poorer.[15]

The preferential attachment model of László Barabási and Réka Albert assumes that the likelihood with which a new node, representing an incoming member of a social network, connects to an incumbent node is proportional to the relative degree of the latter, i.e, the probability of a node i to become attached to a node k is

$$p_k = \frac{\eta_k}{\sum_j \eta_j} \qquad (6.30)$$

In other words, the probability of someone forming a new connection with an individual k is proportional to the number of individuals who have already connected themselves to k. Preferential attachment defines a path-dependent process in which older members of a social network tend to be more connected, in other words: first come, *more* served.

Barabási and Albert's model focuses on degree centrality as the primary driver for the formation of connections. Yet, we may wonder, since the power law is so universal, can it only be reproduced using the degree as an incentive to connect to a member of a social network? Would a different measure affect a network's topology? As we have seen in the discussion in Section 6.4, an individual's importance in a network is not only determined by the degree of her connectedness but also by the quality of her connections. Consequently, individuals do not necessarily connect themselves to a broad networker, but a person who knows *the right people*.

Figures 6.10a–6.10e illustrate sample networks that have been generated with the algorithm based on 6.30, but only the graph in Figure 6.10a uses a node's degree as a basis while the other graphs are generated based on the various centrality measures discussed in Section 6.3. Although the topology is influenced by the centrality measure used to generate the graph, all networks illustrate central nodes that form hubs and are highly interconnected while a majority of the nodes remain sparsely connected. Figure 6.10f plots the degree distribution of each graph and indeed, we can see that the power law distribution is maintained. The simple attachment algorithm is generally robust to variations of equation (6.30), but we can spot minor differences.

Figure 6.11 offers a more detailed account of the differences. It shows the average degree of a percentile range based on 100 simulation runs for each of the five versions of the algorithm, each time creating a network composed of $1,000$ nodes.[16] The mostly small confidence intervals illustrate only minor variabilities between each run. Degrees of nodes at the lowest 40 percentile range are equal to one (i.e. at least 400 nodes in each of the 500 runs have only one neighbour).

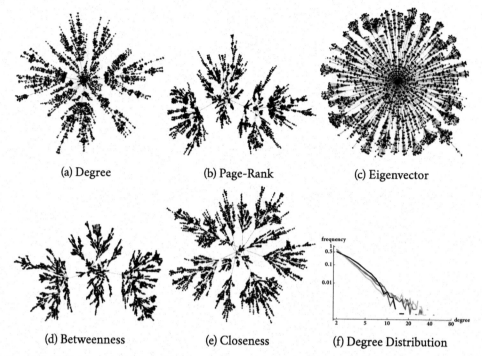

(a) Degree   (b) Page-Rank   (c) Eigenvector

(d) Betweenness   (e) Closeness   (f) Degree Distribution

Figure 6.10: (a)–(e) show a sample graph of 5,000 nodes generated via preferential attachment based on a different centrality measure. (f) illustrates the degree distribution for each of the sample graphs: degree - red, page-rank - blue, eigenvector - green, betweenness - brown, closeness - black.

Betweenness and closeness centrality tend to increase the degree of nodes that are in the middle of the distribution, while degree, eigenvector, and PageRank increase the degree of hubs. Eigenvector centrality creates the strongest imbalances and thus the most highly connected nodes. Remember that eigenvector centrality is a generalisation of degree centrality that does not only take an individual's number of direct connections into account but also the degree of a node's neighbours and their neighbours, etc. Consequently, highly connected nodes that by themselves are connected to highly connected nodes benefit most from the preferential attachment algorithm explaining the stronger concentration of networks.

As indicated previously, power law distributions can be found across various social systems. For example, Zipf (1949) showed that if we rank the largest 100 cities in the USA in 1940 according to their population in a decreasing order – assigning position 1 to the largest city (New York), and position 2 to the second largest city, and so forth until Alabama at position 100 – on a log-log scale with the population of each city on the y-axis (where New York has roughly one million inhabitants and Alabama around 100 thousand), approximately describes a line with a slope equal to -1. Zipf further shows that the rank-size (or rank-frequency) distribution of other social institutions – in the context of human geography, linguistics, musicology, and economics – follows similar regularities.

Consequently, it is interesting to study the predictive power of the simple algorithm based on equation (6.30) in this context. Similar to the preferential attachment model, I assume that the

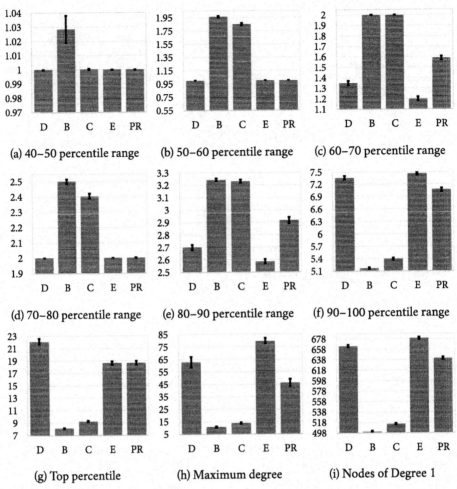

Figure 6.11: (a)–(g) show the average degree over percentile range based on 100 runs per centrality for a graph of order 1,000. (h) and (i) illustrate the degree of the node with highest degree centrality and the number of nodes of degree 1, respectively. Bars indicate confidence interval at $\alpha = 5\%$.

likelihood of an individual to move to city i is given by

$$p_i = \frac{\rho_i}{\sum_j \rho_j} \tag{6.31}$$

with ρ_i being the population of city i. Following Zip's earlier study, Figure 6.12 shows the most recent size distribution of the 100 largest cities in the world and the US. Comparing these graphs to the simulation results that have been generated by algorithm in equation (6.31) shows an astounding similarity. While individuals move to cities for various idiosyncratic reasons, the results suggest that these are only of very minor importance for the growth and size of a city. The growth of cities can be mainly explained by them being more attractive due to their size (and obviously, the benefits that go along with this).

In addition to a power law distribution, social networks tend to exhibit small close-knit communities composed of individuals of the same kind. These small communities share similar

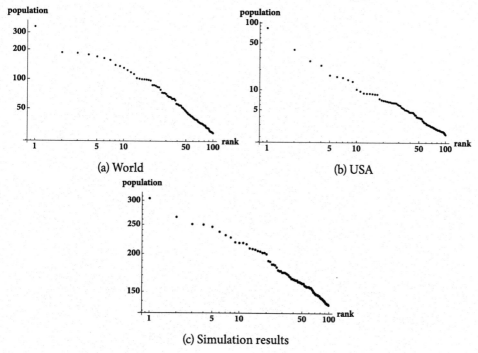

(a) World   (b) USA

(c) Simulation results

Figure 6.12: Size distribution of 100 largest cities in 100,000s.

interests, practices, and identities. While individuals tend to link themselves to more connected and central members of a network, they are, at the same time, also more inclined to associate with others who have a similar identity - *birds of a feather flock together*. Individuals are then torn between linking with their own kind or with hubs that do not necessarily share convictions, practices, and beliefs. The personal inclination to do the former or latter is then driven by what individuals observe among their peers and what they consider socially acceptable. We can adapt the preferential attachment algorithm to take this into account (see also, Ille, 2017).

Assume that individuals can be of one of several types (i.e. identities) given by set I. In addition, an individual observes the number and nature of links that are formed between members of the network. Let the number of uniform links formed between nodes of the same identity $\tau \in I$ be $l_u(\tau)$, and the number of mixed links formed between a node of identity τ and a node of some different identity be $l_m(\tau)$. Assume that the probability with which a new node of identity τ attaches itself to another member with the same identity is given by

$$p_\tau = \frac{l_u(\tau)}{l_u(\tau) + l_m(\tau)} \tag{6.32}$$

for a specific identity τ. Thus, the existence of more mixed connections renders a new node more inclined to connect to another highly connected node of a different identity. The identity of a new node is randomly defined with equal probability. In a first step, the new member decides whether to limit the set of potential neighbours to those that share her type with the probability defined by equation (6.32). In a second step, she links herself to another highly connected node based on the process defined by equation (6.30).

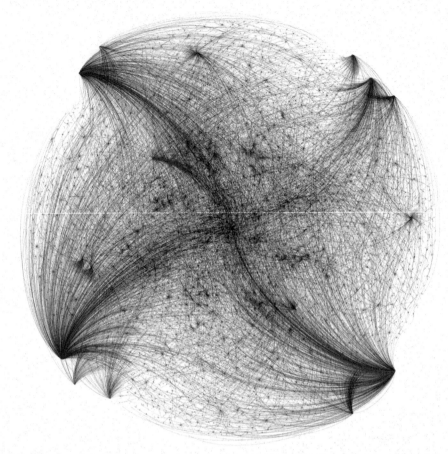

Figure 6.13: A preferential attachment graph with three identities: green, blue, red. Links have the same colour as their parent nodes. Links that connect different types are coloured in black.

This process generates a social network whose degree distribution is characterised by a power law. Yet, in addition, small communities or clusters appear that are marked by the same identity and which become increasingly mixed as their size grows. The graph in Figure 6.13 shows a network of half a million nodes generated by the two-step preferential attachment model with identities.

6.6 Conclusion

In recent years, terms like *fake news* and *super-spreaders* have dominated headlines while online engagements have increasingly dominated our daily lives. Social media platforms have become the main source for sharing and receiving news for a large part of the population (see Kümpel et al., 2015 for an interesting overview). Governments and scholars have traced interactions between individuals during the recent pandemic to develop policies that reduce the reproduction rate of the Coronavirus and decelerate its spread. Weak ties supported by online professional networks increase job opportunities, and political activists have used social media platforms to their advantage.

In short, social networks, both offline and online, dominate social behaviour, beliefs, and expectations of our communities. Our understanding of social dynamics therefore relies crucially on a thorough comprehension of the impact of a network's topology on individual decision-making. The statistical tools in this chapter enable us to identify dominant members of a graph. High centrality measures are not only obtained by those with many connections, but also by those who are able to make the *right* connections. Being linked to an influential member does not only improve the standing of an individual, but in doing so, the latter also promotes the former. The resulting Matthew effect creates power imbalances by which the most influential members of a network tend to become even more powerful.

Social network analysis further enables us to make statements about the network altogether. Measures, such as diameter, density, and characteristic path length help us understand the properties of a network. Centralisations evaluate the differential in centrality between its most influential member and its other members relative to a network that ranks highest in relation to the differential. These measures hence provide knowledge about the dominance of individual members or a small group of members in a social network. Most importantly, modularity identifies communities within a network without the need for further contextual knowledge.

Social network (or graph) analysis is a powerful tool that is used across the social sciences. It is even becoming increasingly popular in the digital humanities where scholars have started analysing the relationships between fictitious characters in the literature, similar to the study in Section 6.4.

Applications and Relation to Other Chapters

This chapter stands apart from the other chapters in this book. Instead of a mathematical approach for modelling social dynamics, it is a statistical approach that provides insights into the characteristics of social networks. Yet it should be clear that social network analysis is complementary to the other approaches whenever we intend to study social interactions that exhibit a topology more sophisticated than the regular networks of the cellular automata which I cover in Chapters 7 and 8. The models in any chapter can be transformed into a spatial version, where interactions occur at a larger scale but the mixing of players is not random and instead, engagements are confined to a small set of peers. Social structure can then have a significant impact on the dynamics and equilibria in these games (but this might not always be the case, as we will see in Chapter 8) and social network analysis supports the other tools discussed in this book and allows us to trace the relation between network topology on the one hand, and dynamics and equilibria on the other hand.

Further Reading

Excellent textbooks that offer a broader introduction to social network analysis are Wassermann and Faust (1994), Borgatti et al. (2018), and Goyal (2007) while the latter is probably the most technical presentation. Another comprehensive overview is offered by Bramoullé et al. (2016). For a broader exposition on the role of social networks and the applicability of social network analysis, the interested reader should refer to Scott and Carrington (2011) as well as the non-technical overview in van Dijk et al. (2018).

Notes

1 We can interpret the adjacency matrix therefore as a transition matrix that demonstrates the diffusion of information or contagion between agents. It thus shares similarities with the probability transition matrix of a Markov process discussed in Chapter 4. However, the adjacency matrix does not show probabilities but the number of times information reaches an agent after a certain number of steps/periods. The total times an agent is exposed to a virus or information after r periods can then be determined by

$$G^{Total} = \sum_{n=1}^{r} G^n \tag{6.33}$$

If we assume that all members pass on information each time, information spread by member 1 reaches member 2 a total of 31 times in the directed network and 637 times in the undirected network.

2 While Travers and Milgram counted the nodes that lie between the end nodes on the path, the length of a path is defined by the number of links, which is equal to the number of intermediaries plus one.

3 A network of minimum size is a tree, which has $n-1$ links. The definition of density given by equation (6.10) implies that its minimum value is always larger than 0. We, therefore, find a definition in the literature that renormalises the density to

$$D = \frac{2|L| - (n-1)}{n(n-1) - 2(n-1)} \text{ for an undirected graph}$$

$$D = \frac{|L| - (n-1)}{n(n-1) - (n-1)} \text{ for a directed graph}$$

4 In a complete network, there must be at least one such shortest path between i to j. However, it is not necessarily unique. If, on the contrary, all shortest paths between any two nodes are unique, the fraction is assigned a value of 1 if the path includes k and zero otherwise. In this case, betweenness centrality corresponds to the stress centrality of k defined by the total number of shortest paths containing k, i.e.,

$$C_S(k) = \sum_{i \neq k \in N} \sum_{j \neq k \in N} \sigma_{i,j}(k) \tag{6.34}$$

On the other hand, if the shortest path between two nodes is not unique (which is likely in larger social networks), both centrality measures can lead to different rankings of nodes and should not be confused.

5 Notice that

$$C_H(i) = \left(\frac{1}{\sum d(k,i)^{-1}} \right)^{-1}$$

In other words, the harmonic centrality is the reciprocal of the sum of the reciprocal distances that define the closeness centrality. The relationship between those two centralities is therefore equivalent to the relationship between the arithmetic mean and the harmonic mean - hence, the name.

6 The literature seems to be undecided on whether to define both the harmonic centrality and the closeness centrality in terms of $d(i,k)$ or $d(k,i)$. I am following here the definition in Dekker (2005, see valued centrality) and Rochat (2009, equation 6).

7 Another interesting extension is presented by Ballester et al. (2006) which allows to identify the key player in a network. Removing the key player from the network changes the optimal behaviour of the other members of that network. The measure is therefore particularly interesting for policy-makers and used in the literature analysing organised crime and terrorism. See also **Key PlayerProblem/Negative** (or KPP-NEG) in Borgatti (2006).

8   If nodes 2 and 3 as well as nodes 1 and 4 in the graph of Figure 6.2b are recombined, the two new communities/nodes are connected by a link of weight 2, since nodes 2 and 3 were each connected to node 4. Notice that the algorithm also works with a weighted graph, i.e, where links possess individual weights.

9   See Smith (1980) for a detailed analysis of the novel and the historical context. Tokugawa Ieyasu was the last of the three unifiers of Japan in the late 16th century after (the former's first enemy then ally) Oda Nobunago and (the latter's general) Toyotomi Hideyoshi. Ieyasu adopted the surname Tokugawa after receiving imperial permission in 1569 to link his lineage to the Minamoto family. His appointment to Tairō (one of five regents) and several political marriages for his sons and daughters significantly strengthened Ieyasu's political network and enabled him to claim the title of Shōgun - the supreme governor and military leader of Japan - after the battle of Sekighara in 1600. Clavell's novel invents a captivating tale around the rise of Ieyasu, renamed to Toranaga, based on the historical events. While Clavell takes a few liberties with the historical facts, (e.g. it was Ishida, not Ieyasu who fled in a lady's palanquin), the power relations are essentially correctly represented – for a short overview, see Turnbull (2012) and for a detailed analysis, see Sadler (1937) and Chaplin (2018).

10 Figures 6.5 and 6.6 as well as Figure 6.13 were generated in Gephi 0.9.2 (Bastian et al., 2009).

11 The exponential scale implies that the distance between 0 and 10 on the abscissa is equal to the distance between 10 and 100. Similarly, the distance between 0.001 and 0.01 is the same as the distance between 0.01 and 0.1 on the ordinate.

12 Such a type of distribution is also referred to as a **double power law**, see Section 6.5.

13 The betweenness distribution of the undirected bipartite graph is roughly equal to the distribution of the unipartite graph. However, in the case of the former the reason is that most nodes do not lie on the shortest path connecting any two nodes while the latter distribution is caused by the redundancy of shortest paths.

14 Since the unipartite projection eliminates the post between two users, the distance between the latter is halved in the unipartite graph.

15 The effect is attributed to Matthew based on the Parable of Talents in the New Testament, which ends with "For to all those who have, more will be given, and they will have an abundance; but from those who have nothing, even what they have will be taken away." (Matthew, 2018, 25:29) Indeed, the economic literature has shown that income and wealth distribution follows a power law (Levy and Solomon, 1997; Gabaix, 2009). The research shows a special type of power law distribution called *Pareto distribution*.

16 Since the graphs are generated by a stochastic process, repeating the simulation 100 times and considering the average of all runs minimises the risk of rare outliers. The process of multiple runs is discussed in Chapter 8 in further detail.

Peer Effects and Spatial Game Theory: Local and Global Efficiency

7.1 Introduction

I N response to the radical social changes imposed by Western colonisation, several cults evolved in Malaysia during the late 19th and early 20th century. Confrontation with the abundance of Western wealth – a seemingly endless supply of canned food, firearms, construction material, machines, and tobacco – led to the belief that through rituals, these goods will be bestowed upon the local population by magical means. While these *cargo cults* were animated by the exogenous cultural and economic transformation under colonial order, their structure, rituals, and underlying belief system are manifold. Some were millenarian movements, others did not believe in revolutionary or catastrophic change, some adopted elements from Christian faith, while others did not demonstrate any Christian thinking or positioned themselves in opposition to Christian belief. Neither did these cults illustrate consistent conjectures about the amount of cargo that would be granted (Trompf, 1991, Ch. 8, see also Iteanu, 2017).

In contrast to the cultural or evolutionary universals, which we studied in Chapter 4, distinct cultures have produced not only a plethora of religious cults and practices but also other forms of behavioural rules to a degree that cultural diversity exceeds biological diversity. Price (2004) lists over 3,500 distinct cultures. Since the Middle Pleistocene, human cultures have become increasingly varied in terms of regional traditions and traits of social function (for details, see Foley and Lahr 2011). Similarly, linguistic fragmentation is equally varied. Eberhard et al. (2021) report 7,139 living languages worldwide. Italy counts 34 living languages in close geographic proximity, and India has over 447 languages, excluding the innumerable amount of local dialects. Indeed, Italy has one of the highest Linguistic Diversity Indices in Europe at 0.593 while India has an index of 0.930 – a value close to the maximum value of 1 which indicates that no two people share the same mother tongue (for more data on other countries, see Matsuura, 2009, Table 7).

In this chapter, I will extend our previous analysis of strategic interactions and discuss an approach that can explain local variations in behavioural rules and strategies. Similar to Chapter 3, we assume that behavioural norms and conventions are considered to be subject to emulation and reproduction. Instead of being randomly matched, which implies an equal likelihood to

DOI: 10.4324/9781003035329-7

encounter and imitate any other member of society, in this chapter, we analyse situations in which interactions are restricted to a limited set of peers. We will see that the localisation of interactions can generate much more diverse and intricate results than the approaches in previous chapters. In our analysis, we will study under which conditions local interactions can also lead to universal conventions, yet we will realise that these are not necessarily the equilibria that evolve under more arbitrary encounters. Additionally, we will discover that local interactions can give rise to and sustain behavioural rules that we previously considered to be strictly dominated strategies.

7.2   Local Imitation on Regular Networks

To simplify our study, I only consider one of the easiest topologies. Each individual occupies a single region on a plane. We can think of the plane as a chessboard or square lattice in which individual squares are ordered along a regular grid. Following convention, I call these squares *cells*. Each agent interacts only with her set of neighbours, and in this particular setting, we can broadly define two variants of neighbourhoods - the **von Neumann neighbourhood** and the **Moore neighbourhood**. Figure 7.1 illustrates the two types of neighbourhoods. The von Neumann neighbourhood includes only the four neighbours in adjacent cells that are situated along the horizontal and vertical axis, while the Moore neighbourhood includes also the diagonally adjacent cells and thus all eight neighbours. Each cell has the same number of neighbours and we can therefore think of the von Neumann neighbourhood as a regular graph of degree 4. Similarly, the Moore neighbourhood defines a regular graph of degree 8. However, the regularity is broken at the edges and corners of the plane. Instead of imagining an infinite plane, I assume that the left edge connects to the right edge of the plane and equivalently, the upper edge connects to the lower edge. The rightmost individuals then have the leftmost players as their neighbours, and the lowest individuals interact with the uppermost neighbours who are positioned relatively below them. This process creates a loop along two dimensions and turns the plane into a torus (i.e. a doughnut) as shown in Figure 7.2. I will use the plane representation for future graphs to simplify visualisation but keep in mind that the actual interaction structure is defined by the torus.

In this chapter, we will focus on the Moore neighbourhood, but results can be easily extended to the von Neumann neighbourhood. Since the square lattice does not explicitly define links between agents (although we can easily redefine the lattice as a graph), the neighbourhood of

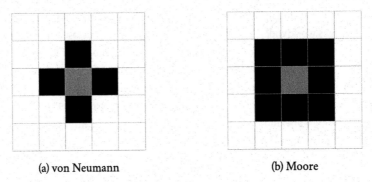

(a) von Neumann   (b) Moore

Figure 7.1: Types of neighbourhood: neighbours of the grey cell are illustrated in black.

(a) Representation as plane. (b) Cellular automata on a regular lattice.

Figure 7.2: (a) flattened representation of the interaction plane, (b) plane warped into a torus.

individual i is defined in relation to the coordinates (x_i, y_i) of her lattice point. Individual j is a neighbour of i, which we denote by $j \sim i$, if $\{j : (x_j = x_i + v, y_j = y_i + w)\}$, with $v, w \in \{-1, 0, 1\}$ and $|v| + |w| \neq 0$. In other words, if i is positioned at coordinates $(5, 7)$, the top-left neighbour is situated at $(4, 8)$.[1] Similar to our definition of neighbours on undirected graphs in Chapter 6, relation $\sim$ is binary (either j is a neighbour or she is not), symmetric (if $j \sim i$ then $i \sim j$), and irreflexive (i is not a neighbour of herself). Given the set of agents N, the set of neighbours of i in lattice g is defined as

$$N_i(g) = \{j \in N : j \sim i\} \tag{7.1}$$

As before, let the pure strategy set for any player i be defined as S_i and her neighbours' strategy set as S_{N_i}. Given a strategy profile of i's neighbours, defined as $s_{N_i} = (s_j)_{j \in N_i}$, the payoff of i is given by $\pi_i(s_i, s_{N_i})$ if she plays strategy s_i against her neighbours. To keep matters simple, assume that the payoff of a player is then the accumulated payoff of playing the same strategy against each neighbour. Further assume that players can only choose among pure strategies. Let the number of neighbours of i playing strategy s_k be defined by $n_k(i)$. If player i plays s_i, her payoff is then

$$\pi_i(s_i) = \pi\left(s_i, \{s_j : j \in N_i\}\right) = \sum_{s_k \in S_{N_i}} n_k(i)\, \pi_i(s_i, s_k) \tag{7.2}$$

In other words, we count the number of neighbours who play strategy s_k, and multiply this number with the payoff that i receives by playing s_i against one such neighbour. The total payoff of i is then the sum of this product over all strategies that is neighbours can choose. Assume that the payoffs are defined by the general and symmetric 2×2 payoff matrix depicted in Figure 7.3.

Using the fact that $n_R(i) = 8 - n_L(i)$, the payoff of player i is defined as

$$\pi_i(s_i) = \begin{cases} n_L(i)\, a + (8 - n_L(i))\, b, & \text{if } s_i = L \\ n_L(i)\, c + (8 - n_L(i))\, d, & \text{if } s_i = R \end{cases} \tag{7.3}$$

	L	R
L	a,a	b,c
R	c,b	d,d

Figure 7.3: Symmetric 2×2 game.

The game is repeated in each period and after interacting with all neighbours and realising a payoff according to equations (7.3), all agents have the opportunity to revise their strategy. Individuals are subject to cognitive limitations and update their strategies by comparing their payoff only to those of their neighbours obtained during that period. Each individual then adopts the strategy of the best-performing neighbour. The updating process is then rationally bounded along two aspects: firstly, players assume that the strategies chosen in the current period are a good proxy for the next period. Thus in contrast to the best-response play in Chapter 2, individuals ignore the strategic correlation between their own and their neighbour's current strategies and future payoffs rendering strategic coercion, such as Tit-for-Tat, infeasible. Contrary to adaptive learning, which we discussed in Chapter 4, a player has no recollection of earlier interactions and therefore does not use past history to derive a probability distribution for future interactions nor is updating driven by random and probabilistic comparisons as in Chapter 3. Secondly, an individual only uses a limited subset of information that is constrained to the neighbourhood. No player has any awareness of the interactions and realised payoffs outside their adjacent cells.

Let $\Pi_i = \{ \pi_j : j \in N_i \cup \{i\} \}$ be the joint set of payoffs of player i and her neighbours in a given period. Notice that although this is a repeated game, individuals choose a strategy only based on the strategies that have been selected during the previous interaction period and the associated payoffs. It should be understood that the strategy chosen for an interaction in some period t therefore depends exclusively on the payoffs in $t - 1$. The strategy that has been played by the neighbour with the highest payoff (including i herself) is defined as

$$s^*_{N+i,t} = \left\{ s_j \big| j \in N_i \cup \{i\}, \pi_{j,t-1}(s_j) = \max \Pi_{i,t-1} \right\}$$

Having played strategy s_i, player i chooses a strategy s^*_i for the subsequent period based on the following imitation rule:

$$s^*_{i,t} = \begin{cases} L, & \text{if } s^*_{N+i,t} = \{L\} \\ R, & \text{if } s^*_{N+i,t} = \{R\} \\ s_{i,t-1}, & \text{if } s^*_{N+i,t} = \{L,R\} \end{cases} \qquad (7.4)$$

In other words, player i chooses the strategy that has generated the highest payoff during the last round of interactions. If both strategies gave rise to the same payoff, player i sticks to her old strategy. For notational simplicity, I am not using a time index for the variables whenever it is irrelevant or obvious in the following. Further, it is important to realise that while is payoff depends on her neighbourhood, the payoff of her neighbours depends on their respective neighbours who, in turn, compare themselves to their neighbours. Neighbourhoods do not entirely overlap. Consequently, the neighbours of i might not opt for the same strategy.

Equivalently to earlier chapters, we define an equilibrium as a state in which no player has an incentive to deviate and all players keep their strategy. If the latter is the same across a vast majority of players, we call it a convention. While earlier a convention required that each player has chosen the same strategy for the entirety of her memory of past play, memory size is now only one period, and a convention is simply a state in which the interaction plane does not show any change in pattern and agents predominantly play the same strategy.

Exercise 7.1

Given that a state in t is defined by $\mathscr{S}^t = \{s_1, s_2, \ldots, s_{n \times m}\}$, show that an equilibrium is reached if $\mathscr{S}^t = \mathscr{S}^{t-1}$.

In the following, we will have a closer look at coordination games and assume that $a, d > b, c$ in the payoff matrix of Figure 7.3.[2] In this case, a convention is reached if all individuals either choose L or all chose R and in this case, the individual payoffs are eight times the respective diagonal payoff. Using the notation established in Chapter 4, the convention in which all choose L is defined by $\mathscr{L}$ and the convention in which all individuals opt for R is denoted as $\mathscr{R}$. We say that $\mathscr{L}$ **payoff dominates** $\mathscr{R}$, if $a > d$. On the other hand, we say that convention $\mathscr{L}$ **risk dominates** $\mathscr{R}$, if $d - b < a - c$. We can think of risk dominance as follows: assume that you have no information about the strategy that another player will choose. Consequently, you must assume that the other player opts for both strategies with equal likelihood. The expected payoff of playing L is then $0.5a + 0.5b$ and of playing R is $0.5c + 0.5d$. Rearranging shows that L grants a higher expected payoff if $a - c > d - b$. Another interpretation of the inequality is that unilaterally deviating from convention $\mathscr{L}$ bears a higher loss than deviating from $\mathscr{R}$ – or put differently, violating a risk-dominant social agreement will cost you dear.

While we wish to study the global convention, it suffices to analyse the local dynamics by realising some direct implications of our assumptions.[3]

1. In a coordination game, the payoff derived from a particular strategy increases with the number of neighbours that select the same strategy.
2. The payoff dominant strategy has the largest value on the payoff matrix's main diagonal. Consequently, the maximum possible payoff is achieved by an individual who chooses the payoff dominant strategy and is surrounded by neighbours who also all play that strategy.
3. Any individual, surrounded only by players choosing the same strategy, never has an incentive to switch, since there is no other strategy that can be imitated. Transitions can only occur at the borders of clusters.
4. A square composed of 3×3 players who all play the payoff dominant strategy will never change their strategy since all compare themselves to a neighbour at the centre of the square with the maximum possible payoff.
5. If all players opt for a strategy at random, i.e. the probability of choosing L or R is $1/2$, the strategy distribution on the lattice during the initial periods is strongly determined by the relative average payoff of each strategy. Consequently, a player more likely adopts the risk-dominant strategy during an initial sequence of interactions.

One of the principal questions is whether this type of interaction can lead to an efficient convention that maximises collective payoff. For the moment, I ignore the element of risk dominance and

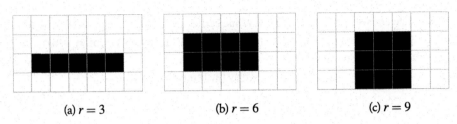

(a) $r = 3$ (b) $r = 6$ (c) $r = 9$

Figure 7.4: Different clusters of size r.

focus solely on payoff dominance. I therefore assume that $d > a$ and $a - c = d - b$. We can then define a payoff premium ρ such that $d = a + \rho$ and $b = c + \rho$. If ρ is positive, $\mathscr{R}$ payoff dominates $\mathscr{L}$. Similar to Chapter 2, we study the stability of $\mathscr{L}$ after the population has been infiltrated by a small number of R players who idiosyncratically shifted to the payoff superior strategy. I define a *cluster of size r* as a set of connected neighbours who all choose the same strategy and all of them have at least one neighbour who herself has $r - 1$ neighbours playing the same strategy. That may sound a bit confusing at first but Figure 7.4 illustrates the idea. For example, suppose that all the individuals that play a particular strategy are positioned along a line as shown in Figure 7.4a. Each player has a neighbour to her left and right choosing the same strategy, except for the corner players. Independent of the length of the straight line, the cluster always has a size of three. Each member of the cluster has at least one neighbour who is neighbouring two players, who choose the same strategy. Hence, each member of the cluster compares any payoff to either $2a + 6b$ or $2d + 6c$.[4] Remember that all players choose the strategy of the player with the highest payoff. Consequently, the length of the line is irrelevant. The same holds for larger cluster. Figure 7.4b shows a cluster of size 6. The cluster will maintain its size if it uniformly increases along the horizontal axis. Cluster size ranges from 1 to 9 and an example of the largest cluster with the minimum required individuals is given in Figure 7.4c.

We can see that any invading cluster of size r playing strategy R can only successfully invade an incumbent population of L players if $8a < (9 - r)c + (r - 1)d$. If neither convention risk dominates the other in a coordination game with $d > a$, we obtain that the minimum cluster size is $r^* = 6$ and furthermore,

$$\rho > \frac{3}{5}(a - c) \tag{7.5}$$

Assuming that idiosyncratic actions occur sporadically, a cluster of size 6 evolves with positive probability and thus, inequality equation (7.5) defines an invasion barrier in terms of the minimum payoff premium. Similar to Chapter 4, a population converges to a more efficient convention as long as it is sufficiently more efficient than the incumbent convention.[5]

Exercise 7.2

Consider that $a < b$ and show that for an invading cluster of size 4 of R players it must hold that $\rho > 3(a - c)$ and the cluster is a square, while any larger cluster always invades the population.

In contrast to previous chapters, the spatial segregation of individuals can give rise to stable local conventions. If inequality (7.5) holds, the payoff dominant convention will propagate across the entire population once the small cluster of invaders is established. Such a cluster is stable if two conditions hold. None of its members who have a neighbour playing the incumbent strategy exceeds the maximum payoff obtained from the payoff inferior strategy (i.e. 8a). Secondly, none of the incumbent players, who is neighbouring the cluster, has a higher payoff than the maximum payoff obtained in the cluster. We can then show that clusters of size r are stable if ρ is defined as follows:

$$r = 5 : a = b \tag{7.6a}$$

$$r = 6 : \frac{1}{2}(a-c) < \rho < \frac{3}{5}(a-c) \tag{7.6b}$$

$$r = 7 : \frac{1}{5}(a-c) < \rho < \frac{1}{3}(a-c) \tag{7.6c}$$

$$r = 8 : 0 < \rho < \frac{1}{7}(a-c) \tag{7.6d}$$

$$r = 9 : \rho < \frac{3}{5}(a-c) \tag{7.6e}$$

> **Exercise 7.3**
>
> Assuming again that $a < b$ but also that $\rho > 7(a-c)$, show that *clusters* of size $r = 1$ are stable if they play the payoff inferior strategy L.

In this setting, clustering is an emergent property and the size of clusters is defined by the inequalities in equation (7.6). Yet these conditions and the invasion barrier hold for the case in which an incumbent payoff inferior convention exists and is invaded. This is a reasonable scenario, if we are interested in studying the organic propagation of new and radical ideas and practices through social imitation after they have been established in some small intellectual circles (see Collins, 1998 for an interesting empirical analysis). Alternatively, we can study the social dynamics in a system without any pre-established convention. In this case, individuals initially choose a strategy at random. However, since clustering is an emergent property, we will then observe some clusters of size 9 after some initial periods of interaction. The $\mathscr{R}$ convention can successfully establish itself if a cluster of R players of size $r = 9$ can successfully invade a cluster of L players of equal size. We therefore need to solve $c + 7d > 8a$ for ρ and obtain that if no incumbent convention exists and individuals randomly opt for one of the two strategies with roughly equal likelihood, the population converges to $\mathscr{R}$ if

$$\rho > \frac{1}{7}(a-c) \tag{7.7}$$

Thus, inequalities (7.5) and (7.7) define the invasion barrier for the payoff dominant strategy depending on how heterogeneously the payoff inferior strategy has been initially adopted.

At this point, we can easily extend our analysis by assuming that the payoff inferior convention is risk superior and see if a trade-off between risk and payoff dominance exists. I assume as before that $d = a + \rho$ but that $b = c + \rho + \mu$. If $\rho > 0$ and $\mu > 0$, $\mathscr{R}$ payoff dominates $\mathscr{L}$ by a value of ρ whereas $\mathscr{L}$ risk dominates $\mathscr{R}$ by a value of μ. In other words, μ defines the *risk premium*. The calculations are a straightforward extension of the previous calculations. If $\mathscr{L}$ is incumbent, the payoff of a member of an invading cluster of size $r = 6$ is $3c + 5d$ which needs to exceed $8a$. The incumbent strategy can invade the cluster if $7a + b > 3c + 5d$. By rearranging, we obtain the following if $\mathscr{L}$ is incumbent

$$\mathscr{R} \text{ is the convention if } \rho > \frac{3}{5}(a-c) \tag{7.8a}$$

$$\mathscr{L} \text{ remains the convention if } \rho < \frac{1}{4}(2a - 2c + \mu) \tag{7.8b}$$

If no convention has yet been established, strategy R takes over the population if $c + 7d > 8a$, while strategy L requires that $7a + b > 8d$. The latter condition only holds if $b > d$ which violates our assumptions. Thus, we have that in the absence of any established convention and a sufficiently random initial distribution of the strategies,

$$\mathscr{R} \text{ is the convention if } \rho > \frac{1}{7}(a-c) \tag{7.9}$$

Conditions (7.8a) and (7.9) are identical to inequalities (7.5) and (7.7). Risk dominance imposes an additional invasion barrier for the establishment of small localised conventions but once the invading strategy is sufficiently payoff dominant, the risk premium is irrelevant and the payoff dominant convention will be universally established. Thus, the trade-off is limited. The results are noteworthy considering that the form of perturbed adaptive learning studied in Chapter 4 establishes the risk-dominant strategy as a convention. One might think that the localised interaction is responsible. Yet, Young (2001) has shown that for a population situated on a four-regular graph (i.e. the von Neumann neighbourhood), the localised version of adaptive play still determines the risk-dominant convention as the stochastically stable state. Similarly, Lee and Valentinyi (2000) and Lee et al. (2003) show that a best-response rule and a state-dependent mutation process converge to the risk-dominant convention in these spatial games. (Exercise 7.4 asks you to show that the risk-dominant strategy is chosen on the long-term in certain social networks if individuals chose a strategy based on perturbed adaptive learning.)

Exercise 7.4

(Note: you will need to have read Chapter 4 for this question.) Assume that individuals interact in a social network, play a symmetric coordination game with two strategies as in Figure 7.3, and choose a strategy according to the stochastic process covered in Chapter 4. With probability $p \in (0, 1)$, a player updates her strategy. If p is sufficiently small, it is rare that two neighbours revise their strategies simultaneously. Consequently, when updating, a player chooses the action that is a best response to their neighbours' past strategy. In addition, players choose a strategy at random with a small probability ε. (a) Assume that players interact on a complete network. Show that the risk-dominant strategy defines the stochastically stable strategy and thus the long-run convention. (b) Show that the same holds if players are situated on a circle.

On the other hand, it is less clear whether only the adoption rule of choosing a strategy with the highest average payoff leads to the efficient convention. We have seen in Chapter 3 that under social imitation, the equilibrium with the larger basin of attraction is the absorbing state given a completely mixed initial distribution. However, Robson and Vega-Redondo (1996) have shown that a process with randomly mixed pairs of agents who adopt the strategy with the highest average payoff identifies the payoff dominant action as the convention.

7.3 Non-Symmetric Interactions and Payoff vs. Imitation Space

We observe here that a population is able to reach a more efficient mode of interaction if interactions are both local and individuals tend to adopt the behavioural rules of their most successful peer. However, this only holds true if both interactions and externalities are confined to a small neighbourhood. Before I discuss this point in greater detail, we will study the case in which two distinct populations interact. The results we obtain will address another problem with the results of Chapter 4. While stochastic stability implies that a population gravitates towards more egalitarian conventions (see alsoYoung 1998), we observe historically that societies establish forms of interaction that are strikingly unequal. For example, ancient Sparta evolved into a class society composed of regular Spartan citizens and Perioikoi on the one hand and state-owned Helots on the other hand. The former two groups served as free men in the Spartan army while the latter were required to work as serfs and acted as prey during the *Krypteia*.

In contrast to adaptive learning with limited recall, which I discussed in Chapter 4, we will see that localised non-symmetric interactions between distinct populations can lead to social dynamics that disadvantage one population in favour of the other population and thus provide an explanation for highly inegalitarian societies. I redefine the payoffs according to matrix Figure 7.5. Assume that two players - one of each population - coexist on each lattice point. The neighbourhoods are defined as before, only that each individual has eight neighbours of their own population and the same number of neighbours of the other population. Notice that for coherence, an individual does not interact with the other player on her own lattice point. Our previous definitions carry over to the two-population case and a player k in population $i = \{1, 2\}$ has the following payoff

$$\pi_k(s_k) = \begin{cases} n_{L,j}(k)\, a_i + (8 - n_{L,j}(k))\, b_i, & \text{if } s_k = L \\ n_{L,j}(k)\, c_i + (8 - n_{L,j}(k))\, d_i, & \text{if } s_k = R \end{cases} \tag{7.10}$$

where $n_{L,j}(k)$ defines the number of L playing neighbours of the other population $j \neq i$. However, each player compares their respective payoff with those neighbours who are of the same population.

While we might expect that the addition of a second population adds considerably to the complexity of our analysis, it turns out that the two-population case is only a minor extension of the single-population scenario. The reason is that given the payoff matrix in Figure 7.5 as well

Player 2

		L	R
Player 1	L	a_1, a_2	b_1, c_2
	R	c_1, b_2	d_1, d_2

Figure 7.5: Non-symmetric 2×2 coordination game assuming $a_i, d_i > b_i, c_i$.

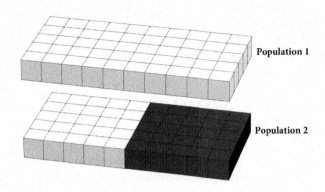

Population 1

Population 2

Figure 7.6: Illustration of the two-player population interaction.

as $a_i, d_i > b_i, c_i$, the strategy distributions of both populations coincide after a brief sequence of interactions. In other words, we only observe *pure* clusters that play the same strategy across both populations after some time, whereas *mixed* clusters, in which populations choose opposite strategies, disappear.

To understand the reason for these dynamics, imagine two different clusters: one cluster is mixed and to its left is a second cluster that is pure. This is shown in Figure 7.6 where the populations are superimposed instead of situated at the same level for visual clarity. Remember that imitation occurs between neighbours of the same population while the individual payoff depends on the strategies chosen by neighbours of the other population. Consequently, members of population 1 do not switch strategy since there is no alternative to imitate since everyone in their population chooses the same strategy. Change in the next period can therefore only happen within population 2 at the border between the clusters. Assume that individuals on white cells play L and individuals on the black cells play R. Every member of the pure cluster will obtain a payoff of $8a_i$ including the members of population 2. In contrast, any individual on a black patch receives only $8c_2$ from choosing R. The member of the mixed cluster in population 2 bordering the pure cluster then compares payoffs with a neighbour of the same population in the pure cluster and switches her strategy to L since $a_2 > c_2$. The logic is analogous if we change the strategies attributed to the black and white patches given that $d_i > b_i$. This implies that institutional change is triggered by a number of individuals that involve all of the participating groups. Keep in mind that here, we only consider organic institutions that are based on spontaneous, uncoordinated and involuntary choice (Menger, 1963) and not pragmatic institutions built on intent nor revolutionary change governed by social dynamics similar to those discussed in Chapter 5.

In the following, we will only look at the scenario in which no clear convention has been established and individuals choose each strategy with roughly equal probability. Remember that the payoff premium $\rho_i = d_i - a_i$ of population i is positive if $\mathscr{R}$ payoff dominates $\mathscr{L}$ and the inverse if ρ_i is negative. The risk premium $\mu_i = b_i - c_i - \rho_i$ is positive if $\mathscr{L}$ risk dominates $\mathscr{R}$ and negative if $\mathscr{R}$ risk dominates $\mathscr{L}$. Since no initial convention is established, we know from our previous reasoning that the population will be mostly defined by pure clusters of size $r = 9$ after a few periods of interaction. Only members at the border of a cluster observe a neighbour choosing a different strategy and therefore we only need to consider these players in our analysis.

A *border* member has a neighbour who is interior to the pure cluster and receives the maximum payoff which is $8a_i$ or $8d_i$, respectively. She compares this payoff to her neighbour who is at the border of the opposite pure strategy cluster and receives a mixed payoff from playing the opposite strategy. A border member switches if the neighbour with the highest payoff choosing the opposite strategy receives a higher payoff than the highest payoff obtained in her own cluster. Define $\eta_{s,i}$ with $s = L, R$ as the number of neighbours in population $i = 1, 2$ that play the opposite strategy and not s. (It will become clear in a second why I flip the notation.) An R player in i switches if $(8 - \eta_{L,i})a_i + \eta_{L,i}b_i > 8d_i$ and an L player changes strategy if $(8 - \eta_{R,i})d_i + \eta_{R,i}c_i > 8a_i$. Solving for n_s, we obtain

$$\eta_{L,i} < \frac{-8\rho_i}{a_i - c_i - \rho_i - \mu_i} \tag{7.11a}$$

$$\eta_{R,i} < \frac{8\rho_i}{a_i - c_i + \rho_i} \tag{7.11b}$$

Note that inequality equation (7.11a) requires that $\rho_i < 0$ (i.e. $\mathscr{L}$ payoff dominates $\mathscr{R}$ for population i) since the denominators in both equalities are positive given $a_i > b_i$. The values of $n_{L,i}$ and $n_{R,i}$ define the maximum number of individuals playing the opposite strategy and thus the minimum number of neighbours that play the same strategy required to induce a switch. In other words, a larger $n_{s,i}$ implies that fewer players of a strategy are needed to be sufficiently attractive for a border player to switch to that strategy. Consequently, $n_{L,i}$ and $n_{R,i}$ simultaneously determine the likelihood at which a border member changes strategy, and also give us a value for the pace at which one strategy takes over both populations. The strategy with the largest pace eventually defines the long-term convention. Since neighbours come in integers, we use the floor function $\lfloor \cdot \rfloor$ to drop the decimal part of a positive rational number (e.g. $\lfloor 6.314 \rfloor = 6$) and to define the set of integers that meet conditions (7.11) given by $\lfloor \eta_{A,i} \rfloor$ for $A = \{L, R\}$. We can then define

$$\eta_L = \max\left\{ \lfloor \eta_{L,1} \rfloor, \lfloor \eta_{L,2} \rfloor \right\} \tag{7.12a}$$

$$\eta_R = \max\left\{ \lfloor \eta_{R,1} \rfloor, \lfloor \eta_{R,2} \rfloor \right\} \tag{7.12b}$$

In other words, η_L and η_R define the largest integers for which equations (7.11a) and (7.11b) hold, respectively, across both populations, and determine the fastest relative pace at which each strategy proliferates. The strategy that is adopted more readily by a population eventually defines its convention. We have the following[6]

$$\mathscr{R} \text{ is the convention if } \eta_R > \eta_L$$

$$\mathscr{L} \text{ is the convention if } \eta_L > \eta_R \tag{7.13}$$

$$\text{The population remains in a mixed state if } \eta_R = \eta_L$$

To summarise the simple logic behind condition (7.13): if no incumbent convention exists and individuals opt for strategies at random, large pure clusters with a cluster of size nine occur after an initial period of interaction and the clusters that expand most rapidly eventually define the convention. However, this is only the case if the average payoff for both strategies does not differ too greatly and the distribution is initially sufficiently heterogeneous.[7]

The results in equations (7.12) and (7.13) offer some interesting predictions. If two populations illustrate a common interest (i.e. the same convention is payoff dominant for both populations), the population converges to the convention or institution that maximises social efficiency.[8] If both populations have conflicting interests and none of the conventions is payoff dominant for both populations, the strategy with the higher *pace of convergence* constitutes the long-term institution. The inequalities (7.11) show a trade-off between the risk and payoff premia. We can further see that these dynamics can lead to an inegalitarian institution that significantly benefits only one population but disadvantages the other population. Under certain circumstances, organic conventions and institutions may illustrate the tendency to become increasingly inequitable.

However, as we shall observe, the importance of the payoff premium depends on the scale of an individual's neighbourhood. Since the chessboard grid can be re-interpreted as an eight-regular graph, we can adapt the notion of an immediate neighbourhood to define a new neighbourhood within a **Chebychev distance** of k. We can think of the Chebychev distance as the geodesic distance but applied to the gridded plane. Remember that the neighbourhood of a node i in an undirected graph is defined as $N_i(g) = \{k \in N | l_{ik} = 1\}$, and on the two-dimensional plane I equivalently defined $N_i(g) = \{j \in N : j \sim i\}$. In the given context, these are the eight neighbours surrounding any agent i at a Chebychev distance of 1. The Chebychev distance of 2 adds the neighbours of the former to the set of neighbours (i.e., all those individuals that are two cells away from some player i). This holds for each larger distance and we can define the neighbourhood of an agent i within a Chebychev distance k as

$$\mathcal{N}_i^1(g) = N_i(g) \text{ and } \mathcal{N}_i^k(g) = \mathcal{N}_i^{k-1}(g) \cup \left(\bigcup_{l \in \mathcal{N}_i^{k-1}(g)} N_l(g) \right) \setminus \{i\} \qquad (7.14)$$

The right equation looks daunting since the neighbourhood within a distance k is defined in an inductive manner. Yet, the interpretation is straightforward. The neighbourhood at distance 1 is simply the neighbourhood in the eight-regular graph we defined in (7.1). The neighbourhood at a distance 2 is the union of the neighbourhood at distance 1 and the neighbours of all those nodes/agents in the former neighbourhood, i.e., the neighbours' neighbours. At a distance 3, the neighbourhood is given by the neighbourhood at 2 and their neighbours. The neighbourhood at the next higher distance is then derived through another repetition of the iterative process. Since she is obviously a neighbour of her neighbours, we exclude node i from the set of neighbours.

Note that individuals interact in two different types of neighbourhoods. The first neighbourhood is defined as the set of individuals who affect a player's payoffs. This neighbourhood therefore represents the size of the externality that an agent exerts. In our example, payoffs were determined by the player's strategy choice and the actions of the eight surrounding neighbours. This also implies that the player's strategy influences the payoff of the eight neighbouring players in turn.

The second neighbourhood is defined by the set of agents a player considers for imitation, and mutatis mutandis, the number of neighbours that consider her strategy. So far, we have assumed that both neighbourhoods are of the same size (i.e. eight neighbours) and perfectly overlap. Both neighbourhoods have a different impact on the likelihood of a payoff dominant convention versus a risk-dominant convention. If the risk-dominant convention is incumbent, an increase in the neighbourhood considered for imitation, i.e. the *imitation distance*, expands the area of appeal of the higher payoff generated by invaders and thus, the latter can take over a population more quickly as long as they reach a sufficiently large cluster size. On the other hand, increasing the neighbourhood that defines a player's payoff, i.e. the *externality distance*, increases the minimum cluster size necessary to invade a population. If the cluster size is too small, the payoff of members of an invading cluster is too low for the latter to proliferate.

Similarly, if no institution is incumbent and individuals choose a strategy initially at random, a player's payoff is closer to the expected value at high externality distances. Since the risk-dominant strategy generates a larger average payoff (remember, $0.5a + 0.5b > 0.5c + 0.5d$ if L risk dominates), most individuals initially shift to the risk-dominant strategy which renders a sufficiently large cluster playing the payoff dominant strategy less probable. Yet, if such a cluster evolves, it will take over the population more quickly since it negatively affects the payoff of those playing the risk-dominant strategy. We should therefore observe a positive impact at moderate externality distances. Similarly, a larger imitation distance disadvantages the payoff dominant strategy if no incumbent convention exists, since such a distribution tends to generate payoffs around the average but it increases the speed at which clusters expand. Figure 7.7 illustrates the interplay between both distances. An imitation distance of 1 (i.e. an individual imitates the 8 adjacent players) strongly

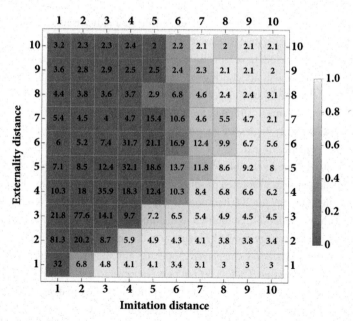

Figure 7.7: Simulation results for $a = 10$, $b = 0$, $c = 4$, and $d = 8$ on a 103×103 torus. Darker colours indicate higher frequency of the payoff dominant convention, lighter colours illustrate higher frequency of the risk-dominant convention. Numbers equal the average number of periods required for reaching a stable distribution.

supports the evolution of the payoff dominant convention while a distance larger than 8 leads to the risk-dominant convention. As expected, moderate externality distances up to a value of 6 encourage a payoff dominant convention, but this does not hold for larger externality distances. We can further observe combinations of distances in which sustainable clusters of each strategy evolve as is indicated by the grey areas in Figure 7.7. However, not all grey areas indicate the existence of both strategies in the final equilibrium state. Only interactions with an imitation distance smaller than 6 and an externality distance smaller than 4 demonstrate such an equilibrium state with persistent subcultures. At higher distances, a population converges to one of the pure conventions depending on whether the initial random distribution allowed for the evolution of a sufficiently larger cluster playing the payoff dominant strategy. Consequently, some simulations converge to $\mathcal{L}$ while other simulation stabilise at $\mathcal{R}$. Notice also that up to an imitation distance of 6, the periods required before a stable state is reached and thus the rate of convergence tends to be highest if the externality distance is one unit higher than the imitation distance. This is caused by the opposing impact of the distances on the pure conventional states. Convergence occurs quickly if one of the distances is relatively large. It takes less than ten periods (and frequently only two periods) on average since the population almost immediately collapses into the equilibrium state after the simulation is initiated.

7.4 Other Spatial Games

So far, we have only studied general coordination games with two strategies. This type of interaction also exhibits interesting properties if applied to other 2×2 games. In Chapter 2, we have seen that the prisoner's dilemma has a dominant strategy that implies it is always a best response to defect, independent of the other player's action. While I already discussed that the prisoner's dilemma is inappropriately specified to represent most social environments, cooperation can also be established if the same actors have a positive chance of being matched again in later iterations of the game. Since players will act contingent on their past experience with another player in this case, an initial defection by one player can entail punishment in the form of defection of the other player in future encounters. Different punishment strategies can then lead to various average payoffs.[9] Yet, not all such strategies are evolutionarily efficient and thus, not all average payoffs will be realised in a realistic context.

Around 1980, Robert Axelrod held a tournament to study the evolutionary efficiency (i.e. fitness) of various strategies in a repeated prisoner's dilemma (see Axelrod, 2006). Each strategy was paired with any other strategy for 200 iterations of the game.[10] The most successful strategy was a very simple algorithm - *Tit-for-Tat*. Submitted to the tournament by Anatol Rapoport, Tit-for-Tat dictates that the response strategy should be identical to the strategy chosen by the opponent in the previous period. In the first period, the player cooperates and then just mirrors the other player's earlier strategy. We can see that Tit-for-Tat is a best response to itself as well as any cooperator, leading to perpetual cooperation, and it is an almost optimal response to defectors. The Tit-for-Tat player only loses in relative terms during the first period, but then does equally well (or bad) as the defector.

Yet, Axelrod's tournament has a shortcoming - interactions are entirely deterministic. Agents never make mistakes, neither while choosing an action nor while identifying the opponent's action.

In noisy environments, however, Tit-for-Tat performs poorly, since it is not forgiving. If players tend to make an error with some positive probability in each round, cooperation in a population of Tit-for-Tat players eventually breaks down leading to universal defection. A sufficiently larger group of cooperators could invade such a population which in turn can be invaded by defectors. More forgiving variations and particularly *Generous Tit-for-Tat* and *Contrite Tit-for-Tat* therefore tend to perform better at high noise levels, and given the right environment, also *Pavlov* tends to perform well.[11] These strategies eventually lead to an environment in which cooperation thrives (see Nowak and Sigmund, 1992; Kraines and Kraines, 1993; Wedekind and Milinski, 1996; Boerlust et al., 1997).

A second drawback of Axelrod's tournament is that it ignores the impact of social structure. We observed that interactions restricted to a subset of the population demonstrate different dynamics than interactions with random pairing. In the latter case, individuals face approximately the same environment over time and local differences disappear. Local interaction, to the contrary, can lead to radically different environments in distinct neighbourhoods. Consequently, while free-riding defectors only benefit from cooperators in their neighbourhood, the positive externalities of cooperation can allow a concentration of cooperators who survive and even invade a population of defectors.[12]

Nowak and May (1992) studied how local interactions change the dynamics and lead to different strategic landscapes. The authors used a bounded lattice structure in which individuals interact with their eight neighbours as well as themselves.[13] The authors studied the dynamics of a particular prisoner's dilemma defined by payoffs $a = 1$ and $b = d = 0$ and different benefits from unilateral defection given by $c > a$ in payoff matrix in Figure 7.3.[14] Neither strategy outperforms the other but cooperators and defectors tend to group together in complex changing patterns if the benefit of defection lies between 1.8 and 2. In this setup, the proliferation of the cooperative strategy requires that the population is neither too much nor too little connected. In the extreme case of a complete network with n players, payoffs are simply defined by n times the average payoff of each strategy. Given that the defective strategy is weakly dominant, since $c > a$, defect has a larger average payoff and thus all players in the complete network will choose to defect. In the other extreme – the one-dimensional circle – the neighbours of some player i are then defined by $N_i(g) = \{i - 1, i + 1\}$. Suppose a string of three players cooperates and is surrounded by defectors. As before, changes only occur at the boundaries between but not within clusters (or strings in this case) formed by players choosing the same strategy. It therefore suffices to compare the payoff of two cooperating neighbours and their adjacent defecting neighbours. The central cooperating neighbour has a payoff of $2a = 2$ while her cooperating neighbours to the left and right receive $a + b = 1$. The adjacent defectors have a payoff of $c + d = c$. Given that to cooperate is weakly dominated, the cooperating string can never expand. As long as $c \leq 2$, the string of three cooperators is stable and will not shrink.[15] At $c > 2$, free-riding on a single neighbour exceeds the combined gain of being a cooperator surrounded by fellow cooperators and the cooperating string disappears. A single defector can invade a population of cooperators, since the former receives a payoff of $2c$, and spawns a string of three defectors. At this point, the surrounding defectors receive a payoff of $c + d = c$ which needs to exceed $2a$ for the string to expand. Thus, the stability condition $c \leq 2$ holds for both invading cooperators and defectors. (Exercise 7.6 asks you to calculate the critical values for c for a two-dimensional torus.)

Exercise 7.6

(a) Show that defectors can spread across the two-dimensional lattice in the von-Neumann neighbourhoods if $c > 15.94$ and the remaining parameters defined by Figure 7.8. (b) Define the critical values for c, such that (i) a cluster of cooperators expands uniformly, (ii) along the axes, (iii) is stable.

If interactions ensue on a two-dimensional torus, a population of cooperators can be infiltrated by a single defector. Similarly, a 3×3 cluster of cooperators can proliferate in a population of defectors. This result is preserved independently of whether or not an individual interacts with herself. Thus, in contrast to Nowak and May (1992), I ignore self-interaction in the following to remain consistent with our discussion in the previous sections. Figures 7.8a and 7.8b illustrate the former case of a single invading defector. After 30 periods, the defector has spawned 2.372 other defectors, but defectors do not form a uniform cluster. Small clusters of cooperators survive between clusters of defectors forming an intricate but symmetric pattern reminiscent of Persian carpets. After another 70 periods, the complex pattern has spread across the entire population. Not only do cooperators and defectors coexist, the pattern is ever changing. Individuals at the borders of clusters change strategy periodically leading to shrinking and expanding clusters of each strategy. Correspondingly, Figures 7.8c and 7.8d show the patterns created by an invading cluster of 3×3 cooperators. After 30 periods, 713 individuals choose to cooperate and the number of cooperators

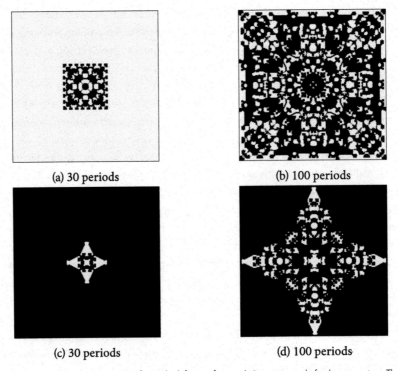

(a) 30 periods

(b) 100 periods

(c) 30 periods

(d) 100 periods

Figure 7.8: The upper row shows the invasion of a single defector of a population composed of only cooperators. The lower row shows the invasion of a 3×3 cluster of cooperator of a population of only defectors. A black cell indicates a defector, a light grey cell indicates a cooperator. The size of the lattice is 199×199, parameters are $a = 10$, $b = 0$, $c = 16.1$, and $d = 0.1$.

continues to increase, yet at a slower rate than in the case of a single infiltrating defector. Again, both strategies coexist in an intricate pattern. At 100 periods, the pattern has not yet spread across the entire population (see Figure 7.8d) but has mainly expanded along the axes. It will require another 125 period before the symmetric pattern has spread across the entire lattice structure.

These results raise two issues. While the fractal structures are beautiful, they are not realistic. Additionally, the patterns are unstable and the population is unable to reach an equilibrium. After only a few interaction periods, the strategy pattern looks remarkably different. In other words, a significant share of today's cooperators are tomorrow's defectors and vice versa. These dynamics seem rather unrealistic and can be addressed by allowing individuals to choose a mixed strategy, i.e. to defect with some probability $p \in (0, 1)$ and cooperate with probability $1 - p$. In this case, the population converges over time to a slowly changing distribution in which roughly 80 percent of the population chooses to cooperate with some fixed probability $p^* \in (0.60, 0.75)$. Figure 7.9a shows such a quasi-stable distribution in which 81 percent play a mixed strategy with $p^* = 0.677$.

Another way to improve the degree of realism of this model is by changing the updating process into a stochastic process. Under reasonable circumstances, not all individuals update their strategies simultaneously. More fickle players question their previous choices at a higher rate than their more steadfast peers. External circumstances that are not captured by the model may make some players question their previous choices. Assume that in each period, a randomly picked share of 66 percent of the population updates their previous choices while the rest sticks to the strategy chosen in the earlier period. At the critical value $c \geq 15.94$, a single defector does not only proliferate as in the previous case, but the strategy is eventually adopted by all players while for any lower values, the number of defectors fails to increase after the first few periods. Therefore, stochastic updating lowers the invasion barrier above which defectors succeed in replacing the entire population whereas at the same payoffs, the population would only maintain a shifting mixed pattern of defection and cooperation under synchronous updating.

A cluster of 3×3 cooperators in turn, can only invade a defector population if $c \leq 15.94$. Figures 7.9b and 7.9c demonstrate the dynamics for $c = 15.9$. Invasion takes significantly more time, yet eventually the system settles on a quasi-stable equilibrium. This equilibrium is defined by an almost fixed structure in which less than 1 percent of the population flips back and forth between strategies. A vast majority of cooperators are segmented by narrow channels of defectors. Hence, a regime shift occurs at the critical $c^* = 15.94$: at smaller benefits from defection, a majority

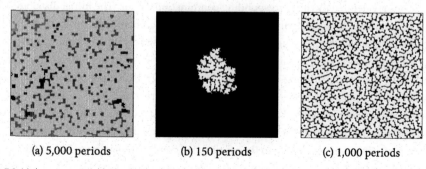

(a) 5,000 periods   (b) 150 periods   (c) 1,000 periods

Figure 7.9: (a) shows a quasi-stable distribution with mixed strategies, (b) and (c) show the invasion of a population of defectors by a 3×3 cluster of cooperators, given a probability that an agent updates their strategy equal to 66 percent. Parameters are $a = 10$, $b = 0$, $c = 15.9$, and $d = 0.1$.

	A	**B**	**C**
Comply	0.25, 0.75	0, 1	0, 1
Renegotiate	0, 1	0.5, 0.5	0, 1
Persevere	0, 1	0, 1	0.75, 0.25

Figure 7.10: 3×3 *zero* sum game with no equilibrium in pure strategies and mixed equilibrium $\alpha_1 = \beta_1 = 6/11$ and $\alpha_2 = \beta_2 = 3/11$.

of the population cooperates but tolerates a few free-riders; at larger values, the entire population eventually defects.

Other 2×2 games illustrate interesting properties on regular lattices. For example, Doves can invade a population of Hawks in a symmetric Hawk-Dove game and create sophisticated regular patterns within a certain parameter range, whereas hawks are able to conquer the entire population. Unfortunately, a more systematic study of these games on regular lattices lies outside of the scope of this chapter. Yet, before concluding this chapter I will briefly come back to our study of coordination and conventions. So far, we have studied situations in which a population coordinates on one of two equilibria in pure strategies. While our previous results extend naturally to more than two strategies, it is interesting to see if spatial interactions can help a population to coordinate in the absence of a pure strategy equilibrium. A variation of the zero sum game with three strategies is given in the payoff matrix in Figure 7.10. Instead of a sum of 0, joint payoffs always sum to 1. We might think here of a situation in which the column population chooses one of three strategies A, B or C, and the row population has only one suitable counter-strategy for each action of the former population. Not all counter-strategies are equally efficient. Strategy *comply* grants the lowest payoff of only one-quarter of the total payoff, *renegotiate* splits the spoils equally and by playing *persevere* against strategy C, the column population receives three-quarters of the total payoff. Based on the discussion in Chapter 2, we can see that the game has no Nash equilibrium in pure strategies, but an equilibrium in mixed strategies (see pages 14–17) at $\alpha_1 = \beta_1 = 6/11$ and $\alpha_2 = \beta_2 = 3/11$, where α_1 denotes the frequency of A, α_2 of B, and for the row players, β_1 denotes the probability to *comply*, and β_2 to *renegotiate*. Consequently, row players will only pick the correct counter-strategy with a probability of $49/121 \approx 0.41$, leading to an expected payoff of $\pi_{row} = 3/22 \approx 0.14$ whereas column players obtain a payoff of $\pi_{column} = 1 - \pi_{row}$.

Figure 7.11 illustrates the outcomes of two different simulations at the first simulation period and at period 30. A primary colour indicates that players on the same patch play one of the strategy combinations on the main diagonal of the payoff matrix in Figure 7.10 and off-diagonal strategy compositions are defined by the corresponding combination colour. The initial distributions in period 1 of both simulations, shown in Figures 7.11a and 7.11c, are indistinguishable. Individuals choose all strategies with the same probability and thus the initial period is not biased towards any strategy at an aggregate level. Yet minor local differences in the initial strategy distribution can lead to significant variations in the long-run dynamics. In Figure 7.11b, the population entirely abandons both strategies *persevere* and C. The blue and green areas represent areas in which row players choose the best response to A and B, respectively. Since the interaction on the lattice turns into a *Matching Pennies* type game, in which neighbouring players cycle through the strategy profiles: column players switch strategies leading to the off-diagonal combinations shown in turquoise, upon which row players switch strategies leading to the diagonal combinations. Hence, the regular patterns keep moving through the lattice. Column players generate profits that are slightly lower than the expected profit of the mixed strategy while row players obtain a small premium of 14 percent.

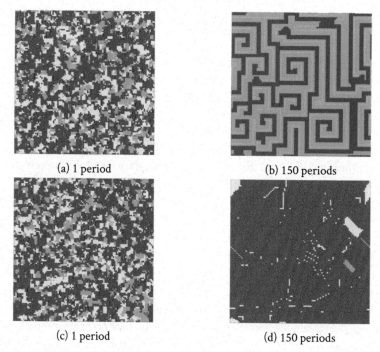

(a) 1 period   (b) 150 periods

(c) 1 period   (d) 150 periods

Figure 7.11: Different equilibrium states of the game in Figure 7.10 starting with a virtually identical initial distribution at which each strategy is chosen with probability $1/3$. Colour code: *blue* = $\{Comply, A\}$, *green* = $\{renegotiate, B\}$, and *red* = $\{persevere, C\}$, remaining colours are the combination of the primary colours: brown indicates either $\{comply, C\}$ or $\{persevere, A\}$, turquoise $\{comply, B\}$ or $\{renegotiate, A\}$, yellow $\{persevere, B\}$ or $\{renegotiate, C\}$.

In the second case, the population has reached the stable strategy distribution shown in Figure 7.11d. In the brown and yellow areas, column players choose C and row players *comply* and *renegotiate*, respectively. In the small turquoise regions, the former opt for B while row players *comply*. The payoff distribution between column and row players is completely different compared to the first case. In other words, column players maximise their payoff while row players leave empty-handed. If, however, updating is asynchronous and stochastic, all strategy combinations occur (not illustrated). Column players have now an additional revenue of 25–30 percent and row players lose 4–5 percent compared to the mixed strategy payoff.

Exercise 7.7

Here is an entirely different game: Mr. and Mrs. Smith join a soirée on a Saturday evening and meet other married couples. Mrs. Smith asks each person, including Mr. Smith, to state the number of different attendees to whom they have been introduced. Each person gives a different answer. Determine to how many people have Mrs. and Mr. Smith been introduced. Use a graph to find your answer - nodes define attendees and a link is formed between two nodes whenever attendees are introduced to each other. (Note: Obviously, spouses need not be introduced to each other nor is any person introduced to herself or himself.) (a) Start with the simplest case in which the soirée is attended by only one other couple. (b) Find the solution if four other couples attend the soirée.

7.5 Extension: Co-evolving networks

While we have studied the impact of social structure on the dynamics and equilibria of various games, I have ignored another important aspect. The regular lattices on which these games are played are outside of the individuals' control. In reality, however, a behavioural rule is commonly not limited to the choice of which action is chosen but also with/against whom the action is implemented. The social network therefore evolves endogenously as individuals not only revise their choices but also their peers. Given the limitation of space, I will briefly discuss a very simple setup based on Thurner et al. (2018) that will help us build a grasp for the dynamics in a co-evolving network topology.

Assume that players interact with their neighbours in a network and each player has to make a binary choice $s_i = \{-1, 1\}$. Since this can be any binary choice, the model setup is broad enough to capture various social setups related to questions of conformity. At each time t, some node i and one of her neighbours, say j, are randomly chosen. Node i then updates her action to the one that j has chosen previously, i.e. $s_i(t+1) = s_j(t)$. In this simplified version of the **voter model**, social imitation is purely stochastic and not based on payoffs. Similar to our previous study, a node has only a positive probability of changing her action if at least one of her neighbours opts for a different action. The highest likelihood of a change in action then occurs in a completely random distribution in which each player has chosen each strategy with equal probability. The likelihood or frequency of change is

$$\rho_D = \left(\sum_{i=1}^{N} \sum_{j=1}^{N} G_{ij} \frac{1 - s_i s_j}{2} \right) \bigg/ \sum_{i=1}^{N} \eta_i \tag{7.15}$$

with η_i being the degree of i and G_{ij} being the element of the adjacency matrix at i, j. Note that $1 - s_i s_j$ has a positive value only if nodes i and j play a different strategy and similarly, the adjacency matrix has only a positive value at i, j if both nodes are neighbours. Following equation (7.15), we count the number of times in which node i chooses an action different from her neighbours and sum this number over all nodes while dividing by the total number of neighbours. Thus, we obtain the relative frequency at which nodes differ from their neighbours. The maximum value of ρ_D is $1/2$, i.e. at a completely random distribution in which on average half of the neighbours play a different action.

In two-dimensional regular lattices, the model converges to one of the two absorbing states, in which all members of the network play the same strategy.[16] However, Vazquez et al. (2008) extend the model by adding a *rewiring probability* p to the model. With probability $1 - p$, a node i updates according to the previous process. With probability p, however, node i does not switch to the action of a randomly chosen neighbour j, but removes the link to the latter (i.e. j is no longer a neighbour of i) and instead, establishes a link to a node m, who is not already a neighbour but has chosen the same action. At $p = 0$, we obtain the initial model while at $p = 1$, members of the network never change action but only rewire. In the former case, as we have seen, the population converges to a state in which all members opt for the same action. In the latter case, the network splits into two components, each playing a different action. Notice that for values of $p \in (0, 1)$, the network topology and the distribution of actions co-evolve. There exists a critical value p^c

at some point in the unit interval, where the system undergoes a **phase transition** from a single component to two network components with opposing actions.

Keep in mind that the model has some limitations. The order and size of the network are constant since a new link is established at the cost of an old link. The decision to connect is based on a node's state or action, but not their position within the network. In chapter 6 on page 141, we have seen a model in which agents connect to others both based on the latter's identity (which we can easily reinterpret as a state or action), and their degree and hence their direct relatedness to other members of the network. We can readily extend the earlier models in this chapter by assuming that individuals are not confined to a fixed set of neighbours and thus a lattice structure, but actions and neighbourhoods co-evolve endogenously. Since both factors can produce intricate patterns of differential behavioural rules, a study of the interplay would generate fascinating results, but such a study goes beyond the constraints of this chapter.

7.6 Conclusion

In this chapter, I introduced social structure to our study of strategic interactions. We have seen that localised interactions can significantly affect social dynamics. Populations are more capable of establishing socially efficient conventions, but spatial interactions also allow for the evolution of local practices and conventions. Depending on the type of interaction and the definition of peers, individuals are able to establish enclaves that adhere to a particular behavioural rule. In deterministic setups, the strategy distribution then creates sophisticated patterns of local rules that resemble fractal structures. These symmetric structures either become more organic and realistic or tend to disappear once we introduce stochastic elements to the replication process. In other cases, we have seen that social structure can prevent the convergence towards a unique equilibrium and social rules are sequentially adopted or abandoned by parts of society. Social structure offers a much richer set of results and a more comprehensive understanding of social dynamics.

Applications and Relation to Other Chapters

The results that we obtained in this chapter stress again a number of important implications. In various scenarios, spatial games exhibit fundamentally different dynamics compared to their counterparts in which a small number of players simultaneously interact or engage in pairwise random matching within a larger population, which we studied in Chapters 2 as well as 3 and 4, respectively. Spatial models can illustrate sudden regime shifts, i.e., phase transitions that are initiated by minor changes to the parameter values or in the initial distributions. Small changes to the initial strategy distribution that are imperceptible at an aggregate level can lead to fundamentally different outcomes. While this may seem similar to a situation in which a population initiates the interaction at opposite sides of but very close to a separatrix, the cause for this variation in dynamics is different. In the simulations in Figure 7.11, the same number of individuals has initially chosen a particular strategy; the critical difference was a minor disparity in the local distributions along the regular grid. However, once we account for random idiosyncratic changes, these differences tend to disappear in some cases, such as in the zero-sum game, but not, for example, in the prisoner's dilemma which we both studied here.

For spatial coordination games, the results are more subtle. While the social system still converges to a coordination convention and thus a Nash equilibrium, the long-run properties differ from the findings of Chapter 4 as long as the fixed neighbourhood of a player is sufficiently small. Instead of the risk-dominant convention, individuals end up in an efficient convention as long as the latter is sufficiently more efficient for the members of society. Indeed, we observe here a result that appears paradoxical. Individuals with limited cognitive abilities, both in respect to their decision heuristic and their understanding of their environment are eventually able to coordinate better than what seem to be more capable actors. Generally, this chapter should convince the reader of the potential importance of studying not only preferences, expectation or strategies, but also the spatial distribution and the social networks in which social actors interact to understand behavioural rules and institutions in a society.

This chapter is undoubtedly connected to Chapter 6, but it extends also to our discussion in Chapter 3. The spatial version of the replicator equation, which I briefly discuss in Appendix A.4.4 ties the latter to spatial interactions which study the social dynamics on regular graphs under stochastic social imitation. Furthermore, social structure can affect the results we obtained in Chapter 5. Similar to the differences between the equilibria obtained in small and large groups, if thresholds are distributed randomly among members (see Figure 5.4 on page 101), interactions limited to peers and thus a subset of the population can make it difficult for heavily structured societies to reach the equilibrium at which the threshold distribution intersects the 45° line (see also Granovetter, 1978).

Further Reading

While there are a number of introductory textbooks, Goyal (2007) probably offers the most elegant presentation of social network analysis. For reasons of space, I have not covered endogenously evolving networks (except for the short discussion in Section 6.5), but the study of the latter has spawned an important literature. Since the study of the role of weak ties in Granovetter (1973), it has become apparent that strategic *networking* entails advantageous outcomes for an individual. By occupying a central position in the network (i.e., one that ranks high in the centrality measures of Chapter 6), an individual improves on her job opportunities, in terms of job positions offered, income levels or choice of partners etc. Goyal (2007, Chapters 7–9) discusses the most common models in the literature during the past two decades. For other literature on the emergence of topologies from a given set of links and agents, see Kirman (1983, 1997) and Kirman et al. (1986) as well as Ioannides (1990, 2006).

Notes

1   Note that the torus constitutes a circle along the x-axis and y-axis, and the loops create an infinite number of possible coordinates for a single cell. For a population of size $n = n_x \times n_y$ (i.e. n_x individuals are arranged in a line along the x-axis, and n_y individuals are positioned along the y-axis) each cell/individual i can then be given a unique coordinate $(\hat{x}, \hat{y})$, with $\hat{x} = x \mod n_x$ and $\hat{y} = y \mod n_y$. The neighbours above some individual k at the upper edge $(n_x - 1, y)$ are then defined by $(0, y + w)$, with $w \in \{-1, 0, 1\}$ and equivalently for individuals at the right edge of the plane at $(x, n_y - 1)$, right neighbours are at coordinates $(x + w, 0)$.

2   For a coordination game, it generally suffices to define $a > c$ and $d > b$. The additional assumption is made as a simplification, but the exercises help you to study the more general case.

3   Further details as well as the proofs can be found in Ille (2014).

4   This also holds for the outer players of the line cluster, since $a, d > b, c$. If this is not the case, these outer players have the highest payoff with either $a + 7b$ or $7c + d$ and strategies L and R are payoff inferior.

5   Ille (2013) provides simulation plots for the results obtained in this section.

6   We can define the measure more in line with the resistances of Chapter 4. Let $\eta_{s,i}$ be the number of players that choose strategy s instead. We then have to solve $\eta_{L,i} a_i + (8 - \eta_{L,i}) b_i > 8 d_i$ and an L and $\eta_{R,i} d_i + (8 - \eta_{R,i}) c_i > 8 a_i$, to obtain

$$\eta_{L,i} > \frac{8(a - c - \mu)}{a - c - \mu - \rho}$$

$$\eta_{R,i} > \frac{8(a - c)}{a - c + \rho}$$

Note that for $\eta_{L,i} < 8$, we still need that $\rho_i < 0$. We obtain

$$\eta_L = \min \left\{ \lceil \eta_{L,1} \rceil, \lceil \eta_{L,2} \rceil \right\}$$

$$\eta_R = \min \left\{ \lceil \eta_{R,1} \rceil, \lceil \eta_{R,2} \rceil \right\}$$

and equivalent to the resistances, we have

$$\mathscr{R} \text{ is the convention if } \eta_R < \eta_L$$

$$\mathscr{L} \text{ is the convention if } \eta_L < \eta_R$$

The population remains in a mixed state if $\eta_R = \eta_L$

7   In fact, I assume that either the populations are sufficiently large or average payoffs are of similar scale. If individuals choose a strategy initially at random, too diverse average payoffs can inhibit the evolution of clusters that are comprised of players of the risk inferior strategy. These clusters do not reach a sufficient size to overtake the player population.

8   If the payoff inferior convention is already established, the convergence speed of one population must be at least three, which is a direct consequence of our previous discussion. Otherwise, the population exhibits a number of stable, rectangular-shaped clusters in which some adhere to locally inefficient conventions.

9   This result has been termed the **Folk Theorem**, since the existence of multiple possible Nash equilibria in repeated games has been commonly known among game theorists and it is unclear who first invented it. More precisely, the Folk Theorem states that if players are sufficiently patient and farsighted, any reasonable outcome can be a subgame perfect Nash equilibrium of the repeated game. A lack of patience implies that players discount future payoffs too drastically which precludes the threat of punishment. Farsighted implies that players take a sufficient number of future interactions into account while subgame perfection entails, simply speaking, that the strategy profile is a Nash equilibrium if we ignore past interactions. The last assumption, reasonable, means that players do not accept to choose a strategy that does not guarantee at least the fall-back payoff. Consider the game in Figure 2.4c on page 15. Players can ensure that they never receive less than an average payoff of 1 if they always defect. Consequently, they would never opt for a strategy that does not ensure at least this payoff. The threat of mutual punishment can lead to a subgame perfect Nash equilibrium with expected payoffs of 2 for both players. Yet, other combinations are also possible, such as $(2.5, 1)$ or $(1.5, 1.5)$.

10 The tournament was repeated with a stochastic/variable game length in a second round.

11 Pavlov implies that a player maintains her strategy if she won (i.e. the opponent cooperated) and switches to her other strategy if she lost (i.e. the opponent defected). Generous Tit-for-Tat only retaliates with a probability of $1 - a/b$ where a is the cost of cooperation (equal to 1 in Figure 2.4c) and b is the benefit of cheating the other (i.e. 3 in Figure 2.4c). Under contrite Tit-for-Tat, a player does not punish an earlier defection by equally choosing to defect if her counterpart has done so after being provoked, i.e. if the player herself has unilaterally defected two periods prior. In other words, the player is willing to pay penance for an earlier mistake.

12 In addition to strategies with memory in repeated interactions and local interaction and imitation, a third type of interaction structure is able to explain the evolution of cooperation and altruistic traits. While defective free-riders obtain an evolutionary advantage over their altruistic peers, a group as a whole benefit from the existence of cooperators. Consequently, selection operates against cooperators within a group but in their favour in the presence of between-group contest or warfare. Thus, multi-level selection can explain the evolution of altruism as long as the selection pressure between groups is relatively strong and groups are sufficiently small, see also Choi and Bowles (2007) as well as Chapter 8.

13 Both in the coordination games and in the prisoner's dilemma used in Nowak and May (1992), results are robust to changes in the boundary conditions as well as the inclusion of self-interaction. Thus, it is globally irrelevant if the plane is warped into a torus with an infinite boundary or is a flat surface in which players at the edges face fewer neighbours. Similarly, the dynamically fractal structures also appear in von Neumann neighbourhoods. See also Axelrod (2006) for additional simulation results showing similar spatial patterns created by Tit-for-Tat players in von Neumann neighbourhoods.

14 Notice that since $b = d = 0$, the prisoner's dilemma has only a weakly dominant strategy, since defect and cooperate grant the same payoff if the other player defects. This assumption does not affect the results, but they are robust if we assume $d = \varepsilon$, with a small positive $\varepsilon \ll 1$.

15 Note that this is consistent with the assumption $2a > c + b$ used in the iterated prisoner's dilemma.

16 At higher dimension, this result does not hold (see Suchecki et al., 2005 for details).

Agent-Based Modelling: Cascades and Self-Organised Criticality

8.1 Introduction

I N summer 376 CE, a group of roughly 90,000 Gothic refugees arrive at the northern Danube banks. Fitigern and Alaviv, rulers of the largest Gothic tribe, the Thervingi, send a plea to the Eastern Roman Emperor to be granted the right to settle in Thrace. Valens, in need of good soldiers in his war against the Persians to the east of the Roman Empire, grants their request and allows the Thervingi to cross the river. Yet, the group is held in the border area for several months, exposed to Roman exploitation, starvation and eventually wintry cold. After tensions grow, the Roman proconsul of Thrace assassinates Alaviv, while Fritigern is lucky to escape. The Gothic group rebels and is joined by other Germanic tribes that remained behind. In August 378, two armies, each comprised 15,000 soldiers confront each other. The Roman forces succumb to the Gothic army and Valens loses his life. The Western Roman co-emperor, Gratian, is too late to join the battle and Fritigern, unhindered, marches on Adrianople and Constantinople.

The Gothic War in the late 4th century is only a single element in a complex chain of events. The Gothic exodus was initially prompted by the Hun invasion of Eastern Europe and their attack on the Alans tribe settling in the Don River. It sets in motion a migration period that will last for almost two centuries. At the same time, the Western Roman Empire had become increasingly politically and economically fragmented. The increase in territory and the reliance on military support from the provinces created economic, political, and military inefficiencies as well as initiated centrifugal forces that broke the Roman Empire apart pushing it to a critical point. Both historic processes are intertwined: the weakness of the Roman Empire promoted the invasion of Germanic tribes while the latter stimulated its fall. In September of 476, the Western Roman Empire ends after Odoacer deposes of the last Western Roman Emperor, Flavius Romulus Augustulus (see Halsall, 2007).

More recently, in 1975, militiamen of the Phalangist Party divert traffic in front of the Church of Notre Dame de la Délivrance in East Beirut. A small commando of the Palestine Liberation Organization refuses to follow the direction of the militiamen and after some commotion, the PLO driver is accidentally shot. This accident, by itself, is tragic but might have only been considered an

DOI: 10.4324/9781003035329-8

unfortunate event. Under normal circumstances, the perpetrators would have been brought to justice and the tragedy would have ended at this point. However, shortly after the event, members of a PLO faction open fire outside of the church and kill a Phalange militant and three of his bodyguards. As a reaction, Phalange militia fire upon a PLO bus a few hours later, killing and wounding not only men but women and children. The *Bus Massacre* is widely considered to be the starting point of the Lebanese Civil War.

The assassination of Alaviv and the shooting outside of the Church of Notre Dame de la Délivrance have something distinctive in common. Both incidents taken by themselves are minor events, yet both trigger a chain of events that develop substantial social momentum. One constitutes the beginning of the *Barbarian Invasions* leading to the fall of the Western Roman Empire, the other triggers 15 years of civil war in Lebanon. Both are examples in human history of complex interlinked social systems entering a critical state after a period of ostensible stability. Once a social system reaches **criticality**, comparatively minor events trigger *cascading dynamics* that culminate in fundamental historic changes. For example, the excessive reliance on forced labour, the high concentration and exploitation of slaves, and the use of gladiators for entertainment during the Roman Republic promoted a state in which the escape of only a small group of gladiators in 73 BCE led to the Third Servile War, also known as the War of Spartacus. The death of Charles IV of France without an heir apparent caused dispute over the succession to the throne of France setting off a sequence of open wars from 1337 to 1453 between the French and English monarchies. Yet, Charles' death was only a trigger that initiated the cascade of events, but the underlying social system was already rendered critical by the events following the Norman conquest of England in 1066. Similarly, the defenestration of two Catholic Lords Regent and their secretary by a group of Protestant nobles in 1618 was not the cause of the conflict between Protestants and Catholics that would last for almost 30 . In fact, similar events happened in Prague already twice before (in 1419 and 1483) without much consequence. It was the growing friction between both sects and the struggle for power since the Peace of Augsburg was signed 63 years earlier.

This list of historical events could be easily extended. Fundamental social transformation is ubiquitous throughout history and induced by changes in the political, social, and economic landscape. The examples illustrate sudden and rapid change, which renders into question the notion of social dynamics and equilibrium convergence of earlier chapters. We have defined institutions as an asymptotically/evolutionarily stable and thus self-stabilising equilibrium once the former are firmly established. This type of equilibrium is only destabilised through repeated idiosyncratic actions, fundamental exogenous shifts or shocks to the interaction environment. Idiosyncratic actions or exogenous shocks must be sufficiently severe or frequent in order to push a social system out of the basin of attraction of its current equilibrium into a state that is part of the basin of attraction of another equilibrium. In this case, social transformation initially occurs gradually and once a social system escapes a basin of attraction it converges to a new set of institutions. In this sense, our previous methods provide some general explanations for the aforementioned events. Indeed, we can interpret a state at the separatrix of two basins as a trigger event since a social system intrinsically converges to a new equilibrium after this point. Such an explanation involves a traceable transition out of the basin of an equilibrium. Yet, the criticality we observe in the above events is characterised by a different dynamic. Initially, shocks to the social system are local and at a macro level, it remains in a metastable state. Once the system reaches criticality, however, it quickly progresses to a new state triggering radical social transformation.

8.2 Critical Systems

In this chapter, we will study two broad models of criticality. I have chosen these models since they replicate a statistical property that we can find in critical systems. We have seen that conflicts, such as those in the late 4th century, are the results of the disruptive forces that are at play once a social system reached the point of criticality. For example, Figure 8.1 shows the fatalities of war since the year 1400 until the First World War. Over the course of five centuries the number of deaths remains low, but now and then we can see sharp spikes. Although warfare is omnipresent, most of the period is characterised by smaller skirmishes while longer, larger-scale battles are rare. In order to better understand the frequency and scale of violent encounters, we can plot the frequency of conflicts as a function of the number of fatalities, similar to Figure 6.12 in Chapter 6. Since the number of deaths is different for most encounters, the frequency at which a conflict of a particular size occurs would be mostly equal to one. We, therefore, need to group encounters of similar scale (e.g., conflicts within a range of 1,000 to 2,000 fatalities) to get a sense of their frequency. The results then depend on the *resolution* we choose. A too high resolution, i.e. too narrow groups, will return a high number of data points mostly clustered around a frequency of one. A too low resolution generates too few data points. For two different resolutions, Figure 8.2 shows the number of fatalities ordered by size along the abscissa and the frequency of the respective size is shown on the ordinate. The resolution is thereby defined by the chosen *bin* size. A bin defines an interval and data points within this interval are grouped together and accumulated. A broader bin covers a larger interval and thus, combines a larger number of data points (i.e., conflicts). We usually assume that bins are of equal size and the smallest bin is plotted as the leftmost element on the x-axis while the largest bin defines the rightmost element on the axis.

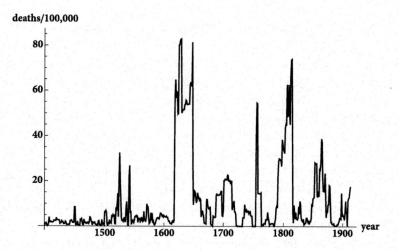

Figure 8.1: Number of death per 100,000 (including military and civilian) from 1400 to 1913. Data based on Roser (2020).

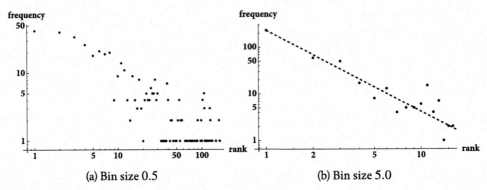

(a) Bin size 0.5   (b) Bin size 5.0

Figure 8.2: Rank-frequency distribution in log-log of war fatalities.

Figure 8.2a uses a bin size of 0.5. In other words, encounters with deaths per $100,000$ ranging between 0 and 0.5 are plotted at rank 1, followed by encounters with deaths ranging between 0.5 and 1.0 plotted at rank 2, and so forth. While this bin size offers a good resolution for small-scale skirmishes, most of the skirmishes beyond rank 30 (i.e. beyond 15 deaths per $100,000$) occur only once within their respective bin. Increasing the bin size to 5.0, as shown in Figure 8.2b provides us with a clearer picture. Note that Figure 8.2 is a log-log diagram, i.e., both axes follow a logarithmic scale. While the distribution at the higher resolution in Figure 8.2a has a more diffuse shape, the data points roughly align along the dotted linear relation in Figure 8.2b. Consequently, we can see that the number of fatalities follows a power law distribution in the latter figure with a slope of around -1.75 (see the previous discussion in Section 6.5). The smallest skirmishes are 73 times more likely than the largest conflicts. However, note that in this context, the slope of our graph depends on the bin size we chose. The absolute value is therefore of minor relevance.[1]

It is important to realise that a power law is only indicative of a critical system, but it is not a proof. The power law distribution in the previous chapter is not caused by cascading dynamics but by preferential attachment. While we cannot exclude that criticality plays a role in defining the size of cities, preferential attachment is also a more plausible explanation for the distribution we observed in Figure 6.12 – especially, since the simple algorithm replicates the data so closely. It is worthwhile to look at another example before we study the mathematical details of criticality. In the introduction, we have seen that population movements are subject to cascading dynamics where displacement can trigger further displacement. The UN provides reliable data on migration since the 1970s which are shown in Figure 8.3 using the earlier log-log representation. The World Development Indicators include the net total of migrants during a five-year period from 1972 to 2017 for 191 countries. A data point in Figure 8.3 represents the yearly average as a share of the population for a specific country during a five-year period, returning a total of $10 \times 191 = 1910$ data points. A bin size of 10^{-4} generates the slightly concave distribution in Figure 8.3a which becomes more linear at lower resolutions.[2] At a bin size of 1 percent, the data points align again on a straight line with a slope of -3.37. Once again, the distribution follows a power law which suggests that migration could be at least partially determined by criticality. We will study this process later in this chapter and will further see that the slight concavity is likely generated by the particular interaction structure of social systems.

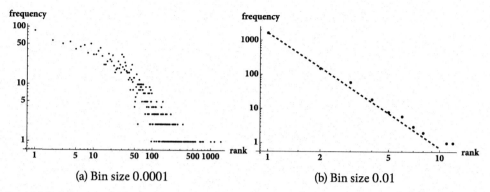

frequency

(a) Bin size 0.0001

(b) Bin size 0.01

Figure 8.3: Rank-frequency distribution in log-log of migration rates. Data based on World Development Indicators (04/09/2020).

8.3 Complexity, Criticality, and ABM

The two models we cover in this Chapter, create criticality in different ways. The first model in Section 8.4, treats criticality as exogenous. In this model, the social system reaches a critical state after a change of the model's parameter values. In the second model in Section 8.5, criticality materialises through an endogenous evolutionary process. In other words, criticality is an emergent property in the second model. The system is not destabilised by some external force, as in the former model, but it converges to a critical state over time. In addition, criticality is robust to changes in the initial conditions and parameters. We shall see that in this system, a critical state is an attractor, i.e., an asymptotically stable fixed point of the dynamical system that is independent of the precise details of the setup. The system is therefore an example of **self-organised criticality**.

In the context of social systems, *self-organisation* deserves some discussion. It suggests an inevitability of the social collapse we have examined in the aforementioned examples. Once the Roman Empire set its strategy on territorial conquest or the Peace of Augsburg was formulated and signed, the crises that occurred decades or centuries later were inescapable. Despite the lack of data that allows us to compare the history of a social system under different scenarios, this interpretation of self-organised criticality appears too stringent. It suggests, however, that criticality is spontaneous and emergent, and the detailed sequence of events is inconsequential. The precise scale and shape of the Roman Empire, the timing of the Huns' decision to move into Eastern Europe, the occasion of the defenestration etc. might have affected the timings of the social dynamics but not the eventual conclusions. Yet, we can say very little about the impact of larger exogenous institutional changes during the process, and whether these might have averted the fundamental social changes that followed.

The two models of criticality illustrate another interesting property. While the dynamics are defined by only a small number of simple mathematical algorithms, the systems illustrate complexity and emergent properties that prevent us from inferring the system-wide dynamics from the underlying equations. Thus, we can trace the dynamics at a micro level but not directly at a macro level and the techniques of previous chapters will not be useful to understand the system's properties. I will therefore need to introduce a different method before we look at the details of the two models.

Agent-based modelling (ABM) provides scholars with a powerful tool for analysing the sophisticated interdependencies in evolving complex systems. These models rely on computer simulations of biological and social systems to replicate the interactions between multiple and diverse interacting and semi-autonomous agents. The availability of dedicated agent-based toolkits (e.g., Swarm, NetLogo, and Repast Simphony) and more accessible programming languages (e.g., Java, Python, Microsoft Visual Studio, and R) since the 1990s made it significantly easier for researchers to simulate biological and social systems. At the same time, computational power has grown exponentially.[3]

We should understand ABM is both an inductive and a deductive approach. It is **inductive**, since ABM can, for example, be used to advance theories about the way a network's topology influences the diffusion of information and the opinions of its members, similar to our previous discussions in Chapter 7. ABM is especially helpful for improving our understanding of **emergent** properties and behaviour in social systems. Emergent behaviour or properties denote characteristics of a social system that are not qualities of its parts but are created by the interaction of the latter. Such emergence is caused by feedback effects between the various agents and the social institutions under which they interact. ABM can make use of the empirical data about the individual parts of the system and test whether a theoretical model of the interacting parts recreates the emergent properties observed at the system's level. In this situation, ABM enables scholar to *tinker* with their theory - by adding new and dropping old assumption, a model can be tuned until it is able to consistently replicate a particular social phenomenon.

Similarly, ABM is **deductive** since it can be used to test and anticipate the implication of a theory. As such, these models open new avenues that have been infeasible to researchers before. We can test the validity of, for example, theories about historical processes by artificially simulating a process using empirical data. Alternatively, we can simulate the macro- and microeconomic implications of development policies in various countries before they are implemented and validate the accuracy of our predictions after these policies have taken effect. However, since ABM does not ensure certainty over the causes of a certain social phenomenon, but an understanding of the hypothetical causes and mechanisms that *would* generate such a phenomenon, the approach is therefore frequently considered to be **abductive**.

Agent-based models not only have several advantages but also have disadvantages over the other approaches discussed in this book. Table 8.1 lists the principal benefits and drawbacks. It is important to realise that contrary to frequent perception, ABM is not a substitute for other mathematical approaches – it is complementary. ABM helps researchers to study and discover dynamics that might remain invisible to other approaches, but at the same time, ABM obscures other elements of interest. It is a particularly convenient approach if either the social phenomenon is too complex to be modelled on the basis of a feasible number of mathematical equations as we have done in previous chapters or the system of equations is not algebraically solvable due to complex interdependencies. Simulations enable us to generate numerical solutions and thus dispense with the problem of insolubility. Yet, these solutions lack the flexibility of **closed-form solutions**. A closed-form solution is an analytical expression composed of a finite sequence of elementary functions and operations. Simply speaking, it is an *exact* solution that is based on a limited number of variables, constants and operators.[4] In this case, it is sufficient to input values into our solution and we immediately obtain a quantitative result. A **numerical solution**, on

Table 8.1

Advantages and disadvantages of ABM

Drawback	Benefit
Absence of closed-form solution	Numerical solution
Recursive dynamics	Can study non-deterministic and aperiodic processes
Lack of transparency and traceability of the model	Can include semi-autonomous, adaptive and heterogeneous agents
Potential lack of tractability and robustness of results	Can model non-linear and co-evolutionary dynamics

the other hand, is only a (more or less precise) approximation of this result and normally does not allow for more general statements. Despite being a second-best option, we can only obtain numerical solutions in specific situations, such as if changes between interaction periods depend on the former period. In this case, dynamics are recursive. Recursiveness may be the result of non-deterministic dynamics. We may wish to analyse the impact of random effects and different parameter values to study whether a system is path dependent or exhibits tipping points.[5] Random initial conditions may lead to different dynamics and push a population to a different equilibrium as we have seen in Chapter 7.4. *Noisy* interaction environments, in which agents are subject to errors due to the lack of clear signals, may also lead a population to a different dynamic path and thus long-term equilibrium. Alternatively and as we will see in Chapter 9, social systems may cycle between a number of equilibria too large to analyse or may not converge to an equilibrium at all and the sequence of results is critically dependent on initial conditions. In the latter case, the system is aperiodic. The sequence of states through which a population passes does not repeat itself even if we measure its path over a sequence of interactions. Since no patterns exist (e.g. the behaviour is not cyclic), we cannot derive any conclusions by looking at a subset of the sequence and a computer will need to iterate the system step-by-step after being given an initial number of values. Changing these initial values requires to rerun the simulation and solutions are limited to the sequences studied.

Additional complexity may arise because we assume that interacting agents do not share identical characteristics but are heterogeneous. Thus, we would require at least one equation per type of agent which imposes a problem of feasibility when using more classical means. Agent-based models do not only enable us to introduce higher degrees of heterogeneity among agents. We can program agents to behave autonomously from each other and any central decision-maker, only restricted by a set of possible actions, their environment, and interaction structure and rules. Agents individually adapt to their changing environment and may be even able to develop new strategies in the form of genetic algorithms.[6] Yet, such complexity does not only originate in the additional sophistication that we add to our agents, but is also due to compound feedback effects between agents and between their environment, actions, and preferences. Consequently, ABM accounts for the interplay between the social structure and institutions in which agents are placed and the repeated interactions between agents. Agent-based models thereby generally

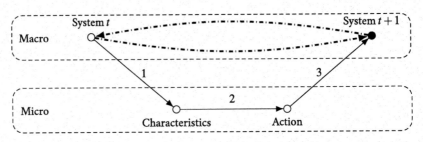

Figure 8.4: Analysis of systemic change based on an adapted version of Coleman's *Boat*.

reflect a process similar to Coleman's Boat (Coleman, 1986, 1994).[7] An adapted version of the Coleman's Boat is illustrated in Figure 8.4. The underlying assumption is that the transformation of a macro structure (e.g. a practice, institution or social contract) can only be understood indirectly by studying the changes which occur at the micro level (i.e. agent-level). Coleman's Boat then provides us with directions for the elements we need to include in our model.

The upper left node in Figure 8.4 defines the starting point of our analysis. The system in period *t* determines the *global* variables of our system. It includes the social structure in which our agents interact and thus, the macro components we consider relevant for our model to explain the social phenomenon under investigation. In simulations, structure frequently takes on the characteristic of physical space, such as a regular two or three-dimensional lattice as we have seen in Chapter 7 or a more sophisticated social network. In addition, the system further includes aggregate variables, such as belief profiles, collective actions, resource distributions, etc.

The lower left node defines the *local* variables of our system and thus, the multi-dimensional characteristics of each agent. These characteristics define an agent's perception, evaluation, capabilities and her possible payoffs. At this level, we outline the agent's preferences and their constraints. The latter may include various factors, such as monetary or natural resources, normative or ideological constraints on possible actions, as well as constraints imposed on an agent's perception, information, cognitive capacity and hence, the capability for learning and autonomous decision-making, such as a limited field of vision or memory about past interactions. Agents may be homogeneous in these characteristics but can also be heterogeneous and endowed with different abilities and resources.

Both nodes determine the crucial variables of our model and require careful consideration to fit the intended analysis and to resist the temptation to add additional complexity to a model that is superfluous for the task at hand. The bridge between micro and macro level is established by linking global variables to local variables, as indicated by link 1. The link is formed by explicitly defining how the components at the system's level feed back into the agents. For example, an agent's information set can be restricted to the actions of her closest neighbours in a social network while her payoff is determined by the actions chosen by the majority of the agent population.

An agent then chooses an action based on her characteristics and behavioural rules. These behavioural rules are modelled explicitly for each agent and are determined by the agent's preferences, constraints, and decision algorithms. These algorithms cover a vast spectrum from simple rules of thumb that are based on a single variable to more complex rules of decision-making based on a multitude of variables. Consequently, link 2 aggregates the local variables of each agent to determine an individual action. We can broadly separate between three mechanisms of choosing an action, examples of which we have seen in earlier chapters. Agents may determine their action

- by adopting a best-response to other actors or by choosing from a set of actions that *satisfice* a minimum payoff, both requiring an optimisation process
- by acquiring an action (trait) via social learning from peers, requiring that agents are able to imitate other agents
- by a hybrid approach during which agents gradually update their existing strategy based on their experience made during past interactions. This process can, for example, take the form of **reinforcement learning** where an action is chosen with a probability proportional to weights based on its accumulated payoffs. It can also follow a genetic algorithm whereby agents create new solution heuristics from a set of existing heuristics via operators akin to biological processes. Both forms require an extended memory and an updating algorithm.

Individual actions aggregate, again affect the system at the macro level (link 4), and lead to a new updated system in period $t + 1$ which will turn into system t in the next interaction period. At this stage, we need to define in which way individual actions aggregate and through which channels they affect global variables. Additionally, individual actions can be coordinated or completely decentralised. In the former case, agents align their current action with the action of others, while in the latter case they ignore the actions chosen by peers once an agent has determined an optimal response.

Once we establish a computer programme based on the process in Figure 8.4, we can use it to evaluate the suitability of our model by running a simulation for a number of periods and confirming that an iterated process is representative of our data and causes the initial system to involve in accordance with the social phenomenon under scrutiny. If necessary, we can refine the individual elements of the code and eventually uncover the conditions and mechanisms that govern the evolution of the underlying social dynamics.

8.4 Segregation

An illustrative example will make this abstract process more tangible. The probably simplest agent-based models are **discrete cellular automata**, an example of which we have already seen in Chapter 7.2. In these models, agents are placed on a regular lattice of cells and interact with their neighbourhood. Since the neighbourhood is normally defined as the adjacent cells (most commonly the Moore or von Neumann neighbourhood, see page 148), agents form a regular network in which all agents are nodes of the same degree. Each agent can be in one of a limited number of discrete states and an agent changes to a new state based on hers and her neighbours' current states. While in the previous chapter, states indicated a strategy and the change to an individual state was initiated by an optimisation process, a state should be seen in a broader context and can denote any type of condition or behaviour. Similarly, a new state can be adopted through rather simple algorithms that do not require individual optimisation. We shall see examples in the following as well as Chapter 9.3.

Thomas C. Schelling was one of the first to use this type of model to study social dynamics in general, and in particular, the reasons for spatial segregation according to ethnic markers.

Figure 8.5: Initial setup of Schelling's segregation model (Period 0).

Agents are placed on a line segment in Schelling (1969) and in later versions (Schelling, 1971), on a two-dimensional lattice. Since the dynamics are very similar for the line segment, we will focus on the two-dimensional lattice setup. A cell on the lattice is either occupied by an agent or empty. Agents are one of two types - blue or red (in Schelling's initial setup, these were pluses and zeros). An agent defines her neighbourhood as the eight surrounding cells and leaves her cell, if the number of neighbours of the opposite colour exceeds the number of neighbours of her own colour. We might imagine an initial setup as in Figure 8.5. On average, an agent has an equal number of red and blue neighbours. Yet, at the individual level, 23 percent of the 69 agents are dissatisfied with their neighbourhood and wish to move (indicated by a cross). Before we have a closer look at the system's dynamics, Coleman's Boat will help us to structure the model. At the system level, the model is defined by the lattice structure and the initial density (the share of occupied cells). The latter determines the number of red and blue agents (each composes 50 percent of the population). In addition, we will need to program as graphical representation of the lattice and to keep track of the dynamics, we might want to record the share of agents that are dissatisfied with their neighbourhood in each period. At the micro level, we define an agent's position on the lattice, her neighbourhood, her (dis)similarity threshold (which may be different from 50 percent) and the share of dissimilar neighbours in her neighbourhood. An agent's action is then given by a simple algorithm to find an empty cell on the lattice if the share of dissimilar neighbours exceeds the individual threshold. Link 2 is then simply a binary decision variable that determines whether an agent is dissatisfied with her neighbourhood.

Link 1 relates an agent's neighbourhood to her state of satisfaction and link 3 connects a movement to a new neighbourhood with the global degree of segregation. It should be clear that links 1 and 3 define a coupled system in which each agent's action has an impact on her neighbours (i.e. they create an externality). In the setting presented in Figure 8.5, the 16 dissatisfied agents will move to an empty spot on the lattice. Consequently, other agents will become dissatisfied as agents of a different colour move into their neighbourhood. This leads to a reshuffling of the neighbourhoods and thus to a change of the agent distribution on the lattice until each agent is satisfied. Figure 8.6 illustrates the dynamics. Since the neighbourhood is very small, it only takes six periods to reach an equilibrium in which all agents are satisfied. We notice a rough form of segregation in Figure 8.6f. In larger groups of agents, the segregation effect requires more periods and is more

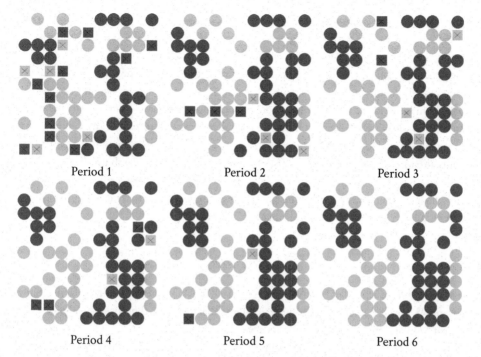

| Period 1 | Period 2 | Period 3 |
| Period 4 | Period 5 | Period 6 |

Figure 8.6: Evolution of Schelling's segregation model.

pronounced, but Figure 8.6 should suffice to understand the general dynamics: in the initial period a number of agents move out of their neighbourhood into a new neighbourhood, which again will lead others to move on and so forth, and over time, segregated neighbourhoods evolve.

The Schelling model shows two important emergent properties that cannot be inferred from its micro-structure. First, segregation occurs even if agents are content to live in a neighbourhood where they are in a minority. While segregation is less pronounced for higher levels of tolerance, it is already noticeable if individuals only move out of neighbourhoods composed of foreign neighbours at a ratio higher than 3 : 1, i.e. if the individual threshold is at 25 percent. Second, even if agents demonstrate a strict preference for a mixed neighbourhood over a segregated neighbourhood composed of only their own kind, segregation still occurs. It is only necessary that agents prefer a neighbourhood in which they are in a majority at least equally to a neighbourhood in which the proportions are reciprocal (i.e. n_i being the number of neighbours of their own kind and m_i the number of neighbours of the other kind in neighbourhood i, then neighbourhood a is at least equally preferred to neighbourhood b if $n_a/m_a = m_b/n_b$ for $n_a > m_a$.)[8] The implications of this result are rather astounding. It suggests that neglecting other factors, such as gentrification, segregation is not simply the product of xenophobia or genophilia, it is a naturally occurring phenomenon if individuals do not want to be part of a too small minority. Since segregation thus also occurs if individuals feel most comfortable if ethnicities are represented in their neighbourhood in roughly equal proportions, the ensuing segregation constitutes an interesting type of coordination failure.

For our purposes, I will concentrate on the impact of *neighbourhood* on the system's dynamics. By extending the definition of a neighbourhood, I also address two drawbacks of Schelling's original setup: firstly, a population is either segregated or mixed while in reality, we observe mixed neighbourhoods next to segregated neighbourhoods, and secondly, segregated neighbourhoods are usually larger in size than those generated by the Schelling model. The assumption is the following: I tend to mostly interact with my neighbours next door and while my interactions with my neighbours become increasingly sporadic as they live further down the road, they still affect me - not necessarily via direct communication but indirectly through their behaviour - the neighbour who parks his second car in front of my house, neighbours who have an appetising barbecue or listen to loud music while my dog joins in and her bark wakes up half of the neighbourhood. Consequently, it is plausible to assume that an agent's decision to move out of her neighbourhood depends also on neighbours living at a distance larger than 1, yet as neighbours live further away they are also less relevant for her decision. We can therefore assume that agents consider all other agents who live within a distance d of their cell as neighbours. Assume that neighbours at a distance of δ (with δ being an integer ranging from 1 to d) have a weight of

$$\frac{d+1-\delta}{d(d+1)/2}$$

A neighbour j at a distance of δ_j has $(d+1-\delta_j)/(d+1-\delta_k)$ times the weight of a neighbour k at distance δ_k, i.e., for a neighbourhood defined by a distance of 5, the closest neighbours have a weight of $5/15$ and the farthest neighbours a weight of $1/15$.

Figure 8.7 illustrates the stable equilibrium distribution given various distances. The initial distribution and setup are identical for all simulations: the individual threshold is defined at 40 percent, the density of population is at 80 percent, and simulations only differ with respect to the size of a neighbourhood. Note that while a higher distance implies that an agent includes a large number of agents (for example, 150 agents constitute a neighbourhood within a distance of 7), even substantial numbers of neighbours are not implausible. Think of the number of residents living in the same block or how many people we tend to cross on our way to the nearest bus stop. Neighbourhoods up to a size of 7 demonstrate dynamics that are rather similar to those of the original model, but larger neighbourhoods lead to larger segregated communities. In smaller neighbourhoods, a relatively large share of dissatisfied agents moves in the first period, while in medium-sized neighbourhoods, migration spikes in the second or third period. Independent of the size of the neighbourhood, the number of dissatisfied agents decreases in each following period until the system reaches an equilibrium.

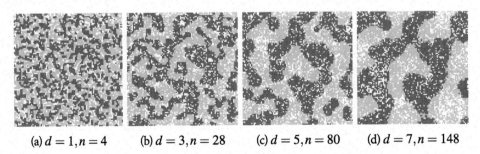

(a) $d=1, n=4$ (b) $d=3, n=28$ (c) $d=5, n=80$ (d) $d=7, n=148$

Figure 8.7: Figures show equilibrium states. Simulations initiated with an identical initial distribution and a similarity threshold of 40 percent and a density of 80 percent. Maximum distance and thus the size of a neighbourhood is defined by d and the number of neighbours included is given by n.

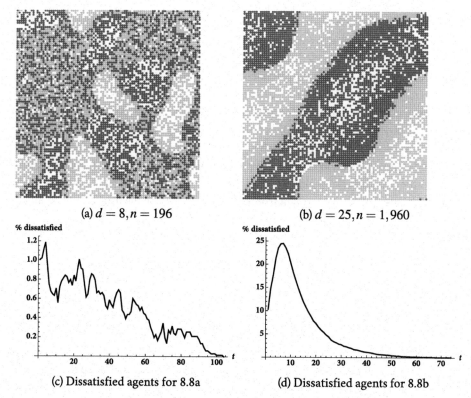

(a) $d = 8, n = 196$ (b) $d = 25, n = 1,960$

(c) Dissatisfied agents for 8.8a   (d) Dissatisfied agents for 8.8b

Figure 8.8: Simulations initiated with an identical initial distribution as in 8.7, a similarity threshold of 38 and 48 percent, respectively, and a density of 80 percent. Parameter d defines the size of the neighbourhood and n the number of neighbours. (a) and (b) show the equilibrium states, (c) and (d) the percentage share of dissatisfied agents over time.

Yet in larger neighbourhoods, some interesting dynamics emerge. Figure 8.8a presents the equilibrium distribution for a neighbourhood of $d = 8$ and an individual threshold level of 38 percent. The distribution shows entirely segregated regions intermixed with desegregated areas. The latter evolve and remain stable for thresholds between 34 and 39 percent. At lower threshold values, all agents are satisfied in the initial period and at higher thresholds, complete segregation occurs (i.e., at a threshold of 40, the distribution looks only a little different from the one shown in Figure 8.7d). Figure 8.8c displays the percentage of dissatisfied agents in each period. Dynamics do not follow the typical decreasing pattern of smaller neighbourhoods but are more erratic. After an early spike in the number of dissatisfied agents, the system seems to initially quickly converge to an equilibrium, but is soon followed by another spike. This behaviour is repeated several times until the system eventually settles on an equilibrium and all agents are satisfied with their neighbourhood.

Further increasing the neighbourhood size reduces the interval of thresholds within which neighbourhoods are mixed. The reason is that the actual distribution of neighbours moves toward an equal distribution as the neighbourhood increases. While the weights in favour of the closest neighbours bias the distribution, the increase in the neighbourhood size brings the initial randomised neighbourhood closer to an equal 50 : 50 distribution. Consequently, more agents are initially satisfied in a larger neighbourhood and the threshold that is required to destabilise the system increases with the size of the neighbourhood. On the other hand, while the number of initially dissatisfied neighbours declines as their neighbourhoods increase, the impact of each movement on the system level is more pronounced, since more neighbours are affected. Starting as a small and localised process, dissatisfaction eventually cascades through the system. Secondly, since the initial number of dissatisfied agents decreases with the size of the neighbourhood, small changes to the threshold may reduce their number to zero. For example, none of the agents is dissatisfied if we drop the similarity threshold from 40 to 38 percent for a neighbourhood of $d = 10$ and thus, the population remains completely mixed. Thirdly, since the larger neighbourhood affects the size of the externality, i.e., the impact of moving agents and the share of affected neighbours, the speed at which segregation occurs also increases with the neighbourhood distance. For a distance of 10, no major changes occur after 170 periods, while for a distance of 25 and 30, the process mostly settles on an equilibrium after 60 and 30 periods, respectively.

Exercise 8.1

Install the latest version of NetLogo from https://ccl.northwestern.edu/netlogo/ and open the *segregation* model from File → Models Library (simply type 'segregation' into the search field at the bottom). Familiarise yourself with the code. Extend the model to include the extended neighbourhood as defined in this chapter and try to replicate the results. (Hint: make use of the *in-radius* function to define an agent's neighbourhood.)

These dynamics have some interesting implication: as the neighbourhood increases, the system becomes both more robust and, at the same time, critical. The process of segregation requires higher threshold levels in larger neighbourhoods and segregation is no longer smoothly correlated with the individual threshold. At moderate levels of tolerance, no segregation occurs but small changes to the individual similarity threshold lead to a fundamental transformation of the population structure. The former also challenges the implication of the original model that segregation can occur even if individuals show relatively high levels of tolerance. At a neighbourhood distance of 25, the minimum threshold needed to set the segregation process in motion, is 48 percent and thus, close to an equal distribution of the neighbourhood. Figure 8.8b shows the final distribution for this case. If we reduced the individual threshold by only 1 percent, no segregation occurs since all agents are satisfied with the initial random distribution. In other words, the system becomes critical at a 48 percent similarity threshold. Admittedly, a number of neighbours equal to 1,960 (minus the empty spaces) in the case of this neighbourhood seems enormous, but in densely populated capitals this number is reasonable; especially if we consider that the farthest neighbours have only one 25th of the weight of the closest neighbours. Furthermore, it requires only a small number of initially dissatisfied agents to set the segregation dynamics in motion. Figure 8.8d illustrates the distribution of dissatisfied agents over time for the $d = 25$ neighbourhood. Roughly 10 percent of all agents are initially willing to move out of their neighbourhood, but after only three periods, the number of moving agents increases to over 23.5 percent and remains at around 24 percent for another three periods. Thereafter, the rate of dissatisfied agents continuously decreases at an ever slower rate until large segments of completely segregated neighbourhoods emerge.

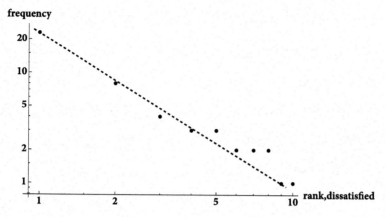

Figure 8.9: Rank-frequency distribution in log-log of dissatisfied agents.

Consequently, in this process, movements of a large number of dissatisfied agents occur more sporadically than small movements. If we group the shares of dissatisfied agents in Figure 8.8d at bins of 0.4 percent intervals and neglect the largest movements (since they would only occur with a frequency of 1 or 0 within the 0.4 percent bins), we obtain the frequency distribution in double-logarithmic scale shown in Figure 8.9. The smallest bin, which comprises movements of 0–0.4 percent of all agents, is plotted furthest to the left and the largest bin, comprising movements of size of 3.6–4.0 percent, is furthest to the right. The dotted line is the fitted trend of the data points indicating a rough power law distribution with a slope of −1.429. The power law is even more apparent if similarity thresholds move beyond the minimum threshold of 48 percent.

The simple cellular automaton which we just discussed has applications beyond the context of migration and residential segregation. Instead of ethnic, social or economic markers, agents are characterised by behavioural patterns and cultural customs. For example, instead of indicating a particular ethnicity, a blue agent might identify, in a different context, an individual that follows a certain action instead. A change in colour of a cell then does not indicate that it is occupied by a new agent but that the agent adopted another custom based on peer effects (while an empty cell implies that no custom is adopted).

While simple cellular automata that follow the micro/macro relationship defined by Figure 8.4 provide a wide range of applications, more sophisticated social dynamics, however, require agent-based models that go beyond simulating the co-evolution of systemic and individual fundamentals. Dynamics are not only defined at the global systemic level and individual level, but by local institutions that operate at the meso level and affect both the overarching elements of the system and the individual characteristics of agents. We can therefore extend Coleman's boat by acknowledging the interactions of social components at various levels of aggregation. In the style of the former model's more materialistic nomenclature, I refer to the model of thought described in Figure 8.10 as the Rooftop model. The micro and macro level are in principle equivalent to Figure 8.4, but both levels may not only be directly linked but depend also on local institutions that are formed by intermediate levels of aggregation. The meso level includes a spectrum of institutions ranging from very local practices (such as my family's recipe for potato salad) to broad norms enforced among a subpopulation and thus at a slightly smaller level of aggregation than the entire

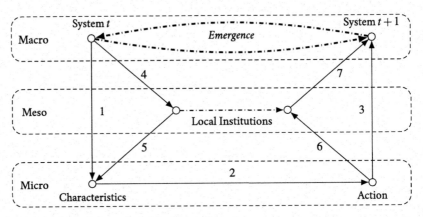

Figure 8.10: Multi-level co-evolutionary change: *Rooftop* model.

system. The interplay between local institutions and agents follows the same fundamentals as Coleman's boat, and both individual actions and dynamic local institutions affect the macro level eventually leading to emergent behaviour.

Again, an application will help improve transparency of the logic underlying Figure 8.10. Pure altruism (or strong reciprocity) as opposed to reciprocal altruism and kin altruism, is not motivated by future returns. Despite such behaviour being open to easy exploitation by free-riders, we frequently observe acts of pure altruism. The evolutionary forces that led to the emergence of this trait have therefore puzzled social scientists in general and economists in particular. A plausible approach suggests that multi-level selection might be the key to explaining that altruism is indeed evolutionarily beneficial.[9] The theory assumes that while being an altruist is not beneficial at the individual level, it is so at the group level. Groups of altruists are stronger and have a higher chance of winning contests with other groups composed of more free-riders, and all members benefit from winning over another group. However, altruists can be exploited by free-riding group members (e.g. during food sharing, hunting, and warfare). If selection between members of one group or tribe acts at a similar frequency as selection between groups (in other words, warfare between tribes is sufficiently frequent), groups are sufficiently small, and the benefits are of roughly equal scale, altruists proliferate.[10]

The overall distribution of altruists and free-riders defines the state of the system at the macro level in Figure 8.10, the composition of each group the meso level and the micro level is again determined by individual preferences and actions. Selection occurs at the inter-group level favouring altruism, and at the intra-group level favouring free-riding. Link 4 determines the expected winning success of a group within the population, link 5 defines the individual benefit of a group member based on the group's composition and link 1 describes the individual advantage or harm of being of a particular type in the winning or losing tribe, respectively. Individual actions determine the group's composition and hence, its relative fitness and ability to win a contest (link 6) while the composition of the collective determines the system's macro structure (link 3 and 7).

We can see that ABM traverses the old structure and agency dichotomy and the question of which aspect should be prioritised seems misguided. While individual actors are socialised and embedded in interaction structures and institutions that constrain or widen their cognition, preferences and actions, these structures are the product of de-centralised individual and collective actions. Emergent properties do not only evolve as macro-phenomena based on aggregated individual actions but feed back into individual preferences and perceptions, thus creating a loop which interconnects individual behaviour and structure. Social behaviour and structure, hence, do not only emerge from individual behaviour but also emerge from the co-evolution of complex and interlinked social components at various degrees of aggregation. The complexity of this process and thus the need for ABM arises from the ensuing non-linear dynamics.

It is surprising that ABM is not broadly used by policy-makers and think tanks, since ABM addresses the critique of economic policy making raised by Robert Lucas (and what thus came to be known as the **Lucas critique**). The critique questions the invariance of policy variables and hence, the formulation and implementation of policies based on aggregated historical data. Policy-makers and advocates should perceive ABM as a useful tool to understand the impact of policies at the micro level as well as their emergent elements and therefore impact on existing institutions.

8.5 Self-Organised Criticality

In the segregation model with an extended neighbourhood, criticality occurred by external intervention. We *manually* decrease the similarity threshold of agents or extend their neighbourhood until some agents become dissatisfied, move, and set in motion a large-scale movement of other agents that fundamentally transforms the position of a vast majority of agents on the lattice and thus, the structure of the system. Yet, in the examples at the beginning of this chapter, we have seen that criticality is an element intrinsically evolving in some social systems. Obviously, we could extend the segregation model and assume some sort of endogenous process that changes the similarity threshold of agents or introduces randomness that eventually causes the cascading dynamics – but that might overextend the aim of this model. Instead, we study the social dynamics of criticality, historical cascades, and rapid social change using another simple model. In its original form, the model replicates behaviour of a pile of sand to which grains of sand are added at regular intervals. Similar to the extended segregation model, the **sandpile model** illustrates system-wide transformations after the system reached a critical state. Consequently, the general dynamics refer to a larger array of social dynamics. I will discuss how the model can be reinterpreted in more detail after we studied the basic assumptions and its dynamics.

Given that most of us played with sand during our childhood, the underlying dynamics and the system's behaviour are intuitive. Imagine you start building a pile of sand. Initially the surface is flat and one by one you add a handful of sand to the surface. It does not matter whether you add sand to the same point or to random locations. Over time a small heap (or several small heaps) build up. With each additional grain of sand, the slope of a heap increases. Eventually, the sides of the heap become so steep that a few grains of sand start to slide off. On their way down, they bounce against other grains of sand and cause the latter to also slide down. As the heap grows into a larger pile of sand, these local landslides turn into larger avalanches. Ultimately, the pile becomes unstable. An additional grain of sand causes an avalanche that is no longer localised but moves along the whole heap to its bottom. At this point, the system has become critical and the pile no longer grows. The addition and following movement of an individual grain of sand leads to

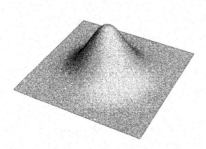
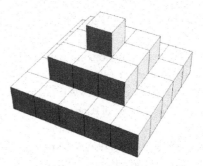

(a) Realistic sketch of a sandpile.   (b) Schematic image of a sandpile.

Figure 8.11: Different presentations of a sandpile.

emergent global dynamics that can no longer be explained by the properties of the individual grain since it now affects the entire system.

Following Bak et al. (1987, 1988) who were the first to study these dynamics as a discrete cellular automaton, I greatly simplify the dynamics of a sandpile but retain the crucial and interesting dynamics. Instead of perceiving a sandpile as illustrated in Figure 8.11a, we rely on the more simplified representation of Figure 8.11b. We can think of the space in which our system operates as a plane separated into cells, much in the same way as the segregation model. Piles of grains of sand are represented as cubes stacked on each cell. Once our stacked cubes reach a certain height, the cubes fall off to the neighbouring cells, thus reducing the height of the stack on the cell and increasing the height of the stack of cubes on the neighbouring cells. For example, the centre cell in Figure 8.11b has a height of 3 and its neighbours have a height of 2. To formalise this, assume that each cell i is defined by coordinate (x_i, y_i) and a height h_i defining the number of sand grains that are stacked on cell i. Further assume that the critical height of a cell is $\bar{h}$. The system is then defined by the following equations

$$h(x_i, y_i) \rightarrow h(x_i, y_i) + 1 \tag{8.1a}$$

$$h(x_i, y_i) \rightarrow h(x_i, y_i) - 4 \quad \text{if } h(x_i, y_i) > \bar{h} \quad \text{and} \tag{8.1b}$$

$$h(x_i \pm 1, y_i) \rightarrow h(x_i \pm 1, y_i) + 1, h(x_i, y_i \pm 1) \rightarrow h(x_i, y_i \pm 1) + 1$$

These dynamics follow the easy and intuitive formulation in Bak et al. (1988).[11] The first algorithm in equation (8.1a) tells us that the height of cell i increases by 1 unit as we add another grain of sand. This is shown in Figure 8.12a. We might start with a flat distribution, all cells have a height of 1 and in the first period, one grain of sand, i.e. a cube, drops on the centre cell. In each period, the process is repeated, and an additional grain of sand drops on the cell. After four more periods, we have the situation depicted in Figure 8.12b - the pile reaches a height of 6. Let 5 be the critical height. The dark cube therefore topples the pile and the distribution changes to the one shown in Figure 8.12c according to the algorithm defined in equation (8.1b).

Figure 8.12c shows a localised reaction. Once the sand toppled on the four neighbours, the system reverts to an equilibrium state. The dynamics are simple but this is not always the

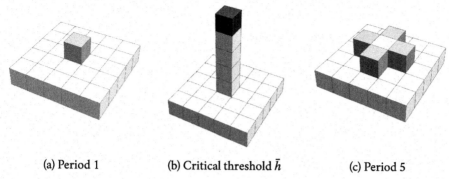

(a) Period 1   (b) Critical threshold $\bar{h}$ (c) Period 5

Figure 8.12: Toppling of sand.

case. If the neighbours as well as the centre cell had a height of 5, the latter would topple after the grain of sand had been dropped on it, leading to a chain reaction that also toppled its neighbour. After the centre had toppled, the neighbours would have surpassed a critical height and the landslide would have further propagated. The complex behaviour arises not because one neighbour topples after the other, but also because multiple neighbours are affected and their neighbours' neighbourhood overlap. Consequently, the landslide is amplified and further demonstrates internal spillovers. Such complex dynamics would not arise in a one-dimensional system (see exercise 8.2).

Exercise 8.2

Show intuitively that a one-dimensional system (i.e. sand can only fall to the left or right) has only one critical state and the reaction of the system after the critical state is reached does not exhibit any complex behaviour, but is characterised by a simple dynamic.

Imagine the current state is defined by Figure 8.13a which is a schematic top-down view of the plane. The numbers in each cell define its respective height. As before, the critical height is 5 and we start in a situation in which the centre cell has just exceeded the critical height. We assume that sand falls off the edges of the 9 cells. Any cell whose height exceeds 5 is marked with a box and spills over to its four neighbours. The eight figures illustrate the entire dynamics of the landslide up to the point where the system reaches a new meta-equilibrium in Figure 8.13h. In total, 8 out of 9 cells reached a critical height. The small world of 9 cells can be studied by hand, but even then, the dynamics are recursive and we have to go through each step. This approach is not feasible for larger worlds and the computer needs to take up the work for us.

Before we look at the simulation results, I will spare a few lines to illustrate the general structure of the program code and its components:

- Definition of global variables/objects: These include the critical height $\bar{h}$ beyond which a stack of cubes collapses, an empty list for the lifetime of the landslides and an empty list for the size of the landslides. The two lists store the information for each period separately and are necessary to study the type of avalanches that the system manifests over time.

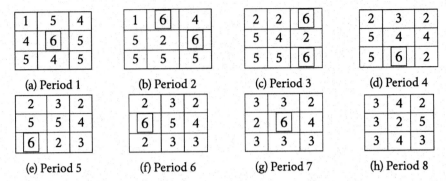

Figure 8.13: Example of a cascade.

- Definition of cell-related variables/objects: These are individual variables for the height, state, and a list to hold the coordinates of neighbouring agents for each cell. The state of a cell indicates whether or not it has reached a critical height and is a binary variable.
- Setup/initiation: The setup routine creates the individual cells, assigns a set of coordinates and a height to each cell, and may define the set of neighbours for each cell. The definition of the latter is not strictly necessary, and the agent set can be calculated during each interaction period. However, since neighbours remain identical in each period, simulation speed is increased if the set of agents is defined once and can be accessed in each period without the need for recalculation.
- Routine: The routine is repeated in each simulation period and follows the general structure:

  1. Define the cell whose height is incremented by one. The cell is either randomly chosen or is a previously specified cell.
  2. Check whether the cell exceeds the critical height: if not, end the simulation period and start the routine again; if it did, change its status to critical and start the following loop:

     (a) Increment a local counter by the number of critical cells (the role of the counter will become clearer later on).
     (b) Reduce the height of any *critical* cell by 4 and increase the height of its neighbours by 1.
     (c) Check whether any neighbour of the critical cells has reached a critical height itself
     (d) Reset the initially critical cells to non-critical and set any neighbour that reached critical height to critical.
     (e) Increment a second local counter by 1.
     (f) If the number of critical cells is positive, restart the loop. If not, end the loop.

  3. Add the first local counter to the *size of landslides* list and the second local counter to the *lifetime of landslides* list.
  4. End the simulation period and start the routine again.

The loop is repeated within the same simulation period as long as at least one cell has exceeded its critical height and thus, the system has not yet reached a metastable state. Since the toppling of a stack only affects a cell's neighbours, it suffices to test only this set of agents. The first local counter tracks the number of cells on which a toppling occurred during the same period while the second counter records the number of times the loop is repeated which we use as a proxy for the lifetime of an avalanche.

You may wonder why I have been discussing a model of statistical physics. The sandpile model can be easily reinterpreted to replicate social and behavioural contagion, and in particular social movements and revolutions. Cells represent individuals, groups of individuals or institutions. A cell's height is the stress that is exercised on the institutions or individuals, or the discontent the latter experience (in the form of, e.g., aggression or push and pull factors, depending on the social dynamics we wish to study). The critical heights represent the specific thresholds of individuals (e.g., the amount of oppression they are willing to bare), and once the threshold is reached, they incite their peers, who in turn become more discontented.

Despite its simplicity, the algorithm generates complex dynamics. Complexity does not arise from a strategic nature of interaction, since agents are simple automata. They are devoid of any repertoire of actions, beliefs or expectations. Yet, complexity is created by two other factors that are common in social systems – *locality* and *externality*. The former applies since each automaton only engages with a strict subset of the population, here its four neighbours. Local variations lead to situations in which the neighbourhood has a distribution of states that fundamentally differs from the population average. This gives rise to localised cascades. Externalities in the form of spillovers then both reinforce and extend the cascade, as previously shown in Figure 8.13.

If we plot the distribution of the lifetimes and the sizes of landslides for a simulation of half a million periods and 100×100 cells, a familiar pattern emerges. Both the size and the lifetime of the landslides follow a power law distribution with a slope roughly equal to -1 as is shown in Figure 8.14. The structure is indicative of a complex system. However, the system defined by equations (8.1a) and (8.1b) is a very rough approximation of a sand pile and even less so of the social systems. Consequently, we need to study whether the power law distribution persists if we make changes to the definition of a neighbourhood, the critical height, and the interaction between agents. We find that the distributions of the lifetimes and sizes are indistinguishable from Figures 8.14a and 8.14b if we extend the neighbourhood to all eight adjacent cells or initiate the simulation with a random distribution of heights. Similarly, if we assume that cells are heterogeneous and have different critical heights, these two distributions are again unaffected and results are robust to these changes.

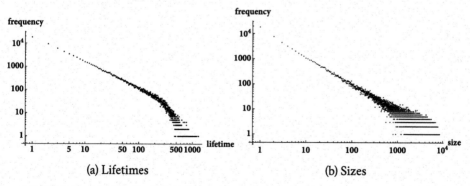

(a) Lifetimes   (b) Sizes

Figure 8.14: Distribution in log-log of landslide lifetimes and sizes.

However, members of social systems interact in networks that rarely correspond even remotely to the regular network formed by the cells in the standard model. The random graphs of Chapter 6 illustrate degree distributions that follow a power law which should affect the impact of an individual reaching a critical state. A highly connected member influences a larger number of other individuals, but each to a lesser degree compared to members of lower degree that are part of close-knit communities.

Figure 8.15 illustrates the size distribution of the landslides if cells are not structured along a regular lattice but as nodes in a network of preferential attachment. I make two additional assumptions: since *sand* can no longer fall off the edges of the plane because agents interact in a network, the system would become satiated and landslides would continue indefinitely. Consequently, one grain of sand is taken out of the system each time the system goes through the loop in the program, i.e. whenever a new agent reaches a critical height and a slide occurs. Further, since the degree distribution is random but follows a power law, agents lose 8 grains of sand when they reach a critical state and distribute $(8/\#neighbours)$ *grains* to each neighbour. Agents of higher degree affect more agents but each to a lesser degree, in line with the earlier reasoning. Ignoring landslides of size 1, Figure 8.15 shows that the power law distribution holds for networks of different sizes. Figures 8.15a and 8.15b present the results for a smaller network of 1,000 nodes. In the former, each agent has the same critical height $\bar{h} = 8$ and in the latter, agents are heterogeneous and their critical heights are randomly distributed between 8 and 15. Both show very similar distributions compared to the larger networks of size 2,500 and 5,000.[12]

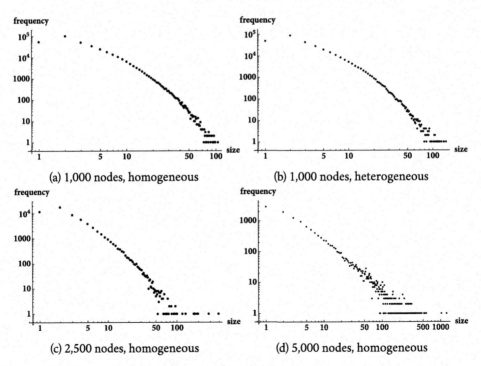

(a) 1,000 nodes, homogeneous

(b) 1,000 nodes, heterogeneous

(c) 2,500 nodes, homogeneous

(d) 5,000 nodes, homogeneous

Figure 8.15: Distribution in log-log of landslide sizes in preferential networks.

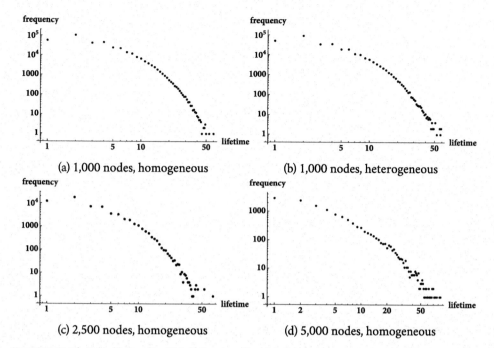

Figure 8.16: Distribution in log-log of landslide lifetimes in preferential networks.

The power law is less evident if we study the lifetime of the landslides shown in Figure 8.16. The distributions are not entirely linear but concave, like the examples in Figure 8.3 at the beginning of this chapter. The concavity is more pronounced in the smaller networks, but changing the scale of the plot recreates the linear correlation. Figure 8.17 plots the two smaller homogeneous networks in a semi-logarithmic plot in which the x-axis has a linear scale. The lifetimes of both networks do not follow a distribution of the form $f(x) = \alpha x^{-\tau}$ but of the form $g(x) = \alpha 10^{-\tau x}$ with τ equal to 0.10 and 0.12 for the networks of order 1,000 and 2,500, respectively. The semi-logarithmic scale implies that in comparison to the lattice/regular network, medium-sized landslides occur with a higher frequency in smaller networks. A cell of higher degree is more likely involved in a landslide and hence, has a higher chance of becoming critical. In turn, the involvement of more connected cells increases the lifetime of a landslide.[13] Correspondingly, other types of random networks with

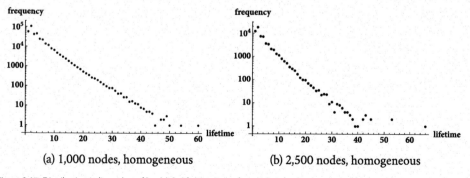

Figure 8.17: Distribution in linear-log of landslide lifetimes in preferential networks.

normally distributed degrees also illustrate a slight concavity in the log-log lifetime distribution, but to a smaller extent than preferential networks. Due to the heterogeneous degree of members in a social network, criticality affects the network at various scales. Depending on their degree, individual actions create feedback effects of different magnitudes. In contrast to other criteria that pertain to the heterogeneity of the agents, the topology of a network therefore influences the dynamics, frequency, and size of the cascades that follow an individual action.

I have previously argued that the sandpile model can be recontextualised by assuming that an individual can be represented as a stack of sand that reaches a critical value and then acts on her neighbours who in turn are galvanised and upon reaching their critical threshold act on their neighbourhoods in return. While this process replicates the essence of social contagion, it misses one essential element: actions are motivated by some unspecified external force that randomly agitates an agent represented by the additional grain of sand. In doing so, I have deliberately ignored the internal decision processes, considerations, or external factors that cause the action, i.e., the question of how stress is exercised on individuals in a social context and more specifically, what causes them to act. Ille (2020) answers the question by suggesting an extension to the sandpile model that includes social imitation and frictions that arise through the exchange with others. While the simple extension renders the model more realistic, it does not change the dynamics and the results of this chapter remain valid.

Exercise 8.3

Bak and Sneppen (1993) developed a simple model of self-organised criticality to explain punctuated equilibria - evolutionary change does not occur gradually, but species exhibit little morphological change for a long time, and now and then evolution illustrates comparatively short periods of strong selection and rapid change. The Bak-Sneppen model is fairly simple: (1) we assume that each species is represented by an agent who is attributed a random number between 0 and 1. This number defines a species' fitness, i.e. its evolutionary success. (2) Agents are arranged in a circle. In each period, the lowest number and the numbers of its two neighbours are replaced by a new number between 0 and 1 (in other words, the least fit species is substituted by a new species and as a result, the fitness of the neighbouring species in the food web is affected.) With the inbuilt functions in NetLogo, it is very easy to build this model: each turtle will only require one variable → fitness (hint: you may use the network functions of NetLogo or define a neighbour as $who \pm 1$). It suffices to determine the turtle with the lowest fitness and substitute the fitness values of this turtle and its neighbours. (a) How do the lowest fitness value and the average fitness change over time? (b) Are subsequent agents with the lowest fitness in the same neighbourhood and what is the distance between these agents? (Similarly to the previous hint, you may make use of the fact that turtles are distributed around the circular network according to their *who* identifier. You can also use NetLogo's network extension to calculate the distance.)

Consequently, the model robustly generates characteristics of social movements and revolutions. Onsets of social contention do not grow gradually over time, but exhibit non-monotonic dynamics. Periods of calm are interrupted by sudden widespread discontent at seemingly random scale (see, for example, Beck 2011, Figure 1). In the sandpile model, we have seen that size and duration of these onsets are distributed according to a power law distribution, something we observe again after plotting the scale and duration of the European revolutions during the past half millennium (see again Ille, 2020) or the fatalities of war like at the beginning of this chapter. These results offer an interesting perspective on the role of micro-foundations when studying social and behavioural contagion. In Chapter 5 individual characteristics critically determined the underlying dynamics. In this chapter, however, individual characteristics, beliefs, and even actions seem less relevant for the general dynamics of the population. The individual still plays a vital role as part of the particular interaction structure that agents form and that allows for the interplay of locality and externality, both creating in conjunction the cascading dynamics we studied in this section.

8.6 Conclusion

In this chapter, we observed two things. Firstly, the dynamics of a social system are defined by the interplay of its components leading to complex behaviour. This complexity creates emergent properties that cannot be easily studied with the conventional approaches we have seen in previous chapters. To model the feedback effects that cause emergent behaviour, an approach needs to account for the link between the different elements of a social system situated at the various levels of aggregation. We therefore studied complex social systems and their feedback effects by using agent-based models which offer the necessary flexibility to replicate the complex interdependencies in social systems, and to generate numerical solutions and predictions. Secondly, some complex social systems illustrate critical behaviour. In such systems, longer periods of stability are followed by rapid and fundamental change of the entire system after the latter has reached a breaking point. What is most interesting is that even very simple behavioural rules can create complex behaviour and criticality as long as individual behaviour implies feedback effects that influence adjacent agents and peers. Localised externalities can then amplify over time and cause a system-wide transformation and complex reactions. We studied two cellular automata – the segregation model with an extended neighbourhood and the sandpile model. Both models illustrate similar distributions but are different in the way criticality is achieved. Both models are therefore a good starting point for social scientists to analyse social systems that exhibit critical behaviour.

Applications and Relation to Other Chapters

In contrast to the previous chapters, ABM does not enable us to find a closed-form solution but can shed light on the intricate interdependencies of complex social systems that generate emergent properties. Agent-based models are, therefore, not a substitute but complementary to other approaches. The chapter is hence distinct from earlier chapters but relates to all of them. It is particularly related to Chapter 9 in which we study complex and chaotic behaviour. We will see that dynamics are highly dependent on parameter values and initial conditions. Consequently, the dynamics of the models discussed in the following chapter exhibit chaotic dynamics that fail to converge asymptotically to an equilibrium state. An analysis of the trajectories of these models requires an iterated process, which necessitates running a computer simulation for each combination of parameter values.

Further Reading

Computational approaches have become common, especially during the past decade with the increase of processing power of simple computers and the availability of readily available agent-based modelling software packages. Classic introductions to the topic are given in Epstein and Axtell (1996) and De Jong (2006). A more general discussion is provided in Miller and Page (2007).

Another interesting example is Axtell et al. (2001). The authors develop a compelling model in which inter- and intra-group discrimination evolves endogenously. Choi and Bowles (2007) explain the evolutionary forces that led to conditional altruism where individual discriminate between in-group and out-group members. Both papers inspired elements of the evolutionary model in Ille (2021) that presents sectarianisation as the result of a coordination game via a public signal by which individuals are attributed social, economic, and political rights based on their religious affiliation.

Notes

1   Imagine we represent the data on the basis of bins x of size l and change the representation to bins of size $10l$. Data in the new bin occurs with frequency g equal to

$$g = \sum_{x=\rho}^{\rho+9} \alpha x^{-\tau} \tag{8.2}$$

where ρ denotes the starting value of the new bin. Due to the exponential relation between the value and its frequency, an increase in the bin size does not lead to a proportional increase in the frequency.

2   Further note that the concave shape disappears at a bin size of 10^{-4} if we plot the net total of migrants as a share of the population between the ages 15 and 64.

3   According to Moore's Law, the number of transistors doubles every two years implying a doubling in performance every 18 months. This prediction, originating in the 1970s, has proven to be roughly correct until now. In 20 years, the number of transistors should therefore increase at a scale of roughly 1,000. Indeed, the number of transistors in a 1995 Pentium Pro amounts to 5.5 million transistors while an AMD Ryzen processor of 2017 has 4,800–9,600 million transistors and an Apple M1 Max of 2021 has 57,000 million transistors.

4   These functions and operators are considered to be arithmetic ($+ \ - \times \div$), nth roots, exponent and logarithm, and (inverse) trigonometric functions. For example, $y = x + 2x^3/(4z + 5w)$ is a closed-form solution while the Taylor series for e^x, equal to $1 + x + x^2/2! + x^3/3! + \ldots x^n/n!$ for $n \to \infty$, is not a closed-form solution since we have to stop the calculation at some point and only obtain an approximation.

5   We have seen examples of path dependency and tipping points in Chapter 3. The equilibrium to which a population eventually converges depends on the basin of attraction in which it initially starts. If the initial conditions position a population in a different basin of attraction, the population will converge to another equilibrium - in other words, the dynamics exhibit path dependencies. In a coordination game as in Figure 3.2a, the interior unstable equilibrium defines a tipping point.

6   A **genetic algorithm** overcomes the limitations of a fixed strategy and renders an agent more *strategically* adaptive to her environment. We have seen previously that a strategy defines an action contingent on the action

chosen by another player. To understand the intuition of these genetic changes to a strategy, consider the following simple example. Assume that two players interact in a game in which they play a Stag Hunt game (Figure 2.4b). Further assume that the two players choose an action conditional on the last three periods of the stage game. In this case, a strategy then has to define an action for the $4^3 = 64$ outcomes over the last three periods (remember there are four possible outcomes per period). We can now define an agent's initial conditional strategy by a string of the same length (e.g. $s_i = (S, H, S, S, \ldots, H)$ where S denotes hunting a stag and H hunting a hare). An agent can be programmed to randomly change one element of the string and thereby obtain a new conditional strategy. Based on the efficiency of this new strategy against the counterpart's strategy during future interactions, the player will be more likely to choose it and eventually might always play an optimal strategy. Axelrod (2006), for example, has used this principle to show that agents tend to play strategies similar to *Tit-for-Tat* in a prisoner's dilemma after some time. For an accessible introduction to genetic algorithms, refer to Mitchel (1999).

7   Also called Coleman's Bathtub. The model probably goes back to McClennan (1967, Ch. 2).

8   There is indeed a substantial literature analysing various preferences and showing how these preferences affect (or not affect) segregation. The reader may refer to Pancs and Vriend (2007) for an interesting study.

9   I am avoiding here any engagement with the almost ancient debate among biologists whether selection occurs only at the individual or also at the group level and the interested reader may refer to Nunney (1999); Williams (1971) and more recently, Nowak et al. (2010). However, the examples in this chapter make it very clear that within the context of social dynamics and human institutions, human evolution has transcended genetic selection and selection undoubtedly occurs at various levels of aggregation.

10   Readers may refer to Boyd and Richerson (1985), Gintis (2000b), and for an interesting extension, see Choi and Bowles (2007).

11   In Bak et al. (1988), the authors did not consider the height of the sand pile on a particular cell but the total height difference with regard to the bonds with the northern and eastern neighbours. Sand falling on a cell at (x, y) increases the height of this cell with regard to cells at $(x + 1, y)$ and $(x, y + 1)$, and reduces the relative height of cells at $(x - 1, y)$ and $(x, y - 1)$. Define $z(x, y)$ as the total height differential of the cell at coordinates (x, y) with regard to its northern and eastern neighbour. We have the following algorithm if sand falls on cell (x, y)

$$z(x, y) \rightarrow z(x, y) + 2$$
$$z(x - 1, y) \rightarrow z(x - 1, y) - 1$$
$$z(x, y - 1) \rightarrow z(x, y - 1) - 1$$

The latter two algorithms imply that the relative height of the southern and western neighbours is diminished by one unit, since (x, y) is their northern and eastern neighbour, respectively. If sand topples off from cell (x, y), it moves into a north and east direction increasing the pile on cells $(x + 1, y)$ and $(x, y + 1)$. At the same time, since the cell loses a grain of sand along each axis, the relative heights of $(x - 1, y)$ and $(x, y - 1)$ increase. We have the second algorithm

$$z(x, y) \rightarrow z(x, y) - 4$$
$$z(x \pm 1, y) \rightarrow z(x \pm 1, y) + 1$$
$$z(x, y \pm 1) \rightarrow z(x, y \pm 1) + 1$$

Notice that the two algorithms are a theoretical extension of the one-dimensional case, and therefore, the algorithms are a bit difficult to interpret within the context of two-dimensional sandpiles: assume that every cell

3,3	3,3	3,3
3,3	3,3	3,3
3,3	3,3	3,3

(a) Initial state

3,3	3,3	3,3
3,3	4,4	3,3
3,3	3,3	3,3

(b) Drop on centre cell

3,3	4,3	3,3
3,3	3,3	4,3
3,3	3,3	3,3

(c) After landslide

Figure 8.18: Example of a cascade following Bak et al. (1988).

has initially the same height and we focus on the centre cell at (x, y) in Figure 8.18a which shows the absolute height of the cells as a tuple of heights along the x-axis and y-axis. Each cell's relative height is the total of the differential along the x-axis and along the y-axis. The centre cell's neighbours are the four neighbours in bold numbers defined by the von Neumann neighbourhood. The cell to the left/west of the centre cell has coordinates $(x - 1, y)$, the one below/south to the centre cell has coordinates $(x, y - 1)$ and so forth. Once sand drops on the centre cell, it is added both to the heights along the x-axis and y-axis. The cell has an absolute height of 4 for each axis as shown in Figure 8.18b. The relative height of the southern and western cell is now $((3 - 4) + (3 - 3) = -1)$, the northern and eastern cells stay the same while the relative height of the centre cell is $(4 - 3) + (4 - 3) = 2$. This describes the first algorithm. Assume, for simplicity, that a relative height of 2 is already critical and the sand topples from the centre cell. We obtain the state shown in Figure 8.18c. The relative height of the centre cell is now $((3 - 4) + (3 - 4) = -2)$ (i.e., it dropped from 2 to -2) while the northern and eastern cell have a relative height of $(4 - 3) + (3 - 3) = 1$, and the southern and western cell lost their negative height differential. Consequently, the neighbours to the north, south, east, and west each gained one unit in relative height, which is the second algorithm. (Notice, however, that we have ignored the relative height differential of the northwestern and southeastern neighbours.)

12   The differences in scale in Figure 8.15 are due to the different lengths of the simulations. The smaller networks were simulated for two million periods, the medium size network for 300,000 periods and the large network for only 85,000 periods.

13   If we increased the minimum degree by imposing that new nodes have more than one link, the network becomes more interconnected and landslides with a higher lifetime would occur regularly, leading to a bump on the right side of the power law distribution.

Chaos Theory: Non-Linear Dynamics and Social Complexity

9.1 Introduction

EDWARD Lorenz decided to put his computer to the test in 1961: could it be used to forecast the weather? The premise seemed both simple and ambitious. If the movement of celestial bodies can be calculated and if atmospheric conditions are governed by similar principal laws, weather can be predicted – at least to some degree. Classical mechanics tells us that roughly correct knowledge of the current state of a system as well as its structure and laws is sufficient to reasonably well predict its behaviour. Indeed, while studying the approaches in earlier chapters, we have depended on a similar perspective – the idea that social systems naturally converge to a fixed point in the state space. Small errors or noise lead to some random fluctuations, but the latter do not cause cascades and intensify over time but probably eventually even disappear. The implicit conclusion is that small variations simply do not matter in the grand scheme of things. But frequently, we observe processes that manifest erratic and non-periodic behaviour and fail to settle close to any apparent equilibrium. Lorenz was among the first to systematically study the chaotic behaviour that he was about to observe when he set out to forecast weather patterns.[1] He came up with a simple model that replicated the empirical data fairly closely. One day of the fateful year of 1961, he decided to rerun part of a simulation to further investigate some of the earlier results. Since Lorenz only needed to inspect the second part of an earlier simulation run, he copied the calculated state values from the beginning of this section and let the computer do its work. This second run should have replicated the data of the earlier simulation, but to his surprise, it did not. When plotted across time, both runs showed significant differences. After some investigation, Lorenz realised that the only discrepancy between both runs was a very minor change in the initial states of the second simulation. Lorenz took the initial conditions straight from the printout of the original simulation and not the internal values of the computer. The printout showed results with three decimal spaces to save space while the computer memory retained six decimal spaces. The rounded numbers were only a little different from the original values, but as the simulation continued, the difference vastly amplified.

DOI: 10.4324/9781003035329-9

Election forecasts share the unpredictable nature of weather patterns. In late June 2016, most betting shops saw *Remain* in the lead, not by much but by a statistically significant margin. Yet, after the votes were cast and to the surprise of many, Britain decided to leave the European Union. The forecasts of the 2016 Presidential Election in the U.S. were even more off target. The New York Times predicted that Clinton would win the election with a probability of 85 percent (Katz, 2016). As we will see, these erratic results may be crucially driven by decision reversals. Affected by the decision and information from others, swing voters can turn from Brexiteers into Remainers (or the inverse). Between 2010 and 2016, the share of *undecided* in the Brexit polls fluctuated widely, reaching peeks of 40 percent. The frequencies of those in favour of remain or leave showed no discernible trend or pattern.

Again and again, time series data do not only show random fluctuations around some mean, but structural breaks leading to new periodic patterns and sudden shifts of what initially seemed to be trends. Inoculation programmes, such as for rubella and gonorrhoea, or the population growth of different species exhibit random spikes. The historical records of the Nile's water level display long periods of stable trends interrupted by random and sudden rapid changes. These dynamics raise the question of whether such fluctuations are indeed just extrinsic noise and stochastic glitches of nature that randomly push a system away from its equilibrium state or whether these variations are inherent to a system. The answer to this question is crucially relevant for determining whether the system is deterministic or non-deterministic. As we shall see, the former type of system generates the same results given identical initial conditions. In this case, chaos is theoretically predictable (which is why we speak of *deterministic chaos*). The latter type of system, on the other hand, is exogenously infused with randomness and is therefore stochastic and impossible to predict with reasonable accuracy. As will become apparent in this chapter, however, it is difficult to differentiate between deterministic systems that are chaotic and non-deterministic systems by just looking at the data. What speaks in favour of deterministic chaos is that despite being seemingly random, the dynamics display regularities, but the debate about what qualifies as chaos, especially in the context of social systems where deterministic and non-deterministic dynamics mesh, is still open. For example, Chapter 8 studied the sandpile model – a deterministic system as long as the cell on which a grain of sand is dropped is not determined randomly. We have seen that the duration and size of landslides follow a power-law distribution consistent with the empirical data discussed in the last chapter. The scale-free nature of this chaotic system implies that the shape of the distribution is unaffected by the length of the simulation. Independent of whether we analyse the data of a run of one million or ten million periods, the distribution's slope remains the same.

On the other hand, commodity prices are generally considered to be subject to random exogenous fluctuations, but they illustrate similar characteristics. In fact, Granovetter and Soong (1986) show that a bandwagon effect in conjunction with decision reversals can lead to demand fluctuations that seem stochastic but are caused by a deterministic process. When Benoît Mandelbrot looked at the historical data of cotton prices, he found that the data lacked the typical symmetry of the hump-shaped normal distribution. However similar to the sizes and lifetimes of cascades in the sandpile model, he discovered scale invariance. The plot of the changes of daily prices fit the pattern created by the plot of the changes of monthly prices.[2]

While I am unable to provide an ultimate answer here as to when and whether a system is deterministic or non-deterministic in reality, I implicitly assume the former whenever I speak of *chaos* in this chapter (with the exception of Section 9.3, which introduces a noise parameter). Indeed, much like the self-organised system that governs the patterns of the Great Spot of Jupiter, chaos occurs and has been studied in biological, economic, and social system. While we have already encountered chaos in Chapter 8, we will see that the continuous systems of Chapter 3, the discrete models of Chapter 5 and the spatial games of Chapter 7 can fail to converge to a state of equilibrium or to recurrent periodic patterns even in the absence of any exogenous forces that create random noise. These systems spawn chaotic dynamics; yet, as we shall see, there is structure to this chaos. Consistent attributes enable us not only to derive the properties of chaos but to make predictions.

9.2 Threshold Models with Decision Reversals

In Chapter 5, we discussed models in which individuals opt for an action (or belief) once the number (or share) of individuals who choose that action exceeds the former's individual threshold. So far, our analyses were based on the assumption that population thresholds follow a random distribution and can be presented by a cumulative distribution function. Since a CDF has a non-negative slope across its domain, the number of individuals x of those following the action at time $t+1$ is positively correlated with x in the earlier period t - simply speaking, a higher following this period implies a *proportionally* higher following in the next period.[3]

However, the introductory example showed that decision reversals occur in voting behaviour and collective actions. We can see such behaviour also when selling and buying assets and stocks, consuming conspicuous goods, considering to vaccinate or to attend venues. This is by no means an exhaustive list of the cases, in which individuals reconsider their previous choice and abandon an act once too many people engage in the same action. Granovetter and Soong (1986) and Granovetter and Soong (1988) introduced a simple extension of their model to account for these dynamics. Imagine that each individual has two thresholds that constitute the upper and lower share of members in the same population within which the individuals choose to take an action. For example, I might consider to join a protest, if say, 20 percent of the other people protest, but I may stay at home, once the share reaches 80 percent. For any individual i, it must hold that the threshold r_i^U at which she drops out must exceed the threshold r_i^L at which she joins an action. Given some current share x_t, the share in the next period is then defined by the difference between the share of individuals who decide to follow the action and those who abandon it. In other words, $x_{t+1} = F(x_t) = F^L(x_t) - F^U(x_t)$, where F^L and F^U are the CDFs of the lower and upper thresholds across all individuals. Since $r_i^U > r_i^L$ (i.e., nobody can abandon an action before having engaged in it), it must hold that $F^L \geq F^U$. The two CDFs can be any non-decreasing continuous function with a domain and range that do not exceed the unit interval. Assume for example that

$$F^L = x_t^{\frac{1}{\alpha}}$$
$$F^U = x_t^{\beta}$$

(9.1)

for some $\alpha, \beta > 1$. Both parameters determine the reactivity of individuals to the choices of others and both CDFs will intersect at $F^L(0) = F^U(0) = 0$ and $F^L(1) = F^U(1) = 1$ and $F^L > F^U$ for any $x \in [0,1]$. The resulting *net-threshold function* $F(x_t)$ then describes a hump-shaped function that

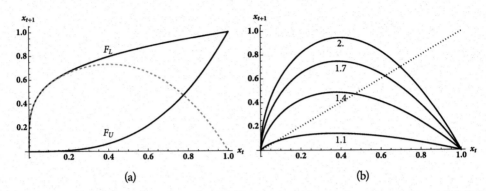

Figure 9.1: (a) shows F^L and F^U in bold given $\alpha = 4$ and $\beta = 3$. The resulting net-threshold function $F(x_t)$ is shown as dashed. (b) illustrates $F = 2\left(x^{(1/\alpha)} - x^\alpha\right)$ for different values of α.

intersects the abscissa at 0 and 1 as shown in Figure 9.1a. The population reaches a stable fixed point at roughly $x^* = 0.636$. Note that $F(x_t)$ is no longer a CDF. For our model, it suffices that the function is non-negative and does not exceed 1 for any $x \in [0, 1]$. It is also not necessary that the net-threshold function $F(x_t)$ is defined as a difference of two CDFs. To make results more interesting and to simplify our analysis to one parameter, I will assume instead that

$$x_{t+1} = F(x_t) = 2\left(x_t^{\frac{1}{\alpha}} - x_t^\alpha\right) \tag{9.2}$$

In this case, the function cannot be split into two CDFs but $F(x_t)$ meets our requirements as long as $\alpha \in (1, \bar{\alpha}]$ where $\bar{\alpha}$ defines the upper bound at $\bar{\alpha} = 2.09845$. The function is increasing in α leading to a higher interior fixed point, as is shown in Figure 9.1b.

For the following discussion, I have chosen the function in equation (9.2) instead of the example in equation (9.1) deliberately, since the former manifests some interesting properties that we would not obtain for $F^L - F^U$. At $\alpha = 1.6$, the system converges to a stable equilibrium at $x^* = 0.5835$ as shown in Figure 9.2a. Since the system requires a few periods to settle on an equilibrium state, the figure shows the x-values for periods 9,950 to 10,000. This result is consistent with our previous analysis in Chapter 5. The slope of $F(x_t)$ is (for convenience, I drop again the time index in the following)

$$\frac{dF(x)}{dx} = \frac{2\left(x^{1/\alpha} - \alpha^2 x^\alpha\right)}{\alpha x} \tag{9.3}$$

At $\alpha = 1.6$, the slope at the interior fixed point is approximately $|-0.786| < 1$ and thus this equilibrium is asymptotically stable by condition (5.3) on page 98. Changing the exponent to $\alpha = 1.8$ returns the dynamics in Figure 9.2b. Since the slope at the interior fixed point is $|-1.211| > 1$, the latter is unstable and the population flips between two states at $x_1^* = 0.3957$ and $x_2^* = 0.8180$ for reasons that I discuss further below. At $\alpha = 2.0$, the interior fixed point is also unstable as the slope is now -1.592, but at this point, the pattern in Figure 9.2c looks more volatile and seems to fluctuate erratically between different states. In addition, small changes to the initial conditions radically alter the trajectory. While the bold graph shows the trajectory starting at the initial condition $x_{01} = 0.100$, the dotted graph presents the orbits for $x_{02} = 0.101$. Two systems,

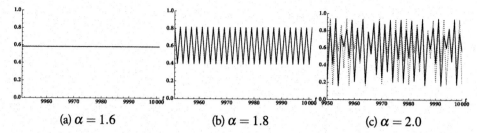

(a) $\alpha = 1.6$ (b) $\alpha = 1.8$ (c) $\alpha = 2.0$

Figure 9.2: Figures show periods 9,950 to 10,000, given different values for α.

which only illustrate minor differences in the initial conditions, manifest substantial differences in their long-run behaviour. This divergence of trajectories that start at adjacent initial states is known as the **Butterfly effect.**[4]

Note that the aperiodic behaviour of the system given by equation (9.2) at $\alpha = 2$ is deterministic, but it lacks a closed-form solution. Similarly to the agent-based models in Chapter 8, we need to iterate the process for each time period since any future state can only be determined by the previous state. Moreover, since trajectories are highly sensitive to changes in the initial conditions, a simulation with some initial condition cannot be used as an approximation for a system that starts at a nearby initial condition, as Lorenz realised by chance on that winter day in 1961. Slight changes to the initial conditions require a new simulation.

When simulating the system in equation (9.2), gradually increasing α escalates the sophistication of the trajectory's pattern. However, this process is not gradual. At values below $\alpha_1^* = 1.69710$, the system converges to a stable interior fixed point that increases in α. At α_1^*, the system bifurcates (more precisely, it undergoes a **flip bifurcation** or **period-doubling bifurcation**) and now cycles between two states which are the fixed points of $F(F(x))$ (also called, a *two-cycle*). Yet, once we increase the exponent beyond $\alpha_2^* = 1.90607$, the system bifurcates again. Now the system periodically fluctuates between four different states. At $\alpha_3^* = 1.95092$, the system bifurcates yet another time and with each bifurcation, the number of states, between which the system cycles, doubles. Figure 9.3 shows the behaviour in greater detail. The **bifurcation diagram** plots the stable equilibrium/periodic values of x in relation to α.

The system bifurcates several times before dynamics seem to turn entirely disorganised. Despite the seemingly chaotic nature of these bifurcations, they are governed by a regularity. Let

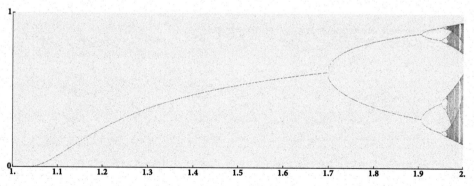

Figure 9.3: Bifurcation diagram for $\alpha \in (1,2]$.

B_n define the n-th bifurcation and let

$$\delta_n = \frac{B_n - B_{n-1}}{B_{n+1} - B_n} \tag{9.4}$$

Feigenbaum (1978) showed that for larger values of n, this ratio between period-doubling bifurcations is equal for all parabolic shapes (or more precisely for all one-dimensional maps with a single quadratic maximum).[5] The **Feigenbaum constant** is defined as

$$\delta \equiv \lim_{n \to \infty} \delta_n = 4.66920\ldots \tag{9.5}$$

If we put the above values into equation (9.4), we have

$$\delta_2 = \frac{1.90607 - 1.69710}{1.95092 - 1.90607} = 4.65931$$

which is already very close to the Feigenbaum constant. We can now use the Feigenbaum constant to predict the next bifurcation, which should occur at around

$$B_4 = \frac{B_3 - B_2}{\delta} + B_3 = \frac{1.95092 - 1.90607}{\delta} + 1.95092 = 1.96053 \tag{9.6}$$

Since this defines a geometric series, we can further calculate at which point the number of bifurcations is infinite and the system turns chaotic

$$B_\infty = \frac{B_2 - B_1}{\delta - 1} + B_2 = \frac{1.90607 - 1.69710}{\delta - 1} + 1.90607 = 1.96302 \tag{9.7}$$

Exercise 9.1

Derive the result in equation (9.7) from equation (9.4).

Figure 9.4 presents a close-up of the bifurcation diagram for the interval between 1.96 and 2.01. The results in equations (9.6) and (9.7) are excellent predictions. At $\alpha = 1.96067$, the system bifurcates a fourth time and oscillates between $2^4 = 16$ states, while chaotic dynamics ensue at $\alpha = 1.963$.

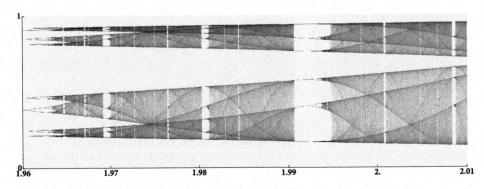

Figure 9.4: Bifurcation diagram for $\alpha \in [1.96, 2.01]$.

From Chapter 5, we know that the fixed point is defined as the intersection of $F(x)$ and the 45° line, and mathematically, it is given by any x^* for which $F(x^*) = x^*$. After a **period-doubling bifurcation**, the system alternates between two points x_1^* and x_2^*. Therefore,

$$x_2^* = F(x_1^*) \tag{9.8a}$$
$$x_1^* = F(x_2^*) \tag{9.8b}$$

Iterating the function another time returns

$$x_1^* = F(x_2^*) = F(F(x_1^*)) \tag{9.9a}$$
$$x_2^* = F(x_1^*) = F(F(x_2^*)) \tag{9.9b}$$

At every other step, the system returns to its original state. To simplify notation, define

$$F^n(x) \equiv F(F(F(F(\ldots F(x))))) \tag{9.10}$$

as the n-th iterate of $F(x)$. The notation in equation (9.9) then simplifies to $x_1^* = F^2(x_1^*)$ and $x_2^* = F^2(x_2^*)$. Since the second iterate maps the state on itself after the first bifurcation, we can graphically find an interior fixed point by plotting $F^2(x)$ for $x \in [0,1]$ as shown in Figure 9.5.[6] The figure helps us understand the origin of the bifurcation as well as why the two new fixed points are stable. Figure 9.5a illustrates $F^2(x)$ for $\alpha = 1.6$ and the function intersects the 45° line at $x^* = 0.5835$, which is the only interior and stable fixed point as shown in Figure 9.2a. At $\alpha = 1.69709$, the function is exactly tangent to the 45° line (see Figure 9.5b). At a value above the critical α_1^*, $F^2(x)$ breaks through the 45° line and intersects the latter at two additional points. These two points are stable fixed points of the second iterate, the system bifurcates as the interior fixed point is now unstable at higher values of α. For example, in Figure 9.5c, an intersection from above occurs at $x_1^* = 0.39572$ and $x_2^* = 0.81798$ which is consistent with the dynamics illustrated in Figure 9.2b. Note that the function also intersect from below at $x = 0.68756$ which is the unstable fixed point of $F(x)$ for $\alpha = 1.8$.

The analysis can be extended to all future bifurcations. At $\alpha_2^* = 1.90607$, the system bifurcates a second time giving birth to four stable interior fixed points of F^4 and at $\alpha_3^* = 1.95092$ the third bifurcation occurs leading to eight stable interior fixed points of F^8. Note that since the system cycles through all stable fixed points, the iterate of $F(x)$ must correspond to the respective number of fixed points.[7] Thus, a bifurcation causing n fixed points to become $2n$ fixed points occurs whenever α is just marginally larger than a value at which the nth iterate of $F(x)$ is tangent

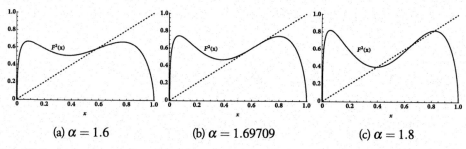

(a) $\alpha = 1.6$ (b) $\alpha = 1.69709$ (c) $\alpha = 1.8$

Figure 9.5: Figures show the second iterate around the critical α value.

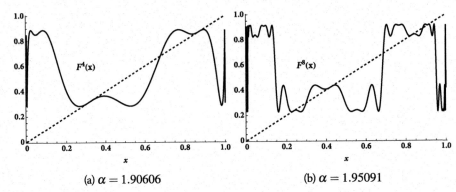

(a) $\alpha = 1.90606$ (b) $\alpha = 1.95091$

Figure 9.6: (a) Plots the fourth iterate $F^4(x)$ below the critical α value. (b) Plots the eighth iterate $F^8(x)$ below the critical α value.

to the 45° line at the n fixed points. Figure 9.6 plots the fourth and eighth iterate of $F(x)$ at values that are marginally smaller than the critical αs. Again, we observe that the function is tangent at two and four points, respectively.

A closer inspection of Figure 9.4 reveals further interesting details. The bifurcation diagram is characterised by broader bands. It seems that the two lower bands join at around $\alpha = 1.95$ to form a larger band. The same seems to hold for the upper bands, but both bands leave out values around $x = 0.7$ for the entire range of α. In addition, the chaotic regions contain a number of more pronounced curves indicating that these values of x are visited more frequently for a given α. Both characteristics are connected to the critical values of $F(x)$, at which the slope of $F(x)$ equals zero. Using equation (9.3), the critical value of x are defined by

$$\hat{x} = \alpha^{\frac{2\alpha}{1-\alpha^2}} \tag{9.11}$$

Trajectories that pass the vicinity of a critical value tend to cluster together for several iterations causing the critical values on these trajectories to appear more frequently. Figure 9.7a present the effect. Note that equation (9.11) is strictly increasing in α, and therefore must lie between

$$\hat{x}_L = \lim_{\alpha \to 1} \alpha^{\frac{2\alpha}{1-\alpha^2}} = \frac{1}{e} \approx 0.36788 \tag{9.12}$$

$$\hat{x}_H = \lim_{\alpha \to \bar{\alpha}} \alpha^{\frac{2\alpha}{1-\alpha^2}} \approx 0.40092 \tag{9.13}$$

Figure 9.7a plots the first four iterations of five trajectories that start at and around the critical value. We observe that the reason for the clustering is that the slope around the maximum of the hump-shaped function is flat, and thus the trajectories follow each other after being projected onto the 45° line. Figure 9.7b plots the x values of the first 16 iterations that start at $\hat{x}$. The first eight iterations outline the main bands in Figure 9.4 and the x of the 9th to 16th iteration retrace its bolder curves in the chaotic region.[8] Since these curves are derived from the critical values, they are called **critical value lines** or **curves**.

Exercise 9.2

The logistic map of the form $x_{t+1} = rx_t(1 - x_t)$ has been studied extensively and it shares the qualitative properties of the system defined by equation (9.2). To test your understanding, apply the previous analysis to the logistic map and study how the quantitative results differ.

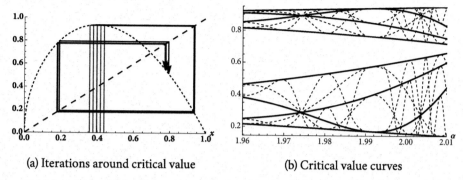

| (a) Iterations around critical value | (b) Critical value curves |

Figure 9.7: (a) shows the first four iterations starting within ±0.04 of the critical value for $\alpha = 1.987$. (b) shows the critical value lines based on the x values of the first eight iterations (bold) and the following eight iterations (dashed) for a trajectory starting at $\hat{x}$.

The critical value curves explain a second phenomenon displayed in Figure 9.4. The chaotic regions are interrupted by small windows in which the system returns to a periodic dynamic. Such a window occurs in the region $\alpha^w \in (1.99066, 1.99264)$ in which the system oscillates between six fixed points. Figure 9.8 graphs the sixth iterate of $F(x)$ at $\alpha = 1.9915$. The six stable fixed points correspond to those instances in which $F^6(x)$ crosses the 45° line from above which are highlighted by the circles in Figure 9.8. At each of these fixed points, the slope of $F^6(x)$ is approximately $-0.30194 > -1$.[9] Looking back at Figure 9.7 shows that at α^w, the interior critical value curves are tangent to the principal critical value curves that define the main bands. Hence, the fixed points are given by the six critical value curves defined by the first eight iterations starting at the critical value $\hat{x}$.

As α decreases to values to the left of the periodic window, the six fixed points disappear once $F^6(x)$ is no longer tangent to the 45° line at these points. If we move α to the right of the window, the absolute slope of the iterate at the fixed points exceeds 1 turning the latter unstable and leading to chaotic behaviour. The areas close to the periodic windows exhibit interesting behaviour. To its left, the system illustrates **intermittency** implying that trajectories seem to switch between chaotic and periodic dynamics. Intermittency arises because the iterate is almost tangent to the 45° line at those points that turn into stable fixed points of the periodic window. Consequently, trajectories stay within the vicinity of the fixed point for several iterations which leads to pseudo-periodic behaviour (see exercise 9.3 and Ch. 10.4 Strogatz, 2015 for details). To

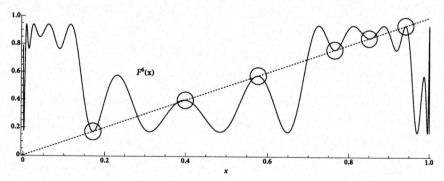

Figure 9.8: Plot of the sixth iteration $F^6(x)$ at $\alpha = 1.9915$. Fixed points ($x_1^* = 0.17081$, $x_2^* = 0.39900$, $x_3^* = 0.57664$, $x_4^* = 0.76423$, $x_5^* = 0.84881$, $x_6^* = 0.93996$) are highlighted by circles.

the right, the chaotic attractor expands in size which gives rise to narrow and well-defined chaotic bands around the former fixed points. Once α increases further, these narrow bands eventually fully integrate again into the major bands. This behaviour is called **interior crisis** or **crisis-induced intermittency** (see Ch. 7 Hilborn, 1994 and Grebogi et al., 1987 for a detailed explanation).

Exercise 9.3

(a) Plot the trajectory for $\alpha = 1.9905$ for several periods. What do you observe? (b) Graph $F^6(x)$. What happened to the stable fixed points of the graph in Figure 9.8? (c) Trace the trajectory for $F^6(x)$ and $x_0 = 0.851$ for ten periods. What do you observe? Link the results in (b) and (c) to explain the dynamics that you discovered in (a).

9.3 An Information Spin Glass

While studying cellular automata in Chapter 7, we have seen that despite their simplicity, these systems demonstrate emergent properties and sophisticated dynamics to the point of being chaotic. In this section, we will study another of these seemingly simple systems. As before, I assume that the interaction environment is defined by a flat two-dimensional plane that is separated into regular square-shaped cells. Each individual is placed on a different cell and interacts with their Moore neighbourhood (see page 148). Each cell on the plane is occupied and for simplicity, the plane is warped into a torus (as shown on page 149) and hence, each individual has eight neighbours.

Any individual i can be in one of two states $\theta_{it} = \{-1, 1\}$ at time t. These binary states can represent a vast array of opposing individual characteristics and behavioural rules, but here, we might assume that the binary state represents opposing individual beliefs. Furthermore, each neighbour j affects the state of an individual i with a randomly assigned weight $w_{ij} \in [-1, 1]$. A negative weight implies that the neighbour's belief discourages an individual from adopting the same belief while a positive weight reinforces the belief. Given is set of neighbours N_i, in each period, she calculates the payoff

$$\pi_{it} = \theta_{it} \sum_{k \in N_i} w_{ik} \theta_{kt} \tag{9.14}$$

Based on the sign of π_{it}, individual i determines her future state θ_{it+1} according to the simple decision-algorithm

$$\begin{aligned} \theta_{it+1} &= \quad \theta_{it} \text{ if } \pi_{it} > 0 \\ \theta_{it+1} &= -\theta_{it} \text{ if } \pi_{it} \leq 0 \end{aligned} \tag{9.15}$$

Consequently, an individual switches her state if the calculated payoff is not positive. In addition, individual i also changes her state with a small probability p_{it+1} even though $\pi_{it} > 0$. Assume that this probability is

$$p_{it+1} = e^{\frac{-\pi_{it}}{\sigma}} \tag{9.16}$$

where σ is an exogenous noise parameter. Such external noise can be caused by new private or ambiguous public information, individual preferences or practices that are not covered by the model. We have $p_{it+1} \in (0, 1)$ as well as

$$\frac{\partial p_{it+1}}{\partial \pi_{it}} < 0 \text{ and } \frac{\partial p_{it+1}}{\partial \sigma} > 0$$

In other words, an increase in the noise raises the likelihood of an erroneous switch, but the latter is less likely to happen if all her neighbours are in the same state as i.[10]

The simple model generates complex dynamics. For higher noise parameters or a mix between positive and negative weights, the system is unable to settle close to an equilibrium and remains in a disorganised state – but this does not hold for all parameter values. To see this, let the share of strictly positive weights across the population be given by ω, thus with probability ω a neighbour encourages the adoption of a state, with probability $1 - \omega$, she discourages an individual. Assume for the moment that all neighbours are connected through positive weights (i.e., $\omega = 1$). We might think here of a situation in which individuals are subject to high-peer pressure or rely mostly on social imitation. Figure 9.9 demonstrates various population states given different parameter values for σ. In each simulation, the population starts with the random initial distribution shown in Figure 9.9a in which half of the population is in state 1 and the other half in state -1. At very low noise parameters, the population eventually settles on a quasi-equilibrium at which most individuals maintain their state. In this case, the population evolves into large extended neighbourhoods that share the same state. As the noise and hence the probability of an idiosyncratic shift increases, these neighbourhoods become less distinct and disappear at higher noise levels. This suggests that if peer pressure on individual choices or beliefs is sufficiently strong, the population converges into distinct camps sharing different beliefs even in the absence of any positive assortment and distinct popular opinion or established practice.[11] The result is intuitive, but what is more interesting is that there is a critical region of peer pressure to noise ratio in which the population switches from the erratic population state in Figure 9.9d to the organised state in Figure 9.9b. The system experiences a **phase transition**.

To better trace the impact of σ on the population state and the phase transition, Figure 9.10a plots the average share of switches across different values of σ.[12] The relation between σ and the frequency of state switches is not perfectly monotonic across all values. However, we can observe that below $\sigma = 0.8$, switching is sporadic, but starts to increase at $\sigma^* \in (0.8, 1)$ and escalates thereafter. For example, at $\sigma = 0.25$ the approximate share of individuals, who switch their state

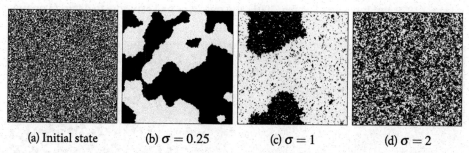

(a) Initial state   (b) $\sigma = 0.25$ (c) $\sigma = 1$ (d) $\sigma = 2$

Figure 9.9: Figures show different population states given $\omega = 1$ on a 201×201 plane. (a) shows the initial random population state, the remaining figures show the population states after 5,000 periods for different noise parameters and thus probabilities of idiosyncratic switching. A phase transition occurs at $\sigma \in (1.0, 1.3)$.

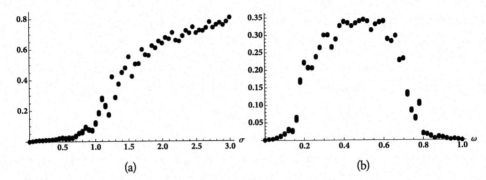

Figure 9.10: Figures plot the average number of switches in periods 500–600. (a) shows the impact of σ, given $\omega = 1$, (b) shows the impact of ω, given $\sigma = 0$.

in each period, is 1 percent and at $\sigma \in (0.8, 1)$, the share increases to around 7 percent. In this interval, the system goes through the phase transition.

Since the noise parameter is positive, the system is not deterministic. However, it can exhibit similar characteristics in the absence of noise and create deterministic chaos. Figure 9.11 illustrates the impact of an increase in the share of positive weights ω on the population states, under the assumption that half of the population is initially in one of the two states, but no idiosyncratic switch occurs by setting $\sigma = 0$. Intuitively, the system converges to a quasi-equilibrium if the beliefs or actions of most individuals are positively reinforced by their neighbours, as shown in Figure 9.11d. If, on the contrary, ω is low and most individuals are discouraged by their neighbours, the population is equally able to settle on a quasi-equilibrium in which homogeneous neighbourhoods only expand along the horizontal or vertical axes, leading to the pattern of regular *canals* in Figure 9.11a. The system therefore sustains two phase transitions. As before, the initial random distribution affects the region of the critical ω values at which the transitions occur, but we can see in Figure 9.10b that the two phase transitions transpire around $\omega_l^* = 0.15$ and $\omega_h^* = 0.8$. Again, this simple model generates the intuitive result that societies form clusters of uniform belief, behavioural rules or practices as long as there is only little antagonism between the members in such a cluster.

We may argue that the existence of only two diametrical states is too simplistic and it is unrealistic to assume that individuals *flip* from one state to the other within a single period. After all, individuals demonstrate a bias towards their prior opinion (known as *confirmation bias*, see Lord et al., 1979 and Jones and Sugden, 2001) and only repeated exposure to different opinions

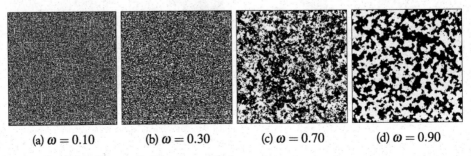

(a) $\omega = 0.10$ (b) $\omega = 0.30$ (c) $\omega = 0.70$ (d) $\omega = 0.90$

Figure 9.11: Figures show the results for different ωs and $\sigma = 0$.

leads to a change of mind. The model can be easily extended to accommodate a continuous individual state space $\theta_{it} \in [-1, 1]$. Whenever $\pi_{it} \leq 0$, individual is state partially moves towards the other end of the spectrum (e.g., from state 0.8 to state 0.6). To render the model consistent, if $\pi_{it} > 0$, the affirmation by peers should reinforce the state (e.g., i moves from state 0.6 to state 0.8). The results of such an adapted model look essentially identical to the simpler case with two states. Similar to the simpler model, the population converges to a quasi-equilibrium if σ is small and ω is either close to 0 or 1. If ω is large, the population is again characterised by larger homogeneous neighbourhoods, in which case most individuals are surrounded by neighbours whose states have the same sign. The endorsement by peers therefore incrementally increases the state of i if the latter's state is positive and decreases her state otherwise. Over time, the population converges to a distribution at which most members are either of state 1 or −1 whereas a small number of individuals remain at an undecided state close to 0.

While these results are interesting, they are not surprising. However, this simple model of interaction demonstrates interesting properties given a more sophisticated interaction structure. So far we have assumed that individuals interact in the well-defined structure of a regular network. Yet, this type of topology is not naturally occurring and preferential attachment fosters the evolution of scale-free networks with a power-law degree distribution as I argued before. We have seen in Chapter 6 that these networks are defined by a majority of nodes with a low degree and a small number of highly connected hubs. A change in the state of one network member might not trigger any other change in the network, but may also cause significant cascades. The former happens if the node is surrounded by neighbours who themselves have a higher degree. The impact of the node's state change has only an insignificant influence on her neighbours and the shock to the system, which the change in her state entails, remains highly localised. The latter, on the other hand, happens if a highly connected node changes her state. It is then likely that a substantial number of her neighbours are of a low degree and thus affected by the state change and subsequently change their state in return. The effect of the state change is then amplified and can pass through the system affecting other individuals at a larger distance. For this to happen, the path between the distant nodes needs to exhibit some degree of fragility (i.e., the neighbourhoods of each of the nodes on the path are as such that the change of the state of one or two neighbours causes another state change). Similar to the sandpile model in Chapter 8, these cascades can be significant. Figure 9.12a illustrates the frequency with which a single state change affects a certain number of members of a network of 1,000 nodes. While the change of the state of a single individual induces a state change in mostly only 30–60 other members, it sporadically has a significantly higher impact.

Additionally, the distance between the member who first switched and the affected individual with the longest geodesic distance can cover the diameter of the entire network. The diameter of the network with 1,000 nodes is 18 and the average shortest path between any two nodes is 7. Figure 9.12b demonstrates that the distance between the node that switched first and the one affected that is furthest away frequently exceeds the average shortest path and can bridge the entire network. Thus, while a single shock mostly does not alter the state of a large share of the population in the network, it tends to spread to distant members. Sporadically, a shock can have a significant impact not only in terms of numbers but with regard to the average state and hence belief of the population. During the simulations, some shocks shift the average state by over 10 percent. An accumulation of such shocks can then entail a complete change in the overall perception after

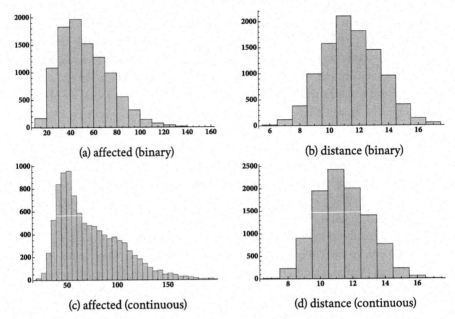

(a) affected (binary)   (b) distance (binary)

(c) affected (continuous)   (d) distance (continuous)

Figure 9.12: Figures show histograms based on the simulation with $\omega = 0.85$ in a network of 1,000 nodes which has been shocked 10,000 times. (a) and (b) refer to the binary case, (c) and (d) show the continuous case.

a few idiosyncratic changes. This effect is not only interesting if we wish to understand sudden and profound shifts in public opinion. The spin glass model is also particularly insightful when applied to other networks in which contagion plays a crucial role, such as those formed by banks through interbank lending or by chains of infection.[13] Figures 9.12c and 9.12d show the results for a continuous state space between -1 and 1 and the same networks. Individual shocks cause up to 256 network members to revise their belief, but the impact on the average opinion is slightly smaller at a maximum of 7 percent. As before, the continuous and the binary model generate essentially the same results.

As a last extension of the model, I assume that instead of the fixed network topology, in which individuals react to a random change in the state of one of their fixed neighbours, shocks are generated by the addition of new members to a network. In Chapter 6, we observed that the typical topology of social networks can be replicated by a simple algorithm (see page 138). Correspondingly, assume that each time a new member is added to the network, she attaches herself to one of the existing members with the probability defined in equation (6.30). The newcomer has a random state and old members react to the state of the new member by updating their states in the previously described continuous manner. This is a plausible situation. New members introduce novel beliefs and practices into established communities and identity groups. These new ideas and habits can possibly be adopted and gradually internalised by incumbent members. Figure 9.13a depicts the share of individuals who switch their state after a new member has been added to the network. The figure shows the result of four different simulations for the periods 1,000–1,100 and the same network size. None of the four runs follows a particular pattern, some cycle widely while others are relatively consistent. All trajectories are different despite being generated by the same attachment algorithm. Different realisations lead to completely distinctive dynamics. In small

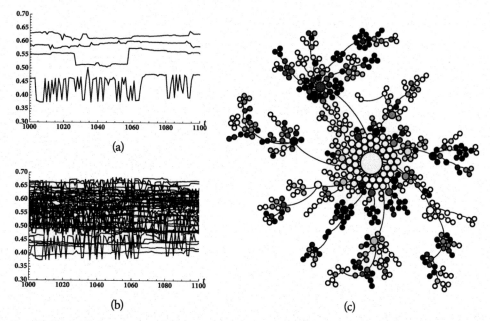

(a)

(b)

(c)

Figure 9.13: (a) and (b) shows the share of individuals who switch their state as a consequence of a new attachment: (a) 4 runs, (b) 50 runs. (c) illustrates the network of order $n = 500$. The size of a node defines its eigenvector centrality, darker colours indicate that a node is more frequently discouraged from its state (i.e., obtains usually $\pi_{it} \leq 0$).

networks, the different trajectories vary across the entire state space. When the network reaches around 1,000 nodes, the trajectories remain within a share of 0.35–0.65 but preserve their arbitrary nature (see Figure 9.13b).[14]

However, parts of the network are robust against the impact of a newcomer with a different state. Figure 9.13c illustrates a network that has gone through the algorithm 499 times. A darker node indicates a higher frequency of switching relative to the age of the node.[15] A larger node illustrates a higher eigenvector centrality. It is apparent from the figure that the changes of the individual states do not occur uniformly across the network but are concentrated within moderately connected clusters. The central nodes in these clusters share the colour shade of their neighbours. For example, the dominant node in the centre of the graph and most of its neighbours are white, indicating that these nodes have changed their state only very sporadically. Since nodes in this cluster are mostly connected to other nodes of the same cluster and hence state, their states are self-reinforcing. The light clusters therefore converge to the boundary states -1 or 1. Darker clusters, nonetheless, are composed of members who do not share the same state. In these clusters, newcomers can tip the balance causing their neighbours to update their state. The shock induced by the newcomer can propagate across the cluster, but its reach is constrained by the more settled white clusters. Due to feedback loops, the darker clusters tend to move randomly across the state space and even flip between a negative and positive state after a new member is added to the network. In essence, the network is composed of tightly knit clusters that illustrate heterogeneous qualities. Some establish a well-defined and consistent belief or behavioural rule, but others are unable to agree. In this case, a conventional belief or practice is not established and disrupted with each new member.

9.4   Chaos in Evolutionary Games

The evolutionary games in Chapter 3 can also illustrate chaotic behaviour. However, if the game is played among members of the same population, the total number of strategies needs to exceed 3. Remember that a game with n strategies in a single population is defined by $n-1$ replicator equations. Consequently, the dynamics of a game with three strategies can be represented in a two-dimensional state space. Yet, chaotic behaviour requires an (autonomous) continuous system with a state space of dimension three or higher (see also the Appendix, Section A.5).[16]

I therefore start our analysis with a generic game of four strategies ($S_i = \{A,B,C,D\}$) given by the payoff matrix in Figure 9.14. Since the game is played between two members of the same population, the payoff matrix is symmetric.[17] The payoff vector of player i is then

$$\vec{\pi}_i = \Pi \begin{bmatrix} w \\ x \\ y \\ z \end{bmatrix} \tag{9.17}$$

where Π is the payoff matrix in Figure 9.14 and $\{w,x,y,z\}$ define the population frequencies of strategies A, B, C, and D, respectively. Simplifying notation by defining $w = 1-x-y-z$, the four replicator dynamics are

$$\dot{x} = x(10z - 5(1-x-y-z) - \phi) \tag{9.18}$$

$$\dot{y} = y(15(1-x-y-z) - 2x - 10z - \phi) \tag{9.19}$$

$$\dot{z} = z(11(1-x-y-z) - 5x - \phi) \tag{9.20}$$

with $\phi = (1-x-y-z)\pi_w + x\pi_x + y\pi_y + z\pi_z$ and $\pi_w = -x+y+5z$.

Exercise 9.4

(a) Show that the game in Figure 9.14 has seven interior fixed points and four corner solutions. (b) Show that only the two solutions above are asymptotically stable.

The replicator dynamics have two asymptotically stable fixed points (or evolutionarily stable states), one at $(x=1, y=0, z=0)$ and the second at $(x=0, y=15/16, z=0)$. The former can be readily inferred from the payoff matrix Figure 9.14. The asymptotically stable fixed point must be a best response against itself and therefore needs to have the highest payoff value on the diagonal

Player 2

		A	B	C	D
		A	B	C	D
Player 1	A	0,0	$-1,-5$	1,15	5,11
	B	$-5,-1$	0,0	0,-2	10,-5
	C	15,1	$-2,0$	0,0	$-10,0$
	D	11,5	$-5,10$	0,-10	0,0

Figure 9.14: A four strategy game.

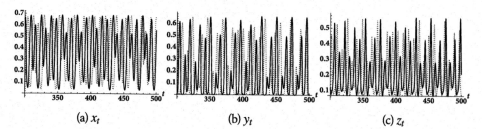

(a) x_t (b) y_t (c) z_t

Figure 9.15: Figures show values of x_t, y_t, and z_t during periods 300–500, with initial values $y_0 = 0.21$, and $z_0 = 0.25$. Full curves are initiated at $x_0 = 0.26$, dotted values use $x_0 = 0.27$.

element (which is 0 in this case) compared to the other payoffs in the same column for Player 1 and the same row for Player 2.

In addition, sufficiently mixed initial distributions lead to chaotic trajectories. Figure 9.15 illustrates an example. The dynamics suggest intermittency in the form of periodic regime changes during which the population seems to follow a cyclic behaviour. Upon closer inspection, we can see that the values are not periodically reoccurring, but change slightly. A by-product of this pseudo-periodicity is that despite the chaotic dynamics, slight variations in the initial conditions initially do not lead to vastly different trajectories but to similar reoccurring patterns. The dotted curves in Figure 9.15 show the values of the population frequencies for a slightly different initial distribution. For periods 300–500, results are fairly similar with one trajectory lagging behind the other. The similarity in the spikes indicates that a population is more likely to visit states in the vicinity of certain locations in the state space.

To see this, Figure 9.16 plots the trajectory in the unit simplex. Since the state is defined by three non-negative frequencies that do not exceed a total value of one, the state space is defined by a regular triangular pyramid. The trajectory exhibits two interesting characteristics. First, individual frequencies do not exceed values of 0.7, no strategy goes extinct, and the trajectory remains within the *spherical triangle*. Second, the darker areas of the trajectory support the previous conjecture

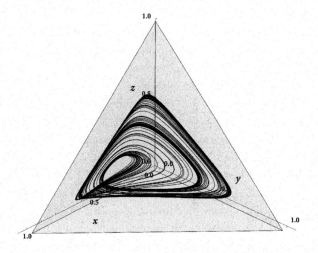

Figure 9.16: Figure shows the trajectory from period 0 to 800 in the unit simplex with the same initial values as the full curves in Figure 9.15.

		Player 2	
	R	P	S
R	1,1	0,2	2,0
Player 1 P	2,0	1,1	0,2
S	0,2	2,0	1,1

Figure 9.17: The two-population rock-paper-scissor game.

that the population moves into the vicinity of certain pseudo-periodic cycles more frequently than other states. For longer periods, the trajectory would cover most of the states in the spherical triangle but will never leave the latter. The observation connects to the question raised at the beginning of this chapter. If we compare the historical data of two different groups, countries, or regions etc. which show similar patterns, it is unclear whether differences in the time series data are caused by some minor external forces and noise, or whether these differences are endogenously generated by a chaotic social system. In the former case, we assume that future data will look similar as long as the external factors remain identical and noise has no cumulative impact. In the latter case, the chaotic dynamics do not allow us to predict the behaviour of the system with sufficient accuracy. Similar to the Nile's historical water levels, structural breaks and significant shifts can occur within short periods of time.[18]

Chaotic dynamics can also occur in interactions between members of more than one population. In two-population games, the number of strategies must exceed two at least for one population to ensure that the state space is of higher dimension than two. Figure 9.17 shows a rock-paper-scissor type game in two populations.[19] A member of one population only plays against a member of the other population, but never against her own kind. The payoff values follow the standard rule of the game: rock beats scissor, scissor beats paper, and paper beats rock. The winner receives a payoff of 2, the loser goes away empty-handed, and if both play the same strategy, the winning amount is split evenly. While rock-paper-scissor is a children's game, it is representative of the essence of a much larger class of negotiations and (not only military) engagements in which each strategy encompasses a suitable counter-measure.

The game is a zero-sum game which we can easily see if we subtract 1 from all elements in the payoff matrix. It is thus straightforward to see that the Nash equilibrium is defined by a mixed strategy in which each player chooses one of the three strategies with probability $1/3$, but the split into two populations adds a catch. The dynamics of the two-population rock-paper-scissor game are highly sensitive to changes in the initial conditions. Given the three strategies in two populations, we obtain four replicator dynamics. To avoid having to deal with a four-dimensional state space, we can split the state space by population and present the dynamics in two equilateral triangles as we have done in Chapter 3.5. Trajectories starting at $x_{10} = 0.5$, $y_{10} = 0.2$, $x_{20} = 0.2$ and $y_{20} = 0.5$ lead to what seems to be an unremarkable periodic behaviour that follows a quasi-stable orbit akin to the one-population version of the game, as shown in Figure 9.18a. Since the game is symmetric, the orbits are regular and identical for both populations. Consequently, the trajectories in the two unit simplices look identical for both populations. Figure 9.18 therefore only present one unit simplex which holds both for population 1 and 2. Note that Figure 9.18a plots the trajectory only for periods 3,000–5,000 during which the trajectory follows a *quasi*-stable orbit, but the latter is not entirely stable over longer periods. Plotting the trajectory for ten million periods will fill the

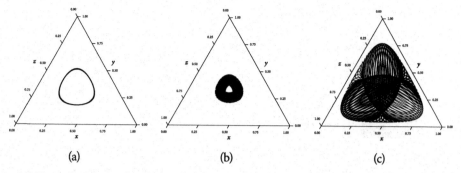

(a)   (b)   (c)

Figure 9.18: Figures show trajectory for periods 3,000–5,000 in unit simplex of population 1. (a) illustrates the periodic behaviour shown in the unit simplex for initial conditions ($x_{10} = 0.5, y_{10} = 0.3, x_{20} = 0.5, y_{20} = 0.3$), (b) for initial conditions ($1/3, 0.25, 0.25, 1/3$), and (c) for initial conditions ($0.6, 0.3, 0.3, 0.6$).

entire interior spherical triangle but the trajectory never leaves the boundaries of the latter. It also stays predominantly within the vicinity of the quasi-stable orbit.

Dynamics change if we alter the initial conditions to the asymmetric initial state $x_{10} = 1/3$, $y_{10} = 0.25$, $x_{20} = 0.25$ and $y_{20} = 1/3$. Figure 9.18b reveals that the trajectory is not perfectly periodic but covers a broader spectrum of the state space while maintaining a spherical triangular shape. Figure 9.19 illustrates the reason for the thicker edges. In addition to periodically cycling through the strategies, the amplitudes of the periodic shifts also change periodically. This process of *super-periodicity* has a period of approximately 1,000 interaction periods and an amplitude of roughly 0.15. The frequencies for population 2 are not shown since again the frequency patterns are identical apart from a horizontal phase shift of 500 interaction periods. Consequently, when the amplitude of the strategy frequency of one population is highest, it is lowest for the other population.

Increasing the initial frequencies of strategies *Rock* and *Paper* for both populations, lowers the initial frequency for *Scissor* and pushes the initial state closer to the boundaries of the unit simplices. The result is shown in Figures 9.19c and 9.19d. The dynamics seem to be going through a bifurcation since both populations now switch between two super-periodic cycles leading to the intricate pattern in Figure 9.18c. One of the two periodic cycles has the same amplitude as the previous case in Figures 9.19a and 9.19b while the second has more than double the amplitude. Similar to the quasi-stable orbit in Figure 9.18a, the trajectories in Figures 9.18b and 9.18c also fill the entire interior of the spherical triangles if plotted over ten million periods. Most importantly, the trajectories maintain their quasi-periodic character.[20]

If we push the initial conditions further to the extremes, dynamics change completely. Figure 9.20 shows the dynamics with the initial distribution $x_{10} = 0.8$, $y_{10} = 0.1$, $x_{20} = 0.8$, and

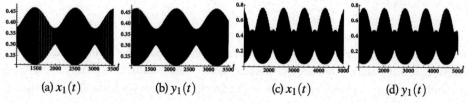

(a) $x_1(t)$ (b) $y_1(t)$ (c) $x_1(t)$ (d) $y_1(t)$

Figure 9.19: Figures demonstrates the super-periodic dynamics of the population frequencies of population 1 in periods 500–3,500. (a) and (b) are based on the initial values of Figure 9.18b, (c) and (d) are based on the initial values of Figure 9.18c.

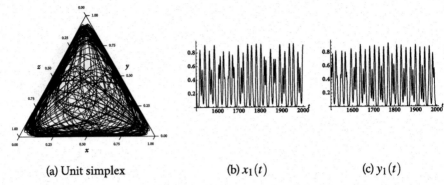

(a) Unit simplex   (b) $x_1(t)$ (c) $y_1(t)$

Figure 9.20: Figure shows the chaotic dynamics for Population 1 for initial conditions $(0.8, 0.1, 0.8, 0.1)$.

$y_{20} = 0.1$. None of the population frequencies follows a discernible pattern and small variations in the initial conditions lead to entirely different trajectories - in other words, the system is chaotic. If we run the simulation for longer periods, the trajectory will eventually cover the vast majority of the state space.

In contrast to Sections 9.2 and 9.3, it is not changing to a parameter that engenders a shift in dynamics but an alteration of the initial conditions. Initial distributions close to the Nash equilibrium induce (relatively) stable cycles, while inegalitarian initial distributions closer to the vertices of the unit simplex produce chaotic dynamics. The simulations indicate that the trajectories do not switch between periodic and chaotic behaviour. While two trajectories belonging to alternative regimes never cross, given the limitation of the state space, they must eventually pass each other in close proximity. Consequently, small random fluctuations caused by external factors and idiosyncratic choices can push a population from a quasi-stable periodic orbit onto a chaotic trajectory.

Exercise 9.5

To get a better feel for how the initial conditions change the dynamics, plot the trajectory in the unit simplex for one population with initial conditions $(x_{10} = 0.6, y_{10} = 0.25,$ $x_{20} = 0.6, y_{20} = 0.25)$, then incrementally increase the values for x_{10} and x_{20} to 0.7 while keeping the values for y_{10} and y_{20} at 0.25 and plot the trajectory after each increase. What do you observe? (Note: The system requires a few periods to settle on a stable orbit, results are clearer when plotted for later periods, say 4,000–5,000.)

9.5 Conclusion

The results of this chapter contrast strongly with most of the previous chapters. Earlier, social dynamics seem to cause societies to gravitate towards stable equilibria that define social, economic, and political institutions. After all, reality corroborates these results. In our daily lives, we are constantly exposed to and constrained by social practices and conventions. Their consistency keeps us grounded, helps us coordinate, and constitutes the essence of our social fabric. It seems unlikely that a few random choices will unravel existing institutions. Yet, in other instances, this stability is less obvious. If the Protestant noblemen had not defenestrated the Catholic regents in

1618, Rosa Parks had decided to vacate her seat in 1955, Archduke Franz Ferdinand had not visited Sarajevo in 1914, or Adolf Hitler had been accepted to the Academy of Fine Arts Vienna in 1907 or 1908, world history might have taken a different turn. The discussion in Chapter 8 suggests that probably some of the essential developments that followed these events would have simply occurred at later instances, but this chapter indicates that their absence might have pushed us onto entirely different historical trajectories.

In earlier chapters, the basin of attraction puts limitations on history dependence. The implication was that if two societies with similar conditions are sufficiently close to an equilibrium state, they will remain similar over time. Yet, the results of this chapter provide us with a different reading. Differences in the initial conditions, as small as they might be, lead to entirely different social dynamics over time. Historically, we can find examples for both interpretations. For example, Argentina and Canada looked very similar before World War I from an economic perspective but have since diverged drastically. During the same period, wealthy countries have demonstrated strong convergence.

These results suggest an incoherence, but this is not so. Instead of posing the question whether social dynamics are defined by convergence or chaos, we should acknowledge that both are two sides of the same coin, as I suggested in Chapter 1. It is a small step from dynamic to chaotic . The current chapter has not introduced any new approaches, since we have modelled social dynamics on the basis of what we have seen before, namely replicator dynamics, individual thresholds or localised social imitation. Instead of a contradiction, the results of this chapter are merely an extension of the previous arguments. We have seen that the shift from convergence to chaos can occur with the change of an exogenous parameter. In these cases, external changes to the natural, political, economical, and social environment may not only unsettle previously persistent institutions, but can have drastic long-term effects as the new environment no longer allows a society to return to the old institutions nor to converge to a new equilibrium. Secondly, we have further observed that the transition between the two regimes can be entirely dependent on initial conditions. Relatively small variations in the composition of a population or the rate of adoption of behavioural rules can mean the difference between chaos and consistency. This adds a new dimension to the role of path dependence on institutional setups and stability.

Applications and Relation to Other Chapters

This chapter relates to all previous chapters, except for Chapter 2 due to the latter's static character. This is easy to see with regard to Chapters 3, 5, and 7, since this chapter is in principle only a small extension of what we already studied in these earlier chapters. In Chapter 8, the self-organising criticality of sandpile model is inherently chaotic, while the character of the interactions in those networks, which I discussed in Chapter 6, depends essentially on the degree and distribution of connections between the various members as we have seen, for example, in Section 6.4 (see also Potts 2000, Chapter 4).

Further Reading

It is difficult to find literature with a clear social scientific focus and most presentations are catered to students of physics and engineering. Nevertheless, excellent introductions to the topics are offered by Hilborn (1994) and Strogatz (2015). Both textbooks are very accessible and provide an in-depth overview. More technical alternatives are Wiggins (2003) as well as the short, but dense and highly analytical exposition in Hale (1963).

Stadler et al. (1993) extend the linear replicator dynamics and introduce the *catalytic network equation*. While it was developed in the context of chemical reactions, the catalytic network equation can be reinterpreted to model a situation in which the interaction of two strategies encourages the adoption of a third strategy in conjunction with the former. A natural application is the division of labour or different forms of governance. The resulting equation is a non-linear differential equation that gives rise to chaotic dynamics.

Replicator dynamics in discrete time tend to generate interesting dynamics in the form of complex attractors with periodic or chaotic dynamics. The *discreteness* of the imitation process leads to overreactions similar to those studied in this chapter. Bischi et al. (2018) study a binary choice models using discrete time exponential replicator dynamics. They show that the position and stability of the fixed points obtained in such interactions critically depend on the reactivity of players, i.e., their propensity to switch behavioural rules after having observed a potential payoff gain.

Notes

1 Strictly speaking, Lorenz was already late to the party. The founding father of chaos theory is considered to be Henri Poincaré who studied the motion of three bodies subject to Newton's law of universal gravitation in his memo *Sur le problème des trois corps et les équations de la dynamique*, which won the King Oscar Prize in 1889 in honour of Oscar II of Sweden. Poincaré's work inspired significant contributions on dynamical systems in the early 20th century.

2 This scale-independent similarity is called **self-similarity**. Some readers may be familiar with so-called fractals or Mandelbrot sets that illustrate the behaviour of a function within some parameter space. These shapes are composed of structures that are just smaller iterations of the larger shape. The recursive pattern creates objects that are within dimension, hence the name fractals.

3 Notice that this does not mean that always $x_{t+1} \geq x_t$, but that $x_t > x_s$ implies that $x_{t+1} \geq x_{s+1}$ for some periods s and t.

4 Indeed the correct technical term is *sensitive dependence on initial conditions*. The butterfly effect goes back to a talk given by Edward N. Lorenz at the American Association for the Advancement of Science in 1972 entitled: *Does the Flap of a Butterfly's Wings in Brazil set off a Tornado in Texas* (see Lorenz, 1972).

5 Feigenbaum discovered a second constant which relates the ratio of the maximum distance between two branches (or pitchforks) of subsequent bifurcations. Remember that the system bifurcates a second time at $\alpha = 1.90607$. Thus, for a marginally smaller value, the two branches obtain a maximum distance before they split again. We define this distance as d_1. Similarly, right before the system bifurcates again, the two adjacent branches (since now we have four) reach their maximum distance. The largest distance between the adjacent branches defines d_2. (The upper branches are closer to each other than the lower branches, so we take the latter.) We calculate the ratio $\Delta_1 = d_1/d_2 = 2.89918$ and do the same for the ratio of the second and third bifurcation and obtain $\Delta_2 = 2.42235$ which is of similar scale. Feigenbaum (see Hilborn, 1994) has shown that

$$\Delta \equiv \lim_{n \to \infty} \frac{d_n}{d_{n+1}} = 2.5029\ldots$$

which is called the **Feigenbaum α**.

6   Note that $dF^2(x)/dx = dF/dx|_{F(x)}dF/dx|_x$. We therefore have

$$\frac{dF^2(x)}{dx}\Big|_{x_1^*} = \frac{dF}{dx}\Big|_{x_2^*}\frac{dF}{x}\Big|_{x_1^*} = \frac{dF^2(dx)}{dx}\Big|_{x_2^*} \tag{9.21}$$

since $x_2^* = F(x_1^*)$. In other words, the slope at x_1^* equals the slope of $F^2(x)$ at x_2^*. We can directly see that this must also hold for the fixed points at higher levels of bifurcation and the corresponding iterate of $F(x)$.

The interval of α in which the system cycles between two stable fixed points is therefore obtained by solving $x_1^* = F^2(x_1^*)$ and $x_2^* = F^2(x_2^*)$ to obtain the fixed points and finding the conditions for equation

$$-1 < \frac{dF}{dx}\Big|_{x_2^*}\frac{dF}{x}\Big|_{x_1^*} < 1$$

The approach extends equivalently to any cycle of order n. Given that $x_m^* = F^n(x_m^*)$ implies solving a higher-degree polynomial which renders an analytical solution infeasible, the Feigenbaum constant in combination with the graphical solution provides better insights.

7   The system describes a periodic cycle of period k, defined by a set of points $C_k = \{c_1, c_2, c_3, \ldots, c_k\}$, such that for $c_i \neq c_1$ and $i = 2, \ldots, k$, it holds that $F(c_i) = c_{i+1}$ and $F(c_k) = c_1$. Consequently, the periodic points are $C_k = \{c_1, F(c_1), F^2(c_1), \ldots, F^{k-1}(c_1)\}$ and hence c_1 must be a fixed point of the composite function, i.e. the kth iterate of $F(x)$, given by $F^k(x)$. Since the system cycles through all points periodically, i.e., the cycle begins again after k iterations, c_1 is chosen arbitrarily and any periodic point of the k-cycle is a fixed point of F^k, i.e. $F^k(c_i) = c_i$ for any $i = 1, \ldots, k$.

8   The same approach is used in Peitgen et al. (2004, Ch. 11.4) to study the logistic map.

9   The slope at the fixed points is identical not by coincidence. Remember that the fixed points are created at the same parameter value through a (fold) bifurcation and become unstable through a (flip) bifurcation. Extending on footnote 7, the stability of the k-cycle C_k can be studied on the basis of one of its periodic points c_i, which we determined as a fixed point of its kth iterate $F^k(x)$. Remember that stability requires that $|dF^k/dx| < 1$ at (c_i). We can use the chain rule to determine the derivative of the composite function, which turns out to be just the product of the simpler function $F(x)$ across the k-periodic fixed point (this follows inductively from footnote 6). We have

$$\frac{dF^k}{dx}\Big|_{c_i} = F'(c_1) \cdot F'(c_2) \cdot F'(c_2) \cdot \ldots \cdot F'(c_k)$$

and thus, the slope must be identical.

10 Some readers may realise that this is a simplified version of the **Ising model** without the influence of an external field, which was developed by Ernst Ising and Wilhelm Lenz to model magnetic dipole moments of atomic spins when arranged on a lattice. The interaction between two spins is then defined by whether they tend to align their state (the ferromagnetic case) or to move to the opposite state (the antiferromagnetic case). This section is inspired by earlier collaborative research with Imre Kondor, Alan Kirman, and Giorgio Fagiolo as part of the INET project on *Correlations in Complex Heterogeneous Networks*.

11 Note that the results are different from Chapter 7. While in the latter, imitation is payoff-based, here individuals strictly imitated a state (i.e. belief or action) but ignore any related payoff or benefit.

12 The simulations were conducted as follows: after the population goes through a state of high noise ($\sigma = 10$) for 100 interaction periods, σ is reduced to the corresponding value (say 0.2) and the population is given time to settle into a quasi-equilibrium for 500 periods. Thereafter, the average is calculated for the interaction periods 500–600. After recording the average, the noise level is set again to $\sigma = 10$ for 100 periods after which it is set again to the corresponding value (i.e. 0.2). After 500 interactions, the average is again computed for 100 periods. This process is repeated to obtain ten average values. After this, the value of σ is incremented by 0.05 and the procedure is repeated ten times, leading to 10×61 data points.

13   The dynamics of the spin glass model in social networks raises additional questions. The notion of *too big to fail* and even *too interconnected to fail* might prove inadequate. If the network structure is *opportune*, the failure of small banks can lead to cascades that are more devastating than the bankruptcy of much larger banks.

14   Note that we cannot generalise this result, since I have not conducted simulations for larger networks. It might be that the trajectories converge further or divert at a certain size. This is left to future research.

15   In other words, the shade of a node corresponds to the number of state switches divided by the difference between the current and the period of creation.

16   Note that there are some exceptions to this rule if the continuous system is discontinuous (i.e., non-differentiable) at the singularity. In this case, also two-dimensional systems can generate chaotic behaviour.

17   A similar model can be found in Sandholm (2010, Ch. 9.4).

18   For example, if we study the game for a longer period and compare the trajectories of the systems with the two different initial conditions in Figure 9.15, we can see that the frequencies are still rather similar after 5,000 periods but differ strongly after 10,000 periods but eventually will look similar again.

19   Sandholm (2010, Ch. 9.4) illustrates an asymmetric rock-paper-scissor game in which population 1 has a slight advantage over population 2. Whenever the pair of players choose the same strategy, a player from population 1 receives a payoff of $1/2$ while player from population 2 receives a negative return of $-1/2$. This asymmetric version of the game demonstrates similar chaotic dynamics.

20   While a simulation of ten million periods is no definite proof, we can assume that it is at least unlikely that these initial condition closer to the Nash equilibrium ultimately lead to chaotic dynamics.

– A –

Appendix

A.1 Elementaries

A.1.1 Derivatives

$$\frac{df}{d\alpha} = f'$$

(A.1)

denotes the *first (order) derivative*

$$\frac{d^2 f}{d\alpha^2} = f''$$

(A.2)

denotes the *second (order) derivative*

$$\frac{\partial f(\alpha,\beta)}{\partial \alpha}$$

(A.3)

denotes the *first (order)* **partial** *derivative* of function f at α

$$\frac{\partial^2 f(\alpha,\beta)}{\partial \alpha^2} \quad \text{or}$$

(A.4a)

$$\frac{\partial^2 f(\alpha,\beta)}{\partial \alpha \partial \beta}$$

(A.4b)

denote *second (order)* **partial** *derivatives* of function f. Equation (A.4b) is an example of a *second-order mixed partial derivative*. Under fairly general assumptions (defined by *Schwarz' theorem*), the second partial derivatives are symmetric, implying that

$$\frac{\partial^2 f(\alpha,\beta)}{\partial \alpha \partial \beta} = \frac{\partial}{\partial \alpha}\frac{\partial f(\alpha,\beta)}{\partial \beta} = \frac{\partial}{\partial \beta}\frac{\partial f(\alpha,\beta)}{\partial \alpha} = \frac{\partial^2 f(\alpha,\beta)}{\partial \beta \partial \alpha}$$

(A.5)

This type of notation is commonly known as *Leibniz notation* (in honour of Gottfried Wilhelm Leibniz). Another approach is to use subscript notation, in which the subscript defines the arguments of the derivative:

$$f_{\beta\alpha} = f(\alpha,\beta,\dots)_{\beta\alpha} = \frac{\partial^2 f(\alpha,\beta,\dots)}{\partial \alpha \partial \beta}$$

(A.6)

Notice that the arguments are inverted in the notation. However, as we have seen above, as long as the assumptions in Schwarz' theorem are met, the order is of no relevance.

A second-order mixed partial derivative (or shorthand: a *mixed partial*) of the form $\partial^2 f(\alpha,\beta)/\partial\alpha\partial\beta$ defines how the slope of a function along the β axis changes after a minuscule change in α.

The logic and notation can be extended to higher dimensions and since the partial derivatives are also functions, the symmetry holds. We can thus write

$$\frac{\partial}{\partial\delta}\frac{\partial}{\partial\gamma}\frac{\partial}{\partial\beta}\frac{f}{\partial\alpha} = \frac{\partial^4 f}{\partial\delta\partial\gamma\partial\beta\partial\alpha} = f_{\alpha\beta\gamma\delta} \tag{A.7}$$

A.1.2 Rules of Differentiation

The following rules of differentiation are used throughout this book:

power rule: $\dfrac{d}{dx}\alpha x^n = \alpha n x^{n-1}$ for any constant $\alpha \in \mathbb{R}$

Consequently

$$\frac{d}{dx}\left(\alpha\frac{1}{x^n}\right) = -\alpha n\frac{1}{x^{n+1}}$$

This holds for more complex polynomials of the form $k(x) = \alpha f(x) + \beta g(x) + \gamma h(x)$ (such as $k(x) = x^3 - 2x^2 + 3x$). We have

$$\frac{d}{dx}k(x) = \alpha\frac{f(x)}{dx} + \beta\frac{g(x)}{dx} + \gamma\frac{h(x)}{dx}$$

For two function, $f(x)$ and $g(x)$, we have

sum rule: $\dfrac{d}{dx}(f(x)+g(x)) = \dfrac{df(x)}{dx} + \dfrac{dg(x)}{dx}$

product rule: $\dfrac{d}{dx}f(x)g(x) = \dfrac{df(x)}{dx}g(x) + \dfrac{dg(x)}{dx}f(x)$

and thus

reciprocal rule: $\dfrac{d}{dx}\dfrac{1}{f(x)} = -\dfrac{1}{f(x)^2}\dfrac{df(x)}{dx}$

quotient rule: $\dfrac{d}{dx}\dfrac{f(x)}{g(x)} = \dfrac{f'(x)g(x) - g'(x)f(x)}{g(x)^2}$

Furthermore, we have

chain rule: $\dfrac{d}{dx}f(g(x)) = f'(g(x))\cdot g'(x)$

Logarithmic derivatives are defined by

$$\frac{d}{dx}\ln f(x) = \frac{f'(x)}{f(x)}$$

A.2 Equilibrium Refinements and Discrimination Criteria

Our analysis of the 2×2 games in Figure 2.4 shows that the Nash equilibrium is not necessarily unique even in relatively simple games. Over the years, theorists have presented numerous refinement criteria that allow us to eliminate implausible equilibria. Here, I will only briefly discuss the maximin strategy as well as risk and payoff dominance. Other notable criteria are trembling hand perfection (which is similar to evolutionary stability), the iterated elimination of weakly and strictly dominated strategies, backward induction and subgame perfection, as well as forward induction (also known as burning money).

A.2.1 Maximin Strategy

Another approach for an optimal strategy is to maximise one's lowest possible payoff. In this way, players guarantee that their payoff never falls below a certain minimum. Formally, we say that the **maximin strategy** for a player i is given by

$$\hat{s}_i = \arg\max_{\sigma_i} \min_{\sigma_{-i}} \pi_i(\sigma_i, \sigma_{-i}) \tag{A.8}$$

and the corresponding guaranteed minimum payoff (the so-called *maximin* value) is

$$\hat{\pi}_i = \max_{\sigma_i} \min_{\sigma_{-i}} \pi_i(\sigma_i, \sigma_{-i}) \tag{A.9}$$

For a game of the form

Player 2

		U	D
	L	a,b	c,d
Player 1	R	e,f	g,h

Player 1 maximises her minimum by

$$\max_{s_1} \min_{s_2} [a\, s_1(L)s_2(U) + c\, s_1(L)s_2(D) + e\, s_1(R)s_2(U) + g\, s_1(R)s_2(D)]$$

where $s_k(H)$ denotes the frequency at which player k chooses strategy H in mixed strategy σ_k. Player 1 has to first compute the minimum, i.e.

$$\min_{s_2} [a\, s_1(L)s_2(U) + c\, s_1(L)s_2(D) + e\, s_1(R)s_2(U) + g\, s_1(R)s_2(D)]$$

$$\Leftrightarrow \min_{s_2} [a\, s_1(L)s_2(U) + c\, s_1(L)(1 - s_2(U)) + e\, (1 - s_1(L))s_2(U)$$

$$+ g\, (1 - s_1(L))(1 - s_2(U))]$$

and then determine the maximising strategy. For the Battle of the Sexes in Figure 2.4a, we have $s_A(Musical) = \alpha$ for Anja and $s_B(Musical) = \beta$ for Bert which implies for Bert

$$\min_{\alpha} [2\,\beta\alpha + (1 - \beta)(1 - \alpha)]$$

From the first-order condition, we have $\hat{\beta} = 1/3$ for Bert guaranteeing a payoff of $\hat{\pi}_B = 2/3$. Note that for $\beta > \hat{\beta}$, Anja chooses $\alpha = 0$ and for $\beta < \hat{\beta}$, she chooses $\alpha = 1$. Thus, any other mixed strategy offers Bert a lower payoff. Using the same approach, we obtain $\hat{\alpha} = 2/3$ for Anja.

A.2.2 Risk Dominance and Payoff Dominance

Assume that two players, A and B engage in the Stag Hunt game discussed in Chapter 2 (see page 15), given by the following payoff matrix

		A	
		Stag	Hare
B	Stag	5,5	0,3
	Hare	3,0	3,3

This game has two equilibria in pure strategies, namely (*Stag, Stag*) and (*Hare, Hare*). Since the former equilibrium assigns the highest possible payoff to each player, the equilibrium is pay-off dominant. However, the second equilibrium has some merit. If a player is unsure about the other player's strategy, it is less *risky* to choose *Hare*. More precisely, following Harsanyi and Selten (1989), a risk-dominant strategy is the best response to a mixed strategy that assigns equal probability to each pure strategy, or more formally, *Hare* risk dominates *Stag* for player $i = A, B$ if $0.5\pi_i(Hare, Hare) + 0.5\pi_i(Hare, Stag) > 0.5\pi_i(Stag, Hare) + 0.5\pi_i(Stag, Stag)$ which is equivalent to comparing the potential losses from deviation, i.e. $\pi_i(Hare, Hare) - \pi_i(Stag, Hare) > \pi_i(Stag, Stag) - \pi_i(Hare, Stag)$.[1]

We have previously seen that the type and structure of interactions can render one or the other equilibrium more plausible. The type of stochastic interaction in Chapter 4 assigns higher likelihood to the risk-dominant equilibrium while the spatial interaction in Chapter 7 gives higher credibility to the payoff dominant equilibrium. However, in the simple interactions of Chapter 2 with only two players, the answer to the question of which equilibrium is more plausible is less obvious. We might assume that communication prior to an interaction should enable the players to coordinate and jointly choose to hunt a stag. Yet, Aumann (1990) argues that the payoff dominant equilibrium is still unlikely in this case. Assume that Anja and Bert agree to hunt the stag. Anja will realise that Bert benefits from this agreement independent of his own strategy. Thus, Bert has an incentive to make Anja believe that he hunts the stag, but he has no commitment. If Anja distrusts Bert, she might still go for the hare.

Payoff dominance is also a weak predictor if the game is played by three players. Assume the following game in which Player 3 chooses between pure strategies S and C, and her payoffs are given by the third element in each cell. The game has two pure Nash equilibria, (L,U,S) and (R,D,C). The former is payoff dominant, but would it actually be played? Assume that Anja and Bert can convince player 3 of this equilibrium in some prior discussion and thus to play S. Playing (L,U) is no longer the optimal choice for both Anja and Bert, but to play (R,D), and thus (L,U,S) is unlikely to be stable (see Bernheim et al., 1987).

		A	A
		U	D
B	L	0,0,20	-10,-10,0
	R	-10,-10,02	,2,-10

(a) S

		A	A
		U	D
B	L	-4,-4,0	-10,-10,0
	R	-10,-10,0	-2,-2,10

(b) C

Figure A.1: A game with three players.

A.3 Derivation of the Replicator Dynamics

In Section 3.4, we have assumed that the general replicator dynamics take the form

$$\dot{x}_h = f_h = x_h(\pi_h - \phi) \tag{A.10}$$

for some behavioural rule h played by a share of the population x_h and the $\dot{x}_h$ indicating the time derivative of x_h, i.e., the change over time. Each player of h obtains a payoff of π_h whereas the population average payoff is $\phi = x_1\pi_1 + x_2\pi_2 + \ldots + x_n\pi_n$ for n different behavioural rules.

In order to derive this result, assume that we have a group or tribe at time t of size p^t (see also Weibull, 1997, Ch. 3.1). Thus, $p^{10} = 1,000$ could indicate the population of a large tribe in the year ten of its foundation. Assume that individuals join the group at a rate of β and leave the group at a rate of δ both for idiosyncratic reasons. The group might follow a behavioural rule that renders membership attractive. Let the attractiveness or benefit of joining the group be ϕ.[2] We can write

$$\dot{p}^t = p^t(\beta + \phi - \delta) \tag{A.11}$$

Thus, as long as $\beta + \phi > \delta$ a group increases in size. Yet, we are more interested in the composition of our group. Let x_h^t be the share of tribal members who follow a certain behavioural rule h at time t. Let us assume that this rule is horticulture in contrast to pastoralism, and further assume that being a horticulturist bestows an additional benefit of π_h. Analogous to equation (A.11), we can write the population dynamics for the horticulturist subpopulation as

$$\dot{p}_h^t = p_h^t(\beta + \pi_h - \delta) \tag{A.12}$$

Payoff π_h then determines the attractiveness or benefit of being a horticulturalist. We have the identity

$$p_h^t = p^t x_h^t \tag{A.13}$$

which simply means that if horticulturists constitute a share of 30 percent and pastoralists a share of 70 percent, the number of horticulturists is 300 given the size of our tribe equal to 1,000. The time derivative of equation (A.13) is

$$\dot{p}_h = \dot{p}x_h + p\dot{x}_h \tag{A.14}$$

For notational ease, I drop again the time index in the following. Rearranging equation (A.14) and substituting by equations (A.11) and (A.12) gives us

$$
\begin{aligned}
p\dot{x}_h &= \dot{p}_h - \dot{p}x_h \\
&= p_h(\beta + \pi_h - \delta) - p(\beta + \phi - \delta)x_h \\
&= px_h(\beta + \pi_h - \delta) - px_h(\beta + \phi - \delta) \\
&= px_h(\pi_h - \phi)
\end{aligned}
\tag{A.15}
$$

We only need to divide both sides of the equation by p to obtain equation (A.10).

If the population is split into horticulturists and pastoralists, we can define x_h and x_p as their respective share. Since we have only two behavioural rules, we know that the following identity must hold

$$x_h = 1 - x_p \tag{A.16}$$

and thus,

$$\begin{aligned}\phi &= x_h\pi_h + x_p\pi_p \\ &= x_h\pi_h + (1-x_h)\pi_p \\ &= \pi_p + x_h(\pi_h - \pi_p)\end{aligned} \tag{A.17}$$

Substituting this into equation (A.10), we obtain

$$\begin{aligned}\dot{x}_h &= x_h(\pi_h - \phi) \\ &= x_h(\pi_h - \pi_p - x_h(\pi_h - \pi_p)) \\ &= x_h(1-x_h)(\pi_h - \pi_p)\end{aligned} \tag{A.18}$$

A.4 Extensions of the Replicator Dynamics

A.4.1 Quasi-Species Equation

Assume that instead of perfect, error-free social imitation, a share of the population randomly adopts a strategy. For n different strategies, we can then define a **mutation matrix** Q that is composed of probabilities q_{ij} indicating the chance that a player of strategy s_i shifts to strategy s_j independent of the relative payoff associated with each of these strategies. Matrix Q is then equivalent to an $n \times n$ probability transition matrix, which we defined in Chapter 4.2 and consequently, we have $\sum_{j=0}^{n} q_{ij} = 1$.

Replicator-mutator equation is then a generalisation of the continuous replicator equation and given by

$$\dot{x}_i = \sum_{j=0}^{n} x_j\pi_j q_{ij} - \phi x_i \tag{A.19}$$

with $\phi = \sum_{i=0}^{n} x_i\pi_i$ (as defined before). The special case of the replicator-mutator equation in which π_j is defined by a constant fitness, i.e., the fitness itself is not affected by the frequency of other strategies, is called the **quasi-species equation**.

From Chapter 3, we know that if a probability transition matrix is irreducible and aperiodic, the simple Markov process has an invariant distribution. If the same holds for Q, the quasi-species equation converges to a unique, globally stable equilibrium which can be shown to be the solution to

$$\phi\vec{x} = \vec{x}W \tag{A.20}$$

with $W = [\pi_j q_{ji}]$ being the mutation-selection matrix (see Nowak, 2006, Chapter 3.3).

A.4.2 Lotka-Volterra Dynamics

The biologist Alfred Lotka and physicist Vito Volterra studied the interplay of different species. The general Lotka-Volterra equation for n different species is defined by

$$\dot{y}_i = y_i \left(\lambda_i + \sum_{j=1}^{n} \alpha_{ij} y_j \right) \qquad (A.21)$$

for $i = 1, 2, \ldots, n$. Parameter λ_i determines the natural growth rate of species i in the absence of any resource limitation and predators. In other words, the population of i grows exponentially according to

$$y_i(t) = y(0) e^{\lambda_i t}$$

Parameter α_{ij} describes the interaction between species i and j. Note, however, that λ_i and α_{ij} can be positive, negative, or zero. Thus, not only can an interaction between species be individually or mutually advantageous or detrimental but also the natural growth rate can be negative if other species are absent.

The most common version of the Predator-Prey model with two species is given by

$$\begin{aligned} \dot{y}_1 &= y_1 (\lambda_1 - \gamma_1 y_2) \\ \dot{y}_2 &= y_2 (\gamma_2 y_1 - \lambda_2) \end{aligned} \qquad (A.22)$$

Hence, survival of species 2 is critically dependent on the presence of species 1, i.e. the former preys on the latter. Simultaneously solving for $\dot{y}_1 = 0$ and $\dot{y}_2 = 0$ provides us with a saddle point at the origin $(0,0)$ and an interior fixed point at $y_1^* = \lambda_2 / \gamma_2$ and $y_2^* = \lambda_1 / \gamma_1$. The equilibrium is neutrally stable, any deviation leads to a limit cycle with oscillatory period $2\pi \sqrt{\lambda_1 \lambda_2}$. (I leave it to the reader to verify this.) The dynamics are illustrated in Figure A.2.

Hofbauer and Sigmund (1998) have shown that the Lotka-Volterra equation (A.21) and the replicator equation are equivalent. Assuming that payoffs are linear in the frequency of the other species (or strategy) and are determined by the $n \times n$ interaction matrix $B = [\beta_{ij}]$ the replicator

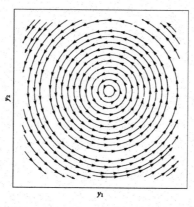

Figure A.2: Dynamics of the Predator-Prey model.

equation is given by

$$\dot{x}_i = x_i \left(\sum_{j=1}^{n} \beta_{ij} x_j - \phi \right)$$ (A.23)

with $\phi = \sum_{i=0}^{n} x_i \sum_{j=0}^{n} \beta_{ij} x_j$. We can redefine $\lambda_i = \beta_{in} - \beta_{nn}$ and $\alpha_{ij} = \beta_{ij} - \beta_{nj}$ to obtain the equivalent Lotka-Volterra equations

$$\dot{y}_i = y_i \left(\lambda_i + \sum_{j=1}^{n-1} \alpha_{ij} y_j \right)$$

We can see that $n - 1$ species or strategies in the Lotka-Volterra expression are equivalent to n strategies in the replicator equations.

A.4.3 Price Equation

Assume that interaction takes place both between members of the same group and between groups. Selection now operates at two levels of aggregation, i.e. the population dynamics are defined by intra-group selection and inter-group selection. In situations in which an action confers a strong negative externality on a group, but is beneficial to the individual (e.g., free-riding) or the action is detrimental to the individual but its externality is positive for the group (e.g. unconditional cooperation), selection pressure at the group level operates in the opposite directions than the selection pressure at the individual level. Typical examples are prisoner's dilemma or tragedies of the commons type interactions. We can then follow Price (1970) and Bowles (2001) to determine the population dynamics of such a behavioural trait.

Let there be n different groups, each group k is of size N_k and the total population is of size N. The relative group size is $x_k = N_k/N$. Furthermore, let p_{ij} be an indicator that defines whether or not individual i in group j follows a certain behavioural rule. A value of 0 indicates that the individual does not follow the rule, while a 1 indicates that she does. The frequency of the behavioural rule in group j is given by p_j. The overall frequency of the behavioural rule in the entire population at time t is simply the frequency in each group weighted by the respective relative size, i.e.,

$$p(t) = \sum_j x_j(t) p_j(t)$$

We can define

$$x_j(t+1) = x_j(t) \frac{\pi_j}{\pi}$$

where π_j is the average number of replications of members of group j (i.e., the expected group size) and π is the average number of replications across the entire population (i.e. the average group size). The change in the overall frequency of the behavioural rule is

$$\Delta p = p(t+1) - p(t)$$
$$= \sum_j x_j(t) \frac{\pi_j}{\pi} p_i(t+1) - \sum_j x_j p_j(t)$$

Note that we can equivalently write $\Delta p_j = p_j(t+1) - p_j(t)$ to obtain

$$\Delta p = \sum_j x_j(t) \frac{\pi_j}{\pi} (p_j(t) + \Delta p_j) - \sum_j x_j p_j(t)$$
$$= \sum_j x_j(t) p_j(t) \left(\frac{\pi_j}{\pi} - 1\right) + \sum_j x_j \Delta p_j \frac{\pi_j}{\pi}$$

Multiplying by π, we have

$$\pi \Delta p = \sum_j x_j(t) p_j(t) (\pi_j - \pi) + \sum_j x_j \pi_j \Delta p_j \tag{A.24}$$

Note that we can extend $\pi_j \Delta p_j$ in the same manner

$$\pi_j \Delta p_j = \sum_i p_{ij}(t)(\pi_{ij} - \pi_j) + \sum \sum \pi_{ij} \Delta p_{ij} \tag{A.25}$$

Furthermore, $\Delta p_{ij} = p_{ij}(t+1) - p_{ij}(t)$. If replication of the behavioural rule is perfect, i.e., the actions and rules associated with the behaviour can be easily observed and imitated, it must hold that $p_{ij}(t+1) = p_{ij}(t)$ and thus, $\Delta p_{ij} = 0$. Simplifying and combining equations (A.24) and (A.25) leads to

$$\pi \Delta p = \sum_j x_j(t) p_j(t) (\pi_j - \pi) + \sum_j \sum_i x_j p_{ij}(t) (\pi_{ij} - \pi_j)$$
$$= cov(\pi_j p_j) + \sum_j x_j cov(\pi_{ij} p_{ij}) \tag{A.26}$$

Let π_{ij} be the number of group members in group j that replicate the behavioural rule of i and define

$$\pi_{ij} = \lambda_0 + \lambda_g p_j + \lambda_i p_{ij} \tag{A.27}$$

The parameters indicate the effect of the behavioural rule on the numbers of replicas in the next period. More specifically, λ_0 indicates a baseline fitness (i.e. some natural growth rate of the behavioural rule), λ_g is the effect that the individual conveys upon the group by following the behavioural rule, and λ_i is the effect for the individual in terms of relative performance (i.e., the partial impact on frequency p_{ij}). The net effect on the frequency is given by $\lambda = \lambda_g + \lambda_i$. We can then rewrite equation (A.26) as

$$\pi \Delta p = var(p_j)\lambda + \sum_j x_j var(\pi_{ij})\lambda_i \tag{A.28}$$

A.4.4 Replicator Dynamics on Regular Graphs

Assume that players can choose from n different strategies and the payoff/fitness of each strategy linearly depends on the frequency of the other strategies. The replicator equation is then given by equation (A.23) on page 230. Defining $\beta_i = \sum_{j=1}^{n} x_j \beta_{ij}$, we can simplify the replicator equation to

$$\dot{x}_i = x_i (\beta_i - \phi) \tag{A.29}$$

Ohtsuki and Nowak (2006) have shown that we can easily extend equation (A.29) to explain the social dynamics on regular graphs of degree $k > 2$, i.e. each individual is linked to k other individuals. It turns out that the replicator equation can be written as

$$\dot{x}_i = x_i(\beta_i + \gamma_i - \phi) = x_i\left(\sum_{j=1}^{n}(\beta_{ij} + \gamma_{ij})x_j - \phi\right) \tag{A.30}$$

The additional term $\gamma_i = \sum_{j=1}^{n}\gamma_{ij}$ determines the local competition between the strategies. The definition of γ_{ij} depends on the replication process.

If we assume that a randomly chosen individual updates her strategy and imitates one of her neighbours in proportion to the expected payoffs, the $n \times n$ matrix $G = [\gamma_{ij}]$ is composed of[3]

$$\gamma_{ij} = \frac{(k+3)\beta_{ii} + 3\beta_{ij} - 3\beta_{ji} - (k+3)\beta_{jj}}{(k+3)(k-2)} \tag{A.31}$$

If a randomly chosen individual compares payoffs with only one randomly chosen neighbour and adopts the latter's strategy with a probability proportional to the payoff difference, the elements of G are given by[4]

$$\gamma_{ij} = \frac{\beta_{ii} + \beta_{ij} - \beta_{ji} - \beta_{jj}}{(k-2)} \tag{A.32}$$

First notice that $\gamma_{ij} = -\gamma_{ji}$ in both equations (A.31) and (A.32), i.e. a payoff gain in one strategy results in a direct trade-off for the other strategy. Furthermore, β_{ii} and β_{jj} define the benefit of playing a strategy against itself and hence, determine the benefit of assortative mixing, while β_{ij} and β_{ji} determine the benefit of playing one strategy against the other and thus, the benefit of disassortative mixing. A strategy i is adopted by more individuals if it does both well against itself as well as against another strategy j compared to how the latter strategy performs against itself and strategy i – a result similar to what we already obtained for evolutionarily stable strategies. Thus while the quantitative relations change in the spatial context, the qualitative results remain identical.

A.5 Dynamical Systems Revisited

We have seen in Chapter 3 that a system of first-order ordinary differential equations is defined as

$$\dot{x}_1 = \frac{dx_1}{dt} = f_1(x_1(t), x_2(t), \dots, x_n(t))$$

$$\dot{x}_2 = \frac{dx_2}{dt} = f_2(x_1(t), x_2(t), \dots, x_n(t)) \tag{A.33}$$

$$\vdots$$

$$\dot{x}_n = \frac{dx_n}{dt} = f_n(x_1(t), x_2(t), \dots, x_n(t))$$

We can write the system more concisely in vector form as

$$\dot{x}(t) = f(x(t)) \tag{A.34}$$

and solve it by finding its roots, i.e. the set of points at which equations (A.33) are all equal to zero. We then study the eigenvalues of the Jacobian matrix at each of these fixed points to determine their respective stability. Yet, sometimes finding the exact position of a fixed point in the state space and/or determining its precise eigenvalues is impracticable, but luckily, neither is it frequently necessary.

If we study a one-dimensional system with two strategies or behavioural rules, like in Chapter 3.3, the dynamics are defined by $\dot{x} = f(x)$. It is straightforward to see that if we can establish that over an interval $x \in [a, b]$ with $a > 0$ and $b > a$, the time derivative $f(x)$ is (weakly) monotonically increasing, and $f(a) < 0$ and $f(b) > 0$, an interior fixed point must exist in this interval and it is a repellor, while if $f(x)$ is (weakly) monotonically decreasing, and $f(a) > 0$ and $f(b) < 0$, the interior fixed point exists but is a node. The logic can be easily inferred from Figures 3.2 and 3.4 in Chapter 3.

In addition, as long as we can establish the number of interior fixed points and for each fixed point, whether its characteristic value is zero or non-zero, we can infer the stability of *all* fixed points (including $x = 0$ and $x = 1$) by determining the stability of a single fixed point. As we move through the unit interval, the stability of the fixed points that are not a saddle point must alternate. A saddle point that attracts trajectories from the left and repels trajectories from the right - a saddle I - lies either to the right of a repellor or another saddle I. Correspondingly, a saddle point that attracts states from the right and repels states from the left - a saddle II - lies either to the right of a node or another saddle II. This becomes obvious when looking at Figures 3.2 and 3.3. In a two-dimensional system, we can make use of Table 3.3 which shows that as long as the trace of the Jacobian is negative and its determinant is positive, a fixed point is stable. In addition, we can make some broad statements about the properties of a system defined by equation (A.34) in general and for the two-dimensional case in particular. Since the mathematical details are not of importance for our purpose here, I will only provide a verbal intuition of these concepts.

Although the dynamical systems of the form given by equation (A.33) which we discuss here are generally assumed to be fully differentiable, these functions need only to fulfil the weaker **Lipschitz condition** (i.e. it is Lipschitz continuous). For the system defined by equation (A.34), the function f is Lipschitz continuous if, for any two states given by points x and y, it holds:

$$\|f(x) - f(y)\| \le \lambda \|x - y\| \tag{A.35}$$

where $\|.\|$ indicates the norm. Equation (A.35) states that the difference in strength and direction of the dynamics at each of the two states defined by x and y does not exceed a multiple of the distance between these two points. In other words, the Lipschitz condition ensures that the dynamical system defined by equations (A.33)–(A.34) creates a vector field that is sufficiently smooth and thus, the dynamics do not change drastically as we move from one point to another point in the former's vicinity. Any system of continuous differentiable equations meets the Lipschitz condition.[5]

The **existence and uniqueness theorem** (Hirsch and Smale, 1974, Ch. 15) tells us that if the system defined by equation (A.34) is differentiable (or more generally, is Lipschitz continuous), then the system has a unique solution.[6] We can write, for example, a simple one-dimensional system of the form $\dot{y}(t) = g(y)$ as $y = \xi(t, y_0)$ for some initial condition y_0. For instance, the solution of $\dot{y} = \alpha y$ is given by $y = y_0 e^{\alpha t}$.

This result implies that starting from a given initial state $x_o = x(t = 0)$, the state $x(t) = (x_1(t), x_2(t), \ldots, x_n(t))$ follows a unique trajectory that satisfies system (A.34) for every period t. Consequently, the future evolution of a state $x(t)$ for any t is solely defined by its current position in the state space and two identical states must evolve in an identical manner. Thus, *a trajectory intersects neither itself nor any other trajectory*.[7] To see this, assume that at period t, two identical states exist at the intersection of the two trajectories – $x_1(t)$ on the first trajectory and $x_2(t)$ on the second trajectory. It must hold that $x_1(t) = x_2(t)$ and $\dot{x}_1(t) \neq \dot{x}_2(t)$ which contradicts the above uniqueness theorem, since

$$\dot{x}_1 = f(x_1(t)) = f(x_2(t)) = \dot{x}_2(t) \tag{A.36}$$

The proof that a trajectory cannot intersect itself is analogous. Figure A.3 illustrates a dynamical system that is characterised by a limit cycle. While all trajectories within and outside the limit cycle converge to the limit cycle, no trajectories intersect.

The former analysis provides an intuition for the **Poincaré–Bendixson Theorem**. Assume that a two-dimensional dynamical system is limited to a bounded region (i.e. the state space is defined by a closed and bounded subset of a plane, such as $x, y \in [0, 1]$), the Poincaré–Bendixson Theorem tells us that a trajectory starting in that region converges to a limit cycle as $t \to \infty$ if the state space does not include any fixed points. For the details of the theorem, you may refer to Hirsch and Smale (1974), but it should be intuitive that since trajectories cannot cross, the limit cycle acts as a barrier that traps the interior trajectory (equivalent to the interior trajectories in Figure A.3). Since the state space is bounded to a part of the plane, a trajectory can only converge to a fixed point or a limit cycle. Furthermore, we can infer from this result that chaotic behaviour can only arise in a continuous dynamical system of three dimensions or higher.

Furthermore, we can make use of a formula in physics that studies the rate at which the volume of flowing liquids and gases changes. The **divergence** for an n-dimensional dynamical

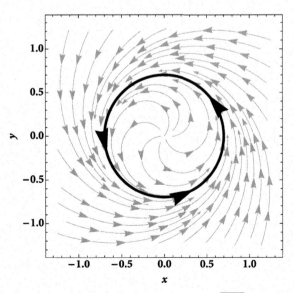

Figure A.3: Trajectories of the dynamical system defined by $\alpha = 0.7$ and $\dot{x} = \alpha x - \sqrt{x^2 + y^2}(x + y)$ and $\dot{y} = \alpha y - \sqrt{x^2 + y^2}(y - x)$.

system (A.33) is given by

$$div(f) = \sum_{i=1}^{n} \frac{\partial f_i}{\partial x_i} \qquad (A.37)$$

If $div(f) < 0$, we can find at least one attractor in the state space (for a two-dimensional state space, this is either a node or a limit cycle). Equation (A.37) implies that we need to study only the sign of the sum of the first-order partial derivatives of equation (A.33) to ensure whether the system has at least one attractor. The details can be found in Weibull (1997, Ch. 6.6), but the intuition for a two-dimensional system is sketched based on Hilborn (1994, p. 99) in the following for illustrative purposes.

We would like to study the behaviour of an initial cluster of initial conditions and see if they converge, given the two-dimensional system $\dot{x} = f_x(x,y)$ and $\dot{y} = f_y(x,y)$. Assume that the initial cluster is given by a small rectangular segment on the two-dimensional plane defined by four states x_1, x_2, y_1, and y_2. The area of the initial cluster is then given by

$$A = (x_2 - x_1)(y_2 - y_1) \qquad (A.38)$$

To study the change of area A over time, we take the first derivative and use the product rule

$$\begin{aligned}\frac{dA}{dt} &= (\dot{x}_2 - \dot{x}_1)(y_2 - y_1) + (x_2 - x_1)(\dot{y}_2 - \dot{y}_1) \\ &= (f_x(x_2,y_1) - f_x(x_1,y_1))(y_2 - y_1) \\ &\quad + (x_2 - x_1)(f_y(x_1,y_2) - f_y(x_1,y_1))\end{aligned} \qquad (A.39)$$

Using the Taylor series expansion, we can write

$$\begin{aligned}f_x(x_2,y_1) - f_x(x_1,y_1) &= (x_2 - x_1)\frac{\partial f_x}{\partial x}|_{x_1,y_1} + \cdots \\ f_y(x_1,y_2) - f_y(x_1,y_1) &= (y_2 - y_1)\frac{\partial f_y}{\partial y}|_{x_1,y_1} + \cdots\end{aligned} \qquad (A.40)$$

Substituting into equation (A.39), we obtain

$$\frac{dA}{dt} = (x_2 - x_1)(y_2 - y_1)\left(\frac{\partial f_x}{\partial x} + \frac{\partial f_y}{\partial y}\right) \qquad (A.41)$$

Simplifying gives us the final result

$$\frac{1}{A}\frac{dA}{dt} = \frac{\partial f_x}{\partial x} + \frac{\partial f_y}{\partial y} \equiv div(f) \qquad (A.42)$$

The result carries over to an n-dimensional system for some n-dimensional volume V

$$\frac{1}{V}\frac{dV}{dt} = \sum_{i=1}^{n} \frac{\partial f_i}{\partial x_i} \equiv div(f) \qquad (A.43)$$

The result can be extended to the existence of cycles. The **Bendixson Criterion** states that a two-dimensional system has no periodic solution (i.e. the system does not follow a closed trajectory) if

$div(f) \neq 0$ and its sign remains unchanged in some given domain D. For example, consider the following system

$$\dot{x} = 3x - y^2$$
$$\dot{y} = y^3 - x^2$$

Since we have $div(f) = 3(1 + y^2) > 0$, the dynamical system has no periodic solution.

A.6 Solving the Roots of Polynomials

We have seen in Chapter 3.4 that the stability and dynamics of a system are defined by the characteristic equation of the Jacobian. In the case of a two-dimensional system, the characteristic equation takes the form

$$\lambda^2 - \lambda Tr(J) + \Delta(J) = 0 \tag{A.44}$$

which is exactly equation (3.23). In this case, the **characteristic polynomial** $\lambda^2 - (f_{11} + f_{22})\lambda + (f_{11}f_{22} - f_{12}f_{21})$ has a degree (i.e. the largest exponent) of two.[8] We can see that the degree of the polynomial is equal to the dimension of the Jacobian and thus to the dynamical system. It is sometimes difficult to find the exact solutions to the characteristic equation, especially if the polynomial is of a higher degree.

Since we are only interested in the sign of the roots, i.e. of the solutions, there are several rules that help us determine their sign without explicitly finding the solutions.

A.6.1 Descartes' Rule of Signs

We order the real coefficients of a polynomial according to the variables' exponents starting with the largest value. Descartes' rule then states the following:

- The number of positive roots equals the number of sign changes of the (non-zero) coefficients or is less than that number by an even number.
- To determine the number of negative roots, we substitute the negative of the argument and repeat the procedure.
- Since the number of roots of a polynomial is exactly equal to its degree, the number of imaginary roots is given by the difference between the degree of the polynomial and the sum of positive and negative roots. Applying Descartes' rule then gives us the *minimum* number.

Furthermore, remember that complex numbers come as conjugate pairs of the form $a + ib$ and $a - ib$ where a (the real part) and b (the imaginary part) are real numbers and i is the imaginary unit, which explains the *less by an even number* element of the rule.

An example will make this clear. Assume the following polynomial

$$-a_5 x^5 + a_4 x^4 - a_1 x + a_0 \tag{A.45}$$

and further assume that any $a_i > 0$. We have three sign changes - one before each coefficient a_i (except for the first). The number of positive roots is therefore either 3 or 1. If we take $-x$

instead of x, only the coefficients multiplied by the variable with an odd exponent are affected (e.g. $x^2 = (-x)^2$). We can therefore repeat the exercise for the polynomial in which we changed the signs for those terms with an odd exponent in (A.45), leading to $a_5x^5 + a_4x^4 + a_1x + a_0$. Since there is no change in the signs, the number of negative roots equals zero. The number of imaginary roots is 5 minus the number of positive roots. Hence, we have a minimum of 2 imaginary roots, since we can have 3 or 1 positive real roots and we have no negative real root. Since $a_0 > 0$, zero cannot be a root of the polynomial.[9]

A.6.2 Vieta's Formulas

Assume that we have a polynomial of degree n, given by

$$a_nx^n + a_{n-1}x^{n-1} + \cdots + a_1x + a_0$$

with n complex (real and imaginary) roots

$$\lambda_1, \lambda_2, \lambda_3, \cdots, \lambda_{n-1}, \lambda_n$$

Vieta's formulas are as follows

$$\lambda_1 + \lambda_2 + \lambda_3 + \cdots + \lambda_n = -\frac{a_{n-1}}{a_n}$$

$$\lambda_1(\lambda_2 + \lambda_3 + \cdots + \lambda_n) + \lambda_2(\lambda_3 + \cdots + \lambda_n) + \cdots + \lambda_{n-1}\lambda_n = \frac{a_{n-2}}{a_n}$$

$$\lambda_1\lambda_2\lambda_3 \cdots \lambda_n = (-1)^n \frac{a_0}{a_n}$$

In other words, the polynomial $a_3x^3 + a_2x^2 + a_1x + a_0$ has roots λ_1, λ_2, and λ_3 for which

$$\lambda_1 + \lambda_2 + \lambda_3 = -\frac{a_2}{a_3}$$

$$\lambda_1\lambda_2 + \lambda_1\lambda_3 + \lambda_2\lambda_3 = \frac{a_1}{a_3}$$

$$\lambda_1\lambda_2\lambda_3 = -\frac{a_0}{a_3}$$

A.6.3 The Jury Conditions

The Jury conditions for a discrete two-dimensional system is given by

$$|Tr(J)| < 1 + \Delta(J) < 2 \tag{A.46}$$

While there are several ways to derive the conditions, the following way is the most straightforward. The characteristic equation is defined by

$$\lambda^2 - (f_{11} + f_{22})\lambda + (f_{11}f_{22} - f_{12}f_{21}) = 0$$

and is thus of the polynomial form

$$\lambda^2 + b\lambda + c = (\lambda - \lambda_+)(\lambda - \lambda_-) = 0 \tag{A.47}$$

with λ_+ and λ_- being the two eigenvalues that solve the characteristic equation. Since the trace of the Jacobian is $Tr(J) = f_{11} + f_{22}$ and its determinant is $\Delta(J) = f_{11}f_{22} - f_{12}f_{21}$, we have $b = -Tr(J)$ and $c = \Delta(J)$.

A stable equilibrium requires that both eigenvalues have an absolute value less than one. Extending equation (A.47) leads to

$$\lambda^2 - (\lambda_+ + \lambda_-)\lambda + \lambda_+\lambda_- = 0$$

and therefore

$$|c| = |\lambda_+\lambda_-| < 1 \qquad\qquad (A.48)$$

Furthermore, we require that $\lambda_+ < 1$, which implies that

$$\left(-b + \sqrt{b^2 - 4c}\right)/2 < 1$$

leading to

$$b + c > -1 \qquad\qquad (A.49)$$

Similarly, it must hold that $\lambda_- > -1$, which implies that

$$\left(-b - \sqrt{b^2 - 4c}\right)/2 > -1$$

and therefore

$$c - b > -1 \qquad\qquad (A.50)$$

Rearranging conditions (A.48), (A.49), and (A.50) and substituting leads to the conditions in inequality (A.46).

The Jury conditions can be calculated for polynomials of higher degree, but these conditions become rather complicated and I will therefore only provide but not derive the Jury conditions for a third-degree polynomial. For a polynomial of the form

$$\lambda^3 + a\lambda^2 + b\lambda + c = 0$$

the Jury conditions are

$$1 + a + b + c > 0$$
$$1 - a + b - c > 0$$
$$1 - c^2 > |b - ac|$$

A.7 Deriving Modularity

Assume that graph g has a size (i.e., the number of links) of $m = |L|$. The sum of all degrees in network g then equal $2m$ (see exercise 6.3). In an undirected network, remember that a degree

$\eta_i(g)$ defines the number of links not only emerging from node i but also entering the latter. If we break the network apart and randomly assign links by keeping the degree distribution of the network, a single emerging link is then faced with $2m-1$ other entry points. If node k has a degree equal to $\eta_k(g)$, the likelihood that one link emerging from i enters into k is then

$$\frac{\eta_k(g)}{2m-1}$$

since k offers $\eta_k(g)$ entry points and thus the same number of chances to connect.

Since node i's number of such emerging links is equal to its degree $\eta_i(g)$, the likelihood that i and k are connected is

$$p(i \leftrightarrow j) = \frac{\eta_i(g)\eta_k(g)}{2m-1}$$

Remember that the adjacency matrix G represents the existence (or lack thereof) of a link between any two nodes in graph g. For simplicity, we write $G_{ik} = l_{i,k}$ and thus, if $G_{ik} = 1$ nodes i and k are linked and $G_{ik} = 0$ implies they are not. The difference between the actual number of links between i and k is then

$$G_{ik} - \frac{\eta_i(g)\eta_k(g)}{2m-1}$$

Note that for simplicity and especially for larger networks, we can change the denominator to $2m$ instead of $2m-1$. We further assume an indicator function δ that is equal to one if two nodes are in the same group, and equal to zero if both are in different groups. Let the group of i be given by c_i and the group of k be given by c_k. We define $\delta(c_i, c_k) = 1$ if both nodes are in the same group and $\delta(c_i, c_k) = 0$ otherwise. Multiplying by this indicator function restricts the modularity measure to nodes of the same community. Summing over all pairs i and k and normalising by dividing with the total degree equal to $2m$ leads to the definition of modularity given in equation (6.26) on page 129.

Notes

1 Based on Harsanyi and Selten (1989, sections 3.9 and 5.4), we can extend the solution to non-symmetric games. Any coordination game can be transformed as shown on pages 17–18 into the game below.

A

		U	D
B	L	l,u	$0,0$
	R	$0,0$	r,d

Equilibrium (L,U) risk dominates equilibrium (R,D) if $l \times u > r \times d$.

2 In the original biological context, β denotes the population's birth rate, δ its death rate, and ϕ the average evolutionary fitness of its members while π_i is the fitness derived from a genetic trait i.

3 Note that Ohtsuki and Nowak (2006) assume fitness under weak selection. The fitness of some individual i is given by $W_i = 1 - w + w\pi_i$ for some payoff π_i. Parameter w determines the intensity of selection and for weak selection, we assume that $w \ll 1$.

4 More precisely, the probability of individual i adopting the strategy of neighbour j is given by $p = \left(1 + e^{-w(\pi_i - \pi_j)}\right)^{-1}$.

5 Applying the fundamental theorem of calculus, we can derive the following sufficient condition for the Lipschitz condition: if $f : D \to \mathbb{R}$ on some domain D and df/dx exists, is continuous and there is some constant κ such that $|df/dx| \leq \kappa \; \forall x \in D$ then (A.35) holds on D with $\kappa = \lambda$.

6 See also the Picard–Lindelöf theorem.

7 To be precise, we ignore the following two cases: (1) the second trajectory started at a state of the former trajectory and (2) the two trajectories approach a point at $t \to \infty$.

8 Note that if the polynomial has more than one argument, the degree is the highest sum of the exponents of the variable. Hence, if we have a polynomial of the form $ax^3y - xy^2$, the highest sum and thus degree is 4.

9 If we abandon the assumption that $x \in [0,1]$ but assume that $x \in \mathbb{R}$, we can further see that the polynomial (A.45) must indeed have at least one real root, since its degree is an odd number, i.e. 5. In fact, any polynomial p with an odd degree, some argument x and only real coefficients, has at least one real root. The intuition is straightforward. As we increase the absolute value of x, the sign of the polynomial is defined by the sign of the greatest exponent. Consequently for equation (A.45), $\lim_{x \to +\infty} p(x) = -\infty$ and $\lim_{x \to -\infty} p(x) = +\infty$. Since $p(x)$ is a continuous function, it must take on any value between $-\infty$ and $+\infty$ and therefore needs to be zero at some point. Note that the logic does not apply if x defines frequencies.

Alvard, M. S. and A. Gillespie (2004). Good lamalera whale hunters accrue reproductive benefits. In M. S. Alvard (Ed.), *Socioeconomic Aspects of Human Behavioral Ecology*, Volume 23, pp. 225–247. Emerald Group Publishing Limited.

Andersen, S., S. Ertaç, U. Gneezy, M. Hoffman, and J. A. List (2011). Stakes matter in ultimatum games. *American Economic Review 101*, 3427–3439.

Appiah, K. A. (2010). *The Honor Code: How Moral Revolutions Happen*. W. W. Norton & Company.

Arrow, K. J. (1951). *Social Choice and Individual Values*. John Wiley & Sons.

Aumann, R. and A. Brandenburger (1995). Epistemic conditions for nash equilibrium. *63*(5), 1161–1180.

Aumann, R. J. (1990). communication need not lead to nash equilibrium. *Mimeo Hebrew University of Jerusalem*.

Axelrod, R. (2006). *The Evolution of Cooperation* (Revised ed.). Basic Books.

Axtell, R., J. M. Epstein, and H. P. Young (2001). The emergence of classes in a multi-agent bargaining model. In S. N. Durlauf and H. P. Young (Eds.), *Social Dynamics*, Chapter 7, pp. 191–211. MIT Press.

Bak, P. and K. Sneppen (1993, Dec). Punctuated equilibrium and criticality in a simple model of evolution. *Physical Review Letters 71*(24), 4083–4086.

Bak, P., C. Tang, and K. Wiesenfeld (1987). Self-organized criticality: an explanation of 1/f noise. *Physical Review Letters 59*(4), 381–384.

———— (1988). Self-organized criticality. *Physical Reviews A 38*(1), 364–374.

Ballester, C., A. Calvó-Armengol, and Y. Zenou (2006). Who's who in networks. wanted: The key player. *Econometrica 74*(5), 1403–1417.

Banerjee, A. V. (1992). A simple model of herd behavior. *The Quarterly Journal of Economics 107*(3), 797–817.

Barabási, A.-L. and R. Albert (1999). Emergence of scaling in random networks. *Science 286*(5439), 509–512.

Bastian, M., S. Heymann, and M. Jacomy (2009). Gephi: an open source software for exploring and manipulating networks. In *Third international AAAI conference on weblogs and social media*.

Basu, K. (1994). The traveler's dilemma: Paradoxes of rationality in game theory. *American Economic Review 84*(2), 391–395.

Beck, C. J. (2011). The world-cultural origins of revolutionary waves - five centuries of european contention. *Social Science History 35*(2), 167–207.

Bénabou, R. and J. Tirole (2011). Identity, morals, and taboos: Beliefs as assets. *Quarterly Journal of Economics 126*(2), 805–855.

———— (2016). Mindful economics: The production, consumption, and value of beliefs. *Journal of Economic Perspectives 30*(3), 141–164.

Bergin, J. and B. L. Lipman (1996). Evolution with state-dependent mutations. *Econometrica 64*(4), 943–956.

Bernheim, B. D., B. Peleg, and M. D. Whinston (1987). Coalition-proof nash equilibria i. concepts. *Journal of Economic Theory 42*(1), 1–12.

Bikhchandani, S., D. Hirshleifer, and I. Welch (1992). A theory of fads, fashion, custom, and cultural change as informational cascades. *The Journal of Political Economy 100*(5), 992–1026.

Bilancini, E., L. Boncinelli, S. Ille, and E. Vicario (2022). Memory retrieval and harshness of conflict in the hawk-dove game. *Economic Theory Bulletin 10*, 333–351. https://doi.org/10.1007/s40505-022-00237-z.

Binmore, K. (1994). *Game Theory and the Social Contract Volume I: Playing Fair*. MIT Press.

——— (2007). *Game Theory: A Very Short Introduction*. Oxford University Press.

——— (2009). *Rational Decisions*. Princeton University Press.

Bischi, G. I., U. Merlone, and E. Pruscini (2018). Evolutionary dynamics in club goods binary games. *Journal of Economic Dynamics & Control 91*, 104–119.

Blondel, V. D., J.-L. Guillaume, R. Lambiotte, and E. Lefebvre (2008). Fast unfolding of communities in large networks. *Journal of Statistical Mechanics: Theory and Experiment 2008*.

Blume, L. E. (1993). The statistical mechanics of strategic interaction. *Games & Economic Behavior 5*(3), 387–424.

Boerlust, M. C., M. A. Nowak, and K. Sigmund (1997). The logic of contrition. *Journal of theoretical Biology 185*, 281–293.

Bonacich, P. (1987). Power and centrality: A family of measures. *American Journal Of Sociology 92*(5), 1170–1182.

Borgatti, S. P. (2006). Identifying sets of key players in a social network. *Computational & Mathematical Organization Theory 12*, 21–34.

Borgatti, S. P., M. G. Everett, and J. C. Johnson (2018). *Analyzing Social Networks*. Sage Publications.

Bossen, L. and H. Gates (2017). *Bound Feet, Young Hands: Tracking the Demise of Footbinding in Village China*. Stanford University Press.

Bowles, S. (2001). *Individual Interactions, Group Conflicts, and the Evolution of Preferences*. Brookings Institution Press.

——— (2004). *Microeconomics – Behavior, Institutions, and Evolution*. Princeton University Press.

Box, G. E. P. (1976). Science and statistics. *Journal of the American Statistical Association 71*(356), 791–799.

Boyd, R. and P. J. Richerson (1985). *Culture and the Evolutionary Process*. The University of Chicago Press.

——— (2005). *The Origin and Evolution of Cultures*. Oxford University Press.

Bramoullé, Y., A. Galeotti, and B. Rogers (Eds.) (2016). *The Oxford Handbook of the Economics of Networks*. Oxford University Press.

Brown, D. (1991). *Human Universals* (Reprint edition ed.). McGraw-Hill Education.

Chaplin, D. (2018). *Sengoku Jidai. Nobunaga, Hideyoshi, and Ieyasu: Three Unifiers of Japan*. CreateSpace Independent Publishing Platform.

Choi, J.-K. and S. Bowles (2007). The coevolution of parochial altruism and war. *Science 318*, 636–640.

Choi, J. P. (1997). Herd behavior, the "penguin effect," and the suppression of informational diffusion: An analysis of informational externalities and payoff interdependency. *The RAND Journal of Economics 28*(3), 407–425.

Clavell, J. (1986). *Shogun*. Dell Publishing.

Coleman, J. S. (1986, 5). Social theory, social research, and a theory of action. *American Journal of Sociology 91*(6), 1309–1335.

———— (1994). *Foundations of Social Theory*. The Belknap Press of Harvard University Press.

Collins, R. (1998). *The Sociology of Philosophies: A Global Theory of Intellectual Change*. The Belknap Press of Harvard University Press.

Congressional Record (1959). Proceedings and debates of the 86th congress. *First Session (July 1, 1959, to July 16, 1959) 105*(10), 12369 – 13656.

Crabtree, S. A., D. W. Bird, and R. B. Bird (2019). Subsistence transitions and the simplification of ecological networks in the western desert of australia. *Human Ecology 47*(2), 165–177.

Darley, J. M. and B. Latané (1968). Bystander intervention in emergencies. *Journal of Personality and Social Psychology 8*(4), 377–383.

De Jong, K. A. (2006). *Evolutionary Computation: A Unified Approach*. THe MIT Press.

Dekker, A. (2005). Conceptual distance in social network analysis. *Journal of Social Structure 6*(3). also available at: https://www.cmu.edu/joss/content/articles/volume6/dekker/.

Dhami, S. (2016). *The Foundations of Behavioral Economic Analysis*. Oxford University Press.

Durlauf, S. N. and H. P. Young (Eds.) (2001). *Social Dynamics*. Brookings Institution Press, The MIT Press.

Eberhard, D. M., G. F. Simons, and C. D. Fennig (Eds.) (2021). *Ethnologue: Languages of the World* (24 ed.). SIL International.

Ellison, G. (1993). Learning, local interaction, and coordination. *Econometrica 61*(5), 1047–1071.

———— (2000). Basins of attraction, long-run stochastic stability, and the speed of step- by-step evolution. *The Review of Economic Studies 67*(1), 17–45.

Epstein, J. M. and R. Axtell (1996). *Growing Artificail Societies*. The Brooking Institution.

Falk, A., E. Fehr, and U. Fischbacher (2003). On the nature of fair behavior. *Economic Inquiry 41*(1), 20–26.

Falk, A. and U. Fischbacher (2005). Modeling strong reciprocity. In H. Gintis, S. Bowles, R. Boyd, and E. Fehr (Eds.), *Moral Sentiments and Material Interests*, pp. 193–214. The MIT Press.

Feigenbaum, M. J. (1978). Quantitative universality for a class of nonlinear transformations. *Journal of Statistical Physics 19*(1), 25–52.

Fischbacher, U., C. M. Fong, and E. Fehr (2009, 10). Fairness, errors and the power of competition. *Journal of Economic Behavior & Organization 72*(1), 527–545.

Foley, R. A. and M. M. Lahr (2011). The evolution of the diversity of cultures. *366*(21357230), 1080–1089.

Foster, D. and H. P. Young (1990). Stochastic evolutionary game dynamics. *Theoretical Population Biology 38*, 219–232.

Fudenberg, D. and J. Tirole (2005). *Game Theory*. Ane Books Pvt.

Gabaix, X. (2009). Power laws in economics and finance. *Annual Review of Economics 1*, 255–294.

Gamble, S. D. (1954). *Ting Hsien: A North China Rural Community*. Institute of Pacific Relations.

Gino, F., M. I. Norton, and R. A. Weber (2016). Motivated bayesians: Feeling moral while acting egoistically. *Journal of Economic Perspectives 30*(3), 189–212.

Gintis, H. (2000a). *Game Theory Evolving*. Princeton University Press.

—— (2000b). Strong reciprocity and human sociality. *Journal of Theoretical Biology 206*(2), 169–179.

—— (2009). *The Bounds of Reason: Game Theory and the Unification of the Behavioral Sciences*. Princeton University Press.

Goyal, S. (2007). *Connections: An Introduction to the Economics of Networks*. Princeton University Press.

Granovetter, M. (1973). The strength of weak ties. *American Journal of Sociology 78*(6), 1360–1380.

—— (1978). Threshold models of collective behavior. *The American Journal of Sociology 83*(6), 1420–1443.

—— (1995). *How to get a job: a study of contacts and careers* (2 ed.). The University of Chicago Press.

Granovetter, M. and R. Soong (1986). Threshold models of interpersonal effects in consumer demand. *Journal of Economic Behavior and Organization 7*, 83–99.

—— (1988). Threshold models of diversity: Chinese restaurants, residential segregation, and the spiral of silence. *Sociological Methodology 18*, 69–104.

Grebogi, C., S. W. McDonald, E. Ott, and J. A. Yorke (1983). Final state sensitivity: An obstruction to predictability. *Physics Letters 99A*(9), 415–418.

Grebogi, C., E. Ott, F. Romeiras, and J. A. Yorke (1987). Critical exponents for crisis-induced intermittency. *Physical Review A 36*(11), 5365–5380.

Guckenheimer, J. and P. Holmes (1983). *Nonlinear Oscillations, Dynamical Systems, and Bifurcations of Vector Fields*. Springer-Verlag.

Güth, W., R. Schmittberger, and B. Schwarze (1982). An experimental analysis of ultimatum bargaining. *Journal of Economic Behavior & Organization 3*(4), 367–388.

Güth, W. and R. Tietz (1990). Bargaining behavior: A survey and comparison of experimental results. *Journal of Economic Psychology 11*(3), 417–449.

Hale, J. K. (1963). *Oscillations in Nonlinear Systems*. McGraw-Hill Book Company, Inc.

Halsall, G. (2007). *Barbarian Migrations and the Roman West, 376–568*. Cambridge University Press.

Harsanyi, J. C. and R. Selten (1989). *A General Theory of Equilibrium Selection in Games*. MIT Press.

Heider, F. (1946). Attitudes and cognitive organization. *Journal of Psychology 21*, 107–112.

Henrich, J., R. Boyd, S. Bowles, C. Camerer, E. Fehr, H. Gintis, and R. McElreath (2001). In search of homo economicus: Behavioral experiments in 15 small-scale societies. *The American Economic Review 91*(2), 73–78.

Henrich, J., R. McElreath, A. Barr, J. Ensminger, C. Barrett, A. Bolyanatz, J. C. Cardenas, M. Gurven, E. Gwako, N. Henrich, C. Lesorogol, F. Marlowe, D. Tracer, and J. Ziker (2006). Costly punishment across human societies. *Science 312*(5781), 1767–1770.

Hilborn, R. C. (1994). *Chaos and Nonlinear Dynamics*. Oxford University Press.

Hirsch, M. W. and S. Smale (1974). *Differential Equations, Dynamical Systems, and Linear Algebra*. Academic Press, Inc.

Hofbauer, J. and K. Sigmund (1998). *Evolutionary Games and Population Dynamics*. Cambridge University Press.

Hoffman, E., K. A. McCabe, and V. L. Smith (1996). On expectations and the monetary stakes in ultimatum games. *International Journal of Game Theory 25*(3), 289–301.

Ille, S. (2012). The theory of conflict analysis: A review of the approach by keith w. hipel & niall m. fraser. *International Journal of Mathematics, Game Theory and Algebra 21*(2/3) also available at SSRN: https://ssrn.com/abstract=2275952.

———— (2013). Simulating conventions and norms under local interactions and imitation. *LEM Working Paper Series, 2013/4*.

———— (2014). The dynamics of norms and conventions under local interactions and imitation. *International Game Theory Review 16*(3).

———— (2015). State-dependent stochastic stability and the non-existence of conventions. *SSRN* available at SSRN: https://ssrn.com/abstract=2652668.

———— (2017). Towards better economic models of social behaviour? identity economics. *Studies in Ethnicity and Nationalism 17*(1), 5–24.

———— (2020). On revolutionary waves and the dynamics of landslides. *Studies in Ethnicity and Nationalism 20*(3), 223–243.

———— (2021). The evolution of sectarianism. *Communications in Nonlinear Science and Numerical Simulation 97*, 105726.

Ille, S. and M. W. Peacey (2019). Forced private tutoring in egypt: Moving away from a corrupt social norm. *International Journal of Educational Development 66*, 105–118.

Imhof, L. A. and M. A. Nowak (2006). Evolutionary game dynamics in a wright-fisher process. *Journal of Mathematical Biology 52*, 667–681.

Ioannides, Y. M. (1990). Trading uncertainty and market form. *International Economic Review 31*(3), 619–638.

———— (2006). Topologies of social interactions. *Economic Theory 28*, 559–584.

Iteanu, A. (2017). *Continuity and Breaches in Religion and Globalization, a Melanesian Point of View*, Chapter 9. Palgrave Macmillan.

Jones, M. and R. Sugden (2001). Positive confirmation bias in the acquisition of information. *Theory and Decision 50*, 59–99.

Kahneman, D. and A. Tversky (1979). Prospect theory: An analysis of decision under risk. *Econometrica 47*(2), 263–291.

Kandori, M., G. J. Mailath, and R. Rob (1993). Learning, mutation, and long run equilibria in games. *Econometrica 61*(1), 29–56.

Kassin, S. M. (2017). The killing of kitty genovese: What else does this case tell us? *Perspectives on Psychological Science 12*(3), 374–381.

Katz, J. (2016). Who will be president? *The New York Times (November 8)*. available at https://www.nytimes.com/interactive/2016/upshot/presidential-pollsforecast.html.

Kelly, R. T. (2013). *The Lifeways of Hunter-Gatherers* (2 ed.). Cambridge University Press.

Kirman, A. (1983). Communication in markets: A suggested approach. *Economics Letters 12*(2), 101–108.

—— (1997). *The Economy as an Interactive System*. Addison-Wesley.

—— (2011). *Complex Economics: Individual and collective rationality*. Routledge.

Kirman, A., C. Oddou, and S. Weber (1986). Stochastic communicationand coalition formation. *Econometrica 54*, 129–138.

Kraines, D. and V. Kraines (1993). Learning to cooperate with pavlov an adaptive strategy for the iterated prisoner's dilemma with noise. *Theory and Decision 35*, 170–150.

Kümpel, A. S., V. Karnowski, and T. Keyling (2015). News sharing in social media: A review of current research on news sharing users, content, and networks. *1*(2), 1–14.

Kuran, T. (1987a). Chameleon voters and public choice. *Public Choice 53*(1), 53–78.

—— (1987b). Preference falsification, policy continuity and collective conservatism. *The Economic Journal 97*, 642–665.

—— (1998). Ethnic norms and their transformation through reputational cascades. *Journal of Legal Studies 27*, 623–659.

Latané, B. and J. M. Darley (1968). Group inhibition of bystander intervention in emergencies. *Journal of Personality and Social Psychology 10*(3), 215–221.

Lee, I. H., A. Szeidl, and A. Valentinyi (2003). Contagion and state dependent mutations. *Advances in Theoretical Economics 3*, 24–52.

Lee, I. H. and Á. Valentinyi (2000). Noisy contagion without mutation. *The Review of Economic Studies 67*(1), 47–56.

Lesourne, J., A. Orléan, and B. Walliser (Eds.) (2002). *Leçons de micréconomie évolutionniste*. Odile Jacob.

Lévi-Strauss, C. (1968). *The Savage Mind* (Paperback ed.). University Of Chicago Press.

Levie, H. S. (1966). *Chinese footbinding: The history of a curious erotic custom*. Walton Rawls.

Levy, H. S. (1966). *Chinese footbinding: the history of a curious erotic custom*. W. Rawls.

Levy, M. and S. Solomon (1997). New evidence for the power-law distribution of wealth. *Physica A 242*, 90–94.

Lord, C. G., L. Ross, and M. Lepper (1979). Biased assimilation and attitude polarization: The effects of prior theories on subsequently considered evidence. *Journal of Personality and Social Psychology 37*(11), 2098–2109.

Lorenz, E. B. (1972). Does the flap of a butterfly's wings in brazil set off a tornado in texas. In *American Association for the Advancement of Science*, 139th Meeting. Available at https://eapsweb.mit.edu/sites/default/files/Butterfly_1972.pdf.

Mackie, G. (1996). Ending footbinding and infibulation: A convention account. *American Sociological Review 61*(6), 999–1017.

Marquis de Condorcet, M. J. A. N. d. C. (1785). *Essai sur l'application de l'analyse à la probabilité des décisions rendues à la pluralité des voix*. de l'Imprimerie Royale.

Matsuura, K. (2009). *Investing in Cultural Diversity and Intercultural Dialogue*. UNESCO World Report, UNESCO.

Matthew (2018). *The New Oxford Annotated Bible - New Revised Standard Version* (5 ed.). Oxford University Press.

May, R. M. (1976). Simple mathematical models with very complicated dynamics. *Nature 261*, 459–467.

McClennan, D. C. (1967). *The Achieving Society*. The Free Press.

Menger, C. (1963). *Problems of Economics and Sociology*. University of Illinois Press.

Miller, J. H. and S. E. Page (2007). *Complex Adaptive Systems: An Introduction to Computational Models of Social Life*. Princeton University Press.

Mitchel, M. (1999). *An Introduction to Genetic Algorithms* (5 ed.). A Bradford Book The MIT Press.

Nash, J. F. (1950). Equilibrium points in n-person games. *Proceedings of the National Academy of Sciences 36*, 38–49.

Newman, M. E. J. (2006). Modularity and community structure in networks. *Proceedings of the National Academy of Sciences 103*(23), 8577–8582.

North, D. C. (1991). Institutions. *Journal of Economic Perspectives 5*(1), 97–112.

Nowak, M. A. (2006). *Evolutionary Dynamics*. The Belknap Press of Harvard University Press.

Nowak, M. A. and R. M. May (1992). Evolutionary games and spatial chaos. *Nature 359*, 826–829.

Nowak, M. A., A. Sasaki, C. Taylor, and D. Fudenberg (2004). Emergence of cooperation and evolutionary stability in finite populations. *428*, 646–650.

Nowak, M. A. and K. Sigmund (1992). Tit for tat in heterogeneous populations. *Nature 355*, 250–253.

Nowak, M. A., C. E. Tarnita, and E. O. Wilson (2010). The evolution of eusociality. *Nature 466*(7310), 1057–1062.

Nunney, L. (1999). Lineage selection: Natural selection of long-term benefits. In L. Keller (Ed.), *Levels of Selection in Evolution*, Chapter 12, pp. 238–252. Princeton University Press.

Ohtsuki, H. and M. Nowak (2006). The replicator equation on graphs. *Journal of Theoretical Biology 243*, 86–97.

Padgett, J. F. and C. K. Ansell (1993). Robust action and the rise of the medici, 1400-1434. *The American Journal of Sociology 98*(6), 1259–1319.

Pancs, R. and N. J. Vriend (2007). Schelling's spatial proximity model of segregation revisited. *Journal of Public Economics 91*, 1–24.

Peitgen, H.-O., H. Jürgens, and D. Saupe (2004). *Chaos and Fractals: New Frontiers of Science* (2 ed.). Springer-Verlag.

Potts, J. (2000). *The New Evolutionary Microeconomics*. Edward Elgar.

Price, D. H. (2004). *Atlas of World Cultures: A Geographical Guide to Ethnographic Literature*. The Blackburn Press.

Price, G. R. (1970). Selection and covariance. *Nature 227*, 520–521.

Quetelet, A. (1835). *Sur l'homme et le développement des ses faculté, ou essai de physique sociale*. Bachelier.

Robson, A. J. and F. Vega-Redondo (1996). Efficient equilibrium selection in evolutionary games with random matching. *Journal of Economic Theory 70*(1), 65–92.

Rochat, Y. (2009). Closeness centrality extended to unconnected graphs: The harmonic centrality index. *Applications of Social Network Analysis, ASNA*. https://core.ac.uk/download/pdf/148005918.pdf.

Roser, M. (2020). War and peace. *Our World in Data*. https://ourworldindata.org/war-and-peace.

Sadler, A. L. (2011 (1937)). *The Maker of Modern Japan: The Life of Tokugawa Ieyasu* (Routledge Library Editions: Japan ed.), Volume 43. Routledge.

Samuelson, L. (1994). Stochastic stability in games with alternative best replies. *Journal of Economic Theory 64*(1), 35–65.

——— (1997). *Evolutionary games and equilibrium selection*. MIT Press series on economic learning and social evolution. MIT Press.

Sandholm, W. H. (2010). *Population Games and Evolutionary Dynamics*. The MIT Press.

Schelling, T. C. (1969, 5). Models of segregation. *The American Economic Review 59*(2), 488–493.

——— (1971). Dynamic models of segregation. *Journal of Mathematical Sociology 1*, 143–186.

——— (1978). *Micromotives and Macrobehavior*. W. W. Norton & Company.

Scott, J. and P. J. Carrington (Eds.) (2011). *The SAGE Handbook of Social Network Analysis*. SAGE Publications.

Scotus, J. D. and M. F. García (1912). *B. Ioannis Duns Scoti ... Commentaria Oxoniensia Ad IV Libros Magistri Sententiarus*. Ad Claras Aquas (Quaracchi) prope Florentiam: ex typographia Collegii s. Bonaventurae.

Sen, A. (2002). *Rationality and Freedom*. Belknap Press.

Skyrms, B. (2010). *Signals*. Oxford University Press.

Smith, H. (Ed.) (1980). *Learning from Shōgun - Japanese History and Western Fantasy*. Program in Asian Studies University of California, Santa Barbara.

Stadler, P. F., W. Fontana, and J. H. Miller (1993). Random catalytic reaction networks. *Physica D: Nonlinear Phenomena 63*(3-4), 378–392.

Strogatz, S. H. (2015). *Nonlinear Dynamics and Chaos* (2 ed.). Westview Press.

Suchecki, K., V. M. Eguíluz, and M. San Miguel (2005, Sep). Voter model dynamics in complex networks: Role of dimensionality, disorder, and degree distribution. *Physical Review E 72*(3).

Sunstein, C. R. (2002). The Law of Group Polarization. *Journal of Political Philosophy 10*, 175–195.

Thatcher, M. (1987). Interview for woman's own ("no such thing as society"). *https://www.margaretthatcher.org/document/106689*.

Thurner, S., P. Klimek, and R. Hanel (2018). *Introduction to the Theory of Complex Systems*. Oxford University Press.

Travers, J. and S. Milgram (1969). An experimental study of the small world problem. *Sociometry 32*(4), 425–443.

Trompf, G. (1991). *Melanesian Religion*. Cambridge University Press.

Turnbull, S. (2012). *Tokugawa Ieyasu*. Osprey Publishing.

Turner, C. L. (1997). Locating footbinding: Variations across class and space in nineteenth and early twentieth century China. *Journal of Historical Sociology 10*(4), 444–479.

Turnovsky, S. J. and E. R. Weintraub (1971). Stochastic stability of a general equilibrium system under adaptive expectations. *International Economic Review 12*(1), 71–86.

Valéry, P. (1942). *Mauvaises pensées et autre: 1941-42* (la bibliothèque numérique romande www.ebooks-bnr.com ed.). Éditions Gallimard.

van Damme, E. and J. W. Weibull (1998). Evolution with mutations driven by control costs. Tilburg University, Discussion Paper, 1998-94, Working Paper, Version: September 29.

van Dijk, J., T. Poell, and M. de Waal (2018). *The Platform Society: Public Values in a Connective World*. Oxford University Press.

Vazquez, F., V. M. Eguíluz, and M. S. Miguel (2008, Mar). Generic absorbing transition in coevolution dynamics. *Physical Review Letters 100*(10), 108702.

Volz, Y. Z. (2007). Going public through writing: Women journalists and gendered journalistic space in china, 1890s–1920s. *Media Culture & Society 29*(3), 469–489.

Wassermann, S. and K. Faust (1994). *Social Network Analysis: Methods and Applications*. Cambridge University Press.

Wedekind, C. and M. Milinski (1996). Human cooperation in the simultaneous and the alternating prisoner's dilemma: Pavlov versus generous tit-for-tat. *Proceedings of the National Academy of Sciences of the United States of America 93*(7), 2686–2689.

Weibull, J. W. (1997). *Evolutionary Game Theory*. MIT Press paperback edition.

Wiggins, S. (2003). *Introduction to Applied Nonlinear Dynamical Systems and Chaos* (2 ed.). Spinger-Verlag.

Williams, G. C. (Ed.) (1971). *Group Selection*. Aldine-Atherton.

Wilson, J. Q. and G. L. Kelling (1982). Broken windows. *The Atlantic*.

Young, H. P. (1993). The evolution of conventions. *Econometrica 61*(1), 57–84.

———— (1998). *Individual Strategy and Social Structure*. Princeton University Press.

———— (2001). *The Dynamics of Conformity*, Chapter 5. Brookings Institution Press.

———— (2008). Self-knowledge and self-deception. *Department of Economics, Discussion Paper Series 338*, University of Oxford.

Zimbardo, P. G. (1969). *The Human Choice: Individuation, Reason, and Order versus Deindividuation, Impulse, and Chaos*. University of Nebraska Press.

Zipf, G. K. (1949). *Human behavior and the principle of least effort*. Addison-Wesley Press.

Fundamental Theorem of Mixed Strategy Nash
Equilibrium, 14

game, 11
    sequential, 12
    simultaneous, 12
game theory
    cooperative, 9
    evolutionary, 42, 65
    non-cooperative, 9, 42
genetic algorithm, 196
global clustering coefficient, 129
Gothic War, 171
graph
    bipartite, 134, 135
    characteristic path length, 123
    complete, 119, 124
    connected, 121
    density, 124, 133, 135, 136, 144
    diameter, 123, 133, 211
    directed, 19, 119
    disconnected, 121
    heterogeneous, 134
    homogeneous, 134, 135
    order, 119
    radius, 123
    regular, 122
    size, 119
    undirected, 119
    unipartite projection, 135

Helots, 155
Hundred Years' War, 172

imitation
    normative, 95
    positive, 94
    preferential, 95
Inanna, 67, 91
inductive, 176
information set, 29
in-set, *see* stable manifold
institutions, 3

interior crisis, 208
intermittency, 207
Ising model, 221
isocline, 58
    see also nullcline, 65
iterated map, 97

Ju/'hoansi, 57
Jury conditions, 103, 237

Key PlayerProblem/Negative
    (KPP-NEG), 144
Kootenai, 41
Krypteia, 155
Kwakwak'awakw, 57

learning
    adaptive, 69, 72, 150, 154
    reinforcement, 179
    social, 42–43, 64, 68–69, 179
Lebanese Civil War, 172
Leibniz notation, 223
Liapunov stable, 47
link, 118
    directed, 119
Lipschitz condition, 233, 240
locality, 191
Lotka-Volterra equation, 229
Lucas critique, 187

Mandelbrot sets, 220
manifold
    stable, 54
    unstable, 54
Markov chain, 71, 144
    aperiodic, 72, 228
    ergodic, 72, 91
    invariant distribution, 73, 228
    irreducible, 72, 91, 228
    time-homogeneous, 68, 71
Markov process, *see* Markov chain
    stationary distribution, *see* Markov chain,
        invariant distribution